MANY VOICES

"ROOTED IN RELATIONAL PSYCHOANALYSIS, enriched by postmodern pluriformity, and reflecting profound theological acuity, *Many Voices* is a nuanced and carefully researched work that captures the most significant features of the kind of pastoral theology that is needed in the twenty-first century. Because it is firmly based in a relational anthropology and theology, the book manages to bring into creative and critical dialogue the deep roots of psychoanalytic and psychodynamic psychotherapy, evocative aesthetic theology, and spirituality and to weave them into a process that is therapeutic and enlivening, as the cases that illustrate the text clearly demonstrate. Pamela Cooper-White has provided pastoral care providers with another vital resource for the theory and practice of pastoral psychotherapy."

—EMMANUEL Y. LARTEY
Professor of Pastoral Theology, Care and Counseling
Candler School of Theology, Emory University

MANY VOICES

Pastoral Psychotherapy in Relational and Theological Perspective

Pamela Cooper-White

FORTRESS PRESS

MINNEAPOLIS

For the many voices
that have enriched my life and helped me to grow,
especially my patients and students

MANY VOICES
Pastoral Psychotherapy in Relational and Theological Perspective

First Fortress Press paperback edition 2011

Scripture quotations are from the New Revised Standard Version Bible, copyright © 1989 by the Division of Christian Education of the National Council of the Churches of Christ in the USA. Used by permission. All rights reserved.

Cover art: "16 People" by Farida Zaman, © Farida Zaman/Images.com. Used by permission.
Cover design: Kevin van der Leek Design, Inc.
Book design: Ann Delgehausen, Trio Bookworks

ISBN 978-0-8006-9870-6
The Library of Congress cataloged the hardcover edition as follows:

Library of Congress Cataloging-in-Publication Data
Cooper-White, Pamela
    Many voices : pastoral psychotherapy in relational and theological
perspective / by Pamela Cooper-White.
        p. cm.
    ISBN-13: 978-0-8006-3957-0 (alk. paper)
    ISBN-10: 0-8006-3957-X (alk. paper)
  1. Pastoral psychology. 2. Pastoral counseling. 3. Psychotherapy—Religious aspects—
Christianity. I. Title.
    BV4012.C66 2006
    253.5'2—dc22
        2006014303

Contents

PART 1
A Theological and Theoretical Framework

PART 2
Practicing Pastoral Psychotherapy

Preface

THIS BOOK is an effort to bridge worlds: contemporary psychoanalytic theory and praxis and pastoral counseling. It offers an overview of pastoral psychotherapeutic theory and practice from a postmodern, relational-psychoanalytic perspective, within the context of a new, postmodern pastoral theology. The book was conceived as filling a gap, both as a textbook for advanced students in clinical training as pastoral psychotherapists and as a conversation piece for colleagues in the practice and teaching of psychotherapy. There is, perhaps today more than ever, a need for new, more relational approaches to pastoral psychotherapy in our pluralistic, technologically driven, and global social context. This project is an effort to address this need.

Multiplicity is the conceptual through-line, or red thread, that weaves from the beginning to the end of this book. First, in part 1, readers will be invited to explore the multiplicity of persons (not only in terms of pluralism and diversity of human beings in our relations with one another but also multiplicity as *internally* constitutive of each individual mind/self/subject, at both conscious and unconscious levels); and the multiplicity of God (grounded in a Trinitarian theology that continually breaks itself open wider and wider toward a constructive theology of limitless love, creativity, and fecundity; of *creative profusion, incarnational desire, and living inspiration*). Then, in part 2, an appreciation for this multiplicity will inform pastoral psychotherapeutic praxis, detailing a method of working with all the varied, contradictory, and creative parts of each patient in his or her many self-states, identifications, and subjective moments.

The corresponding model of psychotherapy offered in this book differs a good deal from a traditional therapeutic model that holds *integration* as a goal. *Integration* as a term may be all too easily (mis)understood as a kind of process of homogenization, in which the unconscious is brought into consciousness somewhat as the contents in the bottom of a blender are brought up and whirled together into a pudding with those on the surface. Note the verticality of this image, which corresponds to a classical psychoanalytic paradigm (Sigmund Freud's "topographical model"[1]) of consciousness and unconsciousness in which the unconscious is "deeper," pressed down and out of sight, beneath the repression barrier. The model in this book turns away—or perhaps, more accurately, turns sideways and three-dimensionally—from an exclusively vertical conception of consciousness and unconscious. In part 1, readers will be invited to consider a more spatially dispersed concept of mind where conscious and unconscious coexist more fluidly on multiple planes or axes. The therapeutic process of tapping unconscious material, then, involves not only a cathartic release of repressed (pressed-down) mental contents, but *all* feelings, thoughts, fantasies, and sensations that have been dissociated, disavowed, projected, and split-off in a potentially infinite number of inner and outer directions. This approach to psychotherapy, rather than aiming toward an integration of unconscious and conscious into a homogenized whole, has as its goal an increasingly harmonious awareness and constructive dialogue among all the disparate parts, conscious and unconscious, of the person who comes for help.

Drawing both from postmodern understandings of the diversity of truths and from the postcolonial notion of *hybridity*—in which dialogue partners join together in new, creative ways without losing their individual distinctiveness—this model of pastoral psychotherapy seeks to help individuals come to know, accept, and even appreciate all the distinctive parts—the many voices—that live within them. This approach to psychotherapy is more orientation than method. While techniques will be discussed, particularly in chapters 4 and 5, this is finally an orientation toward multiplicity, toward an embracing of mystery and of all that remains beyond knowledge, beyond certainty, beyond any singular "truth." By embracing such multiplicity and honoring such mystery, the pastoral psychotherapist may help to facilitate a process by which the patient may discover a more expansive, appreciative, and generous way of living and relating with others, even with the Holy—the source of *all* loves, all mercies, all creativities, all truths, all voices, and all just relations.

A Brief Overview

With multiplicity as its starting point, then, the book is unapologetic in its plea for a return to psychoanalytic concepts and approaches (with a full appreciation for the many changes psychoanalysis has undergone in the hundred-plus years since Freud's landmark *Interpretation of Dreams*[2]). Although pastoral counseling as a discipline has its origins in psychoanalytic thought, since the 1950s it has largely separated itself from psychoanalytic paradigms, often because of conflicts with the hard-line classical ego psychology approach that was dominant in the United States in the 1950s and '60s onward. This book incorporates the many exciting developments in contemporary psychoanalytic thinking, which in turn incorporate postmodern, constructivist ideas—including multiplicity—into a new understanding of *relationality* and *intersubjectivity*.

These ideas unfortunately remain mostly unknown in current pastoral counseling theory and practice. My previous book *Shared Wisdom: Use of the Self in Pastoral Care and Counseling*[3] was an attempt to begin to fill in this gap. Its focus was the single subject of transference-countertransference dynamics, via the use of the pastoral caregiver's own subjectivity in the mutual interplay of a pastoral relationship, as viewed through a contemporary psychoanalytic lens. *Shared Wisdom* addressed professionals occupying the entire spectrum of pastoral care (in both parish and chaplaincy settings), counseling, and psychotherapy. The anticipated readership of this book is somewhat narrower—it is addressed to professionals working at the pastoral psychotherapy end of this spectrum—but the focus here is wider: not only the transference-countertransference dimension of the therapeutic relationship (although this remains central to any relational psychoanalytic practice), but the theory and practice of pastoral psychotherapy more generally. The goal of *Many Voices*, then, is to bring contemporary psychoanalytic understandings back into dialogue with the pastoral psychotherapeutic field, toward a wider application of multiple aspects of postmodern relational theory and practice.

Part 1 lays a theological and theoretical framework for the work of pastoral psychotherapy from this postmodern, relational-psychoanalytic perspective. There were many questions to tackle immediately at the outset concerning the viability of such a hybrid project. For example, Why choose a psychoanalytic approach to pastoral psychotherapy, and why the term *pastoral psychotherapy* as opposed to *pastoral counseling*? How is postmodernism relevant or even applicable to either the "pastoral" or the "psychotherapeutic" domain? Why *relational*, and what is really meant by this broad and increasingly popular term in both pastoral care and theology? Is a "postmodern theology" even possible? And is the phrase "a psychoanalytic pastoral theology" a multiple oxymoron? These questions are taken up in detail in the introduction.

Part 1 continues with two chapters on constructive theology, to undergird the pastoral psychotherapeutic approach detailed in part 2. Chapter 1 investigates the question of theological anthropology—"what are human beings that you are mindful of them?" (Ps. 8:4)—and posits a relational understanding of persons as multiple, mutable, fluid, and always in process. Chapter 2 develops a parallel relational understanding of God, investigating the multiplicity of God and the use of the Trinity as a fluid metaphor for this multiplicity, and offers implications toward a relational pastoral praxis. This chapter concludes with thoughts on a multiple/Trinitarian, relational pastoral theology, with a proposal for a new set of *pastoral Trinitarian metaphors*: God as Creative Profusion, God as Incarnational Desire, and God as Living Inspiration.

Part 1 concludes with chapter 3, a relational understanding of health and unhealth as a framework for pastoral diagnosis. Psychotheological questions of traumatic wounding, shame, and the interrelationship of sin, pathology, and evil are addressed toward the end of this chapter.

Part 2 turns to the actual *praxis* (liberative practice) of pastoral psychotherapy. Chapter 4 offers an overview of the therapeutic process, and practical issues regarding preconditions for a fruitful therapeutic relationship, and the initial phase of therapy. The theme of multiplicity is continued as the concept of meeting with the many varied parts of each individual is explored. Particular challenges for the pastoral psychotherapist are noted. Chapter 5 continues with the middle phase and termination, following the theme of multiplicity in action. Empathy, transference, symbolic communication, dream exploration, enactments, therapeutic failures, and other issues of practice are explored from a pastoral and relational-psychoanalytic perspective. Both chapters are illustrated with detailed case examples, including the challenges of a relational, intersubjective approach to psychotherapy; the many vicissitudes of unconscious relationship in a therapeutic context; and dimensions of sexual, gender, and cultural diversity and multiplicity.

The book concludes with a meditation on the therapeutic sensibility and an appreciation, finally, for the mystery of the Holy, of persons, and of the therapeutic process. We are drawn, finally, into the ineffable dimensions of *un*knowing that enliven each new therapeutic relationship (and all relationships) with the continual, primordial surprises of creation: chaos, silence, and love.

How to Use This Book

This book is intended both as a textbook for pastoral psychotherapists/pastoral counselors at intermediate and advanced levels of clinical training, and also as a book for continuing education of—and, it is my hope, continued dialogue with—experienced pastoral counselors and psychotherapists in professional practice. A therapist needs a theoretical framework out of which to practice in order to have some coherent sense of the nature of human beings, the source and nature of wellness, the causes and remedies for human suffering and illness, and the ways in which the therapeutic relationship can help individuals and families to heal. At the same time, recognizing that all theory is finally metaphor and social construction, and that there is no ultimate "truth," it is helpful to remember that therapeutic wisdom can be drawn from many competing understandings. This book will draw its coherence from putting postmodern theological and relational-psychoanalytic frameworks into dialogue. But every theory, however compelling in its explanatory power, including postmodernism itself, is still just one paradigm, and its vision is still bounded by the questions it knows how to ask. This book, like all creative works, is also certainly bounded by my own social location as author—as a white, professional-class, north American wife and mother, ordained as an Episcopal priest, employed as a multiply-degreed academic in an earnestly-struggling-yet-still-patriarchal institution, with my own personal history of unearned privilege, emotional nurture and deprivation, and voluntary and involuntary joys and sufferings. The reader is therefore encouraged to find additional, multiple points of entry to this long essay, bringing his or her own unique agreement, critique, and application, in dialogue with multiple other theoretical frames and cultural viewpoints.

It should perhaps also be noted what this book is not intended to be: it is not a how-to manual or "cookbook" from which a reader can go directly from the page to practice with actual patients. The heart of psychotherapy training is clinical experience, under the supervision of a senior practitioner. As my own research with pastoral counselors and clinical social workers has shown, therapists at all levels of training and experience know the ethical importance of continuing education in peer settings, and they highly value ongoing professional supervision and peer consultation.[4] The book is therefore intended only as an adjunct to actual supervised experience as a therapist or pastoral counselor-in-training working with real, uniquely gifted, suffering human patients.

You may choose to use this book in several ways. It is recommended to read the book cover to cover, so that the theological and theoretical frameworks for the sections on psychotherapeutic practice will be clear. However, if your interests lie primarily in discovering new theological or theoretical developments in the field of pastoral theology, you may want to focus on the first two chapters. If your interests lie primarily in practice, you may want to begin with chapter 3 and refer back to the first two chapters as needed. Case study material may be especially useful in training and teaching settings. I welcome your feedback from your own experience.

Acknowledgments

A work of this level of detail would not be possible without the support and feedback of many individuals. I am grateful to my many wonderful colleagues who read drafts and portions of the manuscript and gave input from their various areas of expertise: to theologians John Hoffmeyer, Catherine Keller, and Robin Steinke for their thoughtful readings of part 1; to pastoral psychotherapists and psychoanalysts Wallace Fletcher, Florence Gelo, Felicity Kelcourse, and Lallene Rector; to my colleague on the Pastoral Care Team of the Lutheran Theological Seminary at Philadelphia, Eloise Scott; and to spiritual directors Sharline Fulton and Cathy Looker, SSJ. Particular thanks also go to Flo Gelo, Constance Goldberg, and Marilyn Steele for consultation on the ethical use of case material.

I am grateful as well to colleagues in the American Association of Pastoral Counselors (AAPC), especially Douglas Ronsheim, Margaret Kornfeld, Pamela Holliman, Phillip Bennett, and others already named above for their enthusiastic encouragement to undertake this project. And I am thankful for my many colleagues in the Society for Pastoral Theology, and the Person, Culture, and Religion Group of the American Academy of Religion—especially Kathleen Bishop, Valerie deMarinis, Carrie Doehring, David Hogue, Rodney Hunter, Emmanuel Lartey, Bonnie Miller-McLemore, Francesca Nuzzolese, Jeanne Stevenson-Moessner, Teresa Snorton, and many others, including some already named above. Their very thoughtful engagement with my previous book *Shared Wisdom*, continued intellectual stimulation and friendship, and creative leadership in our field have contributed personally to my creative process in the development of this project. I am also grateful for the ongoing partnership with Fortress Press, for Beth Lewis and my editors, Michael West of Fortress Press and Ann Delgehausen of Trio Bookworks, without whose careful attention this book would be much poorer.

I give thanks for my spiritual communities: the Episcopal Church of St. Martin-in-the-Fields, Chestnut Hill, Philadelphia; Christ Lutheran Church, ELCA, Gettysburg, Pennsylvania; and the Sisters of St. Joseph Center for Spirituality at Chestnut Hill College and St. Mary's Retreat in Cape May, New Jersey. Special thanks also go to Teresa Bowers, David Erickson, Mark Mummert, Norman Nunamaker, and the Gettysburg Chamber Orchestra, who have been my musical "holding environment" throughout the time of working on this project.

I have learned so much over the years from my students, parishioners, and psychotherapy patients, who have opened their hearts and minds to me in relationships of trust! They have helped me to grow tremendously, both professionally and as a person. I am also grateful for all my own professors, supervisors, consultants, and mentors, from whom I received not only my formal clinical and classroom training but models for caring, and seeing the world in both a pastoral and a psychoanalytic light. I especially want to thank Margaret Emerson (pastoral counselor and adjunct professor, San Francisco Theological Seminary), Marilyn Coffy (formerly Director of the master's in Pastoral Counseling program at Holy Names College, Oakland, California), Constance Goldberg and Joseph Cronin (faculty, Institute for Clinical Social Work, Chicago), Stephen Joseph and Marilyn Steele (Jungian analysts in private practice in Berkeley, California), Cotton Fite, James Shackelford, the late Bonnie Niswander, and all the staff of the Pastoral Counseling Center at Lutheran General Hospital, Park Ridge, Illinois, and the faculties of Holy Names College and the Institute for Clinical Social Work. Without the multiplicity of wisdom and insight they shared with me over many years, this book would not exist.

Special thanks go to my colleagues at the Lutheran Theological Seminary at Philadelphia, particularly Dean Paul Rajashekar, President Philip Krey, and the Board of Trustees, for granting me sabbatical leave to devote to the completion of this project, and to Thrivent Financial for Lutherans and the Episcopal Evangelical Education Society for sabbatical funding. Thanks to Jon Pahl, loyal mutual reader, and to Katie Day, my neighbor, friend, and LTSP colleague in the social sciences, for innumerable cups of coffee, gourmet meals, carpooling children, and kitchen-table conversations about the demands of juggling family life, teaching, and research. I am grateful for the tremendous spirit of collegiality and support of *all* my faculty colleagues at LTSP—for ongoing conversation, constructive critique, and mutual inspiration. The gender-diverse, multicultural, and urban human context of LTSP in which we live and work is truly "good soil."

Finally, as always, my greatest debt of gratitude goes to my family—especially my husband, Michael, and our daughter, Macrina, who have lived with me through my own multiple self-states, rhizomes, dirt, and "fecundity!" Especially when writing is hard and the woods are dark, you are my Dante, my Virgil, and my Beatrice.

Permissions

Wherever possible, biblical translations are all taken or adapted from *The New Testament and Psalms: An Inclusive Version*, ed. Victor Roland Gold, Thomas L. Hoyt Jr., Sharon H. Ringe, Susan Brooks Thistlethwaite, Burton H. Throckmorton Jr., and Barbara A. Withers (New York: Oxford University Press, 1995). All other biblical quotations are from the New Revised Standard Version Bible (NRSV).

Figure 2: Michelangelo (1475–1564). Creation of Adam; detail of God and surrounding figures. Detail of the Sistine ceiling. Sistine Chapel, Vatican Palace, Vatican State. Photo Credit : Scala / Art Resource, N.Y. Used by permission.

Figure 5: "Meshberger's Discovery of the Brain in Michelangelo's 'Creation,'" Journal of the American Medical Association 264 (1990): 1837–41. Used by permission of the American Medical Association.

Figure 7: Photograph of Frederick Hart, "Ex Nihilo" Tympanum, Washington National Cathedral, from 2006 © The Protestant Episcopal Cathedral Foundation. Used by permission.

Figure 8: The vertical split, reproduced from Heinz Kohut, "The Two Analyses of Mr. Z," *International Journal of Psycho-Analysis* 60 (1979): 11. Used by permission of Dr. Thomas Kohut.

Earlier versions of portions of chapters 2 and 3 appeared as Pamela Cooper-White, "Pastoral Implications" for Easter Sunday, Lectionary Homiletics 15, no. 2 (February–March, 2005): 41ff., and Pamela Cooper-White, "I Do Not Do the Good I Want but the Evil I Do Not Want Is What I Do: The Concept of the Vertical Split in Self Psychology in Relation to Christian Concepts of Good and Evil," *Journal of Pastoral Theology* 13, no. 1 (2003). Both are adapted by permission.

All photographs are by the author, except where otherwise indicated.

Introduction

Introducing Four Case Studies

BEA

Bea[1] first came into my office on a warm September afternoon. She introduced herself nervously, looking downcast. Her voice was very soft and low. She was stylishly dressed and made up, but the overall impression she gave was one of lack of confidence. Long, shiny black hair hung down like a curtain, hiding part of her face. She settled tentatively into the chair I offered and did not hold her head up. She looked uncomfortable in her body.

At the time of our first meeting, Bea was twenty-six years old, the daughter of Korean immigrants living in a large Midwestern industrial city, and mother of one son, Sam. Bea was living with her mother, who often babysat Sam and her other grandchildren. Bea's father had died of a heart attack eight years before. Bea was referred to me by a priest colleague of mine, Paul, with whom she had had sporadic contact. Her first communication with me was a telephone call the previous month in which she tearfully reported that she was in the process of getting a divorce but could not really bring herself to leave her husband, Donny. In his referral to me, Paul had also stated that he felt the marriage was unhealthy, possibly dangerous for Bea, and said he had encouraged Bea to go ahead with the divorce. When she became ambivalent and reluctant, he suggested therapy to Bea, for dealing with "deeper issues that might be getting in the way."

KAREN

Karen, a thirty-year-old daughter of eastern European immigrants, was an accomplished visual artist. She was initially referred to me for therapy because her pastor felt that she was "stuck" in her grieving after the death of her father. It quickly became apparent that in addition to a complicated bereavement, Karen had been suffering for years from major clinical depression with an underlying baseline of moderate depression (dysthymia) even during her "good times." She was working for a temporary employment agency when she entered therapy and was just beginning to devote a major portion of each week to painting and exhibiting her artwork. When she was not working or doing her artwork she spent long hours on the couch in the room she had claimed as her studio, sleeping or staring at the walls in a depressive haze.

Karen was also feeling trapped in a relationship with a man, Alan, with whom she lived, whose behavior she described as introverted, cold, and preoccupied with his work as an information technology specialist. She and Alan lived in the basement apartment of her mother's house, and when they argued, Alan would often go upstairs and sleep in her old bedroom in her mother's quarters. Alan was skeptical and belittling about Karen's art, and her mother was horrified that Karen was wasting her time being an artist and would never be able to make a living. She would sometimes invoke Karen's dead father and yell, "What would your father think of this stupid [expletive] you're doing!?" When Karen won an award at an art show, she felt there was no one in her life who could celebrate her success.

BRENT

Brent was a forty-year-old white middle-class computer programmer who came to therapy because he had experienced suicidal fantasies that had startled and deeply frightened him. These feelings had started when he was reassigned by his boss. The change of job was officially defined as a lateral move, but Brent experienced this as a demotion in responsibility, authority, and power. He felt that coming to therapy was a sign of weakness but, given his depressive thoughts, he had used his considerable analytical skills to convince himself to "get some help." His fright overcame his shame, although he was highly resistant to the idea of "seeing a shrink." Given Brent's reliance on his thinking function, and his interest related to computer work in networks and systems, I suggested that as part of our initial work together, he construct a genogram of his family history. Brent threw himself gladly into this task and soon was observing certain intergenerational patterns in his suburban family. For example, he described both his parents, and the two siblings he identified—a sister Joan, a lawyer, who was three years older, and "my Irish twin," Josh, a self-employed entrepreneur, who was ten months older—as being "workaholics."

JENNIFER

Jennifer was a twenty-one-year-old white single mother of an infant girl. She was working for minimum wage as an uncertified home health aide but hoped one day to go to nursing school. She was also heavily involved in a church that identified itself as fundamentalist Christian and had an international organizational structure. Jennifer was referred by a women's shelter with whom my agency at the time had an ongoing contract for low-fee therapy. Jennifer became homeless when her boyfriend (the father of her child) was caught setting a fire in their apartment building, causing their eviction. Jennifer had difficulty articulating any goals for therapy other than the fact that it was mandated by the shelter: "I don't really need any therapy. I'm doing fine. They just make us do this, you know." She continued by saying, "All my goals now are spiritual. I seek God first. I would like this situation to help me be more forgiving."

Although she took pains to present herself and her situation as "fine," the presenting crisis followed years of ongoing drama and turmoil. Her boyfriend was addicted to drugs, as was her older brother. Jennifer was also involved in an ongoing intense emotional struggle with her parents. Her mother had refused to talk to her for the past five years. Jennifer stated that this was because her boyfriend was black, and therefore her baby was biracial. She said that this conflict with her mother was simply "her cross to bear," and that she now receives her greatest joy from knowing God. She planned to be rebaptized soon, regarding her former sexual relations as a sin. "I'm a serious Christian, very serious, and I tithe, knowing that somehow God will provide even though it's a sacrifice."

The purpose of this book is to provide an overview of pastoral psychotherapeutic theory *and praxis* from a postmodern, relational-psychoanalytic perspective. This book is, at least in part, a response to a need for new, more relational approaches to pastoral psychotherapy in today's pressurized, pluralistic, and postmodern social context.[2] The book is an effort to bridge worlds between contemporary psychoanalytic theory and practice, and pastoral counseling. I use the term *praxis*, rather than *practice*, here at the outset to signal intentionality about the liberative and political aspects of care, which are always implicit, though not always explicitly attended. As in my previous books, I will also continue to integrate this postmodern, relational-psychoanalytic paradigm with constructive work in theology. Because pastoral practice is always a subset of all faithful practice (citing Catherine LaCugna), "Christian orthopraxis must correspond to what we believe is true about God: that God is personal, that God is ecstatic and fecund love, that God's very nature is to exist toward and for another."[3]

Why *Psychoanalytic?*

Why does the world need a book from any sort of psychoanalytic framework, especially in this postmodern era in which eclectic and/or narrative psychological approaches might seem to make the most sense as approaches to pastoral counseling? Although pastoral counseling has its practical and theoretical (though not theological) origins in psychoanalytic thought, over the past five or more decades it has increasingly separated itself from psychoanalytic paradigms because of legitimate problems pastoral theologians have raised with a rigid classical ego psychology approach that had been dominant in the United States since the 1950s and '60s. Rogerian therapy and family systems approaches became the lingua franca of pastoral counseling. Since the 1980s, narrative approaches to pastoral counseling have caught the imagination of many.[4] Nevertheless, knowledge of classical psychodynamic theory, object relations, and Jungian psychology have continued to be valued in pastoral counseling training centers,[5] and there is some evidence that this interest not only continues but is increasing, particularly with the rise of interest in self psychology since the late 1980s.[6]

Why work psychoanalytically? Psychoanalysis is not, finally, only a therapeutic modality but an art, a way of thinking and of looking at the world. It is an *aesthetic* as much as a *hermeneutic*, and certainly more than a science.[7] It is a commitment to the belief that things—including people, faces, words, behaviors—are never only as they seem, and that everything potentially has multiple layers of meaning. It is an aesthetic because it recognizes the power and even the beauty in such a multiplicity of symbolic meanings and nuances, as well as the patterns by which these meanings continue to shift and change over time. It is an art of seeing, complexly, like a painter. Tracy Chevalier describes this process of seeing in a fictional exchange between the painter Jan Vermeer and his servant, the "girl with a pearl earring":

> "Come here, Griet . . . Look out the window."
> I looked out. It was a breezy day, with clouds disappearing behind the New Church tower.
> "What color are those clouds?"
> "Why, white, sir."
> He raised his eyebrows slightly. "Are they?"
> I glanced at them. "And grey. Perhaps it will snow."
> "Come, Griet, you can do better than that. Think of your vegetables . . . Think of how you separated the whites. Your turnips and your onions—are they the same white?"
> Suddenly I understood. "No. The turnip has green in it, the onion yellow."
> "Exactly. Now, what colors do you see in the clouds?"
> "There is some blue in them," I said after studying them for a few minutes. "And—yellow as well. And there is some green!" I became so excited I actually pointed. I had been looking at clouds all my life, but I felt as if I saw them for the first time in that moment.[8]

Psychoanalysis, similarly, helps us to see in new and deeper ways the many phenomena of our lives—people, places, behaviors, emotions, memories, objects, and our own self-states. Through interpretation and *re*membering, it is as if we were seeing them for the first time.

Why Pastoral *Psychotherapy*?

It may be important at the outset to clarify some terms and to situate the subtitle of this book, "Pastoral Psychotherapy in Relational and Theological Perspective," conceptually. Why not "pastoral counseling," for example, or even, since the author of this book is grounded in the Christian religious tradition, "Christian counseling"? Of the five terms currently most in use—*pastoral care*,[9] *spiritual care*, *pastoral counseling*, *Christian counseling*,[10] and *pastoral psychotherapy*—the latter is probably used the least in contemporary pastoral counseling practice. This has been a historic debate within the pastoral field since the nineteenth century, and within the pastoral counseling subspecialty in particular.[11] Carroll Wise, in his 1980 book, *Pastoral Psychotherapy*, argued for the term, stating,

> In using the word psychotherapy rather than counseling we are returning to the roots of our religious tradition. The Greek word "psyche" in the New Testament refers, not to one part of the total person as distinguished from other parts, such as pneuma and soma. It rather refers to the living person as a total reality or unity. It cannot be taken to mean a spiritual aspect as distinguished from the mental or physical. It is man [*sic*] as a whole, an organic unity.[12]

I am reclaiming the term *pastoral psychotherapy* not as a synonym for *pastoral counseling* but as a particular and distinct healing intervention *in its own right*. For the purposes of this book, I am defining *pastoral psychotherapy* as a mode of *healing* intervention (therapy) that is specifically grounded both in *psychoanalytic* theory and methods (psycho-)—that is, with a primary focus on *unconscious* mental and emotional processes—and held in a constructive, creation-affirming theology (pastoral). While all forms of pastoral care and counseling are intended to foster growth, healing, and empowerment for just and loving engagement with the world, the special charge of pastoral psychotherapy is to help, accompany, and support individuals (and couples and families) in recognizing and healing especially painful psychic wounds and/or long-standing patterns of self-defeating relationships to self and others. The primary means of healing is both through the classical goal of understanding, or insight—making the unconscious conscious—and through the process of reviving and "working through" painful experiences and affects. The duration of therapy may range from a few months to several years or more. The focus of this book is on one-on-one psychotherapy because of the emphasis on the formation of unconscious processes, but the methods are applicable to work with couples, families, and groups.[13]

In my previous writings, I have drawn on the schematic of the Johari Window[14] (see Figure 1) to show the distinction between pastoral *care*, *counseling*, and *psychotherapy*. In this diagram, areas 1 and 3 are the usual domains of pastoral care, involving conscious communication between pastor and pastoral-care recipient. Area 2 is also, on occasion, an area for pastoral care, as personal feelings and behaviors are observed by the pastor (even if the parishioner is not fully aware of it). This is an area of risk, and it requires great sensitivity and tact because exposing what is known to others but not known to self evokes shame. Therefore, while occasionally the

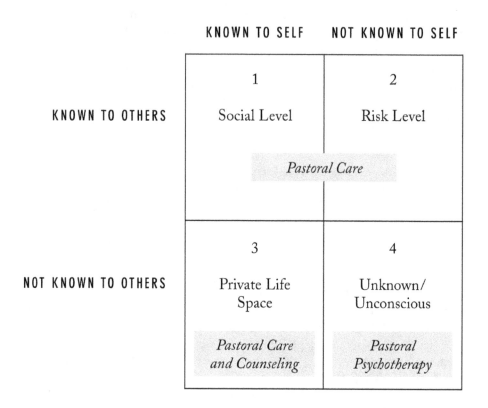

KNOWN TO SELF   NOT KNOWN TO SELF

	1 Social Level	2 Risk Level
KNOWN TO OTHERS		
	Pastoral Care	
NOT KNOWN TO OTHERS	3 Private Life Space	4 Unknown/ Unconscious
	Pastoral Care and Counseling	*Pastoral Psychotherapy*

Figure 1: *Johari Window, adapted for pastoral care and counseling*

domain of pastoral care when gentle confrontation is required, it is more the purview of pastoral counseling and psychotherapy.[15] Area 4 is the realm of pastoral psychotherapy and not pastoral care. It represents the realm of the unconscious. It is here that the unconscious relationship of therapist and patient will be manifested, primarily through transference-countertransference dynamics. An understanding of the intersubjective nature of unconscious communication allows the therapist to enter more deeply with the patient into the unknown, allowing for the unconscious to become conscious as meanings are co-constructed, revised, and shared through empathic exploration.

In this volume, I am further drawing out the distinction between pastoral counseling and pastoral psychotherapy. I have defined *pastoral psychotherapy* above. *Pastoral counseling* is also a mode of pastoral helping that goes beyond short-term and supportive pastoral care, both on the level of risk and intimacy, and in duration.

Like psychotherapy, it belongs in the realm of greater training and specialization of certified (and/or licensed) counselors. However, in contrast to pastoral psychotherapy as defined above, I am defining *pastoral counseling*, for the purposes of this book, as focusing mainly on *conscious* emotional and mental processes (or, at most, *preconscious*—that is, mental contents that may be *temporarily* out of awareness but easily accessible once some attention has been paid), with the goal of solving problems in the client's present situation, often by identifying and building on the client's existing strengths.

The primary means of healing in pastoral counseling is through a cognitive reframing of the client's current situation and the adoption of new strategies for coping, although some focus may be given to antecedents in the client's early life. Pastoral counseling, then—including cognitive, cognitive-behavioral, Solution-Focused,[16] Rational Emotive,[17] and many contemporary narrative approaches[18]—tends to focus on the present and future rather than present and past emotional events, and works through various methods of reframing negative perspectives or meanings to events in order to arrive at solutions to problems identified by clients. Much or all of what is discussed in session—usually about once a week—involves events and feelings of the client that have occurred outside the counseling relationship, in the client's experiences with everyday living during the week. The language used to describe the therapeutic pair in this enterprise is usually (pastoral) *counselor* and *client*, giving emphasis to the respectful, contractual nature of the professional relationship.[19]

In real practice, this distinction between counseling and psychotherapy is not so pure; there is much overlap. The chief difference is most often seen in the focus of attention in the counseling/therapy session—counseling will focus almost entirely on the client's situation and problems *outside* the session; while psychotherapy will increasingly focus over time on the interaction *between* the therapist and the patient in the here-and-now of the therapeutic session in an effort to "catch" unconscious projective processes "in the act," *in media res*, as a mirror for understanding the unconscious processes that are likely also being enacted in the patient's everyday life.

Psychotherapy may be further divided into *psychodynamic* therapy and *psychoanalytic* therapy. Neither form of psychotherapy disregards either the patient's ongoing problems and concerns in everyday life outside the consulting room, or what is occurring intersubjectively between the therapist and the patient. However, the focus of psychodynamic therapy tends to be on the way in which emotional events in early childhood set up patterns of perceiving and reacting as they are carried into current living outside the therapeutic relationship. This is the most commonly known aspect of psychodynamic therapy—the therapist and patient come to make genetic interpretations about present behavior based on experience deep in the past, "bringing the unconscious to consciousness."[20]

Psychoanalytic psychotherapy is distinctive in that it is characterized not so much by interpretation of the past in the patient's everyday life, although this is an ongoing part of the work, but rather on what is happening in the therapeutic relationship, here and now, "in the room." The hallmark of psychoanalytic psychotherapy, then, is not only attention to the patient's early childhood and how it is playing out in relationships outside the therapy, but attention to the multivalent unconscious operations that are present in the intersubjective relationship between patient and therapist—the transference-countertransference relationship. Sigmund Freud framed this in terms of a heroic battle (between the forces of resistance and "rational consideration"), which reflects his fear at the time about the perils of erotic transference. Most contemporary analytic practitioners would say that such struggle only reflects one of many possible dynamics that may arise in the intersubjective working through of the therapeutic relationship. Nevertheless, while it is best to read beyond the militant language of struggle and penetration, as well as the narrowly medical language of "physician" and "cure," Freud's words from the early days of psychoanalysis are still important in establishing the centrality of working in the immediacy of the transference:

> In following up the libido that is withdrawn from consciousness we penetrate into the region of the unconscious, and this provokes reactions which bring with them to light many of the characteristics of unconscious processes as we have learnt to know them from the study of dreams. The unconscious feelings strive to avoid the recognition which the cure demands; they seek instead for reproduction, with all the power of hallucination and the inappreciation of time characteristic of the unconscious. The patient ascribes, just as in dreams, currency and reality to what results from the awakening of his unconscious feelings; he seeks to discharge his emotions, regardless of the reality of the situation. The physician requires of him that he shall fit these emotions into their place in the treatment and in his life-history, subject them to rational consideration, and appraise them at their true psychical value. This struggle between physician and patient, between intellect and the forces of instinct, between recognition and the striving for discharge, is fought out *almost entirely over the transference-manifestations. This is the ground on which the victory must be won*, the final expression of which is lasting recovery from neurosis. It is undeniable that the subjugation of the transference-manifestations provides the greatest difficulties for the psycho-analyst; but it must not be forgotten that *they, and they only, render the invaluable service of making the patient's buried and forgotten love-emotions actual and manifest*; for in the last resort no one can be slain *in effigie*.[21]

Psychoanalytic therapy is therefore often conducted more than once a week because the shifting nuances of feelings in the therapeutic relationship itself unfold in such a way that more time is needed to observe these shifts as they occur, and to explore them in the level of detail needed. Such frequency helps to maintain the focus on—and immersion in—the flow of shared unconscious material, without slipping back into more ordinary social discourse. (Note that psychoanalysis proper involves even more frequent contact, as well as some different techniques that require further intensive training to become certified as a psychoanalyst.[22])

This book will consider both forms of psychotherapy—psychodynamic and psychoanalytic—recognizing that in actual practice, the focus often moves back and forth between psychodynamic and psychoanalytic explorations, depending on what is most pressing for the patient at a given moment.

Pastoral psychotherapy draws its definition from the etymology of the word *psychotherapy* itself. The prefix *psycho-* comes from the Greek word ψυχὴ (*psychè*), which carries multiple related meanings, including "soul/breath," which is similar to the Hebrew sense as "embodied breath" and "animal life" (*nephesh*), and "soul" in the Hellenistic sense as "spirit/breath/wind," πνεῦμα (*pneûma*) in contrast to the body, σῶμα (*sôma*).[23] In modern psychological terms, *psyche* thus refers both to one's embodied self and to the disembodied experience of mind as a separate entity, which may or may not be immediately associated with the body (as in René Descartes's famous seventeenth-century dictum supervaluing rationality above the body: *Cogito, ergo sum*—"I am thinking, therefore I exist."[24] *Therapy* comes from the Greek word θεραπεύω (*therapeúo*), which is usually translated as "to cure or to heal" (e.g., in the New Testament, in Matt. 4:24; Mark 6:5; Luke 6:7; etc.). Therapy therefore takes its primary meaning as the act or work of healing.

The language of the therapeutic pair in this paradigm is (pastoral) "therapist" or "psychotherapist" and "patient." There are problems in this terminology that have been taken up critically in the pastoral literature.[25] Chief among these problems is that a "therapist" may be too easily understood as the one who is doing the acts of healing, and a "patient" may be seen only as passive, as the one being acted upon. Nevertheless, I argue for retaining this language for two reasons. First, somewhat pragmatically, it belongs to the psychoanalytic tradition from Freud's time to the present moment, and thus it has become a "signifier" in its own right of a form of psychological healing work that is rooted in an exploration of unconscious domains—increasingly, as this is understood in all forms of contemporary psychoanalysis—not only of the patient's inner life, but the therapist's as well, in a unique, mutual interaction. As Jungian analyst Virginia Beane Rutter has written:

> In depth psychotherapy there is an unconscious mutuality of exchange, whether or not this mutuality is consciously acknowledged. Although my role as the guardian of the work is mandated and necessary, I am influenced: my psyche is acted upon by the psyches of my patients. On a conscious level, I also learn from my patients—about myself, about life, about culture.[26]

More will be said about this dimension of mutuality, as "intersubjectivity," later in the book. But it is interesting in light of this mutuality to note that the word θεραπεύω (*therapeúo*) also has a second, less well known meaning. In addition to the more obvious English cognate definition "to heal," θεραπεύω also means "to serve" (as in Acts 17:25). Far from being the lofty expert, the therapist, in the etymological sense, is also one who serves, not from above but from *below or alongside*. Like Jesus washing the feet of his disciples in the upper room, the therapist's vocation is not to lord it over the patient, but to *serve* her or him. Only the tools are different. Instead of water, a basin, and a towel, the therapist's tools are, among other things, empathy, honesty, curiosity, experience, a certain amount of life wisdom, a foundation of supervised training, humor, and hope.[27]

The reason for retaining this language of "patient" is that it continues to carry the multiple meanings of soul and psyche; of suffering, passion, the pathos of the human condition (patient), and the meeting of this suffering at a profound level with a movement toward healing (*therapeúo*). As Rutter has written: "I use the term *patient*, rather than *client*, because the Latin root of *patient* means 'to suffer or endure' and 'to be under someone's care,' while the word *client* has a commercial connotation in our society. As a Jungian analyst I feel suffering and caring are fundamental aspects of therapeutic work."[28]

Embedded within this paradigm of suffering as passion and pathos is also a term from the same etymological root that has been increasingly somewhat unpopular in the pastoral literature in recent decades: *pathology*. Pathology, diagnosis, and a medical or "disease" model of psychology and psychotherapy has rightly become suspect in recent decades, to the extent that it sets up an expert–passive patient dynamic, in which patients come to be identified globally and impersonally with their suffering and impairments, or labeled as "problems" in order to impose political and social conformity. However, I believe that to do away with all forms of assessment or diagnosis would be to pretend that various recognizable forms of illness and pain did not exist, in other words, to throw out the baby with the bathwater.

Social workers turned in large numbers to psychoanalytic or "clinical" social work increasingly in the decades after World War I, motivated by this same recognition. They recognized in many situations or "cases" in which individuals and families were struggling to free themselves from genuinely oppressive circumstances, that problem solving, liberal education, advocacy, and supportive case work alone—in other words, approaches that only interacted at the level of clients' conscious awareness—did not eliminate individuals' and families' more deeply entrenched patterns of dysfunction and self-harm.[29] As Freud himself noted, purely educational approaches (analogous in modern times, for example, to self-help books), are not sufficient because they do not address the internal conflicts and unconscious dynamics underlying conscious suffering. In Freud's words:

> If knowledge about the unconscious were as important for the patient as people inexperienced in psycho-analysis imagine, listening to lectures or reading books would be enough to cure him. Such measures, however, have as much

influence on the symptoms of nervous illness as a distribution of menu-cards in a time of famine has upon hunger.[30]

Pathology need not be understood as a pejorative term, by which individuals may be labeled and thus dismissed, but rather as a means of naming a reality of suffering (*pathos-logos*). Understanding pathology in all its nuances requires diagnosis[31] or assessment in order to have some means of categorizing the shapes that mental and emotional suffering tend to take, at least in any given cultural location. Consensus about these categories, and specific terminology, evolves and changes over time as different theories hold sway, but there is a shared language and at least a broadly consensual conceptualization in the field of psychology without which professional communication and consultation regarding practice, research, and training would be very limited. *Diagnosis*, from the Greek word διαγινώσκω (*diaginósko*), simply means to distinguish or inquire, to make a decision, or make something known. In this regard, pathology and diagnosis belong to the practice of pastoral psychotherapy, as one area of disciplined focus, in order to shape care with a thoughtful assessment of "what ails."[32]

It should be noted at the outset that this understanding of diagnosis applies primarily to the understandings and practices of psychology and therapy in the western hemisphere. This consensus taxonomy of mental illness is definitively represented in the International Diagnostic Manual, currently in its tenth edition[33] and, in the United States since 1952, the *Diagnostic and Statistical Manual of Mental Disorders* (DSM), currently in its fourth edition with additional minor text revisions (DSM IV-TR). These are intended as purely descriptive classifications, and do not refer to etiology (the study of causation),[34] although there were certainly underlying theoretical paradigms in order for the classifications to be derived at all.[35] For all their power and authoritative status in the medical and mental health professions, these are nevertheless cultural products that reflect the values and biases of (largely North American and European) Western culture, and continue to carry a rationalist and materialist bias that tends to obscure the variability of phenomena under the rubric of "discovery" and scientific "truth." Every edition of the DSM since the third[36] has involved labels, definitions, and descriptions of disorders as negotiated by separate work groups of specialists and compiled by a senior task force or steering committee.[37] While the "reliability" of its classifications continues to be a subject of some controversy,[38] the utility of having some common clinical vocabulary is valued by most professional counselors and psychotherapists. Sophisticated readings of the DSM and other diagnostic manuals require the clinician to pay attention to their ever-changing and -evolving definitions and underlying theoretical constructs. The introduction to the DSM itself includes cautions on the limitations of a categorical approach, and the still-fledgling efforts of the DSM task force to incorporate "ethnic and cultural considerations."[39] Therapists also should be careful not to use diagnostic labels pejoratively—"the Borderline I see every Tuesday"—nor to confuse uniquely gifted and suffering persons with diagnostic labels—"the bipolar behind curtain 2."

Other constructions and modes of assessment of health and unhealth, including mental and spiritual well-being, are central in other cultures, particularly in the eastern and southern hemispheres. As Nancy Ramsay has written, "diagnosis is not a neutral process; it has both interpretive and constructive functions. Diagnosis reiterates the anthropological and philosophical assumptions of the practitioner and validates the usefulness of those assumptions for naming reality."[40] Optimally, therefore, people who make diagnoses should be always be self-reflective and self-critical, watchful for biases and gaps in their own understanding, and above all, engaged in collaboration with the patient, in an ongoing process of shared reflection, dialogue, and continual revision as the patient's sufferings come to evolve, change, and carry different meanings over time. The issues of pathology and diagnosis will be addressed more fully in chapter 3.

In summary, the distinctions between pastoral counseling and pastoral psychotherapy have to do with the relative emphasis on past, present, and future, and on the patient's strengths, rather than an understanding of the pathology that may be getting in the patient's way. Thus, while pastoral counselors most often ground their explorations in seeking to come to shared understandings of a client's strengths and past coping mechanisms, "psychotherapists" are more likely to ground their explorations with the patient in the patient's strengths but also in an ongoing, collaborative understanding of pathology. This work must be done honestly and empathically at the same time—compassionately and sensitively facing together the truths of those times in the patient's life, especially in early childhood, when experiences of wounding may have caused a fragmentation of the inner life, further resulting in outmoded patterns of survival and coping, and forms of cognition, behavior, and affect (feeling) that cause repeated harm to the person and often to others as well.[41]

Because the revealing of such wounding, often previously hidden from others and from the patient's own awareness, can be accompanied by intense feelings of shame, this work requires the utmost in sensitivity, care, tact, and timing. But to avoid going into this fourth quadrant of the Johari Window at all is to evade the true healing work of psychotherapy, and what sets it apart from all other kinds of helping relationships. Regarding this phenomenon of woundedness from a theological framework, this perhaps also begs the question of the relationship between pathology, sin, and evil. This (perennially controversial) subject will be addressed in chapter 3.

One last note on terminology: the word *patient* also suggests the *patience* that is mutually required between both partners in the therapeutic enterprise to remain steadfast in a process that unfolds little by little, with minute shifts in meaning over time. Pastoral counseling is often time-limited, brief, and solution-focused. Pastoral psychotherapy, in contrast, is a *process*—a minutely detailed, sensitive, and at times extremely delicate uncovering of new and changing meanings that arise between the therapist and the patient over time. It therefore properly tends to be engaged in over years, not weeks or months, although some of its theoretical framework and techniques can be adapted into briefer psychotherapeutic models.[42] It is an organic process, like gardening, that cannot be rushed.

Why *Postmodern*?

For the purposes of this book I am defining *postmodern* as sharing a set of assumptions, critiques, and strategies that arose in the mid- to late-twentieth century in response to a crisis of confidence in the saving power of human rationalism and the scientific method, particularly in the wake of the Nazi Holocaust and the deployment of the atomic bomb. Rationalism, exalted in the scientific paradigm as the source of salvation for humankind, was shown to be a two-edged sword. In particular, rapid advances in technology gave rise not only to methods and machines that improved human health, longevity, and ease for the Western nations sponsoring this research and development. Technology also produced more ruthless, impersonal, and efficient means of genocide and, with nuclear proliferation, for the first time in human history, the capacity to annihilate life on this planet.

While there is no single approach to postmodernism, and no single school of thought or even particular field of study to which it belongs, the following six propositions are central to postmodernism:

1. A recognition that rationalism, or the ability to think about one's own existence—exalted by Descartes as the defining characteristic of the human being in the statement *Cogito, ergo sum* cited above—is in fact limited in its capacity to comprehend fully what is necessary for sustaining both human and planetary life. Descartes found refuge from his dread of ambiguity and relativism in his perception of one seemingly unshakable certainty: the capacity of his own mind to reason about its own existence, and therefore, by inference, the existence of God as the source of such rationality.[43] However, such privileging of the rational over other forms of knowing, including the emotional and the sensate, is in itself a culture- and time-bound notion—a "paradigm"[44] that is capable of answering only those questions that can be conceived within its own cultural, linguistic, sociological, political, and historical horizons.

2. The idea of "objectivity" is thus also called into question, with the recognition of the inevitability of bias in any human perspective. It is not possible to be a neutral, unbiased, or "objective" observer. The subject, or "I," can never be removed from its own observations. Furthermore, as soon as I observe an "object," whether inanimate or animate, I influence the very object I am observing. This principle became known in twentieth-century science as the Heisenberg uncertainty principle.[45] To study something—or, more pertinent to psychotherapy, some*one*—is already to interact with that one, and therefore inherently to have influence or cause change. All research, all communication, involves mutual exchange, and mutual influence, in

which the roles of observer and observed are more interchangeable than most of us were taught to believe by the so-called positivist scientific method.[46]

3. Such categories as truth, fact, and discovery are therefore not necessarily as universally applicable to all people, creatures, things, and places as they were assumed to be in the "Age of Enlightenment." What is considered to be the discovery of "truth" by any group of people is, in fact, circumscribed by the particular set of circumstances and assumptions held tacitly by that group. Truth, and the supposed knowledge of what is true, is therefore not as eternally real, comprehensively understandable, or universal as Enlightenment thinkers proposed. For this reason, priority is given in postmodern thought to the local and the particular rather than the "universal," and "a return from the timeless to the timely."[47] Exactly what, if anything at all, may actually exist in the universe, eternally or momentarily—the "really real" behind our perceptions of reality—is still a subject of intense debate among philosophers, and is probably, finally, an unanswerable mystery. What human beings *can* know, at best, will be partial, fleeting, contingent upon the context of both knower and known, and continually subject to further consideration and revision. All human knowledge, then, far from being a cumulative process of gaining ever more accurate understandings of the world, is better described as a provisional construction of reality that coheres and supports the flourishing of life for those whose constructions hold the most power in a given culture or society. In short, reality is not something that can be fully known—reality is *socially* and *culturally constructed*.[48]

4. To the extent that all knowledge is socially constructed, "facts" are better understood as a combination of beliefs, observations, and theories that hold true for a given group of people in a given context. Such facts must always be examined in light of the biases and assumptions of those who embrace them as true. Postmodern linguistic strategies, such as Jacques Derrida's method of "deconstruction,"[49] constitute efforts to unmask such hidden or unacknowledged biases and assumptions. This is especially important when such biases have been used, as shown by Michel Foucault, to reinforce the power of dominant groups by masking the authority of the powerful in mystifying jargons and naming claims to truth as axiomatic principles rather than the theories that they are.[50]

Just as in George Orwell's saying that history is always written by the winners,[51] that which is considered to be "reality" itself is actually the operative reality, or dominant paradigm, of those who hold power in a given society. Phenomena—including whole groups and classes of people—are named, defined, classified, or disregarded as best serves the interests of the powerful. This construction of reality by those in power is a coherent set of permissible questions and answers that, together, serve to maintain their power and privilege. Dominant perception is disguised as "discovery" of truth. The concept of race itself has recently been demonstrated to function in just this way—as a supposedly scientific method of classifying human beings that has little actual basis in genetic or other scientific evidence but that held sway because of its social and political power to justify the institutional dominance of those classified as "white."[52]

"The way things are" is mystified by naming it "the way things were eternally ordained to be"—either by God or by the laws of nature—while any alternative, contradictory facts or realities, such as those perceived by the less powerful, are disregarded as unscientific opinion (the equivalent in premodern times of heresy). Scientists, philosophers, critics, and others are captivated by this dominant paradigm because we all internalize it from birth, and it might be argued that higher education serves to drill the internalization process even deeper, even while instilling the value of critical thinking. Critical thinking remains captive to the questions that are not only permissible, but fundamentally thinkable, in the dominant paradigm. It therefore requires vision from the margins and not the center of the dominant constructions of reality even to raise the questions that might undermine its hegemony in ordinary people's minds and modes of perception. In the face of every purported discovery, whether in the realm of science, or history, or criticism, etc., it is always useful to ask the question "Who benefits?"[53] Who stands to gain the most according to this statement or version of "truth"?

5. All of the above is not necessarily to "throw out the baby with the bath water." (In this statement, I am staking my own position with those who hold that there is, or at least may be, a reality existing "out there" somewhere, but that it is not possible to know reality positively through the senses because of bias and the continual influence of one's multiple environmental, social, cultural, and political contexts. This is known as a "postpositivist" view,[54] a middle position between the pure positivism of the Enlightenment and pure constructivism, which rejects any notion of a reality "out there" at all, in favor of a view that what we perceive as reality is entirely constructed by ongoing mental and social frameworks of meaning and interaction.) Whether or not there is some ultimate reality beyond our own limited perceptions,[55] we all live according to some construction of reality. This need not be regarded as all bad, even from a postmodern perspective.

Facts, or truths, when acknowledged as contingent and limited, that is, as *theories, beliefs*, and self-limited *observations*, are what enable us to grasp the world in some orderly way, and to move beneficially within it. Everyone lives by some version of truth. The question of ontology ultimately remains unanswerable, but whatever the "real" reality is, it is "imperfectly and probabilistically apprehendable."[56] The issue is not whether it is possible to somehow stand apart from the process of the ongoing internal and social construction of reality, but how aware one is of the contingency and limitations of the truth this ongoing process continually yields. It is important, therefore, to make the daily effort to overcome the seductiveness of prevailing constructions of reality, to remain conscious and paradoxical in one's living out of truth, and to maintain a discipline of wondering how any particular truth might look when viewed from the margins. All truths must be evaluated in light of the particular context out of which they arise, and their generalizability to other contexts must be explicitly questioned and evaluated in light of other truths that may already exist in these other contexts. As a pastoral theologian, moreover, I maintain that this is a spiritual discipline at heart, a *habitus*, in which there is a recognition that all truths must be continually evaluated in the light of post-Holocaust, post-Apartheid ethics: "No statement, theological or otherwise, should be made that would not be credible in the presence of burning children."[57]

6. Finally, the often unnamed *emotional* valency of every truth must be recognized. Truths that invoke fear, in particular, must be evaluated in terms of who most benefits by making others fearful. Fear enslaves, while hope liberates. Postmodernism is not merely a collapse of all values into radical relativism, as is often popularly believed. Postmodernism, having been born in the crucible of disillusionment with Enlightenment ideals of progress in the light of war and the unintended consequences of technological "advances," and having inherited much of the intellectual heritage of nineteenth-century "critical theory,"[58] carries its own—perhaps too little acknowledged—social and political ideals, and therefore holds much in common with Black, feminist, and two-thirds-world[59] theologies of liberation (although these do retain more of a "grand narrative"). Claims to truth should encourage, empower, and embolden, more than they inspire fear. In this new, postmodern approach to what constitutes reality, it is helpful to bear in mind this caveat: that truths should only be accepted *as* true to the degree that their explanatory power is liberative of the marginalized and the oppressed, rather than reinforcing existing structures and institutions of power that continue to harm people, creatures, and the planet through self-serving paradigms of domination and control.

These postmodern questions of what constitutes human knowing has particular significance for pastoral psychotherapists, since our shared human subjectivity is the very medium (whether acknowledged or not) of all therapeutic communication. How do we come to "know" the person who comes to us for help? The very effort, however imperfect, to enter into another's felt experience in order to support his or her growth and healing is to walk on holy ground. As I have written elsewhere,[60] how do we dare to take off our shoes and stand reverently before the burning bush of another's experience? And even if we do, can we ever truly enter another's subjectivity? Even if we perceive, however fleetingly, some truth from our gaze into those flames, have we really perceived a true representation of the other's experience, or merely an idea we have projected from our own experience? And, further, even if we trust that we have come to know at least a fragment of what is true or real to the other person from this reverent encounter, how will this facilitate our being a helper? How will such "knowledge" help us "know" what to do or say from moment to moment in the therapeutic encounter?

These questions, and the postmodern emphasis on subjectivity, will be examined later in more detail. In particular, the *shared* knowing, or "*inter*subjectivity," that arises in any relationship—but perhaps in a uniquely intense and self-reflective way in psychotherapy—is foundational for the relational approach to pastoral psychotherapy being offered in this book. As critic Susan Fairfield has pointed out, most psychoanalytic therapists, even those who identify as postmodern, constructivist, and relational, end up using some form of a mixed model, in which Enlightenment ideals, such as authenticity, cohesiveness of self, and freedom, continue alongside a more deconstructionist commitment to multiply-constituted subjectivities, "paradox, irresolution, and heterogeneity."[61] Nevertheless, the effort not to collapse back into some form of theoretical purity or certainty, the effort to resist simple dualities and to explore the ways in which difference resides within as well as between self and other, is worth the risk of confusion. Such *con-fusion*—such hybridity—is, in the postmodern imagination, a way to new life.

Why *Relational*?

Working even within the more specific definition of pastoral psychotherapy given above, as a mode of healing intervention that is specifically grounded both in psychoanalytic theory and methods ("psychotherapy") and in a constructive, creation-affirming theology (the "pastoral" dimension), there are many possible theoretical frameworks and methods, from more "classical" Freudian and ego psychological, to traditionally Jungian approaches grounded in Jung's own nineteenth- and early twentieth-century writings, to later Kleinian, object-relational, Gestalt, self psychological, and other twentieth-century revisions.

This book, while firmly planted in the psychoanalytic tradition since Freud, is not intended to be an overview of all psychoanalytic approaches to pastoral psychotherapy. My aim here is more modest, and at the same time more geared toward "pushing the envelope" of these older psychoanalytic approaches: I am proposing one theory and method of doing pastoral psychotherapy, not new in psychoanalytic circles, but largely unexplored in the pastoral counseling literature to date. This theory and method is drawn from the contemporary school of *relational psychoanalysis*.

The *relational* school refers to a group of psychoanalysts today[62] who have come together around an approach to analysis and therapy that takes seriously the postmodern critiques of objectivity and scientific rationalism inherited in classical Freudian analysis.[63] In their clinical practice, writing, and teaching, they have begun with the foundations of object relations[64] and interpersonal[65] theory, and developed a contemporary line of psychoanalytic inquiry that emphasizes the reciprocal, co-constructed nature of the therapeutic relationship. While various authors in this school of thought differ on certain particulars, they all emphasize that the therapeutic relationship is a two-person enterprise.[66] *Both* patient and therapist are thinking, feeling, experiencing, interpreting, and mutually influencing one another. Therapy is understood best in this model not as a medical treatment, in which the patient brings an illness for which the therapist then makes a diagnosis and prescribes a cure, but as a *shared hermeneutical task*, in which both the expertise of the therapist and the experience and wisdom of the patient are brought to bear in constructing meanings about the sources of the patient's pain.

Meaning is not "discovered" and then conferred by the therapist alone, as in the rather heroic nineteenth-century therapeutic model most of us have inherited through standard counseling training. Rather, meaning is continually being explored, co-constructed, revisited, and revised by both partners—therapist and patient— through a shared flow of associations that brings healing insight not as a cathartic clap of thunder but as a gradual dawning of increasingly complex awarenesses over time. In the classical paradigm, the therapist was seen rather like the child who plays the game "Operation," fishing with tweezers inside the patient's passive, game board body for objects that are the presumed causes of the patient's illnesses, and occasionally being zapped or zapping the patient by making clumsy mistakes. In the relational paradigm, this image might be helpfully replaced by imagining both therapist and patient sitting in the intimacy of a fishing boat (the consulting room), gently and quietly fishing together for the multiple wondrous life forms swimming just on the other side of consciousness, and brimming with food for thought, images, longings, memories, and healing medicine.

Postmodern Theology?

In the strictest sense, there is an unresolvable contradiction between postmodernism and any theology, if postmodernism is by definition inimical to universals, and God, and therefore words about God (θεὸς + λόγος) (*theòs* + *lógos*) by definition concerns the greatest universal. For this reason, some radical theologians have paradoxically rejected the term *God* altogether.[67] According to some contemporary critics, any faith-based statement may be understood not even as modern—that is, belonging to the rationalist intellectual heritage of the Enlightenment—but as *premodern*— belonging to the ages before Descartes, the eighteenth century, and the scientific method.[68]

For the purposes of this book, I think the argument may be framed somewhat differently. Rather than the distinction of premodern-modern-postmodern, it may be helpful to apply instead the heuristic discussed by Theodore Jennings: first-order, second-order, and third-order theological thinking.[69] First-order religious language is the set of words and phrases that express one's basic sense of relationship to God: "Jesus loves me," "God is punishing me." The emphasis in first-order theological thinking is one's personal faith. Like the mixed model that implicates and compli- cates most postmodern practices of therapy, *prima facie* (first-order) faith statements in this heuristic do not exclusively belong to one theological era, such as the pre- modern or modern, as much as they are personal theological statements, sometimes adopted from external authorities.

Second-order language is the language of systematic/constructive theology per se—words (λόγος, *lógos*) about God (θεὸς, *theòs*), that is, the propositional level within which many first-order statements are gathered, generalized, critically understood, and/or codified as a truth claim—and with which others then may vigorously agree or disagree. So, for example, the first-order statements "Jesus loves me" and "God is punishing me" might be generalized and codified in second-order propositional language as "the Christian God is a God of love" and "God's judgment is expressed in the suffering that humans experience in life." Taken together, such second-order theological statements, when subscribed to by a group of people who identify as belonging to a particular religious tradition, become doctrines. A coherent set of such doctrines comprises a dogmatics, that is, the belief system and/or "the theology of" that particular religious tradition.

Third order theological thinking involves a comparison and critiques of the belief systems, propositions, judgments, doctrines, and theologies constructed under second-order thinking. (This order of thinking, along with second-order thinking, constitute the practice or intellectual discipline of systematic/constructive theology.) In *pastoral* theological reflection, third-order thinking would further examine whether "God is a God of love" or "God's judgment is expressed in the evils that humans experience" are adequately true, sufficient, and coherent faith statements in relation to *understanding the human situation at hand*. As I am using this term, *third-order thinking* is used in pastoral theology, specifically, to evaluate whether and what language and tools of the helpee's and helper's respective traditions, and/or other traditions that might be drawn upon, might be most helpful in guiding praxis—that is, offering direction for *the most facilitative pastoral intervention* in this case. It is the level of *critique* of propositions, not for the sake of critique, but for the sake of determining what set of theological propositions will best help to shape a genuinely facilitative pastoral response. This process of critique, may, of course, at times call into question some of our own cherished beliefs and assumptions, and this is then something we must take back for our own discernment, as part of our continuing spiritual and pastoral formation! Note also that these are not developmentally ordered thinking patterns (although a capacity for critical thinking is required for second- and third-order theological deliberation). We all engage in all three levels across the life span.

I am situating the theological reflections of this book as *postmodern*, then, because *at* the level of third-order theological thinking, I am using strategies and awarenesses that are informed by postmodern critiques of both Enlightenment and premodern assumptions about the immutability and impassibility of God, and by unexamined assumptions of white, western European theologies that certain metaphorical representations of God may approach the status of fact, rather than recognizing their limitations as bound by specific cultures and times.

Included within this perspective are both constructive approaches to the theological enterprise through imaginative visioning of new theological metaphors and images, and recovery and adaptation of earlier sources, including biblical, patristic/ matristic, and medieval. It is my assertion that theology is still possible in keeping with postmodernism, since the very *experience* of God/the divine/the transcendent, and the multiple human attempts to formulate that experience, must be reverenced as a vital dimension of many local, particular cultures. Religion cannot be separated from other truth claims as untouchable or automatically suspect; such automatic dismissal in itself reflects a hegemonic Western bias, in this case, toward atheistic scientific rationalism.

At the same time, truth claims about God should be made with humility, recognizing that if they are not to be automatically dismissed, neither are they automatically to be accorded an elevated status of universal truth or transcendent reality. All claims about the nature of the divine or the transcendent are, like all human products, partial, provisional, and contingent upon the perspectives of the cultures from which they arise. (The nature of God *as* God may be something else altogether, and although it may be glimpsed in part "through a mirror dimly," it remains elusive.) God may be fleetingly apprehended in the collected human experience and discourses about the holy, but it is in the nature of God-as-God to be the horizon beyond which certain human knowledge is impossible—even "beyond transcendence"[70] as "transcendence" itself is a humanly conceived idea. In Catherine Keller's words: "for beyond the nostalgia for a premodern grandeur, or the doomed utopias of modern reason, what is the actual work of theology—but an incantation at the edge of uncertainty?"[71]

Thus, this book represents an effort at a *postmodern pastoral psychotherapeutic*, drawing both from postmodern, constructivist, or poststructuralist models of *psychoanalysis*, and from what might be called both postmodern and late-modern (including contemporary, feminist, and liberationist) *theological* constructions,[72] in which postmodern methods are utilized and epistemological problems addressed, while still valuing biblical and historical sources. The pastoral dimension, and its insistence on primary attention to the human person, will come first. This is not traditionally the order in which *pastoral* and *psychology*, or *pastoral* and *theology*, have often been addressed in the pastoral literature of the late-twentieth century. I am deliberately making the point here that the pastoral/theological is not an addendum—an accusation that has been perhaps rightly leveled at many of the most therapeutically oriented pastoral counseling paradigms in previous decades.[73]

Further, this book will begin with a theological understanding of *human persons* and move from there to an understanding of God that may be most helpful in framing this pastoral psychotherapeutic approach in Chapter 2. (The reason for starting with persons and then moving to God, which may seem radical in some theological circles, will be further argued in chapter 1.) Only then will we turn to psychoanalytic theory and method. But first, there is a serious remaining problem: how can psychoanalysis, in any of its various branches, live compatibly with theology at all?

Psychoanalytic Pastoral Theology: An Oxymoron?

I enter a doctor's consulting room to arrange for my surgery. I am dismayed when he tells me that this will be a very long procedure. The anesthesiologist has said that I will have to be under for a very long time.

This was my "initial dream"[74] when I entered analysis in 1991 with a Jungian analyst who incorporated a rich blend of Jungian archetypal and British object relations theory and technique.[75] I had recently made the decision to reenter ordained ministry after a period of disengagement (coinciding with exploration of other unfinished vocational avenues). I had engaged in a number of years of solid, ego psychology–oriented pastoral counseling. But the dream was clear: to get further on this journey of psychological and spiritual discernment, it was necessary to "go under" (at least, as I thought of it then—more will be said later about the metaphor of "depth" in subsequent chapters). Nothing less and nothing easier would do. So I came to the work of pastoral psychotherapy, both as patient and later as therapist, with the assumption that psychological growth and spiritual formation—the dimension that distinguishes pastoral psychology from all other secular psychologies—belong together.

This may seem obvious, a truth that has become cliché in many counseling and pastoral care circles. In my own professional and personal development, however, I have not found it so easy to reconcile psychology with theology or religious belief. Once one moves beyond the general practice of pastoral counseling and the often comfortable, supportive realm of parish pastoral care toward a depth or psychodynamic approach, specific schools of psychological theory begin to compete and conflict both with a Christian identity and with each other. The spiritual and the psychological cannot be conflated quite so easily or uncritically.[76]

The most obvious contradiction would seem to lie between Freud's seemingly resolute atheism, still espoused by many classical analysts today, and any religious or spiritual perspective. Many counselors, wishing for a more spiritual approach, gravitate toward C. G. Jung because of his apparently more spiritual perspective. But the task of integrating a Christian identity with depth psychology is not really so simple as to trade in a more supposedly atheistic Freudian point of view for a Jungian one in the interests of incorporating the spiritual dimension into psychotherapy.

FREUD

On one hand, Freud is not quite as pure an antagonist toward religion or spirituality as is popularly thought.[77] This is a fundamentalist approach to Freud. It takes too literally certain statements in his writings, such as his scorn for any inherently human "oceanic religious feeling" apart from infantile wish fulfillment,[78] or his analysis of Moses as a father-figure in an oedipal struggle writ large in Hebrew history.[79] As Bruno Bettelheim and others have pointed out, [80] Freud himself embodied a split between the scientific materialist, (the aspect evident in most of his writing, which was for a scientific audience[81]), and the nineteenth-century romantic with a strong interest in culture[82] and in the paranormal[83]—the Freud more subtly revealed in his actual work as a therapist,[84] in biographies,[85] and in correspondence.[86]

A strong ethic, albeit a rather somber, pessimistic one emphasizing the virtue of renunciation, and shorn of any religious origins, is discernible in Freud's writings, as well as a Jewish regard for reciprocity and respect for the dignity of others.[87] As Phillip Rieff famously put it, the atheist Freud had the "mind of a moralist."[88] Freud's Judaism could also be seen as a palimpsest in both his hermeneutical method—the seeking out of latent meanings in manifest material, revealed through linguistic techniques and open to alternative interpretations[89]—as well as many of the philosophical and religious assumptions particularly in his cultural writings.[90] Edward Said points to the "irremediably diasporic, unhoused character" of the postexilic Jewish community as a source for Freud's own resistance toward easy palliatives, whether political or religious.[91] Freud's ethic derived, rather, from a sense of human solidarity founded in a tragic realism regarding human fallibility, desire, and identity complexity.

Freud's critiques of religion tended to caricature some of the worst of Judeo-Christianity's authoritarianism, its denigration of the body—particularly sexuality, and its disregard for insights from psychology and science.[92] Freud objected to religion as an institutionalization of the oedipal conflict and a paternalistic demand on the part of religious authority for infantile, blind obedience to an irrationally moralistic superego rather than a means of rational moral decision-making[93]—an "ethical realism" that Reinhold Niebuhr later affirmed (although as a Christian theologian Niebuhr retained the religious language of sin and redemption that Freud had rejected).[94]

Freud was interested in the feeling of the "uncanny" (*das Unheimlich*), identifying it linguistically as the opposite of the familiar, the "homelike" (*das Heimlich*).[95] The uncanny arouses dread, and in Freud's discussion seems especially to tread in a region in which the distinction between the living and the dead becomes blurred. Freud describes a paradox, that the uncanny, the unhomelike, is always dimly perceived as secretly familiar because it represents a return of repressed infantile fears, and the magical thinking that accompanied them. Thus ghosts and spirits are reprojected onto current reality when infantile dread is reevoked by "silence, solitude, and darkness . . . elements in the production of the infantile anxiety from which the majority of human beings have never become quite free."[96] "The distinction between imagination and reality is effaced, as when something that we have hitherto regarded as imaginary appears before us in reality, or when a symbol takes over the full functions of the thing it symbolizes."[97] Freud similarly rejected a tendency he found in religious believers to concretize religious symbols and metaphors as fixed realities, and further characterized religion as an immature delusion of consolation and gratification of infantile wishes, rather than a mature renunciation of the pleasure principle.[98]

Many of the same critiques have been vigorously prosecuted (though not necessarily using Freud's theoretical language) by theologians and religious leaders within organized religion, and not only in the modern era. As Kirk Bingaman recently suggested, persons of faith can persist in belief, "living in the tension" between religious faith and the psychoanalytic disposition to question:

> Believers, unlike the helpless child who must ultimately capitulate to the stronger oedipal father, have the capacity to imagine something better. We can either settle for an unreflective and insular religious faith of the first naïveté [citing Paul Ricoeur], or we can choose to expose our faith to a hermeneutics of suspicion, which invariably opens the door to a postcritical religious faith of the "second naïveté." This . . . corresponds to . . . the supreme choice facing every person of faith, namely, whether or not to update and transform our psychical image of God.[99]

Freud also advocated that the best preparation for becoming a psychoanalyst was a broad, interdisciplinary background not only in science and psychology, but in the humanities, literature, history, and the arts.[100] He repudiated the trappings and language of religion and spirituality, perhaps, as some have suggested, due to his own early object relations and unconscious associations to religion, the oceanic, and a fear of the maternal,[101] but he did, in fact, value much of what contemporary pastoral theologians and therapists would consider to be pertinent to the spiritual domain.

JUNG

At the same time, Jung offers no easy panacea for a pastoral psychotherapist.[102] Jung has sometimes been appropriated by theologians, pastoral counselors, and spiritual directors as a bridge figure between psychoanalysis and religion.[103] "Transpersonal psychology," an outgrowth of Jungian analytic psychology and the human potential movement (e.g., Abraham Maslow's "self-actualization"[104]), is particularly appealing to some because of its focus on Jung's idea that the edges of consciousness open out toward universal human consciousness and the transcendent. Quoting from the website of the Institute for Transpersonal Psychology in Palo Alto, California:[105]

> Transpersonal Psychology is a psychology of health and human potential. While recognising and addressing human psychopathology, transpersonal psychology does not derive its model of the human psyche from the ill or diseased. Transpersonal psychology looks to saints, prophets, great artists, heroes, and heroines for models of full human development and of the growth-oriented nature of the normal human psyche . . . Another way of putting this is that the

personality is, by design, the vessel or vehicle which enables the soul and spirit to navigate through the world. Thus, the proper role of the personality is to be a translucent window, a servant to divinity within.[105]

However, Jung's attitude toward organized religion *per se*, particularly the constricted moralistic Christianity of his own Protestant upbringing as a Swiss minister's son, was conflicted at best.[106] This bias reflects both Jung's longing for personal authenticity over against blind obedience to external authorities, and his frustration in particular with Western Christian institutions. It has, however, filtered into some contemporary Jungian practice as a (sometimes quite unconscious) privileging, and often romanticization, of Eastern spiritual practices and symbols, and a reverence for ancient pre-Christian mythology, while devaluing, ignoring, or even denigrating Western Judeo-Christian images and stories. This may be overcome as an individual practitioner by choosing elements of Jung's writings that are compatible, remythologizing Judeo-Christian symbols[107] as in the earlier writings of Victor Turner (a Dominican priest who initially corresponded collaboratively with Jung much as Oskar Pfister corresponded admiringly with Freud)[108] and the work of Episcopal priest and Jungian analyst John Sanford.[109]

However, there remains a significant conflict between Jung's thought and mainstream Christian doctrine, originating in Jung's own critique of Christianity. For example, there is a profound dissonance between Jung's concept of the archetype of Wholeness versus Christianity's moral emphasis on purity and goodness. Jung conceived of the process of maturation, which he called "individuation,"[110] as a journey toward wholeness. It requires the bringing to consciousness and embracing of the "Shadow"[111]—aspects of the Self (often imaged in Jungian psychology as the dark, the primitive, the ugly) that are disavowed, disowned, displaced. Even God, Jung posited in *Answer to Job*, must have a Shadow if God is to be whole.[112] This is perhaps nowhere better exemplified in Jung's writings than in the famous fantasy image he recorded from his own childhood:

> I gathered all my courage, as though I were about to leap forthwith into hell-fire, and let the thought come. I saw before me the cathedral, the blue sky. God sits on His golden throne, high above the world—and from under the throne an enormous turd falls upon the sparkling new roof, shatters it, and breaks the walls of the cathedral asunder.[113]

In his struggle to free himself from the constraints of his father's rigid Protestantism, Jung faced a terrifying possibility: even God shits. For the boy Jung, God was a maddening paradox: "God alone was real—an annihilating fire and an indescribable grace."[114] This ambiguous view of God's nature flew in the face of his father's rigid Christian convictions that God was omnipotent, pure goodness, and that the goal of Christian living was purity and obedience.

This Christian drive toward purity and perfection is peculiar when one considers the gore and anguish of human existence actually depicted in both the Hebrew Bible and the New Testament, and is not very compatible with the gospel narratives of Jesus' own life and grisly death. But a Platonic mind-body split emerges in the Bible in Paul's Greek writings, and it pervaded patristic and medieval Christianity.[115] It comes down to us again in the pietistic fervor of some of the reformers, not only in the sixteenth century, but later in the passionate evangelical desire for "perfection," expounded, for example, by John Wesley and Jonathan Edwards.[116] Can one remain a Christian, with all that Christianity has come to mean historically, and still embrace the terrifying ambiguities of the God of scripture? This was at the heart of Jung's personal quest in childhood: what kind of God could be vast enough to contain even the worst imperfections of creation, and still bring forth good?

Jung's attitude toward the question of God's existence represented a departure from Freud's defensive atheism. Jung was agnostic about the question of God's objective existence, but remained open to the traces of the divine in the subjective experience of psychic life.[117] For Jung, the image of God was an archetypal symbol,[118] stemming from the collective unconscious (for Jung, the "deepest" layer or deposit of shared human images throughout history, accessible to every individual via the outer edges of the personal unconscious). The God archetype was closely related to the archetype of Wholeness and its related form, the archetype of the Self.[119] He defined the Self as much larger than the conscious ego[120] (derived from Freud), which is really only a small part of the total person. In this schema, the ego performs an important executive function, but it tends to regard itself as more central than it actually is. The outer boundaries of the Self are transpersonal, contiguous with all other persons, across all generations. The Self contains aspects of the "collective unconscious,"[121] the accumulated deposit of knowledge, wisdom, and patterning of experience shared among all humanity. At its outer edges, Jung believed, the Self flows into the divine.

Jung viewed Christ as an archetypal symbol for the Self[122] (as was the Buddha,[123] and other nonpersonal religious symbols such as the Mandala[124]), bridging the individual and the divine. This was related for Jung to the call of the Self for "individuation," which Jung further perceived to be represented by the symbols of transformation in the Christian Eucharist.[125] Individuation thus incorporated a relational, moral quality. Jung believed that by bringing the unconscious to awareness, and owning the Shadow dimension of oneself, one could withdraw the projections of evil that one had assigned unconsciously to the external world, thereby refraining from demonizing others.[126] (This process psychologically is not unlike the movement described in Kleinian theory from the infantile splitting of the "paranoid-schizoid position" (a developmental position, to be described in more detail in chapter 3 in which negative psychic contents are projected externally[127]), to the "depressive position" (in Melanie Klein's theory, the more mature developmental position in which one is able to psychically hold good and bad together, acknowledging one's own hunger and aggression and mourning one's omnipotent fantasies of perfect goodness and omnivorous control).

The reality of God was, for Jung, a psychic reality, founded in collective human experience, and therefore beyond any sort of empirically grounded debate.[128] The divine was a psychological phenomenon, as manifested in the personal experience of individuals over centuries and across cultures. Jung claimed his own personal acquaintance with "the numinous or divine,"[129] while demurring both from the abstract philosophical question of God's "physical existence," and from the question of faith or personal belief. For Jung, God was a matter of subjective knowledge through personal, psychological experience. It was in this sense that Jung said in a radio interview in 1955, "All that I have learned has led me step by step to an unshakable conviction of the existence of God. I only believe what I know. And that eliminates believing. Therefore I do not take his existence on belief—I know that He exists."[130]

The subjective nature of Jung's construction of the divine has prompted a further critique, particularly from theologians. In Jung's own time, Martin Buber stated that Jung's "new psychology protests that it is 'no world-view but a science,' [and yet] it no longer contents itself with the role of an interpreter of religion. It proclaims the new religion, the only one which can still be true, the religion of pure psychic immanence."[131] Buber objected to a psychological reductionism he found in Jung's writing, a kind of gnosticism in which transcendence and faith were sacrificed to "knowledge."[132]

Contemporary theologians Don Browning and Terry Cooper, among others, are also critical of a close parallel between analytical psychology and the human potential movement—the optimism inherent in both, that the human being is naturally being drawn toward growth, including moral development. According to Browning and Cooper:

> Jung failed to understand the deeper levels of anxiety and inordinate self-concern and how these facts of human nature invalidate all uncomplicated harmonistic metaphysics and the philosophical ethical egoisms that follow from them . . . In the thought of Jung, both the moral selectivity of the individuation process and the redemption of the transcendent function give rise to an image of self-fulfillment that does not go beyond the ethical-egoist actualization of one's own unique potentials.[133]

This critique has a particularly American, Protestant ring to it, as it focuses on the twentieth-century problem of individuation as rampant individualism and targets the human potential movement as tending toward a "culture of narcissism." In my view, Jung was not so much hampered by what to our twentieth-century American eyes looks like subjectivism (although this caution is warranted), as by his own nineteenth-century cultural and philosophical context—the pre–World Wars European confidence in progress (including that of the individual). Both Freud and

Jung viewed psychoanalysis/analytic psychology as liberative tools freeing human beings from the grip of unconscious motivations.

Just as Freud was embedded in a modernist paradigm, continually striving to prove his credibility as a scientific rationalist, Jung was embedded in a premodern/modern Platonic paradigm of ideal dichotomous forms (Anima/Animus, Self/Shadow, etc.) eternally being manifested in partial, dichotomous, earthly representations. Like Freud, Jung was also striving along heroic lines to promote enlightenment and a form of rationalism that, while departing from Freud's own orthodoxy, nevertheless was grounded in a desire to confront unthinking obedience to authorities, whether religious, philosophical, or scientific. Jung shared Freud's confidence in the freedom—including moral freedom—that could be bestowed by recognizing, plumbing, and exploring the depths of the unconscious.

It would be an injustice to accuse either Freud or Jung of simplistic thinking; reading their original works reveals tremendous breadth, complexity, and also social concern. Freud, his daughter Anna, and others of their circle viewed psychoanalysis as a means toward promoting social justice,[134] and Jung saw the raising of the unconscious to consciousness and the withdrawing of projections onto the other as evil, as a way toward world peace.[135] Yet, it is useful from a postmodern vantage point to deconstruct a certain historically bound and culture-constrained naïveté—or at least, perhaps, unfounded optimism—wedded to the heroic, self-confident colonialism that inheres in both men's theories.

Jung, therefore, cannot be uncritically adapted or appropriated by pastoral psychotherapists as an easy antidote to Freud. I would argue, finally, that both Freud's hermeneutic of suspicion and Jung's sensing of the numinous are needed. Freud's skepticism and Jung's openness to unexplained phenomena and the spiritual realm are most helpful to a twenty-first-century pastoral theologian and psychotherapist if taken together. Their theories of religion—its origins, meaning, and function—and their reflections on human constructions of the divine deserve continued attention. Both theoretical traditions are entwined in our psychological inheritance, including the subdiscipline of the psychology of religion. Both offer useful deconstructive (analytic) methods (even when we do not agree with their conclusions) that search beyond the surfaces of things and stand in opposition to the easy answers, superficial consolations, and demonizing of the "other" that may arise from uncritical religious belief. And both engage in exploration of human experiences of the uncanny, the mysterious, and (at least for Jung) the divine.

The tension between Freud and Jung, and their very personal oedipal conflict, is a *relational* tension. It is in such a relational space—even as an arena of conflict, I would argue—and not in coming down firmly on one side of their debate or the other, that our own wrestling with the tension between religion and psychology, theology and psychology, can be most fruitfully played out. This is not to argue for the nineteenth-century solution of resolving a dialectic by somehow discovering a transcendent or overarching solution that encompasses both sides. It is, rather, a shift from the need for *a* solution to the embrace of the tension itself, a shift from content to process, from knowledge (in the form of certainty) to relationship.

Ever the preacher's son, Jung struggled inconclusively throughout his life to reconcile the competing healing claims of psychology and religion. Jungian analyst Murray Stein has even argued that Jung was not interested in demolishing Christianity but, rather, healing it from its historic complexes and transforming it "along lines compatible with the Jungian therapeutic,"[136] encouraging "the development within Christianity of a kind of Hinduistic spirit of ecumenical tolerance for every conceivable image of God and for every possible expression of the self."[137] In his essay "Psychotherapists or the Clergy?" he offered the following concluding paragraph:

> The *living spirit* grows and even outgrows its earlier forms of *expression* [a reference to both religion and psychotherapy]; it freely chooses the men [*sic*] who proclaim it and in whom it lives. This living spirit is eternally renewed and pursues its goal in manifold and inconceivable ways throughout the history of mankind [*sic*]. Measured against it, the names and forms which men [*sic*] have given it mean very little; they are only the changing leaves and blossoms on the stem of the eternal tree.[138]

Although Jung's emphasis here was on a singular spirit, the numinous or the divine as it manifested itself in ever-changing images and symbols of the human imagination across cultures and centuries, it is the relationality of the word *expression* I want to highlight here. I would propose that by standing in the tension *between* Freud's atheism and Jung's archetypal theories, in the realm of expression itself, we may discover a more messy but fruitful realm—a realm of relationality, a livingness of Spirit rather than a rejected totem or a carefully defined archetype. Here we may find, congruent with the more postmodern context of our own time, a "third" domain, always in flux, of relationality, tension, and mutual expression—a transitional domain of imagination.

Potential Space: Object Relations and Standing in the Contradictions

The British pediatrician-turned-psychoanalyst D. W. Winnicott identified religion, together with art and philosophy, as belonging to the realm of "transitional phenomena."[139] Winnicott defined transitional phenomena as "the third part of the life of a human-being, a part that we cannot ignore . . . an intermediate area of experiencing, to which inner reality and external life both contribute . . . a resting-place for the individual engaged in the perpetual human task of keeping inner and outer reality separate yet interrelated."[140] Winnicott (following Klein) proposed that an infant initially makes no distinction between the mother's actual breast and the internal fantasy of the breast that is needed and desired. To the extent that the mother is able to anticipate the baby's needs and provides a breast (and by extension, the provision of food and nurture) "at the right moment," the baby is confirmed in the illusion that s/he has created the breast. The object of desire is simultaneously created (from the inside) and discovered (from the outside). There is thus an intermediate psychic area between "me" and "not-me" that is initially blurred and undefined.

In order to navigate the maturational process by which the mother comes to be recognized as a separate entity outside the infant's control, a child will often adopt a teddy bear, blanket, or other soft object that can stand in for the mother's breast and at the same time can remain totally under the child's control. This is the origin of Winnicott's term *transitional object*. The object helps the child make the transition from believing that everything is a part of him- or herself, to tolerating the loneliness engendered by a realization of his or her separateness. In health—that is, in Winnicott's terms when provided with "good enough" parenting[141] and a "facilitating environment"[142]—the child eventually lets go of the object as the capacity to relate to actual other persons increases.

In Winnicott's concept, maturation brings about a shift from "object relating" (by which he means relating to one's own internal objects and relating to others through projection) to "object usage" (a somewhat utilitarian sounding term for what we might commonly understand as relating to an actual other person, perceived with his or her own separate subjectivity).[143] This process is actually initiated by the child's innate aggression, in which s/he attacks and destroys the object (as s/he perceives the other internally), and is then confronted by the actual object, beyond his or her projections, which survives. During infancy, this is the parent who survives the child's biting and pummeling and continues to care for the child, neither retaliating nor abandoning.[144] As the child grows, fantasy is gradually modulated by the ongoing interaction between internal objects that are loved, hated, tightly held, devoured, attacked, and controlled, and external others who have their own uncontrollable reactions and jar against the child's internal fantasies and projections.

Yet the "reality principle" does not quash internal fantasy altogether. The interplay between inner and outer remains as a third dimension, in the realm of imagination and play, and it continues over the life span, encompassing both personal reverie and creative outward expression. It is also the realm of cultural experience, in which both the capacity for trust and the potential for "creative living" are engendered in the space between baby and mother, child and family, individual and society.[145] As Ana-Maria Rizzuto has pointed out, religious symbols and God-representations do not fade away as blankets and teddy bears do, but continue to mature alongside one's representations of self and other, as an individual continues to engage ultimate questions of mortality, meaning, and the purpose of existence.[146]

Winnicott did not expand upon his brief statements locating religion within transitional phenomena. More recently, however, psychologists of religion have extended Winnicott's ideas to explore human experiences of faith and images of the transcendent. James Jones recently identified all human knowing—including the human project of constructing images of God—as primarily relational, existing in an interactive space analogous to transitional phenomena.[147] William Meissner similarly located religious faith—including God-representations, the use of religious symbols, and the experience of prayer—in Winnicott's "potential space,"[148] in which "the experience of faith . . . is neither exclusively subjective nor wholly objective by reason of its own intentionality; rather, it is a realm in which both the subjective and objective poles of experience contribute to the substance of belief."[149] The child simultaneously finds and experiences him- or herself to be creating the provisions of faith as it is provided by family and community.

Meissner's observation that religious objects are "the vehicles for the expression of meanings and values that transcend their physical characteristics"[150] is important in countering Freud's critiques of religion's tendency to collapse symbols into concrete objects. What Freud viewed as a totem or fetish, we might, with Meissner, more accurately identify from within religious tradition as an idol. Just as in Eastern Orthodox tradition an icon is intended as a "window" into the divine, and not as something to be worshiped in itself, religious symbols participate in the transitional space between the inner world of fantasy, dreams, and images, and the external world of separate reality.

Winnicott and object relations theorists do not solve the question of God's existence. But they make room for the dialogue between psychology and religion by relocating the mystery of human experiences of transcendence from the realm of searching for empirical answers to the realm of relationality. They invite us to "stand in the spaces"[151] *between* inner certainty (which actually belongs to internal fantasy and splitting) and external "truth." Just as Jung found in Christ an archetypal symbol for the Self, object relations theorists have also perceived Christ as a symbol of the object that is destroyed by human aggression, yet paradoxically survives as a genuine object of love.[152] God-in-Christ neither retaliates nor abandons humankind—but on the contrary, by being destroyed, lives to become the very means of forgiveness and redemption. Dodi Goldman also finds in the contemplative religious tradition an analogy with the child's sense of safety with the "good-enough" mother: "The capacity to be alone in the felt presence of the mother parallels the traditional idea of the Presence of God as being both intimate and ultimate."[153]

Good-versus-evil, all-or-nothing fights about absolute truth belong to Klein's paranoid-schizoid position, in which one identifies with the good and projects the bad onto external objects. Holding a depressive position toward religion itself, relinquishing the twin illusions of perfection and certainty, frees us to recognize the ambiguities and unresolvable questions that faith poses.

Regarding God from the transitional space of our own simultaneous knowing/not-knowing, we are thus able to enter into a space of holy imagination—a sacred space in which we experience God through relating. God is both like us and not like us as we simultaneously create and discover God in relationship. God is thus encountered as the "uncanny," the strange, and the unhomelike—as in Rudolf Otto's description of numinous experience, and the Holy as "wholly other," a "mysterium tremendum."[154] It is not surprising, then, that in our Judeo-Christian tradition God is allied with the stranger, the sojourner, the one(s) we ourselves oppress, and that this discovery becomes transformed into an ethical call, to meet and love the stranger as—who is—ourselves.[155]

PASTORAL PSYCHOTHERAPY:
FAITH SEEKING UNDERSTANDING

Wilfred Bion, in his summary of psychoanalytic practice theory, located psychoanalysis at the intersection of "the medical and the religious."[156] By "religious" Bion was not referring to organized religion or theology; he was noting the dimension of the ineffable and the poetic in psychoanalysis, and its engagement with the deep human questions of existence.[157] From Freud's correspondent, the Swiss pastor Oskar Pfister onward, religious therapists and ordained clergy have not only embraced psychodynamic theory, but have made major contributions as psychoanalysts.[158] Anton Boisen's *Exploration of the Inner World* was a foundational work for pastoral theology, in which Boisen's own experience as a mental patient in mid-twentieth-century America prompted him to advocate for the integration of a humanistic, religious perspective into the treatment of mental illness and regarding the patient as the primary textbook for psychotherapy: "the living human document."[159]

More recent analytic writers have also explored the concept of "faith" as it relates to therapeutic practice and a philosophy or psychoanalytic attitude toward human growth and meaning. Psychoanalyst Michael Eigen, whose published musings on the edges of psychosis, union and differentiation, ecstasy, and rage are some of the most thoughtful and adventurous in psychoanalytic writing,[160] brought attention to "the area of faith in Winnicott, Lacan and Bion" in a much-discussed article in 1981.[161] Faith and spirituality have recently become hot topics in psychoanalytic writing,[162] as contemporary theorists have recognized psychoanalysis as a way of touching the ineffable and, moreover, describing the particular form of hope that underlies all psychotherapy even when formulated in the most secular terms—the faith that human beings can grow and change, and that the therapeutic relationship has something to do with the deepest questions of human meaning, purpose, and existence.

New voices have entered the dialogue between religion and psychology from multicultural and interfaith perspectives as well.[163] Even the category of sin, from which psychological theorists tend to shy away, has been readmitted in somewhat different language, like the "return of the repressed." For example, Heinz Kohut wrote a little-known essay validating altruism and moral courage as something more than simply a neurotic reaction formation,[164] and in an interview toward the end of his life, he quoted Eugene O'Neill's statement, "Man is broken. He lives his life by mending. The grace of God is the glue."[165]

In a recent textbook on psychoanalytic psychotherapy, Nancy McWilliams describes this psychoanalytic sensibility as a form of "theology"[166] whose articles of faith include a commitment to authenticity and a belief in the positive power of self-knowledge. In her summary of the "psychoanalytic sensibility," McWilliams also draws further implications for social transformation and political justice:

> It is my deep conviction that the attitudes I have discussed—curiosity and awe, a respect for complexity, the disposition to identify empathically, the valuing of subjectivity and affect, an appreciation of attachment, and a capacity for faith—are worth cherishing not only as components of a therapeutic sensibility but also correctives to some of the more estranging and deadening aspects of contemporary [American] life. Their opposites—intellectual passivity, opinionated reductionism, emotional distancing, objectification and apathy, personal isolation and social anomie, and existential dread—have often been lamented by scholars and social critics as the price we pay for our industrialized, consumer-oriented, and technologically sophisticated cultures. The cultivation of the more vital attitudes that undergird the psychoanalytic sensibility just might be good for the postmodern soul whatever one's orientation to psychotherapy.[167]

Freud called psychoanalysis the "impossible profession"[168] If psychoanalysis was already impossible in Freud's day, then is it plainly unthinkable to integrate it with the also "impossible" profession of full-time vocational ministry (lay and ordained) and the specialized ministry of pastoral psychotherapy? Yet, if *psycho-therapy* is at heart the healing (*therapeúo*) of both mind and soul (*psyche*), can the two vocations of pastoral helper and psychotherapist not somehow find a way to be integrated into one distinctive practice of ministry? Is it not possible to develop, borrowing a term from John McDargh, a "psychotheological perspective?"[169] Jones wrote this invitation to a dialogue between psychoanalysis and theology:

> In this dialogue, theology's role would be to take this psychoanalytic image of inherent relationality and carry it to its furthest reaches, thus connecting psychoanalysis and theology in a common exploration of human relationality and shedding light on the larger implications of a category that psychoanalysts may use unreflectively. The theologian might help see the larger implications of the analyst's implicit image of relationality. The analyst might help the theologian see the unconscious themes at work in the theologian's image of the ultimate reality. Together, they shed light on both the depths and heights of human experience of existing as relational beings.[170]

This book is one effort to continue that dialogue, particularly drawing from a relational-psychoanalytic model that has been considerably elaborated in the decade since Jones made this invitation.

PART 1

A Theological and Theoretical Framework

Chapter 1

A Relational Understanding
of Persons

What are human beings that you are mindful of them,
mortals that you care for them?

Yet you have made them a little lower than God/the gods
and crowned them with glory and honor.

—Psalm 8:4-5

ALL THEOLOGY, but especially pastoral theology, begins with human beings, and in particular, the pain and brokenness of the human condition (and indeed, all creation). Pastoral theology takes suffering as its starting place[1]—in Jürgen Moltmann's words, "the open wound of life in this world."[2] The classic pastoral functions, as articulated in the mid-twentieth century, and amended in recent decades, immerse the pastoral theologian directly in this open wound, through a commitment to ministries of healing, sustaining, guiding, reconciling, nurturing, empowering, and liberating.[3] As Emmanuel Lartey has articulated from a multicultural pastoral counseling perspective, "pastoral care expresses human concern through various helping activities including counseling but also celebrating, commemorating, rejoicing, reflecting, mourning, and being present."[4] A postmodern pastoral perspective, moreover, recognizes that all pastoral encounters will involve a process of *co-creating* of psychological, cultural, and theological meanings. Carrie Doehring[5] has enumerated a postmodern set of criteria for moving within the multiplicity of traditions and approaches available. These include evaluations of their (1) contextual meaningfulness (opening rather than simplifying and closing down the complexity of religious, spiritual, and psychological experiences), (2) interdisciplinary meaningfulness (creating space for a lively correlational dialogue between theological and psychological perspectives—I would add the wider social sciences and other secular disciplines), and (3) pragmatic usefulness[6] (contributing to care and justice, rather than remaining at a level of theoretical abstraction).

Taking human persons as the starting point is a reversal of more traditional theological approaches, in which an image of God is posited, and from that image, a theological anthropology is developed—following perhaps the reasoning that if God is prior to human beings as the Creator, and human beings are created in the "image and likeness of God" (Gen. 1:26, 27), then it makes sense to describe God first. Theologians thus have historically begun their systematic inquiries with the nature of God, drawing on revelation from scripture, which is given *a priori* status as divinely inspired truth, and/or on tradition—the accrual of doctrine over time. Theological anthropology, that is, the theologically informed study of the nature of human beings, has always been addressed second, after the question of God's nature.

All descriptions of God, however, are human fabrications,[7] whether their authors acknowledge this or not, and most theologies carry an unconscious ideal image of the human as the template for a superhuman God. Particular formulations about God are, further, framed in terms of their particular historical and cultural inheritance, including the central symbol systems, of their framers.[8] Cultural norms further tend to predicate and provide cognitive frameworks for how people will (or will not) interpret and ascribe certain anomalous affect states as "religious experiences."[9] The philosopher Immanuel Kant insisted on the limits of human reason and knowledge, in critique of René Descartes's search for some rationally certain foundation for truth. Following Kant and Martin Heidegger, postmodern writers who have addressed the idea of "God" *as* idea (such as Emmanuel Lévinas,[10] Jacques Derrida,[11] Julia Kristeva,[12] Luce Irigaray,[13] Jean-Luc Marion,[14] and Grace Jantzen[15]) have further critiqued any absolute metaphysical construct of God, or "onto-theology."[16] Such metaphysical constructs inevitably fall back on human categories, often while ignoring or mystifying the human limitations of such constructs by calling them unquestionable as belonging to divine "revelation." (Much more will be said about these critiques and elaborations in chapter 2.)

I would therefore argue that the human origin of all theologies extends to all portrayals of God, including biblical ones. Even for those of us as Christians who subscribe to a belief in the Bible as divine revelation, that revelation still had to be filtered through the available images and metaphors of its scribes and redactors, through their imaginative use of language and of oral tradition, and it continues to be filtered further through the lenses of its readers, both historical and contemporary.[17] Sallie McFague has made cogent arguments regarding the metaphorical nature of theology, particularly in the imaging and naming of God.[18] Psychoanalytic studies of the unconscious origins of individuals' God imagoes in the internalized figures of one's parents from earliest childhood[19] further reinforce the suggestion that most attempts to describe God, particularly in anthropomorphic terms, may rest as much in the unconscious regions of theologians' psyches as in any externally verifiable "truth" about what God is like.

In the West, it therefore comes as no surprise given the dual hegemony of patriarchy and northern European—white—physiognomy, that the classic Western portrait of God is a white, muscular male figure, with a flowing beard signifying that "he" is old enough to have existed before the rest of the world (see Figure 2).

Figure 2: *God in the Sistine Chapel, fresco by Michelangelo, 1508–1512*

But if we accept a commonly held belief that human beings (and I would say all creation) are formed in the image and likeness of God (Gen. 1:26), then would it not be possible to begin with human nature (which, of course, *all* God *images* really are to begin with!) and approach the question, "what is God like?" from the bottom up—or, to be less vertical, from the inside out (or outside in?). This approach is not as new or radical as it may at first seem. It resonates with much earlier, more pre-modern than rationalist/Enlightenment, schemas. Augustine, in his treatise on the Trinity, proposed "that the mystery of the trinity can be understood (to some extent) through analogy with the human soul; just as self-knowledge, self-memory, and loving self-affirmation are interrelated, so too are Father, Son, and Holy Spirit."[20]

This book therefore begins with the human being. The subjective experience of the finitude of human life itself has been argued to be a starting point of both theology (e.g., Friedrich Schleiermacher[21]) and philosophy (e.g., Karl Jaspers's "philosophy of existence,"[22] and Heidegger's critique of "onto-theology,"[23] which will be discussed in more detail in chapter 2), in the face of the apprehension (in both senses of the word) of the possibility of an infinite transcendence. To make this assumption explicit entertains theology as a more humble enterprise. We know about the created world and the human condition because we live within these realities. Our powers of comprehension are limited even to describe these adequately, much less to describe God. But to reflect on life in all its minute particularities may be the best starting point for coming to understand what God is like at least "dimly," and "in part" (1 Cor. 13:12).

This approach appeared rather frequently in Celtic Christianity, especially prior to the conforming of the British church to Roman Christianity at St. Hilda's abbey at Whitby, England, in 664 CE. The ancient Celts also knew the ordinary experience of everyday life as a source of both relationship to and revelation about God.[24] If we are truly made "in the image and likeness of God," then we may best glimpse what God is like not in abstract imaginings that purport to convey transcendent, universal truths, but in the mirror of the most minute and particular manifestations of human experience and of creation itself. Like Julian of Norwich's example of a thing the size of a hazelnut, God loves the small and the particular:

> He is our clothing, who wraps and enfolds us for love, embraces us and shelters us, surrounds us for his love, which is so tender that he may never desert us. And so in this sight I saw that he is everything which is good, as I understand. And in this he showed me something small, no bigger than a hazelnut, lying in the palm of my hand, as it seemed to me, and it was as round as a ball. I looked at it with the eye of my understanding and thought: What can this be? I was amazed that it could last, for I thought that because of its littleness it would suddenly have fallen into nothing. And I was answered in my understanding: it lasts and always will, because God loves it; and thus everything has being through the love of God.[25]

This view also resonates with the postmodern critique of grand theories; "humanity" cannot be known as a whole, but only in its local particulars, like the drops of dew on a spider's web—each interconnected with all the others by the web, perhaps a metaphor for the matrix of life itself, yet distinct, crystalline, reflecting each other in the surrounding diversity. "Humanity," then, cannot simply or simplistically be defined by those particular humans by whom "humanity" has been normed, particularly in post-Constantinian Christianity. The marginalized and the invisible are re-valued as equally precious and equally definitive of what it means to be human.

Now we will turn to the ancient question, addressed to God by the psalmist: "what are human beings, that you are mindful of them, mortals that you care for them?" No work by a single author can begin to unpack all the possible answers to this question. The purpose of this chapter is more modest: to offer one possible *pastoral* theological anthropology that helps to inform and undergird a theory and practice of pastoral psychotherapy.

What Are Human Beings That You Are Mindful of Them?

In this section, I will propose characteristics of human beings as part of divine creation, recognizing that such a proposed outline can be partial and imperfect at best, and cannot escape being conditioned by my own social location as a white, married, professional-class, middle-aged woman, and Anglican priest and pastoral theologian:[26]

1.　Human beings are part of creation and creation is good, therefore *human beings are good*. Before original sin, there was original blessing, and we all still retain that spark of what the Quakers call "that of God within each person."

2. *Human beings are vulnerable.* Fragile, easily wounded, confused and tempted by the complexity of the world, and susceptible to straying away from our own highest good, we know ourselves to be "sinners from our mother's womb" (Ps. 51:5)—living in a condition of alienation even while yearning for wholeness and light.

3. *Human beings are embodied.* Creation—with its atoms, molecules, cells, skin, leaves, scales, feathers, fur, hair, and flesh (σὰρξ)—is embodied. Therefore, human beings live by, with, and in the enfleshed reality of our bodies.

4. *Human beings are both alike and unique.* All parts of creation, animate and inanimate—stars, grains of sand, amoebas, newts, blue jays, elephants, cats—and therefore humans, are simultaneously, as Lartey has highlighted, "like all others, like some others, and like no others."[27]

5. *Human beings are intrinsically relational.* All creation is interconnected. Human beings thus are connected with all creation and with one another, knit into the entire fabric of creation, and interwoven in an unfathomably deep and wide "living human web."[28] Therefore, each human communicates with/communes with and participates in a common humanity and a common existence with all creation, and also longs inwardly for connection and communion with God/the source of creation.

6. *Human beings are multiple, not unitary.* The human person is more multiple, variegated, and fragmented than has traditionally been understood, either in traditional Western portrayals of the human person as a somewhat heroic, solitary figure, or our own subjective sense of ourselves as a single, unified "I."

7. *Human beings are mutable, fluid, and in process.* Creation continues to evolve, change, and adapt, and new life springs up while old parts of creation decay and die. Each individual life, including each human life, is likewise in a continual state of flux and transition.

8. *Human beings are loved beings.* Finally, creation is loved by the creator. The very act of creation is the motion of Love itself, extending beyond itself, generously self-giving and spilling over into tangible and animate forms. So human beings, like all creatures, are loved beings. To be human *is* to be loved.

9. *Human beings are loving beings.* Therefore, above all, as creatures made in the image of God, human beings are endowed with the capacity for love.

To sum up in one sentence, then, human beings are *good, yet vulnerable; embodied;* both *alike* and *unique; intrinsically relational; multiple; mutable; loved,* and therefore *loving* beings. Examining these attributes one at a time, what might be said drawing from the fields of psychoanalytic psychology and theology, to support these assertions? Especially for the purposes of this book, how is each of these statements helpful to me, a pastoral psychotherapist, in understanding each particular human person who comes to me for help and consultation, and with whom I have committed to be in a uniquely safe and intimate pastoral therapeutic relationship?

Human Beings Are Good/Human Beings Are Vulnerable

Christian theologians beginning with Paul (arguably the first Christian "systematic theologian") have struggled to come to terms with the seemingly immutable reality that human beings "do not do the good [we] want, and the evil [we] do not want, [we] do" (Rom. 7:15, 19). No pastoral theology, grounded in the care of suffering human beings, can ignore the problems of sin and evil. These issues will be discussed more thoroughly in chapter 3, in relation to issues of psychological health and unhealth, and a pastoral theology of good and evil. The doctrine of original sin, particularly as elaborated by Augustine, is foundational in most mainline Christian theological traditions. This doctrine, and what Paul Ricoeur calls the "Adamic myth"[29] of the primeval Fall of humans from perfect goodness, offer powerful metaphorical descriptions of the pervasive human sense of two simultaneous "truths" of existence: that there is a divine or transcendent force or reality in the world; and that human beings are somehow inescapably separated, even alienated from that reality and often feel themselves to be caught up in the subjective existential experience of defilement, sin, and/or guilt (Ricoeur's "primary symbols" for the human experience of evil).[30] At our most nakedly honest moments, we experience ourselves, in Paul Tillich's words, to be "standing under judgment,"[31] and therefore deserving our mortality. Bonnie Miller-McLemore's recent work on sin as "frailty" adds fresh poignancy to this dimension of humanness.[32]

Nevertheless, original sin need not be understood as the primary or *defining* characteristic of the human person. Different strands of theological tradition over the centuries have taken differing understandings of the degree to which the Fall (or the primal alienation this myth describes) damaged or utterly eradicated the human capacity for goodness.[33] Reformed theologian F. LeRon Shults has reflected, "reforming theological anthropology will require that we follow Augustine not by repeating exactly what he said [i.e., his doctrine of original sin], but by doing what he did: articulating the illuminative power of the gospel by engaging contemporary scientific and philosophical understandings of human agency."[34] For Shults, this means a turn to the centrality of relationality. Sin is not an essential, innate, or inherited trait of humanity, but it is an observable aspect of human life in its social dimension—a dynamic reality of "the concrete historical and communal nature of human existence."[35] As liberation and Asian theologians have emphasized, sin involves not only individual guilt, but communal power relations, oppression, and shame.[36]

There are numerous Christian approaches to human sin, with views of human agency spanning a wide spectrum between a belief in total human moral freedom and a belief in total human depravity. These views relate to a parallel spectrum of beliefs about the relativity or absoluteness of the separation between human beings and the divine.[37] Christian theology, in all its many forms, however, is fundamentally rooted in the belief that God has acted and is still acting in creation, in the life, death, and resurrection of Christ, and continues to act in the present movement of the Holy Spirit in the present world. There is in Christianity a deep-seated and essential affirmation of goodness in creation, understood as occurring in the original primordial creation event, in the many accounts of God's saving and healing acts in human history, and in the ongoing movement of God in creating, renewing, redeeming, and blessing the world.

Even within the metaphorical account of the Fall, the goodness of creation was primary and included human beings. God saw what God had made and declared everything "very good" (Gen. 1:31). Before there was original sin, there was original goodness and "original blessing."[38] The human being was and is created in God's image (Gen. 1:26). Before any doctrine of original sin, there was original goodness. Sin is a condition of woundedness, alienation from God and from others in creation, but goodness is prior. Goodness is the foundation of all creation and the essential core of humanity. The human person is a dynamic being, moving toward growth and life through relationship with one another and with God, who is love and relation. (Much more will be said about the relationality of God in chapter 2.)

This affirmation of the primary goodness of the human person is a foundation for all good therapy. Without taking a naïve attitude toward the suffering and hurt that humans cause to one another and to the planet, having an appreciation for the spark of goodness and the *imago Dei* that exists in every human allows for a more generous, freeing, and respectful therapeutic stance. The Indian greeting, in Sanskrit, *"Namaste,"* ("The God in me greets the God in you")[39] is the fundamental place from which we seek to greet every patient (and, one hopes, everyone else in our lives as well). No matter how muddied and dim that spark of goodness may seem to the outside observer, however buried under layers of suffering, fear, and negative, even evil, behavior, this primordial goodness is the original inheritance of all created beings from the beginning of time.

Human Beings Are Embodied

The Christian theological tradition also struggles, as noted in the introduction, with the Platonic idea of the separation of soul and body. As early Christianity imbibed Greek philosophy, so it also absorbed a Platonic conception of a soul that had its origins outside or above human flesh, and at death would be freed from captivity in the body. This notion that human beings were constituted of two substances continued well into the Reformation[40]—rational nature in an individual substance (Boethius), a rational soul that rules over the body (Augustine), an incorruptible human soul within a corporeal substance (Aquinas), an immortal substance ruling the body in which it "dwells . . . as in a house" (Calvin).[41] The Enlightenment, with its emphasis on rationality, further widened the gap between mind and body. Descartes' dualism emphasized reason—the *res cogitans*—as what was central to human nature, in contrast with the body as merely the *res extensa* (the "extended thing"). He stated, "I am truly distinct from my body, and can exist without it."[42] Abstract thought, cultural creativity and mastery over nature were elevated, while things of the body, nature, and mortality—including sexuality, childbirth, blood, and hence Woman—were denigrated.[43] Whatever one's bias for or against Sigmund Freud's views of the human person, Freudian theory must be taken seriously precisely because of Freud's insistence on the reality of life lived in the body—our animal nature, including sexuality and aggression as prime motivators of human behavior.[44]

Contemporary neuroscientists have challenged this mind-body split from the perspective of recent brain research. Antonio Demasio, in his work on the relationship of the brain to consciousness, refuted "Descartes' error" by showing the direct relationship between body chemistry, brain chemistry, and subjective sensation and experience.[45] V. S. Ramachandran (who coined the term the "God module" for an area of the temporal lobe),[46] Nancey Murphy, Eugene d'Aquili, Andrew Newberg, Carol Rausch Albright, and pastoral theologian James Ashbrook have further investigated in various ways the connection between neurological functioning and religious consciousness.[47] As a philosopher of science and a Christian, Murphy has newly addressed the question of mind-body dualism head-on, taking a physicalist approach to human nature, but at the same time affirming morality, will, and religious sensibility as arising from a combination of neurobiological complexity, culture, and relationships to self, other, and God.[48]

The biblical witness itself is less dualistic than the philosophical tradition imbibed by the church fathers. The linguistic unity in the Hebrew Bible of body, soul, feeling, desire, and life is well known. Biblical scholars also have refuted a hard division in the New Testament between spirit and body. Even in Paul's writings, with his distinction between living according to the flesh (σάρξ, *sàrx*) and the spirit (πνεῦμα, *pneûma*), these are not separate substances as in Plato, but different orientations of the whole person.[49] Paul's emphasis on resurrection of the body (σῶμα, *sôma*) gives evidence to his regarding "the body as the person and the person as the physical body . . . placing it at the parousia of Christ in which personal redemption is coupled to and is a part of the redemption-by-transfiguration of the whole physical cosmos."[50] Anthony Thistelton even places relationality at the center of this biblical view of *sôma*. He states that the author of the Epistle to the Hebrews "does not think of σῶμα [*sôma*] as one component of human nature over against the soul, but for an explicit theological purpose: to refer to the relationality of the whole person as called into a temporal movement toward salvation as he or she relates to others and God."[51]

Finally, feminist theologians have also challenged Enlightenment mind-body dualism as perpetuating the subjugation of women's experience and glorifying disconnected rationality at the expense of the lived experiences of childbirth, sexuality, dying, suffering, and surviving.[52] God is *in* the body, not disembodied. A feminist theologian, Sallie McFague has offered the metaphor of the world itself as "God's body."[53] Womanist and Black feminist theology in particular celebrate the power of sheer survival as a source of knowledge to inform and sustain faith.[54] God is thus experienced both in the community of solidarity, and within the embodied self, as in Ntozake Shange's often quoted line of poetry: "I found God in myself and I loved her/I loved her fiercely."[55]

Human Beings Are Both Alike and Unique

Each human person is unique, and can be known in his or her particularities, and at the same time shares experiences, emotions, physical and cognitive capacities, genetic origins, and species memory that are common to all human beings. We are all simultaneously "like all others, like some others, and like no others."[56]

Like No Others

Perhaps one of the most compelling contributions of postmodern philosophy has been the investigation of ways in which established powers in the West subsumed or obscured individuals' differences and particularities under the rubric of what is "natural" (natural law), what is "normal" (based on various scientific or medical taxonomies), what represents the Ideal (the Platonic strain in western philosophy[57]) or "essential" characteristics by which entire groups of people may be categorized and labeled (again, as defined by the dominant culture). Furthermore, such assumptions are codified and embedded in language itself, so that the very acquisition of language becomes the medium by which the developing child also acquires the dominant culture's worldview. Both the set of assumptions about what is good, right, normal, and real, and the hegemonic nature of dominant discourse, are reflected in the term used by French philosophers (borrowing from Plato), "the logic of the Same."[58]

Sameness reinforces prevailing power structures. In her study of Paul's discourse of power in his letter to the church at Corinth, Elizabeth Castelli writes:

> Sameness serves the interests of the superordinate in a hierarchical relationship of power. Multiplicity destabilizes the certainty of the very claim to superordinate status. Unity is most often called for by those whose authority will be undergirded by it, and matters most to those for whom identities are problematized and for whom boundaries are at risk.[59]

Much of Western thought up through the nineteenth century gave lip service to individuals' differences, often framed in terms of rights and responsibilities. But the voices of those who did not conform to white, masculine models of humanity (until recently, labeled uncritically as "man"), remained largely unheard. Twentieth-century theorists have begun to propose strategies for the investigation of what is left unsaid and obscured in written texts and in speech, and for opening genuine dialogue with the silenced, the romanticized but disempowered Other—in postcolonial terms, sometimes referred to as the "subaltern." Interpersonal analyst Harry Stack Sullivan was one of the first analysts to identify how groups, such as racial groups, unconsciously come to represent the "not-me,"[60] and then are projectively distorted (whether through denigration or romanticization) as "the unconscious, the disowned, the uncannily strange, the powerfully fascinating."[61]

Emmanuel Lévinas's philosophical explorations of the relationship and ethical responsibility of the subject to the Other,[62] Jacques Derrida's "deconstruction,"[63] Michel Foucault's discourse analysis (of power),[64] Luce Irigaray's psychoanalytic interpretation of woman as the Other, mystified and silenced in Western cultural, philosophical, and psychological discourse;[65] and Gayatri Spivak's critical reflections on the question "can the subaltern speak?"[66] all point to the recognition that each individual human being is unique. S/he cannot be summarily categorized, homogenized (as in the North American myth of the "melting pot"), or defined, either by societal norms or by any other particular individual presuming to stand in the place of a subject in relation to her as an object—even an object of sympathy or concern. Each individual is irreducible and undefinable. It is in this sense that Lévinas identified the Other as the horizon of the infinite—beyond the scope of ordinary understanding, analysis, or "objective" evaluation.

The immediacy of genuine encounter between "I" and "Thou," as Martin Buber described,[67] transcends or eludes rational, categorical thought. Rational thought about the Other already objectifies him or her into an "It." Lévinas extended Buber's reflections on the "I-Thou" encounter to focus on the immediacy of the human face. In psychoanalytic theory, the "mirror" has become a rich metaphor for one's face-to-face encounter with oneself, mediated through the empathic gaze of the other[68]—but also, as emphasized by Jacques Lacan,[69] the alienating and solipsistic encounter of one's own gaze in reverse through cold glass. Thus, life-giving face-to-face encounters are also flesh-to-flesh. All studies of human development emphasize the early recognition of the mother's face and of human facial expressions, and the crucial importance of face-to-face interactions in constructing the capacity for relationship.

For Lévinas, moreover, the face poses an ethical imperative. It is the face of the other in all its particularity, naked and unmediated, that confronts us with the absolute separateness and difference of another human person. Lévinas insists that the uniqueness of this face automatically calls an ethical response from us, which takes priority over (and for Lévinas, even exists prior to) our claim to our own autonomy or freedom. We cannot use, degrade, or objectify another if we truly see his or her face.

How is communication possible between persons, given such radical difference? I have described the relational-psychoanalytic concept of intersubjectivity in detail previously.[70] Briefly, the term *intersubjectivity* refers to the shared wisdom—both conscious and unconscious—that resides in the space between persons. Perception of reality and the interpretation of events is not an isolated phenomenon that belongs to an "I" alone, but is co-constructed in the interstices of relationship. Thus, in any relationship, knowledge of self, other, and events is not encapsulated in each person's individual subjectivity, but flows back and forth between "I" and the

"Other" who faces me and whom I am facing. Reality itself is co-constructed in a third space between the supposed polarities of "I" and "Thou."

The idea of a "third space" has also been explored by postcolonial writers such as Homi Bhabha,[71] with particular attention to the restoration of voice to those regarded in the West as "Other." The "third space" refers to an in-breaking of space for speech by those previously silenced by Western hegemonic discourse. Such speech would not be conditioned by Western definitions of those who were colonized, or by monolithic self-definitions based on a desire to return to one's roots. It would be free to form identifications and create meanings based on present experience, simultaneously acknowledging heritage, and historical colonial patterns and influences:

> The intervention of the Third Space of enunciation, which makes the structure of meaning and reference an ambivalent process, destroys this mirror of representation in which cultural knowledge is customarily revealed as integrated, open, expanding code. Such an intervention quite properly challenges our sense of the historical identity of culture as homogenizing, unifying force, authenticated by originary Past, kept alive in the national tradition of the People.[72]

It is a cultural space, opened by global interchange, "where the negotiation of incommensurable differences creates a tension peculiar to borderline existences." Bhabha relates this to another concept, that of *hybridity*, in which "other 'denied' knowledges enter upon the dominant discourse and estrange the basis of its authority—its rule of recognition."[73] Hybridity is used in this sense to represent a joining together of two different entities without sacrificing either's distinctiveness. Cultural identities can emerge from stereotypes generated both by colonialists and nationalists "who have sought authority in the authenticity of 'origins.'"[74] "Hybrid hyphenisations emphasize the incommensurable elements as the basis of cultural identities."[75] Bhabha also differentiates between "diversity" as a liberal value, and "difference."[76] The former perpetuates an idea of consensus in which difference is tacitly contained and controlled by the dominant culture; the latter is "based on unequal, uneven, multiple and *potentially antagonistic*, political identities," multiple identities that "articulate in challenging ways, either positively or negatively, either in progressive or regressive ways, often conflictually, sometimes even *incommensurably*—not some flowering of individual talents and capacities."[77]

This emphasis in postmodernism and postcolonialism on restoring the speech and subjective stance of the "other" has lifted up previously unheard and unseen individuals, and created a strong case for respect for the uniqueness of each human person and subgroup within the larger society. At its most promising, this perspective encourages a celebration of difference, and offers both a language and a method for the overthrow of previously unchallenged hegemonies of thought and political practice. It might be argued that this emphasis on particularity is simply another version of Enlightenment insistence on individual rights and freedoms. Dwight Hopkins,[78] Robert Bellah,[79] and others have critiqued the individualism of

Northern American culture in particular. Hopkins names the dominant theological anthropology of the United States as a "demonic individualism" that "reveals itself in a kind of American cultural trinity: historical amnesia, instantaneous fulfillment of desire, and 'we're number one' mythology."[80]

If taken superficially, the postmodern emphasis on the local and the particular, and the resistance to universals or *total*ity as (at least potential) *total*itarianism,[81] this could be seen as a swing to radical ethical relativism, and a kind of simplistic "I'm OK, you're OK" social psychology. Late-modern (such as Lévinas), postcolonial, and postmodern thought need not collapse into a bland or nihilistic relativism, however. Enlightenment values enshrined in the French revolution's motto "*liberté, fraternité, egalité*" (liberty, brotherhood, equality), although originally framed by and applied only to those with privilege (the white male voting "brother" citizen), need not be discarded in a postmodern era. The challenge of postmodernism and postcolonialism, rather, is always to ask the question (and not fail to ask it because of the inertia and the self-interest and ready self-deception of dominant culture): what is the perspective of those who have traditionally been excluded by what Spivak terms "hegemonic discourse"?[82] And at what point does "equality" devolve into enforced conformity to a dominant and dominating ideology of the Same? Lévinas writes compellingly of the disruption, even the "violence" of the face,[83] as it shatters preconceived notions and even political structures in its absolute ethical demand for recognition as a uniquely separate and different subject. To take seriously the demand of the Other for recognition automatically engages the question of multiple individuals' competing cries and demands, hence the question of justice:[84]

> I have always described the face of the neighbour as the bearer of an order, imposing upon me, with respect to the other, a gratuitous and non-transferable responsibility, as if the I were chosen and unique—and in which the other were absolutely other, i.e., still incomparable, and thus unique. But the [people] round me are multiple. Hence the question: 'Who is my neighbour?' The inevitable question of justice.

Finally, there is also a difference *within* difference. Psychoanalytic object relations thinkers have highlighted the difference between the actual, external other, and the other as perceived internally. "Objects are not people."[85] As Melanie Klein first emphasized, the "other" that is represented in the internal world is much more a product of fantasy, idiosyncratic perception, splitting, and autistic distortion than an objective representation of other people. The "joyous shock of difference"[86] is often accounted for by the difference between one's habitual thinking about the other in a relationship, with all its internal resonances and projective assumptions, and the occasional inbreaking of something coming from the actual other person that so interrupts these assumptions that it has the character of something entirely new, disruptive, and therefore potentially transformative of one's old inner reality. D. W. Winnicott called this "object use," differentiating it from "object relating."[87]

By experiencing the shock of the "real" other, not as one projectively has perceived him or her, but having both his or her own *subjectivity*—his or her own internal world—and *subjecthood* or independent existence,[88] the internal other is "destroyed," or broken down so that a new and potentially more genuinely related other can emerge both internally and interpersonally.

More recently Jessica Benjamin[89] has clarified that the recognition of this "real" other (as opposed to the internal object of fantasy) does not result in a collapse into sameness, but rather makes room for a dialectically organized negotiation of difference—a reciprocal process of mutual recognition. Negation is as important to this process as recognition, since the intersubjective interplay of fantasy and reality is an ongoing, negotiated process—in Benjamin's words, "there is a dialectic between breakdown and restoration of recognition—the destruction and survival necessary to psychic life."[90] In the process, one's own capacity to negotiate difference further enhances one's own relationship to one's self and sense of identity. One becomes more capable of recognizing not only the difference of the external other, but also the "nonidentical" selves within.[91]

LIKE SOME OTHERS

The anthropologists' assertion that human beings are not only like no others, but also like some others and like all others, serves as a further check on the potential for radical relativism and individualism. Human beings are not isolated, but relational, as will be described further below. In this apparently innate yearning for affiliation, human beings also choose mates, form families and tribes, and identify themselves not only with other individuals but groups. Some of the ways in which human beings have been categorized, such as race, class, sexual orientation, and gender, have been convincingly shown to be social and political constructs that may serve to keep certain groups in power over others—especially when these are described in terms of binary oppositions that obscure nuances and shades of difference among individuals.

Yet, in spite of the fictive element of many supposed demographic "realities," human beings both seek and find similarity and kinship with one another. Cultures, like individuals, have distinctive features that are nevertheless fluid and permeable. People also generally participate in many cultural systems that overlap. As Hopkins notes, culture permeates multiple aspects of life including labor and economics, aesthetics and art, and religion and spirituality.[92] Individuals in non-Western and Southern-hemisphere cultures, as well as nondominant cultural groups in the West, tend to identify with culture and a collective sense of identity.[93] Relationality and one's sense of accountability and responsibility for others in the community is an ethical and moral definer of self, even in North American culture where individualism is prized. One's agency is always codetermined by that of others, whether this mutual communal influence is acknowledged or not.[94]

Bonds of group and culture can create powerful communities and societies, knit together by ready empathy based on shared values and perceptions, and affection based largely on mutual identification. These bonds can function for both good and ill—creating group pride and motivation for positive achievement, shared energy for altruism, resistance by disempowered groups against oppression, but also the dangers of clannishness, xenophobia, or shared delusional thinking, and mob psychology as Freud described in his *Group Psychology and the Analysis of the Ego*.[95]

Persons are not only born into cultures; they also participate in and continually co-construct the cultures in which they are embedded. As anthropologist Clifford Geertz asserted, cultures are not monolithic.[96] Cultures are too often described in terms of general characteristics that do not adequately depict the richness of variations within their communities.

Further, cultures themselves do not simply exist, they also evolve, and not in a vacuum. Multiple national, ethnic, and linguistic groups coexist and comingle, and each new contact has the potential for genuine encounters in which new meanings may be made, and thus, new realities. Idealized or "pure" cultures that are invoked to represent the identity of individuals, families, and groups actually function as "imagined communities."[97] As Seyla Benhabib has pointed out, recent debates about culture have tended to operate upon four faulty assumptions: regarding cultures and value systems as "self-consistent, pre-reflexive wholes; as sealed off from one another; as internally unified; and as systems of meaning, value, and interpretation which must also be reproduced over time by individuals under the constraints of a material way of life."[98]

Individuals within cultures are therefore not only embedded in them, but act upon them and create new variations within them. As an individual grows and develops, he or she makes meaning of the cultural surround. Some of these meanings will subtly or even radically shape the culture itself. As members of a culture are exposed to other cultures and worldviews, the capacity for empathy and mutual perspective taking increases, as well as the capacity to apply critical thinking to one's own cultural norms and values.

Perhaps, then, it is this middle definition—that human beings are *like some others*—that poses the greatest ethical challenge. It is easier, perhaps, to assert the rights of the unique individual, or to fall into a bland moralism that "in the end, we are all the same." Jesus' radical commandment, to love the enemy as well as the neighbor, simultaneously acknowledges the ease of relating to those with whom we identify, those "like us," and its dangers—and he poses the most challenging ethical requirement: to reach out beyond bonds of commonality and ease of relating, to the stranger, the Other, even the one whose differences most threaten us, and whom we most fear.

Like All Others

Finally, although postmodernism rightly challenges assumptions about universals—particularly as such "universals" are defined by certain groups and exclude the experiences of others—there are some ways in which human beings are like all other human beings. This is the fundamental basis for all empathy and all human relationship. In the vastness and multiplicity that constitutes each human person, each of us is capable of feeling, experiencing, and knowing everything that human beings can feel, experience, and know. (More will be said about the multiplicity of the human person below.) In spite of the dangers of being subsumed under an oppressive expectation of conformity to a dominant Same, there are still basic human characteristics, needs, and emotions that form a bond of common human experience.

Pioneering social worker Charlotte Towle's book *Common Human Needs*,[99] Abraham Maslow's theoretical hierarchy of human needs,[100] and the work of Silvan Tomkins[101] on innate or "primary" human affects that are observable in infants across cultures, all point to certain dimensions of the human condition that are shared across time and cultures. Humans are 99.9 percent identical genetically, and the superficial differences that are used to justify social and political constructions of racial inferiority, such as skin color, are not correlated scientifically with more complex traits such as intelligence, personality, artistic aptitude, or athletic ability.[102] Culturally, while C. G. Jung's elaborate system of archetypes is heavily imbued with a Neoplatonic notion of eternal Ideas or Ideals, and can easily devolve into essentialism (particularly, as feminist critics have shown, with respect to gender, as in the *anima* and *animus* archetypes[103]), his explorations of common symbols, themes, stories and myths across many disparate cultures and civilizations point to the richness of certain aspects of shared human experience.[104]

The danger, of course, is to overextend such arguments. Jung, like Freud, was a romantic explorer in nineteenth-century heroic mode. In the zeal to discover what human beings share in common, it is all too tempting to assert one's own group's interpretation of such phenomena as "universal," and then, in a colonizing move, to impose this interpretation as normative. Yet, an opposite danger also exists. Denying another the possibility of sameness, of humanity held in common, is as much a feature of unconscious oppression as insisting upon a homogenized universality in which the other must conform to the dominant group's values, norms, and identifications.[105] Barbara Johnson, in her reading of a 1950 Zora Neale Hurston essay, "What White Publishers Won't Print," states that "the resistance to finding out that the Other is the same springs out of the reluctance to admit that the same is Other. If the average man [*sic*] could recognize that the Negro was 'just like him,' he would have to recognize that he was just like the Negro."[106] Unconscious projective processes are thus implicated both in denying otherness, and denying commonality.

While any theory identifying what may be "basic" to human life is inevitably influenced and limited by the cultural biases of their authors, contemporary efforts at cross-cultural research suggest at least some validity to such theories, particularly in the realm of human affect and human needs. Human beings seem universally to feel interest/excitement, enjoyment/joy, surprise/startle, distress/anguish, fear/terror, anger/rage, shame/humiliation, dissmell (reaction to bad smell), and disgust (which are

Tomkins' observations of primary affects expressed at two levels of intensity). Infants fail to thrive when the natural processes of attachment to a primary caregiver are interrupted.[107] As Maslow articulated, we not only need physiological requirements such as air, food, drink, sleep, and basic safety, but also love, a sense of belonging, and *perhaps* some form of growth or "self-actualization"—such as having an impact, or fulfillment of one's gifts and potential (the most vague, interculturally contested, and individualistically framed "need" in Maslow's hierarchy). Attunement by primary caretakers to infants' affects appear to be essential not only for the development of a child's capacity to relate, but also to the development of the brain itself.[108] Such commonality does not create, but perhaps provides a primary basis for the next characteristic of human beings, which is our *relationality*.

Human Beings Are Intrinsically Relational

Winnicott once wrote "There is no such thing as a baby . . . If you set out to describe a baby, you will find you are describing a baby and someone. A baby cannot exist alone, but is essentially part of a relationship."[109] If we extrapolate beyond the language of his time and place, of mothers and babies, or all *parents* and babies, we can understand this to mean that none of us is born in isolation. We all have our personal beginnings in the very body of another human being, and as infants we "fail to thrive" without human touch. The object relations theorists were correct in their reframing of Freud's basic instincts, beyond the two drives of sex and aggression—to the fuller understanding that human beings are driven first and foremost by their desire to connect and remain connected to other human beings.

To quote Martin Buber, "in the beginning is the relation."[110] Life begins in the matrix of "I and Thou."[111] Buber wrote, "It is not as if a child first saw an object and then entered into some relationship with that. Rather, the longing for relation is primary, the cupped hand into which the being that confronts us nestles."[112] Thus, even our knowledge of self and others is not something we either discover or invent in a vacuum, a pure subjectivity, but is characterized by the multiple, subtle interactions and influences that we exchange with others every moment, from the time of our birth. "Personalist" philosopher John MacMurray[113] distinguished between a "self," as an isolated individual, agent, or doer, with self as subject and world as object, and a "personal being," who is simultaneously both subject and object: "The unity of persons is found in the community of You and I, in which the intention is to regard all others as Selves."[114] For MacMurray, personal existence cannot be understood apart from relations with other persons.[115] Our consciousness is better described as not just subjectivity, but as one dimension of, and participating in *intersubjectivity*. MacMurray also finds the origins of this capacity for intersubjectivity in the relationship of the infant with the mother (primary caretaker).

Human beings are also, therefore, creatures who live in communities. No person, however seemingly isolated, does not depend upon other humans, and on the wider creation, for his or her existence. Humans cannot survive alone. Humans live in *contexts*, which include both the natural environment, and human-generated cultures.

Our relationality and our longing for connection finally extends to our deep desire for God, and to God's loving desire for us. God uniquely created and bestowed human beings with the capacity for this relation, however obscured it may be by the brokenness of creation and the consuming preoccupations of daily human existence. This intrinsic relationality between human beings and the divine may even be hardwired into the human brain, as some neuroscientists have argued.[116] Through prayer, and other ways in which we may become aware of the flow of connection between ourselves and the divine, we are able to enter into God's passionate desire for us in relation. To quote Augustine:

> There is a light I love, and a food, and a kind of embrace when I love my God—a light, voice, odour, food, embrace of my inner [person], where my soul is floodlit by light which space cannot contain, where there is sound that time cannot seize, where there is a perfume which no breeze disperses, where there is a taste for food no amount of eating can lessen, and where there is bond of union that no satiety can part. That is what I love when I love my God.[117]

While the patriarchal and vertical (top-down) elements of Michelangelo's Sistine chapel fresco may be critiqued in light of contemporary feminist and liberation theologies, this desire is depicted well here as intimacy, connectedness, and mutual reaching between God and Adam.

Human Beings Are Multiple

The two of us wrote Anti-Oedipus together. Since each of us was several, there was already quite a crowd.
                    —Gilles Deleuze and Félix Guattari[118]

With the related concepts of relationality, mutuality, and intersubjectivity in place, we begin to engage more fully the contemporary postmodern "relational" psychoanalytic critique of classical psychoanalytic conceptions of the human. At the heart of all psychoanalytic theories of human persons, or of personality, is a fundamental conception of the mind, and of human consciousness, as being constituted by regions of both *conscious* and *unconscious* mental contents. Regardless of how each psychoanalytic school of thought theorizes the mechanisms by which certain thoughts, mental representations, or mental constructs are removed from conscious awareness, all psychoanalytic approaches to understanding the human mind, and how psychotherapy heals, depend upon the fundamental belief in an unconscious region of the mind, and by extension, the existence of unconscious dynamics between and among human persons.

For the most part, this model of consciousness and unconsciousness has been conceived of vertically, following Freud's so-called topographical model[119] (see Figure 3) in which *conscious*, *preconscious*, and *unconscious* reside in successive layers from top to bottom, with *repression* as the central mechanism for removing mental contents from consciousness. The unconscious was privileged in this model, metaphorically, as the place of "depth." The process of psychotherapy was a heroic act of plumbing the depths and returning with the prize of new knowledge—*in*sight. The project was conceived, in keeping with Freud's own time and context, as a heroic colonial journey to conquer and plunder the hidden recesses of the mind, which were imagined as both deep and dark. This was the model—antedating Freud's later formulation of ego, id, and superego—that was first transmitted to pastoral caregivers in America, such as the Emmanuel Church movement in Boston in the early 1900s,[120] and it has had a powerful influence on pastoral psychology from its earliest days.

While this model represented a powerful metaphor for depicting the forceful influence and seeming independence of unconscious mental processes, its hegemony is now increasingly being challenged within psychoanalytic schools of thought. These challenges are arising from a number of separate theoretical and clinical spheres, generating ideas that are just now increasingly converging toward a new, more multiple, dispersed, and spatially conceived (horizontally or 3- or even 4-dimensionally) model of mind.

The sources of these challenges are numerous. Common to all these contemporary movements is a challenge to the centrality of the function of psychic *conflict* in Freud's concept of the formation of the unconscious. Freud's concept of repression relied on *drive theory* to explain why mental contents had to be removed from conscious awareness. Repression was a by-product of psychic conflict—between the inner drives of sex and aggression, and the social demands of family and civilization—pressing the drives *down* and out of awareness for the sake of getting along with other people (and not being killed or castrated by them!).

CHALLENGES FROM PSYCHOANALYTIC THEORISTS AFTER FREUD

In the generation after Freud, a theory called "object relations theory," beginning with Melanie Klein, challenged the centrality of repression in favor of a model of *splitting*, motivated not by forbidden drives or terror of castration, but by unresolvable contradictions among fantasied and real experiences of parental provision and lack, our need for *attachment* to others, plus our real hunger and aggression. (See Figure 4 below.) It is unresolvable relational contradictions that create splits in mental life, over time populating an entire inner landscape with "objects"—that is, strongly cathected (attached-to) people, part-people, and other objects of attachment that dwell in both conscious and unconscious regions. To borrow from Jungian analyst James Hillman, the internal world is "an inscape of personified images."[121] These inner objects are further understood both to inhabit and to provoke different states of consciousness with different accompanying affective (emotional) atmospheres and

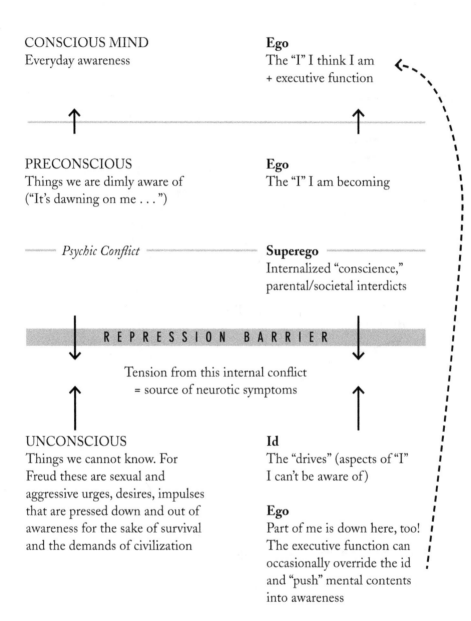

CONSCIOUS MIND
Everyday awareness

Ego
The "I" I think I am
+ executive function

↑   ↑

PRECONSCIOUS
Things we are dimly aware of
("It's dawning on me . . . ")

Ego
The "I" I am becoming

——— *Psychic Conflict* ———   **Superego**
Internalized "conscience,"
parental/societal interdicts

↓   R E P R E S S I O N   B A R R I E R   ↓

Tension from this internal conflict
= source of neurotic symptoms

↑   ↑

UNCONSCIOUS
Things we cannot know. For
Freud these are sexual and
aggressive urges, desires, impulses
that are pressed down and out of
awareness for the sake of survival
and the demands of civilization

Id
The "drives" (aspects of "I"
I can't be aware of)

Ego
Part of me is down here, too!
The executive function can
occasionally override the id
and "push" mental contents
into awareness

Figure 3: *Freud's "topographical model" of consciousness*

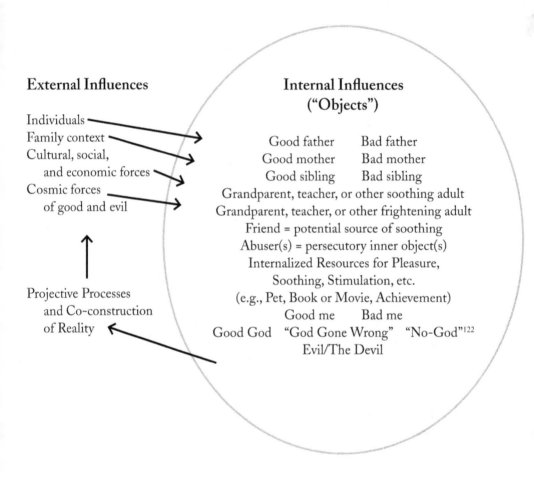

External Influences

Individuals
Family context
Cultural, social,
 and economic forces
Cosmic forces
 of good and evil

Projective Processes
 and Co-construction
 of Reality

**Internal Influences
("Objects")**

Good father   Bad father
Good mother   Bad mother
Good sibling   Bad sibling
Grandparent, teacher, or other soothing adult
Grandparent, teacher, or other frightening adult
Friend = potential source of soothing
Abuser(s) = persecutory inner object(s)
Internalized Resources for Pleasure,
 Soothing, Stimulation, etc.
(e.g., Pet, Book or Movie, Achievement)
Good me   Bad me
Good God   "God Gone Wrong"   "No-God"[122]
Evil/The Devil

Figure 4. *An object relational view of the self*

cognitive capacities, and also to be *in*voked by various shifts in the external environment that may have resonance with them.

Contemporary psychoanalytic theory is increasingly replacing Freud's vertical
"depth" model of consciousness/unconsciousness with an even more sweeping re-
conception of the mind as a multiplicity of mental states—a "normal nonlinearity
of the human mind,"[123] conceived as more spatially or horizontally dispersed, and at

varying levels of conscious awareness.[124] In relational theory, a psychoanalytic movement that has emerged in the last two decades, the traditional psychoanalytic focus on repression as a by-product of conflict has been replaced or at least set alongside an interest in *dissociation* as a nonpathological phenomenon. Jody Messler Davies summarized this aspect of relational theory "that has begun to conceive of self, indeed of mind itself, as a multiply-organized, associationally-linked network of parallel, coexistent, at times conflictual, systems of meaning attribution and understanding."[125]

> Not one unconscious, not the unconscious, but multiple levels of consciousness and unconsciousness, in an ongoing state of interactive articulation as past experience infuses the present and present experience evokes state-dependent memories of formative interactive representations. Not an onion, which must be carefully peeled, or an archeological site to be meticulously unearthed and reconstructed in its original form, but a child's kaleidoscope in which each glance through the pinhole of a moment in time provides a unique view; a complex organization in which a fixed set of colored, shaped, and textured components rearrange themselves in unique crystalline structures determined by way of infinite pathways of interconnectedness.[126]

Dissociation is no longer being regarded in this model solely as a pathological outcome of trauma, or an irremedial state of alienation from one's self, as in Lacan's concept of the illusion of a unified self as seen in the mirror defending against the infantile experience of being a "body-in-pieces" (*corps-morcelé*), "sunk in motor incapacity, turbulent movements, and fragmentation."[127] As Philip Bromberg, another relational thinker, has observed,

> The process of dissociation is basic to human mental functioning and is central to the stability and growth of personality. It is intrinsically an adaptational talent that represents the very nature of what we call "consciousness." . . . There is now abundant evidence that the psyche does not start as an integrated whole, but is nonunitary in origin—a mental structure that begins and continues as a multiplicity of self-states that maturationally attain a feeling of coherence which overrides the awareness of discontinuity. This leads to the experience of a cohesive sense of personal identity and the necessary illusion of being "one self."[128]

A way of explaining this more concretely might be that at any given moment, each of us experiences ourselves in one particular "self state," or state of consciousness that is laden with thoughts, memories, physical sensations, emotions, and fantasies. Our subjectivity is not monolithic. In this sense, none of us at any given point in time is a unitive "Self" or "Being." This accords better with non-Western conceptions of the self, which tend to understand selfhood and identity more in terms of one's belonging in community, and not as an isolated individual defined by his or her own consciousness or will.[129] In fact, as Geertz wrote,

> The Western conception of the person as a bounded, unique, more or less integrated motivational and cognitive universe, a dynamic center of awareness, emotion, judgment, and action organized into a distinctive whole and set contrastively both against other such wholes and against its social and natural background, is, however incorrigible it may seem to us, a rather peculiar idea within the context of the world's cultures.[130]

We are more accurately understood in this theory as a conglomerate or web of self-states, affect-states, personalities formed in identification with one or more of our inner objects or part-objects, and especially a multiplicity of "selves in relation."[131] At any given moment, we may experience ourselves as a subject, an "I," but behind, beyond, or alongside every subject-moment, are all the other subject-moments that comprise the whole of this web.[132] We experience ourselves as intersubjectively constituted both in our own internal relationship or "primary subjective experience"[133] of our multiple selves, and in relation to others—particularly as we are formed from infancy onward through identification with others' responses to us.[134] In a postmodern conception, what is outside of consciousness at any given moment is not necessarily repressed, suppressed, or disavowed, as in other models of the unconscious. These are all potential parts of the web, but there are multiple varying degrees of accessibility and inaccessibility between and among the different parts.

Quantum physics now provides us with better analogies for this web of subjects that is illusorily labeled "myself" than Newtonian physics. Rather than a mechanistic hydraulic system, which some of Freud's language implied, this conception is better understood as a cloud or a swarm of subatomic particles—not without parameters, but no longer with certainty as to what space any individual subpart may occupy at any given moment as all the parts continue in dynamic internal relation. Development itself, rather than being linear, is better described in terms of "complex multiple spirals." Ken Corbett suggests that we reimagine the classical concept of "developmental lines"[135] in terms of "a weblike substance . . . a spiral web or tissue that can be stretched, twisted, elongated, folded in on itself—and that springs back . . . but is never quite the same . . . like taffy but each having a different tensile strength (some spirals are more flexible than others)."[136]

Further, this web develops relationally, not in isolation. Like Gilles Deleuze's notion of the *implex*, which will be explored in chapter 2, development occurs in a mutual process of enfolding and unfolding, even, as we will imagine theologically, "God folded in all things and all things enfolded in God."[137] While Corbett does not take this theological turn, his words leave room for the pastoral theologian to conceive of multiplicity in quantum theological terms: "The lacework of a web articulates the confluence and coadaptive dependence of the interlacing on the context; it is not a Newtonian a priori structure, or a fixed form, but rather a structure that is never fixed and is always in transition, always moving in accord with the atmosphere."[138] The very illusion of seamless going-on-being from one self-state to another, then, is a developmental achievement, and represents the fluidity of mental contents.

This shift in conceptualization of consciousness and unconsciousness, from a vertical to a more horizontal plane, in which mental contents are not necessarily privileged as "deeper," parallels the recent work in infant observation by Robert Emde,[139] Daniel Stern,[140] and Beatrice Beebe and Frank Lachmann.[141] These researchers have proposed that the earliest experiences of the self appear to be organized around a variety of shifting self-states that encompass cognitive, affective, and physiological dimensions, and appear to include internalized representations of relational or interactive experiences.[142] A central aspect of the developmental process consists of being able increasingly to move smoothly from one self-state to another, with increasing self-continuity and self-regulation. This developmental process is aided or impeded by the responsiveness of primary caretakers, particularly in earliest childhood. The sense of boundaries between self and other parallel this internal development, again, aided or impeded by the others in the child's early environment. Both the internal sense of continuity, or in Heinz Kohut's relevant terminology here, "*cohesion*,"[143] and the external sense of healthy, permeable boundaries are thus socially constructed, not an intrinsic trait, and its construction can be incomplete and enfeebled by neglect, or shattered or deformed by traumatic injuries.

THINKING RHIZOMES

Another image that is helpful in considering this multiplicity of the human person is Gilles Deleuze's and Félix Guattari's image of the rhizome. A dictionary definition of a rhizome is "a horizontal, usually underground stem that often sends out roots and shoots from its nodes."[144] It is different from a root in that it extends horizontally, in network-like fashion, and biologically carries on multiple functions—for example, reproduction as well as nourishment. A root, by contrast, normally grows downward, and when used as a metaphor signifies such unitive meanings as depth, foundation, source, and origin (even though roots, too, if not the taproot, can be multiple). Deleuze and Guattari use the rhizome metaphor to challenge the privileging in Western philosophy and in capitalism of images that tend to reinforce or justify hegemony, as if the natural order itself privileged "the one" or "unity" over multiplicity and difference.[145] They state, "We're tired of trees. We should stop believing in trees, roots, and radicles. They've made us suffer too much . . . Thought is not arborescent, and the brain is not a rooted or ramified matter."[146]

The principles or properties Deleuze and Guattari identify with the rhizome are useful in conceiving of the mind as similarly multivarious and complex:

1. *Connection.* "Any point of a rhizome can be connected to anything other, and must be."[147] One of the reasons we do not experience ourselves from moment to moment as a disparate jumble of perceptions is that the mind—and neuroscience confirms this in the form of the networking of brain cells as well—is continually creating and renewing *connections* among mental representations and constructs. The "whole" is constantly shape-shifting, but usually the changes are so gradual as to be hardly noticed, as certain memories and percepts are stimulated by new experiences, while allowing other unused or unstimulated connections to decay.

2. *Heterogeneity.* Here Deleuze and Guattari are actually referring to language (contra Noam Chomsky, whose linguistic theory involves treelike models of grammar[148]), but the principle also fits well with the concept of a multiply-constituted mind, particularly in relation to mental development. Quoting Catherine Clément: "It evolves by subterranean stems and flows, along river valleys or train tracks; it spreads like a patch of oil."[149]

3. *Multiplicity.* Here Deleuze and Guattari's theory corresponds most closely to the relational-psychoanalytic conception of mind as multiple and spatially rather than vertically imagined:

    > There are no points or positions in a rhizome, such as those found in a structure, tree, or root. There are only lines. When [pianist] Glenn Gould speeds up the performance of a piece, he is not just displaying virtuosity, he is transforming the musical points into lines, he is making the whole piece proliferate ... The notion of unity appears only when there is a power takeover ... All multiplicities are flat, in the sense that they fill or occupy all of their dimensions ... [and] the dimensions of this "plane" increase with the number of connections that are made on it.[150]

4. *Asignifying Rupture.* "A rhizome may be broken, shattered at a given spot, but it will start up again on one of its old lines, or on new lines."[151] Here, perhaps inadvertently, Deleuze and Guattari's theory relates to the felt sense of *dis*continuity that occurs in mental life because of trauma, crisis, or other acute disruption of one's habitual thought processes or modes of coping. One does go on thinking, except in cases of literal unconsciousness, as in a coma, but the ordinary illusion of continuity is broken. Even so, whether through dissociative coping patterns or the attempted construction of a new subjectivity following amnesia, mental life continues. It springs up, like the shoots and tubers on a rhizome, from nodes of earlier wounding, or perhaps even places of earlier creative potential. Such shatterings, while not desired, can even become places of new life for those who survive—"strong at the broken places."[152]

5. *Cartography*. Deleuze and Guattari contrast the metaphor of a map with a genealogy. All psychoanalytic theories until recently tended to frame self-understanding and insight in terms of tracing the "genetic origins" of neuroses and other pathology. It was assumed that, with enough analytic persistence, the roots of a given pathology would be uncovered, and the pathology would be cathartically healed. Guattari, himself a trained psychoanalyst who turned away from his Lacanian theoretical foundations, specifically challenges psychoanalysis (especially in its French Freudian/Lacanian forms) with this fifth principle. While a *genealogy* attempts to fasten relations to particular origins in a hierarchical fashion, a *map* constructs relations spatially and is continually "detachable, reversible, susceptible to constant modification."[153]

6. *Decalcomania*. The last principle relates to this critique of Lacanian genetic analysis: "A rhizome is not amenable to any structural or generative model. It is a stranger to any idea of genetic axis or deep structure."[154] (*Décalcomanie*, in French, referred to the nineteenth-century craze for transferring tracings or designs to glass or metal[155]—in other words, images that are traced on the surface, rather than something involving deep structure.) Deleuze and Guattari invented the term *schizoanalysis*[156] in opposition to *psychoanalysis*, to suggest a form of mutable, open, experimental exploration that "rejects any idea of pretraced destiny, whatever name is given to it—divine, anagogic, historical, economic, structural, hereditary, or syntagmatic."[157]

The rhizome presents an alternative model to the classical psychoanalytic assertion that all thought, all behavior, proceeds genetically and to some extent deterministically from a deeper root cause in the past. With Deleuze and Guattari's rhizome image held in tension with the image of roots, the psychoanalytic importance of tracing associations is retained, but now we can see the possibility for a different kind of associational chain of events—horizontal, at times more randomly selected, and linked by present conditions as well as past. This image can also be held in tension with traditional psychoanalytic conceptions of the mind in terms of psychogenetics, tree-like tracings of pathology, and heroic metaphors of plumbing the depths of a single, vertically conceived unconscious.

The metaphor has its limits, of course.[158] Like many postmodern thinkers, Deleuze objects in general to modernist, binary oppositions, but there is no doubt that the rhizome-tree dichotomy presents another logical dualism of its own.[159] By placing the rhizome in opposition to the root, Deleuze and Guattari again posit a kind of contest. The humble potato wins out over the formerly exalted tree.[160] This, too, however, is problematic in psychoanalytic thinking, it seems to me, since some events, some behaviors and feelings, do appear to be "generated"—"rooted" in early childhood experiences and wounds. Yet to assign *all* problems in daily living to a theory of infantile origins may be too reductionistic as well.

It might therefore be most useful to take a both-and approach: rhizome and tree, horizontal and vertical, spatial associational chains and the repetition that can arise out of repressed early childhood experiences and wishes—taking seriously Deleuze and Guattari's caution to never lose sight of the more uncontrollable rhizome in favor of the seductively analyzable tree. Imagine mind and self in terms of a three-dimensional multiplicity (or more)—neither vertical "depth" nor purely horizontal "plane," but an infinitely dimensional, quantum substance, with internal indeterminacy and some fluid external parameters. Imagine a subjectivity, a multiple self, identifiable as both an "I" and a "Thou" simultaneously, and with a mobile consciousness that scans and networks various parts of the "self," in an illusory but functional sense of self-cohesion, self-regulation, and self-continuity.

This larger, more spatial, multidimensional model of mind takes some getting used to! As unfathomable and at times frightening the idea of "the" unconscious always was in traditional psychoanalysis, this model proposes a multiple conscious/unconscious even more freewheeling, impossible to grasp, infinite in its "extensity"[161]—in Graham Ward's words, the mind and self as "an undefined spatiality, like the contours of a perfume."[162] There was a hopefulness in Freud and his followers that the unconscious could be in some sense conquered, brought to light, and the irrational outbursts of the id sublimated and contained—anyone who has experienced psychoanalytic psychotherapy has participated in this hope of increased rationality, self-control, and self-awareness. This postmodern model, while not doing away with the value of exploring the regions of unconsciousness, presents analysis (whether formal therapy or personal self-reflection and introspection) as a much more slippery and never-ending process—truly a life's work, "terminable and interminable."[163]

What, then, is the value of this model, if it consigns us to a perpetual unknowing, a compassless journey with a map that changes like the landscapes Alice encountered after going through the looking glass? Shouldn't we either take refuge back in the modernist models of self where we felt grounded, or throw up our hands and embrace a nihilistic attitude that "ignorance is bliss"? No, as breathtaking and perhaps even "mind-blowing" the expanded scope of this multiple model of mind may be, it also expands, I believe, the potential in psychotherapy (and in life!) for a more creative, inviting process of exploration of subjectivities, "self," "other," and the possible meanings that can be generated between them. Freud's dictum, borrowed from Socrates, that the "unexamined life is not worth living,"[164] while perhaps exaggerated, still rings true. A multiple and variegated unconscious is no less dangerous or prone to self-sabotage than a single one was! The effort to explore, even if one knows that the exploration will always be provisional, contingent, and unfinished, bears fruit, both in expanded self-knowledge and in expanded openness to the "other," both within and without.

There is a political and ethical dimension to this reconceptualization as well. Being open to a variety of "others" within the web that constitutes oneself, it seems to me, should potentiate a greater openness to "others" beyond oneself. The idea of a multiple self as emancipatory also relates to the dimension of time, and to the flow of selves in relational process as well.

Human Beings Are Mutable, Fluid, and in Process

Human beings move through the medium of time more changeably than even widely adopted developmental psychologies may have suggested. To be human is to be in a continual state of flux and transition. "A rhizome has no beginning or end; it is always in the middle, between things, interbeing, *intermezzo*."[165] This interbeing, this fluidity has social and political implications—a freeing of subjectivities from monolithic conceptions of oneself as conforming to a single, rigid structure—especially as that structure is given and reinforced by the prevailing social hierarchies and dominant culture. In the words of French social psychologist Jean-Michel Oughourlian, "What one customarily calls the *I* or *self* in psychology is an unstable, constantly changing, and ultimately evanescent structure . . . only *desire* brings this self into existence."[166]

As Freud understood, much of psychological life bears the imprint not only of parental prohibitions, but through them, the "civilizing" forces of culture as well.[167] Both the parental "no," and the "no's" of culture, live internally in the form of the superego (in object relations terms, a constellation of critical inner objects that can generate aspects of both a healthy conscience and neurotic inhibitions). The gain is being able to adapt and get along with others in spite of competing desires and impulses; the corresponding loss is the loss of contact with one's own inner drives and wishes, and in some cases, a loss of vitality or spontaneity, and the construction (in Winnicott's term) of a "false self."[168] The postmodern proposal of a multiple self goes hand in hand with a more fluid, dynamic, flexible going-on-being. Drawing from Luce Irigaray, feminist postmodern theorist and psychoanalyst Jane Flax describes the multiplicity and fluidity of subjects as emancipatory:

> I believe a unitary self is unnecessary, impossible, and a dangerous illusion. Only multiple subjects can invent ways to struggle against domination that will not merely recreate it. In the process of therapy, in relations with others, and in political life we encounter many difficulties when subjectivity becomes subject to one normative standard, solidifies into rigid structures, or lacks the capacity to flow readily between different aspects of itself . . . No singular form can be sufficient as a regulative ideal or as a prescription for human maturity or the essential human capacity . . . It is possible to imagine subjectivities whose desires for multiplicity can impel them toward emancipatory action. These subjectivities would be *fluid rather than solid, contextual rather than universal, and process oriented rather than topographical*. Emancipatory theories and practices requires *mechanics of fluids*[169] in which subjectivity is conceived as process-

es rather than as a fixed atemporal entity locatable in a homogeneous, abstract time and space [Flax's reading of the Cartesian idea of the self]. In discourses about subjectivity the term "the self" will be superseded by discussions of "subjects." The term "subject(s)" more adequately expresses the simultaneously determined, multiple, and agentic qualities of subjectivity.[170]

Such postmodern writers choose the term *subject* rather than *self*, following Foucault. Whereas the term *self* suggests substance, essence, and autonomy, the term *subject* conveys contingency and relatedness. It refers simultaneously to the "subject" of a sentence, the experiencing "subject" in subjectivity, and, politically, the participation in a complex web of power as "subject" to dominance, and more broadly, to any power or influence excercised from outside oneself by others, as power moves fluidly through relationships.[171]

In Irigaray's feminist exhortation to women to "stop trying" (to conform to oppressive definitions and prohibitions), she frames emancipation in terms of both multiplicity of self and an open-ended, ongoing process of exploration:

> Your impulses may change; they may or may not coincide with those of some other, man or woman. Today, not tomorrow. Don't force yourselves to repeat, don't congeal your dreams or desires in unique and definitive representations. You have so many continents to explore that if you set up borders for yourselves you won't be able to "enjoy" all of your own "nature."[172]

IMPLICATIONS FOR ETHICS

Such postmodernist writers highlight the *emancipatory* implications of a nonunitary conception of self and mind, especially as they influence the social construction of self and others, and the resulting social construction of categories such as gender, race, and class, and the distribution of power.[173] Again, such a model is not without any parameters at all. It is not a call for unlimited license or self-centered freedom. Conscience is not discarded, but rather conceived as expanded—beyond the singular dictates of dominant discourse, and informed by the potential for expanded consciousness of the multiple aims, desires, and subjectivities of the other. The expanded appreciation for one's own being-in-motion can lead to a corresponding respect for the dynamic life of the other. Such an ethic is not anarchical or nihilistic—"I" and "Thou" are balanced internally and in relation to external others. Yet an ethics of fluid, multiple selves may no longer be understood *exclusively* in terms of rules, and rights of individuals, but more as like dancing, in which the movements of others are given space, even as one finds one's own freedom to move in multiple ways. Bodies breathe and weave together, in and out, in the imagery that is generated by this kind of vision.[174] This corresponds well with the Trinitarian image of *perichoresis*, the "divine dance,"[175] which will be explored in the next chapter.

IMPLICATIONS FOR HUMAN CREATIVITY

The "return of the repressed" gives way to a more variable process in which we move in and out of multiple areas of our own knowing and unknowing. "Knowing" itself may be understood, then, as more than cognition (the work of the prefrontal cortex) alone, or even cognitive and affective experience together, which can usually be put into words, but also as "unformulated experience."[176] Living in flux makes a space for those nonverbal mental contents that are only symbolic, or even presymbolic—the knowledge of the body and physical sensation—or, in Christopher Bollas's words, as "the unthought known."[177] Such nonverbal and presymbolic ways of knowing belong to the same regions of mind from which creativity springs. Most of us who have been engaged in any kind of creative process, whether in music, art, or writing, or the "aha!" of nonlinear scientific "intuition" or "discovery," will acknowledge the subjective experience of ideas, notions, and images, coming to us as if from beyond our everyday cognition, not necessarily from outside ourselves (although that is sometimes said, as in reference to inspiration by God or a muse), but from a different region of consciousness, of which we are only dimly aware, except perhaps in our dreams—and perhaps multiple regions simultaneously.

This relates to the therapeutic process as well. There are many "ahas" in the course of therapy. Perhaps it is useful to think of these as the in-breaking of one area of consciousness into another—not as a heroic exercise in vertical drilling into "the" unconscious—"deep inside"—but, rather, the sometimes gracious, sometimes frightening, but always broadening influx of awareness, flowing *across* previously separate regions of awareness. Through the shared reflection that occurs in therapy, cracks and fissures appear in the dams we have built among our different selves and self-states, and new awareness is created as these waters begin to flow more freely.

Human Beings Are Loved Beings

Living in flux, and recognizing our multiplicity, opens a door finally to the ways in which God also might be conceived of as a fluid, multiple being whose very multiplicity is a dance and a loving embrace. This is true poverty of the spirit: recognizing that it is not through our own power, or accomplishments, or control over others, that we are constituted, but through a recognition of the unconditional healing love of God that flows in us and through us to others in our lives. Episcopal priest, psychoanalyst, and spiritual director Phillip Bennett wrote:

> In letting ourselves be loved, we return to our true Center, surrendering our fears again and again, discovering a new strength rising up within us even as our old false confidence falls away. At the very point of failing at our own self-invented fantasies of success, power and control, we find a small opening into the Greater Life—the narrow entrance through which we pass into the vast spaciousness of Love.[178]

Human beings are profoundly known and loved by God. This is the promise of Christian baptism—that we are beloved as God's own children. Drowned in the waters that symbolize the death of old fears and restrictions, and drenched in the waters of new life, we are moist, softened, and refreshed—permeable to one another and to the inflowing renewal, wisdom, and en*courage*ment of the Spirit.

> O God, you have searched me and known me,
> You know when I sit down and when I rise up;
>> you discern my thoughts from far away.
> You search out my path and my lying down,
>> and are acquainted with all my ways.
> Even before a word is on my tongue,
>> O God, you know it completely.
> You hem me in, behind and before,
>> and lay your hand upon me . . .
>
> For it was you who formed my inward parts;
>> you knit me together in my mother's womb.
> I praise you, for I am fearfully and wonderfully made.
>> (Ps. 139:1-6, 13-14a)

"Drenched in the waters of new life"

It is the juxtaposition of being known and being loved—in all our multiplicity, changeability, fragility, and flux—that perhaps most distinguishes the love of God for each human person from the experience of human love, which is rarely so unconditional. Human beings have experienced and described divine love as that love that does not depend on performance, perfection, or any human criterion. God's love for the creation, which includes human beings, is not blind to any of the particularities of each life, but is poured out freely. God does not turn a blind eye to human failures, disappointments, and negative behavior. But God's judgment is not condemnation or rejection. God lifts up the weak, and God is the power of emancipation for those who are unfree (and from a psychological standpoint, we may understand unfreedom as caused by both internal and external forces of oppression). God provides unconditionally, and this abundance of love is rendered best not in theological dogma, but in doxology:[179]

> I will extol you, my God and Sovereign,
>   and bless your name forever and ever.
> Every day I will bless you,
>   and praise your name forever and ever.
> Great is God, and greatly to be praised;
>   the greatness of God is unsearchable . . .
>
> God is gracious and merciful,
>   slow to anger and abounding in steadfast love.
> God is good to all
>   and has compassion over all that God has made . . .
>
> God is faithful in every word,
>   and gracious in every deed.
> God upholds all who are falling,
>   and raises up all who are bowed down.
> The eyes of all look to you,
>   and you give them their food in due season.
> You open your hand,
>   satisfying the desire of every living thing
>   (Ps. 145: 1-3, 8-9, 13b-15)

Human Beings Are Loving Beings

Finally, because human beings are loved beings, they are also *loving* beings. As creation is loved by the Creator, and created in the image of the first Love, creation itself is inherently capable of sharing that Love, receiving its abundance until it spills over in the form of continuing to live and propagate new life, into an ethic of love of creation and the Creator. A multiple, fluid, free, and breathing person is freed to both receive and share the inpouring of love from the Creator.

The "summary of the law," to "love the Sovereign your God with all your heart, and with all your soul, and with all your mind" (Matt. 22:37), and to "love your neighbor as yourself" (Matt. 22:39), is not only something that comes from beyond ourselves, as a Word to be learned and acted upon, but a part of the very definition of what it means to be fully human—the gift of desire for the other, the innate capacity for love. We do internalize this, from birth, in the form of parental prohibitions and society's rules, as noted above; this is the psychological rendering of the process of acquiring the capacity for love and altruism. Yet, the human being also seems in some sense hard-wired to receive this teaching. As the object relations theorists expanded upon Freud's discussions of the acquisition of a superego, the innate human desire for attachment suggests an inherent capacity at least for connection—including reparation when one recognizes that one's own appetites have caused harm to the other.[180]

Even at the beginning of life, we (and other animals) are not only milk-seeking, as in a search for raw survival, but seeking tenderness and warmth.[181] Is this not, even at birth, a rudimentary form of love? Human love is ultimately expressed both in the erotic movement toward life and its propagation, and in the care and stewardship of "the neighbor"—both the human neighbor and the whole creation as neighbor. What does love require but to "do justice, to love kindness, and to walk humbly with our God?" (Mic. 6:8). I include this finally in a theological anthropology because ethics is not simply a secondary move after one understands what is the nature of the human being. It is intrinsic to human-being. In the words of Irenaeus, "the glory of God is a human being fully alive."[182] The ideal image of the fully human person, as exemplified for Christians in the life and witness of Jesus of Nazareth, is a person freed from the shackles of both sociopolitical and psychological oppression, who enters freely and generously into the dance of creation, receiving and giving abundant love in communion with the Holy and with all other created beings.

Conclusion

The intertwining of the human and the divine is part of the essence of whatever we can possibly know both about what it means to be human, and what that implies for what God is like. As we embrace a model of greater complexity and multiplicity of the human mind, and an appreciation for the intersubjective, vulnerable, loving relation between and among human beings and the divine, this will lead us, in turn, to a more variegated, fluid, vulnerable, passionate, and intersubjective image of God, or *imago Dei*.

Chapter 2

A Relational Understanding of God

IT WAS ALREADY IMPOSSIBLE in the preceding chapter to describe the human person without making reference to God. As psychoanalysis, postmodern philosophy, and brain science all converge on a conception of the human being—and indeed, creation—as more multiple, complex, and in motion than we had previously thought (or been able to think because of our Enlightenment conditioning to unitary and reductionist models of truth), then might this not suggest a conception of a multiple, complex, and dynamic *God*?

The word *God* itself cannot be taken to mean one thing, or point to one fixed doctrine about "God." As Gordon Kaufman and Francis Schüssler Fiorenza have argued, "There is simply no single right or correct meaning—no 'essence'—of the word 'God'":

> [It] has been open to a great variety of uses and interpretation, and those who wish to think clearly about how it can or "should" be used today—and what we "should" take it to mean today—must be prepared to give reasons for their preferences; no one is in a position to take for granted that they know definitively what the word "God" means and that their use of this word should therefore be assented to by all other English speakers.[1]

This chapter, then, is not an effort to produce a comprehensive "systematic theology" or dogmatics, which enterprise in any case is suspect in a postmodern context. Rather, it is, again, a more modest effort to explore one possible avenue of "constructive imagination,"[2] from an avowedly Christian perspective, about the divine in which we say we "live and move and have our being" (Acts 17:28)—that of the multiplicity of God, for the specific purpose of framing an approach to pastoral theology and pastoral psychotherapy.

The Multiplicity of God

In a rather straightforward analogy of multiplicity, pastoral theologian James Ashbrook and historian of science Carol Albright have proposed the brain as a metaphor for God's various ways of being God: "the upper brain stem for an attending, ever-present God, the limbic lobes for a relating, nurturing God, the limbic system for a remembering and meaning-making God, the neocortex for an organizing and versatile God, and the frontal lobes for an intending and purposeful God."[3] They conclude with the concept of the "mind-producing brain" as an analogy for God as All-in-All, using the image of Frank Lynn Meshberger's[4] discovery of the brain in Michelangelo's "Creation of Adam" first published in the *Journal of the American Medical Association* in 1990 (see Figure 5). The way these authors have drawn out this analogy of brain and God is both playful and respectful of the complexity of human experience.

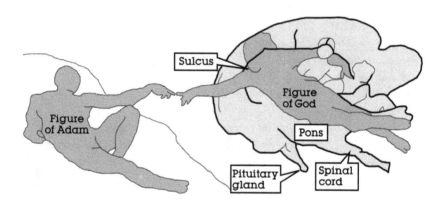

Figure 5: *Meshberger's discovery of the brain in Michelangelo's "Creation"*

Contemporary philosophers and theologians have gone much further in challenging certain axioms of orthodox theism, in which God was posited as One, omnipotent, omniscient, unchangeable, "impassible"—that is, unfeeling, unsuffering, impervious—or having certain essential characteristics that could be positively known through direct divine revelation (either through scripture or nature). There were at least two significant philosophical catalysts for this deconstruction. One was the nineteenth-century philosopher Friedrich Nietzsche's assertion that "God is dead" in his masterwork of romantic self-authorization, *Thus Spoke Zarathustra* (1891).[5] Another was the influential critique by twentieth-century philosopher Martin Heidegger of what he termed "onto-theology,"[6] asserting that the search for certainty about the existence of God as a subject is in itself a form of idolatry, objectifying God as something one could possess through knowledge. Heidegger's critique extended the work of Immanuel Kant, who had already asserted that human reason cannot grasp the infinity of God, skewering the medieval scholastic "proofs" of God's existence, while retaining a concept of God as "a regulative idea or transcendent ideal" that could inspire morality.[7]

These two trajectories of philosophical critique of rational certainties about God pointed toward two very different logical conclusions. Nietzsche's atheism pointed toward nihilism (from the Latin *nihil,* meaning "nothing"—the belief in nothing, or that life is meaningless). Taking a variety of forms in the twentieth century, Nietzsche's nihilism occupied the atheistic dimensions (though not the humanist moral dimensions) of French existentialism; it rationalized for the Nazis the obscene inflation of human powers as an Aryan super-race, based on Nietzsche's concept of the *Übermensch*; it funded the twentieth-century "death of God" theological movement, represented by Thomas Altizer, whose book *The Death of God*[8] sent a frisson (inspiring both dread and a tiny thrill of naughtiness) down the spine of middle-class American churchgoers; and it took root in less popularly known twentieth-century philosophers' rejection of "God" as a viable category for speculation. "Is God Dead?" appeared in stark red letters against a black background as the cover of *Time* magazine for April 8, 1966.[9] Yet, from the vantage point of the twenty-first century, nihilism was itself a dead end. Its cynicism could be seen as paving the way, in part, for terror and oppression, as in the horrors of the Stalinist regime in Russia.

Heidegger's critique of onto-theology, on the other hand, opened up new possibilities for a G/god not graspable in traditional theological terms, but nevertheless possible precisely in the deconstruction of old classical certainties about "Him." As Reformed philosopher Merold Westphal has suggested, Heidegger's critique was less about the existence or nonexistence of God per se, as it was a critique of the idolatry inherent in all human efforts to define God, and in so doing, objectifying the Holy.[10] For Westphal, the faithful human response to God is not onto-theology, but *praise.* Faithful theology—language about God—is not an effort to define God, as if God were a commodity to be possessed, but rather to accept that we see God "through a mirror dimly," and then to "accompany our 'wise silence' with 'songs of praise.'"[11] Catherine LaCugna, too, in her probing book on Trinitarian theology, *God for Us,* names praise—doxology—as the "form of language that best serves the mystery of divine-human communion . . ."[12] Such awe-touched praise is akin to Jacque Derrida's own "prayers and tears,"[13] the faith of the philosopher who paradoxically averred that he might be taken for an atheist, and yet who spoke eloquently of

> a prayer and tear for the coming of the wholly other (*tout autre*), for something impossible, like a messianic prayer in a messianic religion, *viens,* like a vast and sweeping amen, *viens, oui, oui.* Like a faith in the coming of something we cannot quite make out, a blind faith where knowledge fails and faith is what we have to go on, which even believes in ghosts or specters. *Il faut croire.* [One must believe.][14]

Such praise, prayers, and tears perhaps do forge a "third way" between positive and negative theology—positive attempts to know and define God (the "kataphatic" tradition), versus the mystical way of silence before God (the "apophatic" tradition)—as a response that should be evaluated not on the basis of its capacity to "master" the real, as Westphal put it,[15] is not only "*what* we say about God but . . . *how* we say it, to what purpose, and in the service of what project."[16] In LaCugna's words,

> Theology itself is the fruit of communion with God and also can be a means of union with God. Pursued in the mode of doxology, the scope of Trinitarian theology appears to be without boundaries. Understood as a way of rendering praise to God, Trinitarian theology of God reconnects spirituality with theology, orthodoxy with orthopraxis, the contemplative with the speculative, apophatic with kataphatic, the pastoral with the academic.[17]

Ludwig Wittgenstein perhaps stated it most succinctly: "Practice gives the words their sense."[18]

Postmodern philosophers interested in the problematic and complex issues surrounding the idea of "God" have begun to see, beyond the *aporia* ("no-way") of absolute atheism, an impossibility that in itself, paradoxically, pointed again to a wholly transcendent God escaping all human categories of "possibility." In further exploring the inversions of impossibility and transcendence, some philosophers have begun to generate another, theological "third." They have begun to recuperate for postmodern philosophy a series of questions around God as the paradoxical "transcendence and beyond."[19] French philosopher Jean-Luc Marion, especially, has explored the dimension of the "impossible" as the dimension where speculation about God can begin again.[20] If God cannot be known, captured, possessed, owned by rational inquiry, then the impossibility of God is the starting place.

In particular, Marion and Derrida have pondered the impossibility of the idea of "gift"—the problem that once given, a gift sets up an obligation, or at least an unequal relation between the giver and the recipient, which turns the gift into its opposite—a moral demand. The idea of gift relates to Christian theology in particular in the idea of *kenosis*, God's out-pouring of God's own self, in the form of the incarnation and the cross, as God's ultimate gift to humanity. While many would argue that such divine gift does, indeed, constitute a moral demand, or at least prompts a response of gratitude from the human recipients, there is in this postmodern discussion another implication as well—that divine self-giving, pouring out, or *kenosis*, is beyond the pragmatism of human transactions, giving and receiving as quid pro quo. Marion terms this divine giving a "saturated phenomenon,"[21] which defies all positive theological powers to name it, and which fills mystical *not*-knowing, or negative theology, to a point where not-knowing is a result of joyful overflow, not simply lack of resources to name it. This is yet another third way between positive knowing and apophatic unknowing, toward an image of almost mystical abundance—in Marion's words,

The excess of intuition overcomes, submerges, exceeds, in short saturates, the measure of each and every concept. What is given disqualifies every concept. Dionysius [the Areopagite] states this to the letter: "It is stronger than all discourse and all knowledge—and therefore surpasses comprehension in general and therefore [is also excepted from] essence."[22]

This emphasis on transcendence is in its own way, of course, highly rational, "heady," and disembodied, much in the Enlightenment tradition itself. Derrida, the primary source for this line of discourse, defines himself not as postmodern, but as a "man of the Enlightenment, albeit of a new Enlightenment, one that is enlightened about the Enlightenment and resists letting the spirit of the Enlightenment freeze over into dogma."[23] As an outsider in many ways—both an Algerian and a Jew studying and writing in Paris, the center of western scholasticism—Derrida was perhaps "overdetermined"[24] both to wrestle with and to embrace a philosophy of *"l'invention de l'autre* (the incoming of the other),"[25] which is constantly undermining its own avowed sources. However, American philosophers John Caputo and Michael Scanlon, who have hosted a number of conferences bringing the questions of theology and philosophy into public dialogue for several years, make explicit a connection between the apparent heady rationalism of Derrida's method of deconstruction with the very down-to-earth project of transformation and emancipation from dominant discourses of greed and oppression.

Derrida seeks an Enlightenment "of our time," here and now, in the sprawling wealth and bottomless poverty, in the uncontainable plurality and virtual reality of this very late-modern, high-tech, televangelist, free-market, multi-media, millennial fin de siècle, this time of need and greed, in which the "certainties and axioms" of the old Enlightenment require reconsideration, translation, and transformation. That, if we may say so, is pretty much all we meant by "postmodernism."[26]

Critics of postmodernism sometimes confuse the deconstructionist methods that characterize much of what is now collectively called "postmodern" thought with nihilism itself. However, there is a strong emancipatory impulse underlying postmodernism as a *movement* (again, an inheritance from the Enlightenment itself in some sense) that seeks to liberate previously unheard voices from the oppressive hegemony of dominant discourses that are posited (untruthfully) as natural, self-evident, unquestionable, and unitary. Postmodern critiques of rationalist certainties were born in the crucible of disillusionment with nineteenth-century confidence in modernist notions of progress, as the most technologically advanced Western nation coolly and systematically used its scientific knowledge to accomplish the genocidal murder of 6 million Jews, as well as Poles, Russians, Slavs, Roma, and Sinti ("Gypsies"), and other groups deemed "undesirable," including Roman Catholics, Jehovah's Witnesses, homosexuals, political dissidents, the disabled, and the mentally ill—totaling at least 11 million people.[27] Derrida's own writings include a vision using deconstructive arguments, informed by his own experience of migrancy, for human rights.[28]

As a western philosophical movement, postmodernism addresses itself in particular, then, to the hegemony of white, Western, patriarchal explanations of "truth" in the service of the subjugation of all those labeled as Other. Derrida's invented word *différance* holds our feet to the fire by demanding that every text (including both written texts and the "texts" of political rhetoric and of cultural products) be examined for what is different/deferred—excluded, demeaned, and/or erased through naming as "Other" or not naming at all. *Différance* notices, reinstates, and values the previously invisible, voiceless Other. As described in chapter 1, the concept of the Other has been explored by feminist postmodern writers, especially Luce Irigaray,[29] and in the emerging field of postcolonial studies,[30] in which the situation of "alterity"—difference, or living under the sign of the Other—is investigated and critiqued. The idea of a "third space," in particular, has been explored by postcolonial writers such as Homi Bhabha.[31]

Vietnamese American filmmaker and feminist cultural theorist Trinh Minh-Ha, in particular, has drawn this postcolonial concept together with religious reflection to posit a third space within her own tradition of Taoism, between yin and yang—conceived as "the interval" between them, "a state of *alert in-betweenness and 'critical' non-knowingness*, in which the bringing of reflective and cosmic memory to life—that is, to the *formlessness of form*—is infinitely more exigent than the attempt to 'express,' to 'judge or evaluate.'"[32] This idea of the "third" further resonates with D. W. Winnicott's idea of "potential space"[33] and analyst Thomas Ogden's further conceptualization of the "analytic third"[34] currently being explored in relational psychoanalysis.

As postmodern discussions about the concept of God thus break down traditional assumptions about God, positing God as Other to all our cherished doctrinal assertions, so the idea of the multiplicity of God has been opened up to further theological exploration. In my view, this exploration need not completely subvert faithful expressions of God as a transcendent unity, a loving "All-in-All," but it does challenge any use of the totalizing metaphor of the One as the tacit approval or justification for schemes of domination (the One, Holy, and Awesome God as "God of our Fathers,"[35] God of our nation, God of our religion only, God of our football team, God on *our* side). Under this critique, the exploration of alternative metaphors of God's multiplicity break open old assumptions about "*our* God," and make space for alternative visions and voices, particularly those from the underside of dominant culture and politics. Derrida's own work suggests that the seeds of contradiction or subversion lie buried within or behind the self-identities and certainties of every tradition.[36] Rather than nihilistic negation, however, Derrida arrives, *through* deconstruction, at a different kind of *abundance*, "a politics of heterogeneity."[37]

Derrida[38]—and a growing number of other theorists from varying perspectives including feminist theorist Ellen Armour,[39] African American theologian Dwight Hopkins,[40] postcolonial theorists Edward Said[41] and Homi Bhabha,[42] and feminist theologian Catherine Keller[43]—have drawn variously from this trajectory of thought to challenge and deconstruct essentialist theological themes of "light and dark," as a previously mystified racist privileging of whiteness over dark/"Black" skin as akin to purity and sin/stain. Deconstruction has also been fruitfully used by a number of twentieth-century feminist philosophers and theologians[44] to challenge the oppression of women under the appeal of patriarchy and heterosexism to the unquestionability of so-called natural law. Earlier, Karl Marx and Friedrich Engels engaged in a similar critique, pointing to the pervasive promulgation of ruling-class ideology and its consequent internalization by workers, blinding them to their own exploitation.[45] Thus, the seemingly abstract domain of postmodernism and deconstructionist methodology circles again back toward emancipatory theologies that are not abstracted from human history and contemporary political life. Paraphrasing Emmanuel Lévinas, "if philosophy is love of wisdom, it is also, and primarily, the wisdom of love."[46]

The most radical explorations of the multiplicity of God have drawn from Gilles Deleuze and Félix Guattari, whose image of the rhizome[47] was discussed in chapter 1. Deleuze's discussions of "difference and repetition" have prompted theological meditations on the nature of God's creativity as "non-identical repetition."[48] Deleuze links difference to "original depth," a chaotic, plenary source from which all being does not so much emerge, upward, as it "unfolds." For Deleuze, the idea of "God" is constrained even by such "deep" formulations such as the "Ground of Being,"[49] since "ground" itself is not exempt from deconstruction—there yet must be a deeper deep or preceding *profond* (French, "deep"), a "*pro/fond*," a bottomless or groundless pre-origin that precedes the stable "foundation" implied by the term "ground."[50]

This resonates well with the psychological construct of the unconscious as more a matter of horizontal or spatial multiplicities of subjectivity and affect than of Freud's nineteenth-century heroic plumbing and conquering of a single vertical "depth."[51] For Deleuze, depth itself is a matter of "extensity," heterogeneity, and the horizontal play of differences, not defined by any shared "root," origin, or ground: "the (ultimate and original) heterogeneous dimension is the matrix of all extensity, including its third dimension, considered to be homogeneous with the other two."[52] (In other words, what we perceive as the three dimensions, represented by a point, a line, and volume, are to be conceived in Deleuze's philosophy as spreading out spatially, and depth is therefore more than simply vertical. It is depth as in our depth perception.) Deleuze's rhizome is an image of such horizontal extensity.

The fluid multiplicity of the created universe is neither chaos nor cleaned-up composition, according to Deleuze and Guattari, but a "chaosmos"[53] (a term borrowed from James Joyce, meditating in turn on Aquinas's "wholeness," "harmony," and "radiance").[54] As Annie Dillard has written,

Certainly nature seems to exult in abounding radicality, extremism, anarchy. If
we were to judge nature by its common sense or likelihood, we wouldn't believe
the world existed. In nature, improbabilities are the one stock in trade. The
whole creation is one lunatic fringe. If creation had been left up to me, I'm sure
I wouldn't have had the imagination or courage to do more than shape a single,
reasonably sized atom, smooth as a snowball, and let it go at that. No claims of
any and all revelations could be so far-fetched as a single giraffe.[55]

Dillard frames this anarchy, however, not in cosmic insanity, but in divine love.
These sentences precede the above quotation: "What is man, that thou are mindful
of him? This is where the great modern religions are so unthinkably radical: the love
of God! For we can see that we are as many as the leaves of trees. But it could be
that our faithlessness is a cowering cowardice born of our very smallness, a massive
failure of imagination."[56]

Deleuze and Guattari further describe this bottomless origin, "chaosmos," as a
"matrix" (which literally means "womb") and a "milieu of milieux,"[57]—suggesting, or
at least resonating with, maternal imagery for the divine as creator. So—extrapolat-
ing from this discussion of a multiple, heterogeneous, bottomless origin—God, from
a Deleuzian framework, must similarly be bottomless, *unfathomable* not in the sense
of abdication from all attempts to relate to and with the divine, but superabundant,
impossible to reach the depths and thus objectify or possess it.

In a brilliant work on the theology of creation as *creatio ex profundis*, titled *Face of
the Deep*, Catherine Keller[58] exegetes the book of Genesis to develop a "tehomic theology"—a theology of the primordial waters/deeps (*tehom*). God did not, she argues,
create ex nihilo, as an act of power and mastery upon an external sterile void, but
as a messier act of unfolding, germinating, and forming out of the chaotic, unruly,
primordial *tohu vabohu* ("formlessness") that preexisted creation. God, like the chaosmos, for both Deleuze and Keller is infinite in possibility. Creation, states Keller,
is not a "function of power and order, upholding transcendent power-structures," but
the ancient scriptures

imagine a messier beginning, with no clear point of origin and no final end . . .
The heteroglossic Deep—the Hebrew *tehom* or primal oceanic chaos—already
marks every beginning. It leaks into the Bible itself, signifying a fluid matrix
of bottomless potentiality, a germinating abyss, a heterogeneous womb or self-
organising complexity, a resistance to every fixed order. It sweeps away myths of
abstract potency—of the paternal Word—in a tumultuous jumble of neglected
parts whose creation is material and laboured.[59]

God, as infinite, multiple creativity itself/themselves, is such potential. God is
pure implication, as "*implex*" ("in-fold")—another expression of Deleuze, drawing
on the mutual enfolding and unfolding imagined by the medieval church theologian

Nicholas of Cusa.[60] God is folded in all things and all things are enfolded in God[61]—or, in Trinitarian language, infinite in creativity, incarnation, and inspiration.

Keller has also discussed the multiplicity of God in terms of the "plural-singularity of creation."[62] Following Hebrew Bible scholars Danna Fewell and David Gunn, she explores the "curious slippage" in the grammar of Gen. 1:26a, 27, literally: "Then God(s) (*Elohim*—plural) said (singular) 'let us make humankind in our image, after our likeness' . . . So God(s) created (*bara*—singular form of the verb) humankind in his own image, in the image of God(s) he created him, male and female he created them . . ."[63] "God 'himself' is unsure whether he is plural or singular, echoing the narrator's grammatic confusion of a plural name (*elohim*, which may or may not be a proper noun!) and a singular verb."[64] Does the plural *Elohim* refer to a proper name, having evolved from an earlier thought world before monotheism?[65] A "plural of intensity" indicating that YHWH is the "sum of all gods?"[66] An earlier pantheism? Keller states that "registered in the theogram of the plural *Elohim* . . . there remain traces of another interpretation—not of a polytheistic reading but of one which took residual *multiplicity* with theological seriousness." (In consonance with the multiplicity of human beings described in chapter 1 above, Fewell and Gunn also noted that not only God[s] but humankind are both singular and plural [him/them]).[67]

In Gen. 1:20, further, "Let *us* create . . .," *Elohim* takes the plural verb form. Keller cites rabbinic sources that suggested that God needed here to consult a heavenly court, the angels: "The role of the angels is to suggest 'a many-ness of viewpoints, a spectrum of opinions' . . ."[68] Keller reads philosopher of science Michel Serres, in his reflections on the "angelic swarm,"[69] to support a "divining" of "the multiple" as the "Manyone [many/one]"[70]—"an elemental power of creativity, articulate, humble, kenotic, almost democratic, in its delegations; and effusive in its delights."[71] This multiplicity is always in relation, both internally, as the plurality of God(s) and the angelic court, and in relation with the creation/humanity. Concluding a meditation on the multiplicity of God, Keller brings this "matrix of possibilities" back full circle to the multiplicity of creation, and what I have described above in terms of the intersubjective relation between humanity/creation and the divine:

> Can we say with process theology that the creator emits an eros, a "lure to novelty," an "initial aim"—the beginning condition, the "prevenient grace," to which every creature willy-nilly responds? . . . Some respond more *responsibly* than others to the cosmic desire. Committees and democracies make a lot of messes. The creature either responds in creative sensitivity to its own context; or it blocks the flux of its own becoming.
>
> In other words, our responses become us. They generate our own plurisingular inter-subjectivities—out of the multiples of elemental energies, codes, socialities, ecologies that any moment constellate our cosmoi. Elohim would live among the effects; a becoming God, who inasmuch as we have language

for it/them/her/him is at minimum an irreducible effect of language. But not an effect ex nihilo. For this divinity arises out of those unruly depths, over which language catches its breath. The creator, creating, becomes. In singular plurality.[72]

Trinity as Fluid Metaphor

As an Anglican/Christian theologian, I also continue to find inspiration in an evocative and compelling metaphor of multiplicity that is already present in ancient Christian theological resources, namely, the Trinity.[73] One of the most compelling images, from the fourth-century Cappadocian theologians (including Gregory of Nyssa, Basil "the Great," Gregory of Nazianzus, and Macrina—the sister of Gregory of Nyssa and Basil[74]), is the image of the Trinity as *perichoresis*—the complete, equal, and mutual interpermeation of the three persons or dynamic dimensions of the Trinity. LaCugna gives a beautiful, clear description:

> Perichoresis expressed the idea that the three divine persons mutually inhere in one another, draw life from one another, "are" what they are by relation to one another. Perichoresis means being-in-one-another, permeation without confusion. No person exists by him/herself or is referred to him/herself; this would produce number and therefore division within God, Rather, to be a divine person is to be by nature in relation to other persons. Each divine person is irresistibly drawn to the other, taking his/her existence from the other, containing the other in him/herself, while at the same time pouring self into the other. Cyril of Alexandria called this movement a "reciprocal irruption." While there is no blurring of the individuality of each person, there is also no separation. There is only communion of love in which each person comes to be . . . what he/she is, entirely with reference to the other. Each person expresses both what he/she is (and, by implication, what the other two are), and at the same time expresses what God is: ecstatic, relational, dynamic, vital. Perichoresis provides a dynamic model of persons in communion based on mutuality and interdependence. The model of perichoresis avoids the pitfalls of locating the divine unity either in the divine substance (Latin) or exclusively in the person of the Father (Greek), and locates unity instead in diversity, in a true communion of persons.[75]

Although technically not a translation for *perichoresis*,[76] its popular rendering into English as the "divine dance" is a compelling image for the dynamism, energy, and multiplicity-in-unity inherent in the symbol of the Trinity.

> Choreography suggests the partnership of movement, symmetrical but not redundant, as each dancer expresses and at the same time fulfills him/herself

towards the other. In interaction and inter-course, the dancers (and the observers) experience one fluid motion of encircling, encompassing, permeating, enveloping, outstretching. There are neither leaders nor followers in the divine dance, only an eternal movement of reciprocal giving and receiving, giving again and receiving again. To shift metaphors for a moment, God is eternally begetting and being begotten, spirating and being spirated. The divine dance is fully personal and interpersonal, expressing the essence and unity of God. The image of the dance forbids us to think of God as solitary. The idea of Trinitarian perichoresis provides a marvelous point of entry into contemplating what it means to say God is alive from all eternity as love.[77]

Perichoresis has been adopted in feminist theology as an image for "an ethics that upholds three central values: inclusiveness, community, and freedom. Since these ways of relating are the hallmarks of divine life, they should characterize the patterns of human persons in communion with one another."[78] LaCugna's critique of perichoresis as an organizing metaphor for the Trinity—that it can become too focused on what God may be like as God (known as the "immanent Trinity"), and not connected to the relationship between God and creation (the "economic Trinity," the Trinity as revealed through salvation history)—is effectively answered by this ethical turn. Moreover, the image of the dance is not an image of an exclusive club or divine committee of three. The imagery of motion and spontaneity would seem to invite others—humanity, creatures, all living beings—to join in the "dance of all creation."[79] In Andrei Rublev's fifteenth-century icon, which depicts the Trinity as the three mysterious visitors to Sarah and Jacob under the tree at Mamre, the three figures incline democratically toward one another, but there is also a space at the table for us, as we gaze on the icon (see Figure 6). And on the table directly in front of us is a vessel full of cakes made of choice flour (Gen. 18:6), representing simultaneously (and we might say reciprocally) both Sarah's and Abraham's human hospitality and the divine hospitality of the Eucharist.

The effort—not to repristinate, but to find new, nonessentializing movements and metaphors in such ancient Christian sources—is also being taken up by more explicitly postmodern theologians, perhaps best exemplified in the work of the "Radical Orthodox" theologians, especially John Milbank. Milbank's "postmodern Christianity" emphasizes diversity or plurality as a central organizing concept, in which the Trinity is a sign of *"God as community* . . . in process, 'infinitely realized. . . .'"[80] He writes:

Christianity can become "internally postmodern. . . . I mean by this that it is possible to construe Christianity as suspicious of notions of fixed "essences" in its approach to human beings, to nature, to community *and to God*, even if it has never fully escaped the grasp of a "totalizing" metaphysics. Through its belief in creation from nothing it admits temporality, the priority of becoming and unexpected emergence. A reality suspended between nothing and infinity is a reality of *flux*, a reality without substance, composed only of relational differences and ceaseless alterations (Augustine, *De Musica*). Like nihilism, Christianity can, [and] should, embrace the differential flux.[81]

Figure 6: *Icon of the Trinity, Andrei Rublev, fifteenth century*

Milbank finds the expression of this Christianity not in formal creeds and doctrines, which he (pejoratively) calls "Greek knowledge," but in *practices,* and more specifically, practices of *community.* Although he does not specifically say so, Milbank is elaborating an incarnational theology at this point, a kind of "theosis" (a doctrine especially elaborated in eastern Orthodoxy, that we are made divine by Christ's becoming human). This "pattern" of Jesus' life can be repeated in each new context and individual.[82] Milbank elaborates the divine Trinitarian movement itself as one of "nonidentical repetition:"[83] "For the 'patterns' or 'coherencies' of our lives never belong to us, are not 'completed' at our deaths, and can be repeated, or even more fully realized, by others: This is supremely true of a pattern that is taken to be canonically normative, as excathologically coinciding with the identities of all of us, as omnirepeatable and so as 'divine.'"[84]

It is precisely with this emphasis on diversity in community that Milbank draws the distinction between his postmodern theology and nihilism: community embodies a commitment to difference, but unlike nihilism, envisions the possibility of difference *with harmony*—borrowing from Augustine, a *concentus musicus.*[85] This idea echoes earlier formulations of the "social Trinity," such as those of Jürgen Moltmann[86] and Leonardo Boff.[87] In Milbank's attempt to work within a postmodern framework, a subtle shift has occurred, parallel to the feminist postmodern writings of Luce Irigaray, in which *equality* is no longer the implicit value underlying an ethic of justice[88] (since the valuing of equality always runs the risk of homogenization, or submersion of difference under a new totalism), but rather *nonviolence* based on the valuing of *differences.*

For Milbank, further, it is the relational impulse of *desire* (drawing from Augustine), rather than knowledge or dogma that is the mediator of reality,[89] even, I would add, the sacred. Desire for the other reaches across the gaps, across difference, (including, I would add as well, the intimate gap between "I" and "Thou" as Buber intuited,[90] and even the ineffable gap between humanity and God), to create a dynamic, intersubjective arena of creation.

It is certainly not only in Radical Orthodoxy that we find emancipatory, even postmodern, impulses toward a multiple, fluid, relational God. In contemporary Trinitarian, process, and feminist theologies, we find resources that support a Trinitarian theology of complexity, diversity, and mutability. Many contemporary theologians have reflected on the Trinity not in terms of a static, or "frozen"[91] dogma—positing three fixed essences as a complete description of God's nature—but, rather, in terms of a fluid *metaphor* that challenges such singular, totalizing images of God.[92] The Trinity, as described by a number of twentieth-century theologians from a variety of schools (including Moltmann,[93] Boff,[94] LaCugna,[95] Johnson,[96] and David Cunningham[97]) thus continues to offer a fertile ground of symbols or images, even as it helped the Nicene theologians to get beyond the seemingly static binary contradiction posed by the Incarnation, of Christ as *either* human *or* divine. Trinitarian theology is an act of sacred imagination, spanning the centuries of Christian thought, in which perhaps we could say that the very *motion* of God—rather than some fixed essence of God—may be "divined," intuited as alive, flowing, and flowering, multiple in activity and in all the ways in which human beings may catch fleeting glimpses of the Holy, and above all profoundly relational and loving.

In her masterpiece of feminist exegesis of the Catholic theological tradition, *She Who Is*, Elizabeth Johnson describes how the image of the Trinity is one that does not perpetuate, but in fact refutes all monolithic, totalizing tendencies of theology to define God: "At its most basic the symbol of the Trinity evokes a livingness in God, a dynamic coming and going with the world that points to an inner divine circling around in unimaginable relation . . . Not an isolated, static, ruling monarch, but a relational, dynamic, tripersonal mystery of love."[98]

Citing Hildegaard of Bingen, Johnson elaborates:

> The threes keep circling round. Whatever the categories used, there is reflected a livingness in God; a beyond, a within, and a within to the world and its history; a sense of God as from whom, by whom, and in whom all things exist, thrive, struggle toward freedom, and are gathered in. To use one more model, this time from the eleventh-century theologian Hildegaard of Bingen, there is a brightness, a flashing forth, and a fire, and these three are one, connecting all creation together in compassion. All these metaphors express the Trinitarian structure of Christian belief in God.[99]

In addition to the "social Trinity" developed by Moltmann and Boff, numerous other twentieth-century articulations of Trinitarian theology could be considered relational, as Johnson herself exhaustively catalogs.[100] As theologians have begun to play more freely in the late twentieth century with the metaphorical potential of the Trinity, new relational formulations have begun to appear, for example in Sallie McFague's feminist Trinity of mother-lover-friend,[101] and in John Macquarrie's rendering of the Trinity as primordial source, expressive dynamism, and unitive Being in Love.[102] While Macquarrie's emphasis on "Being," from his philosophical roots in existentialism, could be critiqued for tending toward new framings of old essentialisms, his elaboration on the Trinity conveys a warmth of relationality, self-giving, and motion: being as outpouring, expression, and uniting, an "immensely rich diversity-in-unity of God."[103]

The Trinity expresses both the mystery of the relational nature of God-as-God, and in community with us, in creation, as LaCugna has written: "revealed there is the unfathomable mystery that the life and communion of the divine persons is not 'intradivine': God is not self-contained, egotistical and self-absorbed, but overflowing with love, outreaching desire for union with all that God has made."[104]

Most expressions of the Trinity, and all traditional Western conceptions from the third century onward, also invoke a radical equality among the three persons.[105]

"There is no subordination, no before or after, no first, second, and third, no dominant and marginalized. There is only 'a trinity of persons mutually interrelated in a unity of equal essence.'"[106] This image seems, in light of our reflections on Deleuze, to be more like a rhizome than a tree!

Johnson emphasizes that it is relationality that becomes most important in this understanding:

> From the Cappadocian theologians through Augustine on up to Aquinas and beyond, the affirmation is made that what constitutes the Trinitarian persons is their relationality. Aquinas crystallizes this development with his definition of the persons as "subsistent relations." This means that the persons are persons precisely as mutual relations and not as anything else apart from their mutual bonding. Relationality is the principle that at once constitutes each Trinitarian person as unique and distinguishes one from another. It is only by their reciprocal and mutually exclusive relationships that the divine persons are really distinct from each other at all. Their uniqueness arises only from their *esse ad*, from their being toward the others in relation. Holy Wisdom is a mystery of real, mutual relations.[107]

So divine nature, for Johnson, is not an essence, but a *primordial communion*.[108] This parallels Deleuze's own concept of differences, that is, not arising as separate outcroppings or representations from some prior unitary Source or Ideal, but constituting difference through mutual interplay in a weblike horizontal extending ("extensity"[109]) of relation.

The Trinity is, then, a spacious room—even a matrix/womb, in which multiple metaphors can flourish, honoring simultaneously the relationality and the multiplicity of God. In its constantly shape-shifting play of images, I would want to argue that the Trinity itself can become a third space between theological certainty (as a classically posited finiteness of precisely one *ousia* [essence] and three *hypostases* [immutable characteristics of God], and a vacuumed-out negative theology—Anselm of Canterbury's three inscrutable and completely unknowable "*nescio quids*" or "I know not what's."[110] In this Trinitarian third space for theological imagination, the three "persons" of the Trinity are deconcretized, no longer to be understood as a literal "Father," "Son," and "Holy Ghost." The threeness of the classical Trinitarian metaphor is, rather, opened out into multiple images and symbols for the generativity, the incarnational presence, and the continuing aliveness and activity of the divine. Nor is this a collapsing back into the heresy of "modalism," in which the three "persons" of the Trinity are collapsed merely into divine functions or modes of being—as simply creating, redeeming, and sanctifying activities of the One God.

The Trinity, as a third space for metaphorical play and imagination, is, itself, *kenotic*.[111] It is an image that continues to empty itself of fixed essences, not cascading into a nihilistic nothingness of divine absence but an ever-shifting kaleidoscopic pattern. It is like a waterfall, *full* of light, color, and dancing shapes, that provide continual refreshment, a long cool drink for parched feelings and hardened thinking, cleansing for the perceived wounds and stains, cooling for fevered human hubris, and the occasional deluge for those who become too comfortable with the delights of any particular tributary of sacred ideology. Who would dare to enter into such danger-ous, wet, creative contemplation? And yet, who would not be drawn by the beauty of such overflowing abundance? Moreover, as a pastoral theologian, who would not be drawn by the promise of growth, healing, and empowerment that springs from such a multiple image?

Implications toward a Relational Pastoral Praxis

If we are willing to explore these multifaceted efforts toward a multiple concept of God, and a corollary construction of a mutual, co-constructive, cogenerative yearn-ing *between* humans and the divine,[112] then we are led back again to a pastoral con-struction of human beings, consciousness, and its construction in mutual relations (potentially resonating with a variety of faith traditions, not just orthodox Christi-anity), and to an appreciation of this multiple, fluid, relationality of both God and human persons as underpinning all relational approaches to pastoral praxis—through the spectrum of care, counseling, and psychotherapy.

As we embrace a model of greater complexity and multiplicity of the human mind, this will lead us to a more complex and nuanced appreciation for the diversity and mutability of human persons in the way we understand pastoral care, counseling, and psychotherapy.[113] What is *pastoral*—that is, what protects and promotes human growth and helps to heal psychic and interpersonal wounds—from this relational perspective, then, is not a vision of ultimate or reified *oneness*, as in a homogeniza-tion of all "patients" (as objects) into a single uniform model of health and whole-ness, but rather the capacity for a pluriform and diversely just and loving human *creativity*. This creativity is grounded/surrounded/infused in the creative profusion, incarnational desire, and pulsing, living inspiration of the Trinity/loving God, which is the "source, wellspring and living water"[114] of mutual desire that bridges, through the very embracing of difference, toward the creative multiplicity of the other. This, then, becomes the new starting point for an emancipatory praxis of pastoral care, counseling, and psychotherapy, wherein the goal of care is to provide a space in which the person can be freed from the constraining myths of oppression (whether individual, intrafamilial, or social and cultural) toward a freer exploration of her own multiform creative potential.

What might the three traditional aspects of the Trinity say, in a *nonessential-ist* key, particularly as a source for a healing and liberative pastoral praxis? With an ear toward metaphors that resonate with the pastoral functions of healing, sustain-ing, guiding, reconciling, and empowering, I have begun playing with the following

Trinitarian language: *God as Creative Profusion, God as Incarnational Desire,* and *God as Living Inspiration.*

GOD AS CREATIVE PROFUSION

> Glory be to God for dappled things—
>> Or skies of couple-colour as a brinded cow;
>>> For rose-moles all in stipple upon trout that swim;
> Fresh-firecoal chestnut-falls; finches' wings;
>> Landscape plotted and pieced—fold, fallow, and plough;
>>> And all trades, their gear and tackle and trim.
>
> All things counter, original, spare, strange;
>> Whatever is fickle, freckled (who knows how?)
>>> With swift, slow; sweet, sour; adazzle, dim;
> He fathers-forth whose beauty is past change:
>> Praise him.[115]

The English poet Gerard Manley Hopkins captures the multiplicity and fecundity of the chaosmos in his poem "Pied Beauty." Hopkins's nineteenth-century "father" language recedes in importance amid the swirling alliterations and the crunch of consonants that capture the wildness, unpredictability, and perfect imperfection, "dappled . . . fickle, freckled," of creation. I am drawn to Gordon Kaufman's metaphor for God as "serendipitous creativity,"[116] as creativity itself rather than "creator," or anthropomorphic terms "lord and father"—not that God does not "love" as the parental word "father" (or, better, Jesus' word *abba,* "daddy,") implies, or that "God's relation to us, *agape*-love" must be rejected.[117] But, as Kaufman suggests, the anthropomorphic quality of images such as "Father" and "Lord" may tend to concretize a transcendent separation of God from creation,[118] as in a heavenly "Him" and an earthly, separate, us. God's creative activity, then, may be conceived not as something that is being done *to* the creation, but rather an intimately, intrinsically involved and continual process, unfolding around, above, under, and within the creation. Creation is not solely novelty, forever creating new things ex nihilo, but also a process of evolution, unfolding from what already is and is becoming, which Kaufman acknowledges as an indissoluble and unreducible mystery.[119]

Frederick Hart's creation sculpture for the central tympanum over the west portal of the Washington National Cathedral beautifully depicts the turbulent, roiling dynamism of creation.[120] (See Figure 7.) The tenacity of life gives further evidence of the irrepressible nature of God's creativity. One of my own most powerful experiences of the realization of God's presence was in the Oakland, California, hills one late afternoon. I suddenly "saw," in a nonordinary way of seeing, the tremendous force and thrust and determination of the trees jutting out of the soft, seemingly precarious hillside soil and leaning vertiginously out over the landscape far below.

Figure 7: *Creation tympanum by Frederick Hart, "Ex Nihilo" (1974–1982), West Portal, Washington National Cathedral*

The terrible scarring of those same hillsides by fire a few years later, and the rising again of tiny trees out of the seeds broken open by the ferocious heat of the fire, was a powerful sign of the force of new life, even resurrected life. Yet every day, if I pay attention, I am given the gift of reminders of those moments of seeing—in my urban setting in Philadelphia, and in among the historic walls of my Gettysburg home, I see it again: another tiny green spike or tendril, seemingly frail and tender, but with the force to gnaw and snake its way through concrete and brick until it finds the sun and opens.

I love the fact that even if I accidentally dig up a tulip bulb in my garden while planting summer flowers, and stick it in upside down, again by accident, it will figure out how to send its shoots down and around and up again, and in the spring, the tulip will rise once more to animate and color its own tiny patch of winter-deadened space. Here is the unstoppable force of both tree *and* rhizome—on flat sidewalks, vertical walls, on the ridges and cliffs overlooking San Francisco Bay, or curled upside down in the dirt of my garden—who can say where vertical ends and horizontal begins? Life, in all its fecundity, is three-dimensional, unruly, not bound by any compass but God's own greenward direction: Up! Out! Forward! Sideways! Grow!

God, then, *is* creative profusion, and the creation is no longer conceivable as a pristine product by a supernatural maker, but an irrepressible fecundity. This fecundity, this turbulent swarming of creation, it seems to me, is a much more consoling, liberating, and empowering image for pastoral relations than a singular, authoritarian God-the-Father. To liberate the first "person" of the Trinity from a concretized identity as "Father," or even "Creator," opens the way to affirming the dappled, fickle, freckled multiplicity of the real human persons who come to us for care and healing.

We are accepted, confirmed, loved in our complexities and contradictions. It is not the attainment of a shiny, polished perfection that will save/salve us, but the increasing consciousness of our own intricacy—in Annie Dillard's words: "intricacy is that which is given from the beginning, the birth-right, and in intricacy is the hardiness of complexity that ensures against the failure of all life."[121] Our own inner landscape, like the landscape as Dillard describes it, is "'ring-streaked, speckled and spotted,' like Jacob's cattle culled from Laban's herd."[122]

> Anything can happen; any pattern of speckles may appear in a world ceaselessly bawling with newness. I see red blood stream in shimmering dots inside a goldfish's tail; I see the stout, extensible lip of a dragonfly nymph that can pierce and clasp a goldfish; and I see the clotted snarls of bright algae that snare and starve the nymph. I see engorged, motionless ants regurgitate pap to a colony of pawing workers, and I see sharks limned in light twist in a raised and emerald wave.
>
> The wonder is—given the errant nature of freedom and the burgeoning of texture in time—the wonder is that all the forms are not monsters, that there is beauty at all, grace gratuitous, pennies found, like mockingbird's free fall. Beauty itself is the fruit of the creator's exuberance that grew such a tangle, and the grotesques and horrors bloom from that same free growth, that intricate scramble and twine up and down the conditions of time.
>
> This, then, is the extravagant landscape of the world, given, given with pizzazz, given in good measure, pressed down, shaken together, and running over.[123]

This first "person" of the Trinity, this creating God of abundance, "broods over" every person, and every relationship. If it were possible to extract a single quotation from scripture as a motto or guidepost for pastoral praxis, it might be John 10:10: "I came that they might have life, and have it abundantly." Pastoral care, counseling, and psychotherapy all share the aim of restoring individuals (and couples and families) to the full potential, the fullness of life, for which they were created.

This appreciation of infinite abundance in and from God has also been expressed in terms of the "size of God."[124] God is not useful to pastoral theology as a two-dimensional image of Platonic perfection or purity. Such a perfect, pristine God is not big enough to be God. Following process theologian Bernard Loomer, the wholeness—I would add from the above discussion, the chaosmos—of God requires an image not of perfection, but of *size*. This is the God of the mysterium tremendum, the God before whom Moses hid his face on the mountainside. This is not the God of the quick fix but the God in whose vastness no human experience, however terrible, is ever lost or rejected. Perhaps especially in a post-Holocaust Western world, this God, the God of solidarity in whose embrace nothing and no one is lost, is the only God that is still possible.[125]

This theology also has resonance with an expansive and noncondemning view of the human person as messy, multiple, in process, loved (in spite of and/or because of all his or her chaos), and therefore also loving. This is where all pastoral praxis has its beginnings and its endings: in learning to know and love *all* the messy, conflicted, chaotic parts of ourselves, even as God has loved us from our beginnings "made in secret and woven in the depths of the earth" (Ps. 139:14b), and springing from that knowledge of being so deeply loved, growing in the capacity to love others. So the creation stirs in us and brings us into the awareness of God-with-us in our daily lives: God as incarnational desire.

God as Incarnational Desire

In all three aspects of the Trinity, God is love: the power of the erotic, of life breaking through and insisting upon newness, change, growth. This is true in a particular way as God is imaged in the second dimension of the Trinity—God willingly and lovingly present, *in* the flesh, fur, feathers, sea, and soil of the creation. The name *Emmanuel* ("God-with-us") signifies God's own promise to be *with* us, even "to the end of the age" (Matt. 28:20) and more, to be *in* us and in all creation. Just as *perichoresis* was used by the Cappadocians to describe the interpenetration of the three "persons" of the Trinity, *perichoresis* also applies to the relationship between God and the world. God is in us and we are in God—not on some disembodied or theoretical or "spiritual" plane apart from or above daily life, but deep in our blood and our bones. As we walk forward in time and space, loving, working, watching, weeping, rejoicing, God is the whole energy of both justice and mercy, struggling forward through us and in us, in the historical movement of the world. God walks with us and in us, incarnate in history, and intimately involved with us through the very human (and hence animal) experience of living and suffering in the body.

This is the miracle of Incarnation, most clearly embodied for us in the Christian tradition in the life, passion, and resurrection of Jesus of Nazareth. The particularity of the astonishing revelation to the early Christians, that *this Jesus* was God, further tells us about what God is like. Jesus' character, as depicted over and over in the palimpsest of multiple Gospels and overlapping stories, was preoccupied with two central aims: to heal and restore to community those who were ill and/or outcast; and to reverse the social order so that the oppressed would be liberated and the poor lifted up. In the belief that spread from the earliest eyewitnesses to the appearances of Jesus after his crucifixion, Christians even came to the astonishing conviction, read through the prophesies of scripture and the messianic fervor of their times, that Jesus, the Messiah, had been raised from the dead. Whatever one believes about later dogmatic arguments about substitutionary atonement, or the imagery of God sacrificing "His" son, a Trinitarian understanding of the cross points to the astounding assertion that the God who created the universe was so intimately bound up in the fullness of human experience that God allowed *God's own self* to experience excruciating torture and to die, and in so doing, conquered death. Christians thus discern through God's actions in the *personality* of Jesus of Nazareth that God's own nature is to stand in solidarity with all who suffer, and that God not only created the world but offers a continuing promise of transformation from death to new life. And this promise of resurrection is not only a promise about the end of our lives, but also a promise that permeates all the deaths and all the losses we experience, big and little, with the hope that new life can and will come out of even the most desolate and wounded places in our lives. God, as revealed in the second dimension of the Trinity, comes to be known by us as the power of life—*eros*—which infuses our lives, our bodies, with new energy, zest for living, and hope for the future.

The erotic dimension of this *in*carnation, in particular, has been revived in feminist theology.[126] Rita Nakashima Brock specifically identifies the "heart of erotic power" with the incarnation in her book *Journeys by Heart: A Christology of Erotic Power*.[127] She writes:

> Feminist insights about erotic power intersect with the Christian confession that divine reality and redemptive power are love in its fullness. Using feminist experiences and analyses of male dominance and a feminist hermeneutic of erotic power on the biblical texts, it is possible to catch glimpses, within androcentric texts, of the important presence and influence of erotic power within the Christa/Community. Erotic power in the texts sustains and cocreates the whole and compassionate being . . . Christology constructed on the assumption that divine erotic power liberates, heals, and makes whole through our willingness to participate in mutuality. What follows is a Christology of interconnection and action for justice, love, and peace, not of authority, heroism, and proclamation.[128]

LaCugna further identifies sexuality as a holistic dimension of "living a trinitarian life," that is, "living God's life with one another":

> Sexuality broadly defined is the capacity for relationship, for ecstasis, and for self-transcendence. Sexuality lies at the heart of all creation and is an icon of who God is, the God in whose image we were created male and female (Gen. 1). Sexuality is a clue that our existence is grounded in a being whose To-Be is To-Be-For. Sexual desire and sexual need are a continual contradiction to the illusion that we can exist by ourselves, entirely for ourselves. One of the greatest challenges to us is that our sexuality become catholic; sexual desire is specific and tends toward exclusivity, but exclusivity must transcend itself toward inclusivity—for example, openness to a new child or hospitality to the stranger . . . Sexuality is also a vital path of holiness, creativity, fecundity, friendship, inclusiveness, delight, and pleasure . . . Sexual practices and customs can be iconic of divine life, true images of the very nature of the triune God. The person who has "put on Christ" in baptism has put on the capacity for erotic self-expression

that is free and that serves the communion of persons. The person whose sexuality is "eucharistic" regards it as the gift that it is: one of the many ways that God has inscribed upon us the vestiges of God's very life.[129]

The Gospel narratives, and Christian images of Jesus in the manger, in his mother's arms, and later on the road to Golgotha, on the cross, and in his mother's arms again in a Pietà, also emphasize that God, like us, is vulnerable, is wounded. This is perhaps the greatest mystery of the Incarnation. For Christians, there is no clearer depiction of God's vulnerability than that of God being born in a manger, on a dusty straw bed surrounded by the breath of curious animals and frightened, uprooted human parents. And for Christians, there is no clearer depiction of God's woundedness than that of God hanging, tortured, on a first-century imperial Roman cross, betrayed and murdered by earthly powers and principalities. This is one of the more remarkable features of the Christian faith—that the God of the universe is not a God who lords it over us, but participates in the bloody realities of concrete, fleshy living and dying. Further, God's vulnerability is not an illusion, or greatness stooping to meet us, a condescension, as many classical traditions assert in order to preserve the greatness of God's sovereignty.[130] This vulnerability is what God is, as God is revealed to us in the second dimension of the Trinity. And it is in and through such vulnerability, such at-oneness with the creation, that God continually acts to bring healing, justice, and transformation—new life!

This promise of transformation is at the heart of the pastoral enterprise. It heralds that change, however improbable, is never impossible. Much of what impedes growth, healing, and reaching out for new possibilities, new life, is fear. A Trinitarian-informed pastoral psychotherapy holds out the belief that hope is possible and fear does not need to have the last word.

Fear is where the Easter story always begins.[131] Easter begins as the day dawns, a thin, salmon streak of light over the hills where the three crosses stand, empty but still forbidding, mute instruments of torture in silhouette against the sky. Easter begins in the tomb, as a pale light begins to filter into the cave where world-weary security guards doze in boredom to forget the cold of the night, the horror of the dead, the isolation of their post, and the sheer banality of the aftermath of horror. Easter begins as a subtle tremor of hope begins to warm the hearts of the women, stone cold from days of weeping until tears ran dry, bled of hope, exhausted by trauma and anguish. Easter begins in this desolate place of the triumph of death over every aspect of life, every hope. Easter begins in this place of nothingness, where whatever it is that goes on is not life any more for those who have witnessed holocaust, but a numb going-through-the-motions, stripped of sense or purpose. Easter begins in the place of death.

Strange as it may seem, then, Easter dawns as fear. The guards are so frightened they shake and are paralyzed. The women, who have come to the tomb in the shock of early grief, to care for the body of their loved one, are suddenly shaken by a terrifying vision of a massive angel who looked "like lightning" (Matt. 28:3). And he utters the improbable words, "do not be afraid . . ." (28:5).

Our fears, and those of our patients, may seem to pale in comparison to this dramatic story. And yet, when we are truly afraid, we know the power of fear to seize our hearts, to bore into us, and to control our thoughts and actions. This is where Easter begins. With the words "do not be afraid," we are ushered into a new rhythm of transformation that pulses under the whole liturgical year, and our whole life. The rhythm begins with fear, and the impossible but real angelic message: "do not be afraid." Like a gold thread throughout the entire Bible, God, angels, and Christ himself utter these words—thirty-nine times in all—to frightened and astonished believers.

Then the dance picks up in earnest. "Do not be afraid" leads to a feeling, and an action. Joy becomes possible—not the shallow happiness of contentment, but a deeper *ek-stasis*, the feeling of being outside oneself or one's own narrow preoccupations, being opened up for new beginnings. The women "left the tomb quickly with fear" (Matt. 28:8)—but now this "fear" was no longer terror, but wonder, awe, and amazement—"and great joy . . ." (28:8). Hope, brutally smashed, suddenly blossomed again in their hearts. With joy, comes a call to action: "Go and tell . . ." (28:7). The women ran to tell the disciples. And again they were given the same blessing by Jesus himself: "Do not be afraid; go and tell . . ." (28:10).

A similar rhythm is enacted in the Eucharist. Jesus said the blessing, broke the bread, gave it to his friends, and said, "Take, eat; this is my body, which is given for you. Do this in remembrance of me" (Matt. 26:26 and Luke 22:19). This is the Easter rhythm again: Christ's body broken, then given for us, the story of his Resurrection remembered, and the joyful Good News told for generations. We ourselves are afraid/broken, then given the gift and promise of new life, and then energized once again to go and share the gift, which is Love.

Although Easter dawns in fear, it never stays there. The angel's message is "do *not* be afraid." In Henri Nouwen's words, if we make the "house of fear"[132] our permanent dwelling, we find our choices narrowed, and our capacity for love constricted until we can hardly breathe. Staying in our fear causes us to try to control everything, to become preoccupied with ourselves, our safety, until we may even come to hate others because of threats we vaguely perceive. The rhythm of Easter is the movement of pastoral care and psychotherapy—it is the movement out of this house of fear, this house of bondage, to a "house of love."[133] Nouwen asks, "How can we live in the midst of a world marked by fear, hatred and violence, and not be destroyed by it?"[134] The Easter message is that, even at the times of our greatest fear and need, if we listen to the message of the angel ("do not be afraid") we will be led in the dance from fear and trembling to joy and freedom, until our feet, too, are running with the women disciples' feet. This is the central aim of pastoral psychotherapy—not to be healed for our own contentment, or a solipsistic "self-actualization," but to be fully human, even as God-in-Jesus was *fully* human, which is to-be-for-others. Pastoral psychotherapy clings to a belief that we can live again for others, in the power and the mystery of the risen life, which is Love.

Incarnational theology in Christian practice is always sacramental. Like the rhythm of the Eucharist, in which we ourselves are broken, shared, and given, baptism profoundly enacts the rhythm of dying and rising to new life that is at the heart of the Gospel. And the sacraments are "performative"—they bring about what they enact.[135] Further, sacramental life, sacramental living, is not confined to the literal sacraments of the church. The promise of the second dimension of the Trinity is that God is in every moment of our living and doing. One of the gifts of increased awareness that is possible from immersion in the psychotherapeutic process is increased awareness, as well, of the Holy in everyday life. Giving the dog a bath, sitting with arms around a weeping friend, standing with lighted candles at a peace vigil on the Washington Mall, playing a game of pick-up basketball, wrestling with a strenuous intellectual problem, playing music, pushing a child on a swing, digging in the dirt, making love—God is in and around and entwined with it all.

The Incarnation, finally, is about God's desire. Not condescension but love of the creation draws God to us. The promise of the Incarnation, the promise of the transformation from fear to love, and from death to new life, lived vigorously, joyfully *in* the body, the promise of God's desire to be "as close to us as our own breath," leads in turn to the third aspect of Trinitarian imagery, that of the Holy Spirit as living inspiration, the ongoing energy that infuses and empowers the wonder of our relationships.

God as Living Inspiration

If the second dimension of the Trinity depicts God incarnate, the erotic living presence of the Holy in our embodied lives, the third dimension brings God to us in the very rhythm of our breath. The "Holy Spirit" is what we experience as the movement of God in our lives, simultaneously in us and among us, binding us together with each other and the whole created world. The Spirit has been variously thought of as breath, power, energy, wind. In the Bible, numerous words convey this energetic sense of the breath of life: the breath of God (*neshamah*) animating the earth-creature Adam in Gen. 2:7, the power of animal life/breath/soul within us (*nephesh*), the spirit/wind/breath of God (*ruach*) brooding (hovering/nesting) over the waters in Gen. 1 and animating the dry bones in the desert in Ezek. 37, the spirit/breath/wind in the New Testament (πνεῦμα, *pneûma*): "The wind blows where it chooses, and you hear the sound of it, but you do not know where it comes from or where it goes. So it is with everyone who is born of the Spirit" (John 3:8).

Asian Christian theologians have increasingly found a connection, with some qualifications, between this Spirit of life and the Chinese concept of vital energy, or *ch'i*.[136] As *in*spiration, the Spirit is also associated with taking in breath as wisdom and knowledge—enlightenment, to cross over to a different metaphor. Breath, air, and light come together in this aspect of the symbol. As God comes to us and moves in and through us as Spirit, we are given new knowledge, the power to speak, and the courage to stand and to act on behalf of God's priorities—those qualities that the Spirit helps us to see in the life of Jesus and the goodness of creation—mercy and love, healing, and justice.

Images of spirit as wind, breath, life force, and inspiration collide and combine to form an impression of great power and energy, space enough for air to swirl, a feeling of freedom and release. The metaphor of wind suggests both gentle breezes and ferocious, awesome storms. There is power here, power for healing, power for change, power for revolution. Although Irigaray states that a "feminine god is yet to come,"[137] much in Irigaray's language about women's embodied experience is already present in the ecstatic language used to describe the Spirit. The Spirit conveys "multiplicity, difference, becoming, flows, rhythms, and 'the splendor of the body' . . . the god of fluidity and transient boundaries, of the amorphous elements of fire, air, earth and water."[138] While assigning gender to any of the three persons of the Trinity runs the risk of collapsing into essentialism, such fluid images defeat a reified masculinist reading. As feminist theologians have emphasized, *ruach* itself is a feminine noun. "The divine is a movement . . . a movement of love."[139]

In classical Trinitarian theology, if Christ is the ultimate manifestation of God on earth, in human form, then the Spirit is the power by which we are given the ability to understand God's self-revelation in Christ. By extension, the Spirit is the power by which we are given the ability to see the Holy and experience the presence of the Holy incarnate in the world around us, in our everyday lives, and in our relationships. As we breathe in, we experience new life in every moment, and as we breathe out, we experience the holy rhythm and flow of life, which is the most primal form of participation in God's creation—a participation that we neither accomplish by our own will, nor can stop, until our bodies cease to live. And even then, we may discover that the Spirit continues to be involved with us in some other form, perhaps as an infinite pool (of consciousness? of being?). We cannot know. But perhaps just as in creation God is the originating force and nurturing parent of all life, God the Spirit is the pool from which we emerge as creatures, and into which we fall again in all the big and little deaths of our lives.

Just as baptism and Eucharist are practices that reflect the Incarnational dimension of the Trinity, prayer might be seen as the practice that most closely opens our awareness to the third dimension of God-the-Spirit. Just as Jesus asked the disciples, "what are you looking for?" (John 1:38), prayer and meditation can bring us to that place where we not only become aware of our own desire to be closer to God, but of God's infinite desire to give joy and pleasure to us and to the whole creation. The Trinity is not a symbol of a self-sufficient, self-contained exclusive party of three, but rather a symbol of God's self-giving *ec*static motion of love and a reaching toward us and all the created world. Prayer is our reaching toward God, and opening ourselves to God's reaching-toward us, which was already in motion from before our birth. And yet, the mystery of prayer as communion with the Spirit is that it is impossible to tease apart to what extent it is we ourselves, and to what extent it is the indwelling Spirit, who is actually doing the praying in us when we pray: "the Spirit intercedes for us with sighs too deep for words" (Rom. 8:26). Here we encounter the aspect of the Spirit that is described in the Gospel of John in the most personal terms, as the gift of truth the disciples will receive after Jesus' death—translated variously as both "comforter" and "advocate" (John 14:16-17, 25; 16:7).

Augustine describes his experience of coming into relationship with God in mutual, relational, and highly sensual terms:

> Late have I loved you, beauty so old and so new: late have I loved you. And see, you were within and I was in the external world and sought you there, and in my unlovely state I plunged into those lovely created things which you made. You were with me, and I was not with you. The lovely things kept me far from you, though if they did not have their existence in you, they had no existence at all. You called and cried out loud and shattered my deafness. You were radiant and resplendent, you put to flight my blindness. You were fragrant, and I drew in my breath and now pant after you. I tasted you, and I feel but hunger and thirst for you. You touched me, and I am set on fire to attain the peace which is yours.[140]

Not coincidentally, human practices of prayer often involve a deepening and calming of the breath (whether intentionally or unintentionally through the physical relaxation that often comes with a shift in brain state during the focusing or clearing of the mind in prayer). The combination of calm, cleansing breathing, and intentional focus on God or bringing one's life, one's questions, one's feelings, one's problems before God, helps us to become more clearly aware of the presence of God/Spirit in us and in the various concerns and actions of our lives.

Not all forms of prayer are quiet and contemplative. Prayer may be any activity in which we practice awareness of the presence of God. This is the Benedictine rhythm of prayer and work, in which work itself becomes a form of prayer—going about our daily tasks, even seemingly "mindless" chores such as washing the dishes, in a state of "mindfulness" of the presence of the sacred, as Thich Nhat Hanh described: "washing each dish as if it were a baby Buddha."[141] Whatever form it may take, prayer enhances our awareness of our relationship with God, which is always in motion, but not always something we attend fully. Prayer is the human practice of attending to the inspiration of the Holy in our daily existence—as lived in community.

Finally, because the Spirit is not an isolated manifestation of the divine, but conceived as one partner in the Trinitarian dance, the Spirit is in its own distinctive way yet another symbol of the *relationality* of God, and of our life in and with God. As we breathe in, we know that we are not isolated. We do not live in bell jars; we breathe in the entire world. And as we breathe out, if we are aware, we realize that we are reaching even with our breath beyond the confines of our own physical being.

Our very existence affects others. Our very breath ties us to one another, and to the planet. Even our breath, then, is unavoidably a matter of ethics. We cannot extricate ourselves from the very atmosphere in which we and all others live. Breathing reminds us that our very lives are intrinsically *ec*static. We cannot live only for ourselves, but in and for one another, even as the Spirit swirls around and in and through us and all living beings in one great dance—a dance so great that it encompasses the entire cosmos and beyond.

The relational sign of the Spirit, then, is this motion of God, around and in and through, because it invisibly binds us together in one life, one community of creatures. Like it or not, believe it or not, we cannot help but participate in the dance of creation. And so our actions have consequences, not only for our own lives and those closest to us, but for the whole planet. The Spirit infuses all relationships, then, with God's own care, God's creativity, God's incarnational presence. We stand in relationship with this dynamic presence. The Spirit urges, whispers, prompts, and occasionally shoves us in the direction of God's priorities of love and justice. The image is a fluid one, like the air, not dominative and coercive but *in*fluential—always in-flowing. This flow of urgent love can be impeded, by human sin or the thick scar tissue of woundedness, but can it ever be entirely blocked?

This in-flowing relates to the other image of the Spirit, as fire—like the tongues of fire experienced by the followers of Jesus at Pentecost in Acts 2:2-4. The Spirit as fire surrounds, flickers, illuminates, penetrates, consumes, and releases energy as it moves. It connects with Hebrew Bible images of the "refiner's fire" in Mal. 3:2b that purifies and strengthens the people: "thy dross to consume, and thy gold to refine."[142] The healing, persuading flow of God's Spirit is as tenacious as the image of God's irrepressible creativity as the plant breaking through the concrete sidewalk. The Spirit's relationship with us is one of continual healing and impetus for positive growth and change.

The pastoral relationship, then, encompassing the full spectrum of care, counseling, and psychotherapy, is no less fundamentally infused with this energy of God to help heal, grow, strengthen, and promote just flourishing of all persons and creatures. As with all relations among living beings, the pastoral relationship is characterized by a fluid intersubjectivity, where each partner in the relationship is simultaneously both "I" and "Thou" to both self and other, and where meaning is co-constructed, not on either "pole" of the I-Thou duality, but in the third space that exists as a bridge of communication (the ancient Greek word μεταξὺ, *metaxù*), a place of potential but as yet unformulated understandings, and a continuum of shared experience between them. In the pastoral relationship, given the asymmetry of roles between "helper" and "helpee," the psychoanalytic categories of transference (the helpee's subjective experience of the relationship and projections upon it) and countertransference (the helper's similar experiences and projections) become but one symbol of this dynamic interrelation, filtered through the separate subjective experiences and asymmetry of responsibilities of each partner.[143]

The psychoanalytic perspective adds the significant insight that this mutual relation never operates only at the conscious, interpersonal level of ordinary communications and transactions, but encompasses the full range of unconsciousness in and between the participants as well—and encompasses the "unformulated experiences"[144] and co-constructed meanings that lie only in potential, in the realm described by Christopher Bollas as the "unthought known."[145] This is the foundation of *relational* psychoanalytic therapy. But in pastoral psychotherapy in particular, we are further convinced that we do not do this merely by our own powers of reason or intuition, but with the help of the pulsing, energizing breath of God dwelling in both partners in the therapeutic dance, and dwelling in the intersubjective space *between* us, which then opens up as a further space for God's creative profusion, God's incarnational presence, and God's living inspiration.

Conclusion: A Multiple/Trinitarian, Relational Pastoral Theology

A pastoral perspective, "oriented" (paradoxically not just toward a singular "east," but toward a multiplicity of compass points and unfixed directions) toward a God conceived as fluid, vulnerable, multiple, in motion, and in perpetual relation both with us and within us, emancipates us from constraining, static, monolithic notions of both God and human beings. A multiple/Trinitarian, relational pastoral theology, it seems to me, is hospitable to a roomy conception of mind and self that makes new breathing space—space for each human person that can heal narrowness of vision and the constraining hardness of psychic scars, to encompass an ever-widening capacity for relationality, both with other people, and with and among the *inner* selves that inhabit the time and spatial dimensions of one's own lived life.

Theology and psychology meet in this pastoral third space between certainty and unknowability, where rigid hierarchies of both deity-humanity and consciousness-the unconscious begin to collapse, as we recognize that our creativity, art, and human nature itself, contain spheres of both divinity and humanity, rationality and irrationality, knowability and unknowability, of abstract thought, emotion, and animal sense, both within ourselves and in our relations with one another and with God. In the words of T. S. Eliot, "The hint half guessed, the gift half understood, is Incarnation."[146]

Chapter 3

A Relational Understanding of Health and Unhealth

I dream that I have just awakened to discover frightening, cancerous-looking lesions on my forehead. I go to the house of a friend who is a priest, and ask her to recommend a doctor to call because I have none. As I am calling her family physician, I discover to my horror that small, tuberous roots are growing out of the lesions, and a double row of roots is also growing in a straight line down the middle of the top of my head.

THIS DREAM CAME TO ME years ago when I was still a graduate student in pastoral counseling, two nights before I first tried to write a summary of my understandings of psychological health and unhealth. My immediate association was to an orchid plant given to me as a congratulations gift after passing the Episcopal ordination examinations. This plant, which I therefore associated strongly with my sense of vocation, had just begun to bloom. Growing out of the top of the plant were beautiful, creamy white blossoms with mysterious pink interiors. In contrast to their ravishing beauty, there were greedy, ugly, finger-like roots growing everywhere from the pot itself—out the bottom, and crawling up over the edge.

The orchid is a perfect image of health. The purity and beauty of the blossoms could not exist without the ravenous, ugly roots below the surface. In the dream, they frighten and repulse me. However, the dream came as a reminder to me to heed the dark, instinctual aspects of myself, the parts that may not be pretty or pure, even the parts I may wish not to see. They will rise up anywhere and everywhere, even splitting right through the rational mind. The orchid in its totality—blossoms, roots, and all—is a rich symbol for health, which is not perfection but which encompasses everything—dirt, roots, and all.

By contrast, splitting is the hallmark of all psychospiritual unhealth. Pathological splitting should not be confused with inherent rhizomatic multiplicity and fluidity of human persons, as described above in chapter 1, nor should it be confused with the normal mental process of dissociation—that "multiplicity of self-states that maturationally attain a feeling of coherence . . . and the necessary illusion of being 'one self.'"[1] Pathological splitting occurs when either one's sense of self-cohesion, or the capacity to maintain an average, expectable level of stability in relationships, breaks down. Unhealthy splitting exists on a spectrum from milder, more neurotic processes of repression, anxiety, and the employment of a variety of defense mechanisms, to virtual loss of contact with reality in the form of primal projective processes and/or fragmentation in one's ongoing sense of self.

Human Beings Are Vulnerable;
Human Beings Are Both Alike and Unique

It should be remembered, as discussed in chapter 1, that pathology should not be a means by which individuals may be labeled, dismissed, and denigrated. It is in the nature of human beings to be vulnerable, to fall ill, and also to be injured. Pathology (*pathos* + *lógos*) is the study of human suffering, which requires an equal measure of diagnostic acuteness and capacity for *com*passion (suffering-*with*). *Diagnosis* (again, from the Greek διαγινώσκω, *diaginósko*) is the art of distinguishing and making inquiry. It therefore belongs to the practice of pastoral psychotherapy, as one area of disciplined focus, in order to shape the care given with both competence and empathy.

Again, it must be remembered that *human beings are both alike and unique*—all of us are like all others, like some others, and like no others. Part of the art of diagnostic distinguishing is recognizing how our own models of pathology and assessment are bound by time and culture. Other constructions of health and unhealth prevail in other cultures, particularly in the eastern and southern hemispheres. We must always be open to reexamining our hidden assumptions and cultural, class, and gender biases. The more we engage the patient's own perceptions, the more likely we are to understand his or her pain, including the contextual dynamics that have caused or contributed to it.

The Role of Diagnosis in Pastoral Psychotherapy

Diagnosis, like theory itself, has fallen on hard times in some therapeutic quarters. *Pastoral* diagnosis in particular has seldom been addressed as a topic per se. The two major exceptions to this are Paul Pruyser's now classic text, *The Minister as Diagnostician,*[2] and Nancy Ramsay's recent important contribution, *Pastoral Diagnosis: A Resource for Ministries of Care and Counseling.*[3] Because of reductionistic and sometimes sexist misuses of diagnosis to label, (mis)define, and pathologize patients, some therapists are wary of diagnosis.[4] Resistance against intrusive oversight by managed care and third-party payers can also play into this distrust. Some therapists therefore prefer to take a more intuitive approach to assessment, allowing the therapeutic process to unfold without formal evaluations or case formulations. Implicit in this resistance sometimes is a parallel resistance to the notion of pathology itself, as discussed in the introduction to this book, with some therapists feeling that to identify problems with living as pathology is automatically to assume a superior position to the patient and to *pathologize*.

I agree that concepts of pathology, diagnosis, and a medical or "disease" model of psychology and psychotherapy have rightly become suspect in recent decades, to the extent that they set up an expert therapist–passive patient dynamic, in which patients come to be identified globally and impersonally with their suffering and impairments, or labeled as "problems" in order to impose political and social conformity. However, I believe that to do away with all forms of assessment or diagnosis would be to pretend that various recognizable forms of illness and pain did not exist.

If *pathology* is the study of suffering and passion, and *diagnosis* simply means to distinguish or to make something known, then pathology and diagnosis have a place in the practice of pastoral psychotherapy, as one area of disciplined focus, in order to shape the care given and receiving with a thoughtful assessment of "what ails."[5] As discussed earlier, it is not simply a process of plucking diagnostic labels out of the DSM—although the DSM has its uses as a general guide to current (Western) thinking about psychopathology and a common vocabulary for collegial consultation. A good preliminary assessment, however, goes far beyond the DSM's taxonomy and must take into consideration issues of culture, ethnicity, and social context that are still only barely recognized in the DSM. Pastoral psychoanalytic diagnosis, therefore, must always be entered into with humility and vigilance for gaps in one's own understanding, and engaged thoughtfully with the patient, as described above. Diagnosis is not a once-and-for-all procedure carried out only at the outset of therapy but, rather, it is a collaborative process that continues throughout each treatment to its very end.

The value of theory for diagnosis, therefore, lies beyond—often far beyond—the descriptive shells of DSM categories. Fluency in psychological theory helps the clinician to move beyond such quantitative measures toward a more subtle and nuanced, empathic interpretation of the causes of an individual's distress. Such interpretation (which must always be recognized as such, and not clung to as a factual account) may be summarized a *case formulation*.[6] Such a formulation is a working sketch of a patient's inner world and external relations, for the purpose of offering the best, most sensitive therapeutic response. As such, it is always provisional, and subject to ongoing revision. As psychoanalytic supervisor Nancy McWilliams has written,

> it is a more inferential, subjective, and artistic process than diagnosis by matching observable behaviors to lists of symptoms . . . [A] good tentative formulation . . . attends to the following areas: temperament and fixed attributes, maturational themes, defensive patterns, central affects, identifications, relational schemas, self-esteem regulation, and pathogenic beliefs.[7]

Case formulation, while often associated with psychoanalytic therapy, is a valuable tool for counselors practicing from variety of theoretical orientations, ranging from family systems to cognitive-behavioral therapies. A good formulation, regardless of the practitioner's theoretical orientation, is one that begins with a nuanced and detailed understanding of the patient's concerns, in the patient's own language, and connected to the patient's own sensibilities.

Pastoral Assessment and Theological Reflection

Pastoral psychotherapy, with its sensitivity to the spiritual and religious concerns of patients, and further grounded in the theological training of its practitioners, introduces a further, unique element to pastoral diagnosis—that of theological reflection. As I have described in much greater detail in my book *Shared Wisdom*,[8] pastoral assessment involves several steps or movements (which an experienced practitioner may experience more fluidly or even simultaneously). These steps include (1) self-care and centering, which is preliminary to all sound reflection; (2) an examination of one's countertransference in the classical sense, that is, one's own unhealed wounds, "unfinished business" in life, and unresolved issues that may be triggered into reactivity by the patient's concerns; (3) a preliminary assessment of the patient's concerns and problems (as a clinician, this step would include consulting the DSM and other diagnostic resources to provide a tentative formulation); (4) in-depth reflection on one's countertransference in the contemporary or "totalist" sense—that is, all the thoughts, feelings, fantasies, sensations, and reactions that are being felt by the therapist in relation to the patient—as a clue to those dimensions of the patient's inner life that may not have been verbalized, but nevertheless may be present, via unconscious, nonverbal, symbolic, and projective communication, in the intersubjective relationship between patient and therapist; and (5) theological reflection—sitting quietly and free associating to the question "what spiritual or theological images or themes arise in relation to this patient?" This movement in the assessment process draws not only on what can be discerned "objectively" about the patient, but relies heavily on the felt experience of the therapist and the therapist's countertransference, especially in the totalist sense. Theological reflection is not distinct from the therapist's sense of the patient and what it feels like subjectively to be in relationship with him or her, but rather draws on all the senses in an associative fashion. The images, thoughts, and allusions (which may or may not include explicitly biblical references, symbols, or narratives) that arise from intentional theological reflection may in turn surface new insights for treatment.

The Role of Theory in Diagnosis

A good pastoral case formulation, then, is one that begins with a nuanced and detailed understanding of the patient's concerns, in the patient's own language, and connected to the patient's own sensibilities. In order to cultivate an empathic diagnostic sensitivity, therapists must go beyond the categories of the DSM to theoretically sophisticated understandings of certain recognizable patterns of human suffering—and their infinite variations. Theory that is up to this task is what I have called "thick theory,"[9] (borrowing from anthropologist Clifford Geertz's term for good ethnographic observation, "thick description"[10]). Only a thick theory aids the pastoral psychotherapist in thick description (encompassing what is observed in fine detail both about the other, and about one's own affective experience within the flow of the therapeutic relationship). Only such a thick description, in turn, can sensitize the counselor to the minute, specific, and detailed vicissitudes of the patient's speech, behavior, affect, and communication—expressing the delicate turns of his or her life, both inner and outer. And as observations are shared and explored with the patient, the formulation of what ails, and why, is mutually constructed. Diagnosis becomes a relational process rather than a product created by an expert solely for communication with other experts. Relational diagnosis leads naturally to relational treatment—and theory becomes helpful once again as an empathic tool.

With all the above caveats and sensitivities in mind, it is possible to proceed with an overview of psychodynamic theories of health and unhealth. While there are many helpful psychological theories, it is my perspective that psychoanalytic theories, because of their appreciation for the life of the unconscious and the role it plays in human relations, offer the richest nuances for theoretical formulation—they are thick theory at its most multilayered and multifaceted. A "pluralist"[11] approach to psychoanalytic theories (which will be discussed in the next chapter) further enriches the potential for complex diagnostic reflection.

A number of theories will be explored briefly below, including traditional psychoanalytic categories, object relations theory, Self-psychology, trauma theory, and emerging theories about primary affects and shame. To begin, psychoanalytic understandings of pathology have traditionally made a distinction between neurotic, characterological, and psychotic forms of pathology.

NEUROTIC PATHOLOGY AND REPRESSION

The concept of neurosis draws directly from Sigmund Freud's formulations, which are well known and need not be reiterated in great detail here. Much of Freud's clinical theory centered around the "oedipal" crisis, the struggle of a child generally around age five or six to win the love of the parent of the opposite sex. In Freud's work, this is mostly described in terms of the boy's wish to kill his father and possess his mother.[12] Feminist theorists have since shown that the development of girls at this stage, because they are the same gender as the mother, is not exactly parallel, and that attachment to mother is never challenged in the same way as the boy's rivalry with the father in Freud's theory.[13] This difference may result in different gender proclivities in relating,[14] working,[15] and even moral reasoning.[16] Nevertheless, for both boys and girls, neurotic disturbances, particularly anxiety disorders, obsessive-compulsive tendencies, and certain forms or aspects of depression may be generated by unresolved struggles at this stage.

It should perhaps be noted that many disorders once thought by psychoanalysis to be generated entirely by unconscious mental conflicts are now treated success-fully—at least in part—by medication. It is clear that there is a physiological or ge-netic predisposition for the psychotic disorders, and for many of the problems once labeled as neuroses as well—including both anxiety and depression. However, it is not helpful to reduce all psychological disturbances to a purely physiological level. The mind-body connection is subtle and still not well understood.[17] A combination of psychotherapy and medication is often indicated for many disorders because there is almost always a combination of psychological and physiological sources for an in-dividual's distress. Most disorders can be traced to a combination of *three* factors: (1) a physiological predisposition, (2) particular environmental influences or stressors, and (3) internal emotional/psychological processes—the individual's unique feel-ings, thoughts, fantasies, and memories, and the meanings he or she makes (includ-ing images, symbols, and language). Further, most symptoms or problems in living are "overdetermined,"[18] that is, there are multiple causes and influences both in early childhood and in present circumstances that underlie the present difficulties, and therefore there are multiple meanings that any given symptom may be attempting to communicate or express.

In ego psychology, an extension of classical Freudian theory based in America in the mid-twentieth century, neurotic symptoms came to be further classified in terms of unconscious defense mechanisms. Based on the work of Anna Freud and her followers, ego psychologists identified a variety of common defenses as they related to more or less adaptive personality functioning. George Vaillant, who also conducted a well-known longitudinal study of men from their college days across the lifespan,[19] formulated a hierarchy of defenses,[20] which are still used as one standard tool in many practitioners' diagnostic formulations. These range from mature de-fenses (humor, suppression, ascetisim, altruism, anticipation or delayed gratification, and sublimation), to higher-level (neurotic) defenses (introjection of a significant person as a means of coping with loss, identification, displacement, intellectualiza-tion, isolation of affect, rationalization, sexualization, reaction formation, repression, and undoing), to the so-called primitive defenses (splitting, projective identification, projection, denial, dissociation, idealization, acting out, somatization, regression, and schizoid fantasy).[21]

There are significant conceptual problems with this schema, notably, the ten-dency to reduce human behaviors to a neat taxonomy, and even more troubling, the racism implicit in the term *primitive*, in which Freud's nineteenth-century anthro-pological assumptions about "primitive peoples" in "dark continents" came to be at least unconsciously conflated with immature and pathological modes of living and relating.[22] Nevertheless, if one keeps such caveats in mind and reads Freud with an awareness of the cultural and contextual limits of his own conceptual frame, Freud's early formulations are still relevant and worth understanding because they continue to shed light especially on the third domain of pathology listed above, that of internal emotional/psychological processes—how the individual internally processes his or her experiences, and the unconscious mental contents that influence daily living. It is well to note, however, that all psychological theory is most usefully applied in combination with the insights of medical research (psychiatry), brain science, and more contemporary psychoanalytic theory.

That being said, it is important to recognize that the oedipal crisis seems to manifest very differently for girls than boys. It still represents an essential developmental stage for both sexes, but it is less about the child stereotypically wishing to kill one parent to possess the other, as it is essentially the critical point of navigating the transition from dyadic to triadic relationships. Parental failure *either* to acknowledge the child's understandable wish to keep one parent all to him- or herself, *or* to set age-appropriate limits that help the child to be incorporated into a wider sphere of relationships while learning to relinquish grandiose unilateral desires, can result in a variety of painful internal states and external compensatory behaviors. Both acknowledgment of the child's desire *and* firm though compassionate boundary-setting are needed at this crucial developmental juncture.

The splitting involved in neurosis is a splitting off of one's own spontaneity, desires, and impulses via the mechanism of repression. At the heart of neurotic disturbances, there is a wish or drive that had to be repressed—"forgotten" and pressed back into the unconscious (see Figure 3 in chapter 1). For Freud, such repressed wishes were related to the two primal drives (sometimes translated as "instincts") of sex and aggression. The specific aim of such a wish, and its target (the parent one wants to possess for one's own, the parent or sibling one wishes to kill), and the quality and evocativeness of that wish, will vary from one person to the next, resulting in the tremendous variety of forms of personality and of neurotic symptoms. Because civilization requires that we learn to control our impulses for the sake of getting along with others, the unconscious mechanism of repression is probably universal, as Freud proposed.[23] To some extent, all but perhaps the most disturbed or sociopathic individuals learn early in life to sacrifice spontaneity for peace, and perhaps in that sense all of us who are more or less adapted to this society are "neurotic."

Repression is intimately bound up with the formation of a *superego*, Freud's term for the inner dynamic force of conscience or self-control. In healthy individuals, the superego is formed in identification with healthy parental and societal prohibitions, such as "thou shalt not kill." Neurosis only becomes a problem when it becomes chronic and severe enough to interfere with one's "social or occupational functioning"—the DSM threshold for any disorder. If the superego, for example, becomes too harsh or punitive, having been formed in identification with an overly controlling, critical, or punitive parent, an individual can become too inhibited to live a full and productive life. Neurotic symptoms, because they express repressed wishes that would be unacceptable to the person's sense of self and morality, appear as persistent distressing patterns of thought, feeling, and/or behavior that the individual experiences as alien to his or her sense of "my normal self."

A neurotic symptom paradoxically accomplishes two things simultaneously: it performs an act of purification or self-punishment for having the wish, while simultaneously expressing or gratifying the wish in disguised form. So, for example, in classical psychoanalytic thinking, a person who compulsively washes his hands simultaneously purifies himself of unconscious guilt for forbidden unconscious thoughts, yet also "soils" his hands in a different way by scraping them raw and bloody.[24] A person develops a phobia of elevators, which are unconsciously associated for her with sensations of forbidden sexual arousal, so avoiding elevators relieves her of her phobic dread (her sexuality), but also keeps the wish active by making something more of elevators than the nonphobic person would normally experience. A neurotic symptom "binds" the intolerable anxiety by keeping it in some way circumscribed to one aspect of the individual's life, and keeps the wish unconscious (i.e., maintains the repression barrier intact), but the relief one gains temporarily from such symptoms comes at a high price—usually in the form of some kind of inhibition.

Because neurotic symptoms have multiple origins—in Freud's terminology, they are "overdetermined" by several factors in early life—they also usually carry multiple meanings. They therefore may mutate many times over the course of a treatment—or a lifetime. This is why a psychodynamic formulation of a patient's problems presents a more complex picture than a DSM diagnosis alone can do. Psychoanalytic diagnosis should incorporate attention to at least three domains—(1) external, environmental factors (stressors with which the patient is trying to cope, including interpersonal, social, cultural, and political stressors), (2) inherited biological factors, and (3) the patient's intrapsychic dynamics as they can best be understood empathically—as well as the way in which these domains uniquely interact in the patient's inner and outer worlds.[25] This is also why psychodynamic therapy can be so helpful, in addition to whatever symptom relief may be afforded by medication and cognitive-behavioral therapeutic techniques—although these also can be effective and useful. A both-and approach is warranted.

CHARACTEROLOGICAL PATHOLOGY

Unlike neurotic disturbances (which Freud felt more optimistic about healing), *characterological* disturbances, especially borderline and narcissistic conditions, have their origins in an earlier period of development, sometimes referred to as "pre-oedipal." Characterological disturbances may be described as problems that involve not only certain discrete aspects of an individual's personality or behavior, as with neuroses, but permeate the entire personality and functioning of an individual. "Personality" is an all-encompassing way of describing a person's characteristic functioning in both social and occupational arenas. Personality is thus a more or less enduring complex of habitual modes of thinking, feeling, and behaving. One useful contemporary theory identifies the four basic components of personality, drawing synthetically from across various psychoanalytic theoretical traditions:[26]

1. a "biologically based temperament" (e.g., in the work of developmental researchers Stella Chess and Alexander Thomas: "easy," "slow to warm," "difficult," and "undifferentiated," based on nine behaviors observed in children, which are activity level, rhythmicity/regularity, approach or withdrawal, adaptability, threshold of responsiveness, intensity of reaction, quality of mood, distractibility, and attention span and persistence [27]);
2. a "constellation of internal representations of self and other" than are linked to affect states and are externalized in interpersonal relationships (in other words, one's internal object world);
3. a "characteristic set of defense mechanisms"; and
4. a "related cognitive style" (typical ways of thinking).

Because personality is so all-embracing, characterological problems are therefore thought to be caused by wounding at an even younger stage than the oedipal crisis that underlies neurosis—as far back in some cases as early infancy. They are represented in the DSM under the category of "personality disorders," and in formal diagnosis they are coded on a different axis than neurotic and psychotic disorders—in part, because they sometimes coexist with these other problems. Characterological disturbances often are not as distressing to a person him- or herself as neurotic symptoms. Most often, a person with such very early wounding will perceive that the problems s/he is experiencing lie outside or beyond him- or herself. Nevertheless, such disturbances often cause severe problems, particularly in relating with others, and can wreak havoc with both work and social life. The individual is often puzzled why s/he seems to have repeated experiences of conflict or alienation in relation to others, and often feels victimized by others or by his or her circumstances. Sometimes such individuals will come to therapy because "I can't seem to keep a relationship," or "I keep getting fired and I don't know why." In other cases, individuals come to therapy under duress—because their partners have threatened to leave them unless they seek help, or because their behavior has gotten them into serious trouble and they have been court-mandated to seek treatment.

To understand the problems that arise from wounding in earliest childhood, two theoretical orientations—object relations and self psychology—are most helpful. Both offer useful metaphors and frameworks for understanding the fragmentation of consciousness that occurs with very early wounding. There are no medications specific to characterological disorders, although some medicines can alleviate some of the associated symptoms, particularly in the realm of anxiety and depression. Cognitive therapy alone is also ineffective in dealing with the deeper issues involved, although, again, it can be very helpful in managing behavior and teaching impulse control. Psychodynamic therapy is the only mode of therapy that addresses the long-standing internal dynamics that underlie characterological problems such as borderline and narcissistic personality disorders. More will be said about these specific problems below.

Object Relations Theories, Early Wounding, and Splitting

As described by the object relationists, the central mechanism of characterologi-cal pathology is splitting. Melanie Klein, an analyst from Freud's own circle who emigrated to London, proposed a theory of the infant's inner experience that did not entirely replace Freud's view of the centrality of sex and aggression but placed far more emphasis on the formative nature of the infant's earliest inner experience of his or her caretakers. Based on reconstructions from her adult patients' memories, fantasies, and projective processes observable in the therapeutic setting, Klein pro-posed that the infant's basic experiences (such as hunger, thirst, satiety, pain, fright, soothing, and pleasure) are stored by the infant as unarticulated memories divided into "good" and "bad." The infant's experiences of the primary caretaker (for Klein, this was always the mother) are "good" if perceived to be adequately responsive, or "bad" in either of two ways: overwhelming and intrusive, or depriving and unrespon-sive. These good and bad experiences coalesce in the realm of fantasy into symbolic mental representations, or "objects."

The "clinical baby"[28] (the early childhood experience that is recollected in ther-apy) is not identical to whatever a patient may have "actually" experienced internally (and multiply) as an infant, nor is it identical to the "empirical baby"[29] of infant observation research. Nevertheless Klein's intuitions and reconstructions from her adult patients' memories and reenactments are being validated as consistent with the findings of contemporary infant research.[30] This model, elaborated in the work of theorists like W. R. D. Fairbairn—with his system of internal objects, the "libidinal ego," "anti-libidinal ego" or "internal saboteur," and "central ego"[31]—conceives of the inner world as populated with a vast multiplicity of mental representations. Most of these have their origins in real external figures in the individual's life, especially the formative first months and years of life. But, following Klein,[32] they are not neces-sarily derived from a pure, undistorted internalization of external figures, taken in whole. They are digested and metabolized by the infant's own inner mechanisms—fantasized or perceived experiences of the other that may correspond only to varying degrees with external "reality," and shaped by constitutional predispositions, prior experiences, bodily sensations, fears, and wishes, etc.

Further, in infancy, good and bad are absolutely split apart from each other, each having an all-or-nothing quality. A primary caretaker, or even in the earliest months a part of a caretaker, particularly a breast, may come to exist in multiple representations in the interior fantasy world of the child as both a good object and a bad object or objects. Klein called this early period of development the "paranoid-schizoid position," in which the infant's early mental life was organized around this absolute split between good and bad. Of course, the psychological purpose of such splitting is to split off and avoid experiencing the bad, in order to feel secure enough to survive.

Thomas Ogden, a contemporary Kleinian analyst, describes the paranoid-schizoid position or "mode" as follows:

> The paranoid-schizoid mode of generating experience is based heavily upon splitting as a defense and as a way of organizing experience. Whereas the depressive mode operates predominantly in the service of containment of experience, including psychological pain, the paranoid-schizoid mode is more evenly divided between efforts at managing psychic pain and efforts at the evacuation of pain through the defensive use of omnipotent thinking, denial, and the creation of discontinuities of experience.
>
> In a paranoid-schizoid mode, the experience of loving and hating the same object generates intolerable anxiety, which constitutes the principal psychological dilemma to be managed. This problem is handled in large part by separating loving and hating facets of oneself from loving and hating facets of the object. Only in this way can the individual safely love the object, in a state of uncontaminated security, and safely hate without the fear of damaging the loved object.[33]

This explains both the omnipotence and grandiose ideation of the narcissistic personality, and the extreme idealization-devaluation pattern of so-called borderline pathology. In its extreme, Ogden believes such splitting is evidenced in schizophrenic disorders.[34]

Klein further posited a "depressive position" as the most mature form of psychological development, with origins in the second quarter of the first year of life.[35] At this stage, objects begin to be perceived as "other," separate from the self. At this time, Klein proposed, the infant begins to realize on some level that her/his aggression could harm this other, this breast/source of nourishment, and result in the loss of the sustaining object. The child thus begins to gain a rudimentary experience of the destructive potential of his or her own hunger and need. With this sense, Klein suggested, may come a feeling akin to sadness, and a desire for reparation. She called this the "depressive position," and considered it the lifelong foundation for emotional and psychological health. In contrast to the paranoid-schizoid position, it is in the depressive position that the opposites of good and bad begin to be held together in the infant's mind. The same parent who at times provides too little or too much is also the parent who sometimes is soothing and "just right." The sibling who makes me feel furious with jealousy is also the same sibling who is fun to play with.

In time, then, this capacity to hold good and bad together, and the rise of depressive feelings, initially over the loss of a possession (the breast), begins to open into a capacity for empathy for the object as a separate self. Perhaps the poignancy of the oedipal phase may be precisely that it occurs after the development of the depressive position, so that the wish to kill the father must coexist with love for him, and within a context of growing awareness of the separate subjectivity of others—"a dilemma rooted in subjectivity, whole object relations, ambivalence, and historicity."[36]

Klein did not use the term *stage*, like some developmental theories, but rather *position*. Because her theorizing was based on adult clinical cases, she saw that *both* positions fluctuate in dominating a person's thought processes over the lifespan. She saw the paranoid-schizoid position as one in which some adults still predominantly function in spite of their chronological maturity, and to which others might regress during times of stress or trauma.

Later object relations theorists extended Klein's theories, notably, British psychoanalysts Fairbairn,[37] D. W. Winnicott,[38] and Harry Guntrip,[39] and more recently, the "relational" and "intersubjective" psychoanalytic theorists who have pointed to the mutual construction of meaning and reality that occurs in all relationships from birth.[40] For these theorists, the inner world is continually being constituted by the internalization of one's experiences of other people, or "objects," whom one meets over one's lifetime. Note that these internal objects do not have a one-to-one correspondence with the actual others in one's life. They are the representations of the subjective experiences of these others as they are subjectively perceived, and mediated by the affect states and prior perceptions, experiences, and projections, as the individual's inner world grows over time. The inner world is further complicated by multiple representations of one's own self, or aspects of oneself, at different times and under different circumstances.

There is thus an entire inner landscape, populated by a potentially enormous group of internal objects, which bear traces, in whole or in part, of both one's own self-states, and the memories and representations of others. These inner mental representations function somewhat like templates, against which new experiences, particularly relational ones, are tested. As a child grows, s/he begins to expect certain kinds of behaviors from others, based on these internalizations of earlier experiences. The earliest internalized objects, or representations, furthermore, are laid down in the preverbal stages of infancy and toddlerhood and are therefore not necessarily attached to any sort of narrative or verbal memory. They take shape in the form of symbols, images, and sensations—body memories. Narrative meaning, when applied to these early representations, is therefore necessarily retrospective because it comes from the vantage point of an older, verbalizing self. Not all early representations are ever explored or processed verbally, but nevertheless exist as powerful forces governing behavior and experience. Some of our earliest childhood experiences may never reach the cognitive level of symbolization, but may remain at the level of behavior patterns or bodily sensations.[41]

No part of this process is pathological. The large quantity and diversity of inner objects and related affect states is a normal part of human development and is not pathological per se. Human beings are multiple, as described in chapter 1. This multiplicity of internalized objects or mental representations is part of the natural process of "mentalization"[42] that begins in infancy. Current brain research and infant observation studies both lend evidentiary support for this theoretical construction.[43] Problems arise not because of this inherent multiplicity but because of a confluence of early injuries and/or deprivation, certain biological predispositions or vulnerabilities, and the consequent early development of patterns of psychic self-defense and self-regulation that become self-defeating in later life. Healthy mentalization includes a capacity to reflect on one's own complex subjectivity and to recognize empathically the complexity of others' subjectivity as well. Problems arise when splitting becomes chronic, the fluidity of passage among various self-states is impeded, and inner representations, feelings, and sensations that are intolerable are evacuated through projection onto or into others in an individual's environment.

Particularly in the case of trauma, researchers have observed that overwhelmingly terrifying or painful events are not processed cognitively as other narrative memories, but are stored in fragments that split up one's cognitive thoughts from affective or emotion-toned experience, behavioral patterns, and/or visual, auditory, olfactory, taste, and tactile sensation. Some traumatic memories exist—at least initially, until there is some opportunity to process them verbally—only in the form of unsymbolized body memories.[44]

Inner objects or representations are also not inert. As object relations theorists have proposed, inner objects carry on *their own dynamic life*. They function energetically, as motivating forces from within, with varying degrees of autonomy, acting and reacting in relationship with external and internal others. A person may feel "fragmented" or "divided" as different internal forces are stimulated and come into play based on various childhood experiences and internalized significant others. S/he will often have little or no conscious awareness of these inner forces or parts of the self. The less aware s/he is, in fact, of these inner forces, the more likely they are to be projected, as a movie is projected, onto the "screen" of other people. The more negative the inner object, the more likely it is to be expelled through the process of projection. Projection thus distorts our perception of others and causes us to misperceive a new reality as an old (usually painful or self-destructive) one. When early experiences have been consistently painful or depriving enough, projections tend to be negative, and tend unconsciously to motivate behaviors that may cause even more pain in an ever more self-defeating spiral of actions and reactions. Anticipations of mistreatment by others, and related self-protective strategies, which in childhood might have been helpful or even life-saving, often outlive their usefulness as an individual grows into adulthood. In adult life, these entrenched but unconscious patterns of perceiving and reacting begin to create more problems than they solve.

When childhood experiences have been too consistently depriving or traumatic, particularly in the first two years of life, an even more intensely projective process called "projective identification"[45] may occur. According to object relations theory, in projective identification, perceptions and inner objects are not only projected *onto* the screen of another person, where they may set up a barrier in the form of a distorted picture of the other, but they are actually projected *into* the other person.

Intolerably frightening or negative inner objects and related affects are split off and evacuated into the other. As mysterious as this process may seem, it is evidenced by clinical experience. The "other" who is on the receiving end of such projections will experience something alien—a thought, feeling, sensation, or impulse that is unusual for him or her—as having entered them and actually changed their behavior in relation to the person doing the projecting. The process is probably not as mysterious or quasitelepathic as it sounds. It is really carried out by a series of subtle or not-so-subtle affective and behavioral cues that invoke reciprocal affects and behaviors in the other person. The person on the receiving end, moreover, must have some resonance (often unconscious) with the split off and projected material coming into him or her. There must be some "hook" on which the person doing the projecting can "hang" the projected material in the other. Thus, a form of self-fulfilling prophecy often results, in which the inner fears and expectations of the person doing the projecting become incarnated in the other.

A vicious cycle often ensues in the person's life, in which expectations based on negative experiences from early childhood are reconfirmed and reinforced again and again in ongoing living. This pattern is seen most repeatedly and intensely in the so-called borderline personality disorder. This disorder is characterized by a pattern of unstable and often turbulent relationships ("I hate you, don't leave me"[46]), fear of abandonment, intense and shifting moods and feelings, a tendency toward self-destructive behaviors, and extremes of idealization and devaluation of others (splitting)—in other words, living chronically in a paranoid-schizoid position.

The term *borderline* has come to carry pejorative and sexist connotations because therapists have had negative experiences with such patients, a majority of whom are women (who seek therapy for all forms of emotional distress at a much higher rate than men), and a psychiatric lore has grown up around the agonies of treating "borderlines." This unkind and disrespectful pattern of denigration needs to be kept conscious and resisted. It is probably invoked to some degree at a countertransferential level, as an enactment of the splitting and devaluation inherent in the disorder itself. Because of its generally accepted relationship to early childhood wounding, "borderline" pathology is best understood under the broad spectrum of post-traumatic stress.[47] Splitting, projection, and projective identification are the hallmarks of this pathology.

The cycle of projective identification is hard to break because projective processes are not only powerful but frequently are mutual, as individuals become captive to reciprocally reinforcing negative patterns of projection. Particularly in ongoing relationships, a destructive interlocking pattern of mutual projection and internalization may occur, devolving into ever more negative and unconsciously driven interactions. The cycle can usually only be broken, and not easily, by the inbreaking of new and unexpected relational experiences that are powerful enough, repeated enough, and feel real enough to the person to overcome the veil of projections. Such new experience allows for the internalization of a new, more positive reality, a new object that neither abandons nor retaliates.[48] Sometimes this can happen in everyday living, in relationship with an unusually healthy other, but more often, especially when inner representations are too painful or persecutory, a therapeutic relationship is needed to allow for and contain the projective processes at the level of intensity and duration required for healing to take place. Much clinical work in object relations–oriented psychotherapy is founded on this principle. The projective processes that develop in the intersubjective transference-countertransference dynamic of the therapeutic relationship become the focus for exploration between therapist and patient.

Psychotic Pathology

Psychosis is mostly beyond the domain of this book, so little will be said specifically about psychotic process here. From a contemporary object relations perspective, psychosis represents the outer extremes of splitting off inner mental representations from external reality. It involves delusionally intense projective processes in which the person has no capacity to reflect on the possibility that s/he is projecting. Such psychotic projective processes have their origins in the earliest infantile experiences of inner annihilation (feared or actual). Because such early experiences of fear of annihilation are more common in infancy than we like to suppose, it has been posited that everyone has a "psychotic core"[49] or an "autistic capsule"[50] in which inner affects, images, sensations, and symbols are so encapsulated from real, external experience that they form a delusional inner space. Sometimes this region is touched upon in intensive psychoanalytic psychotherapy. It differs from a true psychiatric diagnosis of psychosis, however, in that it is transiently experienced and is not representative of the person's normal, daily experience and behavior.

Fully manifested psychotic disorders include schizophrenia, brief reactive psychosis, delusional disorder, and schizoaffective disorder (in which there are both psychotic and mood symptoms). The distinguishing features of these are cataloged in the DSM IV-TR. Understood theoretically in terms of splitting, the term *schizophrenia* itself means "split-brain." This does not refer to multiple personalities, but rather to a splitting off of reality. It is therefore a thought disorder, characterized by hallucinations (most often auditory) and/or delusions (unshakably held false or impossible beliefs), as well as a variety of other disturbances of thought, self-expression, and behavior as detailed in the DSM. In addition to the schizophrenias, certain other severe mental disorders such as bipolar disorder and major depression can involve psychotic episodes. Certain medications, certain illicit drugs, and some medical conditions may also mimic or bring about a psychotic state. So-called reality testing, the ability of a person to distinguish between reality and fantasy or projection, may also be weakened in persons suffering from so-called borderline or post-traumatic wounding, especially under increased stress or restimulation of traumatic memories. A pastoral psychotherapist who suspects the possibility of a psychotic crisis should always seek psychiatric consultation and may need to help the individual to be hospitalized—particularly if s/he poses a danger to self or others.

Ongoing treatment of the psychotic disorders nearly always involves psychiatric medication and often hospitalization, at least for the purposes of stabilization during crisis. Schizophrenia and schizoaffective disorder usually manifest as chronic, disabling disorders that generally require a lifelong regimen of medication and supportive therapy. Pastoral counseling can productively function as a form of supportive therapy, used as an adjunct to medical treatment, for the purposes of helping the individual with issues of life management and relational coping skills. Intensive psychodynamic therapy, however, is usually considered counterproductive, as it can stir up feelings that may further destabilize the individual's sense of cohesion and grounding in reality.

Self Psychology and Narcissistic Pathology

Heinz Kohut contributed a different but complementary understanding of early wounding that has many features in common with object relations but also offers some distinctively helpful theoretical constructs. Self psychology, the branch of psychoanalysis that evolved from Kohut's theory, has proven particularly helpful in addressing the characterological problems of individuals suffering from narcissistic wounding.[51] In Kohut's view, pathology is a problem with structure and self-cohesion.

The structure of the self, for which Kohut had a very particular schema, is either insufficiently strong or lacking in part. Initially, needs are met from the outside, by objects who in Kohut's terminology function as "selfobjects": simply stated, "objects we experience as part of ourself."[52] This function is provided at first by parents and close caretakers and then, as the child grows, by others in the environment as well. Thus, the structure of the self is formed as the child gradually internalizes what s/he needs from those who are close to her/him.

Kohut initially proposed a "bipolar structure of the self"[53] (not to be confused with bipolar disorder), which can be visualized as a continuum with two poles:[54] the "mirroring" pole, in which the child should receive recognition, warmth, unconditional affirmation, "the gleam in the parent's eye;" and the "idealizing" pole, in which the child experiences the parental selfobjects as reliable, admirable, and idealizable—the core of values around which adult aspirations and ideals are formed. A distinctive aspect of Kohut's theory is that we continue to need selfobjects throughout the lifespan in order to continue to shore up and build our sense of self cohesion.

Structure is built on the mirroring end of the spectrum when the parent sees and responds warmly to the child's being and growing accomplishments. Self psychologists Howard Baker and Margaret Baker have written:

> In the context of a generally responsive environment (the "good enough" parents), the intensity of the grandiose self is diminished but not destroyed. In other words, given reasonable care, humans are so constituted that they preserve a "piece of the old grandiose delusion" . . . , in spite of the fact, and even

because of the fact, that from the beginning of life a countless number of inevitable in phase ("optimal") frustrations and injuries begin to modulate and
transform these delusions by teaching us the limits of our own and other's
power. It is these optimal failures which require the child to develop or invent
internal means to maintain self-esteem, tolerate unavoidable failure, and pursue appropriate ambitions with vigor. The developing child's self-object needs
can then mature from archaic demands for perfection and constant attention
to self-confidence and the healthy self-object need for occasional, thoughtful
appreciation and praise. Clinically, we do not see the results of the "failures" of
good enough parents. Instead, we see people for whom the parent-child interaction seriously failed to meet the child's self-object needs.[55]

As in object relations theories, this development occurs in the earliest period of life
and largely in connection with the infant-mother/parent dyad. Characterological
disturbances are all understood in some way to be derived from this wounding of the
child's primary narcissism.

The second pole, the "idealizing" pole, tends to be built later. This pole involves
the need for a selfobject that the child can emulate and that embodies goals and ideals to which the child can aspire. Later in childhood and in adolescence, as the child's
autonomy increases, there is a related "twinship" need, thought of as a third "pole"
by some,[56] through which the child can organize her/his alikeness and difference
with parents and peers. As self psychology has evolved, six different selfobject experiences are now theorized as necessary to establish, maintain, or restore the sense
of self. Ernest Wolf[57] has identified these as follows: (1) merger, which parallels the
earliest stage in object relations theory; (2) mirroring; (3) alter-ego, or "twinship,"
formed during latency age; (4) idealizing; (5) creativity/efficacy, which is a special
merger with a selfobject needed to sustain particularly taxing creative tasks; and (6)
adversarial, the "ally-antagonist" who can help mediate the separation-individuation
stage characteristic of toddlerhood by accepting the two-year-old's "no" as a gesture
of growing autonomy.

When all goes well, mirroring allows infantile grandiosity to be fed and gradually modified into a mature sense of affirmed identity, self-confidence, and appropriate pride in one's capacities and achievements; and idealizing allows infantile
dependence to evolve into mature interdependence with others in relationships,
and pursuit of goals founded in a secure sense of ideals, values, and purpose. When
all does not go well, however, the result is an inner experience of fragmentation,
lack, and depressive emptiness, a sense that inside oneself "there is no there, there."
This deep insecurity is often disguised by an external presentation of inflated self-
importance, sensitivity to criticism, and narcissistic grandiosity and entitlement.[58]

While self psychologists certainly recognize the impact of trauma on development, the theory overall presents itself as a *deficit model*—pathology is a result
primarily of what an individual did not receive enough of in childhood, rather than

an insertion of active, persecutory "objects" into the child's inner landscape as in object relations theory.[59] The self-psychological model of personality is more *structured* than *peopled*, and pathology results from insufficient structure or structural defects, rather than the presence of something, someone, or some*ones* "bad" inside. The subjective experience of patients from whom Kohut first derived his model was one of lack, "the center cannot hold," and frantic efforts to fill the void.

In actual clinical application, a Winnicottian approach and a Kohutian approach to doing therapy are very similar. (More will be said about therapeutic technique and practice in the following chapters.) The understanding of intersubjectivity that grew out of self psychology is parallel in most respects to the relational school of psychoanalysis that grew out of object relations. Both theories are characterized by their emphasis on relatedness as the primary ongoing motivation of human thoughts, feelings, and behavior. Moving into our postmodern era, both theories also lead easily to an appreciation of the complexity and multiplicity of self-states that constitute the inner landscape of one's self and subjectivity, and to the importance of understanding the mutual co-construction of reality, including perceptions of self/selves, other/s, and the world. Intersubjectivity theory and relational psychoanalysis have not replaced these frameworks, but rather have expanded upon them to conceive of a more genuinely mutual "two-person" therapeutic encounter—understood as operating at both conscious and unconscious levels.

These are the foundational theoretical frameworks for this book. Three other fields of research have added further to our understandings of human development and human pathology. Neuroscience, or the study of the human brain and its development, has already been mentioned above as providing new scientific evidence for the model of human development proposed by object relations theory. In addition, it is useful briefly to review contributions from the fields of traumatology and of "attachment theory" and the study of primary human affects, particularly the affect of shame.

TRAUMATIC WOUNDING

Both object relations theories and self psychology, as noted above, share a common assumption that the psyche is largely developed in the earliest years of life—certainly by age three or three-and-a-half. This early direction is set for the continued development of conscious and unconscious structure. This of course includes the shaping of the self from the positive provisions received from the primary parent. Disturbances of the self, however, are laid down at a similarly early phase. The wounds and resulting blockages, developmental arrests and habitual defensive mechanisms, all begin *before* the child's cognitive and verbal ability and capacity for narrative memory are formed in the brain.[60] Thus, all work on characterological issues can be understood as working with trauma. And much of this trauma has occurred at preverbal stages, and therefore it cannot likely be fully retrieved or cognitively known; but it can be deduced from interactions in the transference.

Trauma became a subject of passionate concern and debate in all branches of psychotherapy during the 1980s and '90s. While the most heated controversies about trauma, abuse, and memory recovery have somewhat abated, attention to the effects of trauma on development continues to be important in clinical training and practice. Current research, including neuroscientific studies of trauma, reinforces the importance of recognizing traumatic *sequelae* ("after-effects") in pastoral care, counseling, and therapy. I use the term *trauma* in its technical sense, following trauma specialists[61] to mean not simply *any* hurt, distress, or injury (the popular sense of the word) but, rather, the deep injury caused by an experience of horror perceived as life-threatening. Trauma involves extreme pain, horror, and/or forced confinement, combined with the terror of being overwhelmed or annihilated, and in which normal coping mechanisms fail or are unavailable. In normal adulthood, it often takes a major horrifying event—such as rape, physical assault, wartime exposure to brutality and horror, an experience of violence or an ongoing threat of violence, torture, or captivity—to constitute the level of helplessness needed to be truly traumatic. Even in later childhood and adolescence, to be experienced as trauma an injury requires a serious invasion or assault on bodily integrity, a threat to life, restriction of freedom, or isolation from help because adolescents are bigger than small children and have more fully developed cognitive faculties.

However, in infancy and early childhood, trauma can be much more subtle because the infant is already in a state of helplessness and total or near-total dependency. Trauma in infancy can be as subtle as a look or the absence of a look, a subtle pattern of unconscious inattention, neglect, or hidden hostility. In the earliest state of infant-parent merger, it has even been suggested that the infant is able to perceive, in a preverbal or presymbolic way, the unconscious of the parent.[62] Because trauma can be so subtle, actual physical or sexual abuse, devastating enough to an older child, can be experienced by a small child as annihilating.

The most severe trauma, especially seen in repeated or chronic abuse or traumatization, creates the most severe splitting, or dissociation. There is a strong, demonstrated etiological link between borderline and dissociative disorders and severe early childhood trauma, especially sexual abuse. An illuminating and non-victim-blaming approach to many of the characterological disorders is to understand them within a broad spectrum of post-traumatic disturbances.[63]

Psychoanalyst Leonard Shengold describes the internal process of an abused child as follows:

> If the very parent who abuses and is experienced as bad must be turned to for relief of the distress that the parent has caused, then the child must, out of desperate need, register the parent—*delusionally*—as good. Only the mental image of a good parent can help the child deal with the terrifying intensity of fear and rage which is the effect of the tormenting experience. The alternative—maintenance of the overwhelming stimulation and the bad parental image—means

annihilation of identity, of the feeling of the self. So the bad has to be registered as good. This is a mind-splitting or mind-fragmenting operation. In order to survive, these children must keep in some compartment of their minds the delusion of good parents and the delusive promise that all the terror and pain and hate will be transformed into love.[64]

Thus, the child's sense of self-cohesion and going-on-being is profoundly shattered by severe trauma and abuse. The developing multiplicity of the child's mental life is hijacked by the trauma, and the healthy capacity for multiplicity turns into chronic, pathological splitting. Internal objects become cut off from one another, as amnestic walls are formed to seal off bad from good and preserve a (sometimes delusional) sense of security in order to survive.

Normal development, in which there is a fluency among inner objects and self-states, is replaced by an overemphasis on the mechanisms of repression (using the meaning this term is given by trauma specialists, as the process by which the conscious mind forgets or presses what has happened back out of awareness), and dissociation (a comprehensive term for a number of processes that help the child to survive what otherwise might overwhelm her or him to the point of psychic or even physical annihilation). At the time the abuse is being experienced, both repression and dissociation must be viewed as normal, not pathological responses to extreme trauma. Carried into adulthood, they need to be seen not so much as pathology as outmoded methods of coping. Once these mechanisms become habitual, they can create havoc in the adult survivor's efforts to love and work. The therapeutic process helps by working through the original traumata and freeing the individual from living in a state of continual vigilance, operating as if the abuses of her childhood were still present. This is spiritual work, as the title of Shengold's book, *Soul Murder*, implies. Nothing strikes more deeply at the sacredness of life and at one's sense of spiritual health/wellness/holiness than trauma and violence. To engage in the treatment of trauma is to engage in nothing less than a priestly journey of companioning toward healing and new life.

PRIMARY AFFECTS AND SHAME

Beyond trauma theory, there is still one more area of research that may offer useful complementary insights into our understanding of normal human development and the sources and treatment of pathology. This research involves the study of human affects and emotions—with particular growing interest in the affect of shame. A closely related area known as "attachment theory" also provides useful corollary concepts to our object relations/relational-psychoanalytic theory and practice.

To begin, affect theory distinguishes between affect, feeling, and emotion,[65] and mood.[66] Michael Basch, one of the first Self psychologists following Kohut, became fascinated with the emerging field of neuropsychology and in particular with the development of emotions in the brain. According to Basch, *affect* is a narrow technical term applied only to our innate biological reactions, not yet in symbolic or verbal form, but simply as they are *experienced* in the body as autonomic response. *Feeling* takes affect one step higher in cognition, as the conscious *awareness* of affect. *Emotion* represents the highest level of cognition, constituted by the memories triggered by the feeling. "Affect is biology while emotion is biography." Emotion is the nuanced *meaning* we give to feeling. More recently, Donald Nathanson (whose primary work has been the investigation into the affect of shame) built upon this set of definitions to add one more term, *mood*.[67] Mood, according to Nathanson, is the enduring experience of some affect, usually due to biochemical factors in the brain.

According to this theory, affects are innate. While the cognitive processes involved in feeling, emotion, and mood are likely to be culturally conditioned, recent cross-cultural research has suggested that the primary affects (those affects observable in infants from birth) may be virtually universal to human experience. Silvan Tompkins[68] identified nine innate or primary affects, based on extensive studies of infants (with particular attention to facial expressions, eye contact/eye aversion, and head movements). Each of these is expressed in terms of a mild and a more intense version of the same affect (mentioned in chapter 1): interest/excitement, enjoyment/joy, surprise/startle, distress/anguish, fear/terror, anger/rage, shame/humiliation, dissmell (reaction to bad smell), and disgust. Basch has further identified boredom as a separate primary affect,[69] and Nathanson has added contentment.[70]

In addition, these researchers have identified shame as a significant negative affect.[71] Unlike guilt, in which we feel we have done something bad, shame is the feeling of *being* bad. This definition was popularized by John Bradshaw[72] especially during the 1980s. Bradshaw's well-known self-help books and television shows drew on the work of Helen Block Lewis[73] (one of the first researchers specializing in the affect of shame and, notably, the mother of trauma researcher Judith Lewis Herman), as well as Alice Miller's theories on the prevalence of toxic shame-based child-rearing practices.[74] Shame is a strong affect, and often comes on suddenly. As Nathanson describes it, "the gaze is averted; tonus in neck and shoulder muscles is reduced and head slumps; vasculature of the facial skin dilates to produce blush; whatever communication had been produced by interaffectivity is now terminated."[75]

Shame strikes at one's sense of oneself and involves a blow to our sense of self-esteem—in self psychological terms, it is the result of narcissistic injury. Tomkins stated that "shame affect is recruited any time desire outruns fulfillment. Any time we reach higher than our grasp and are disappointed, that failure, that impediment to the positive affect that had powered our reach will now trigger shame affect."[76] Frank Broucek,[77] Andrew Morrison,[78] Michael Basch, and most Self psychologists view shame as related to narcissistic wounding early in life, subsequent vulnerability, and reinjury. Lewis further nuanced the definition of shame as the affect triggered by having raised our self-esteem unrealistically or coming to believe we have attributes beyond what we really do; the blush that accompanies the affect of shame is "a signal to others that we recognized our error and wished to be accepted back into the herd."[79]

In addition to being related to a sense of basic badness, shame often involves a sense of exposure. Leon Wurmser theorized that shame is triggered by exposure of something we would have preferred left private, and we are safest being exposed when protected either by love or sexual desire.[80] In a similar interpretation, pastoral theologian Carl Schneider has written that "human beings are the creatures who need some sort of covering" (Gen. 3:7).[81] The etymological root of the word *shame* itself means "to cover." A shame response, according to Schneider, is a natural aspect of our need for privacy and for protection from judgment: "[the shame dynamic] protects human development, which is a process of emergence and unfolding."[82]

Robert Karen, whose research has focused on the study of attachment and how relational bonds early in life influence development, has further suggested three different types of shame:[83]

1. *Existential shame* arises from suddenly seeing yourself as you really are. This is like the shame arising from narcissistic injury described above. Karen suggests that to the extent self-reflection is possible, this type of shame can be a spur to growth and basis for stronger identity. On the other hand, pathological shame can result from too much vulnerability, impeding self-reflection and causing fleeting moments of negative self-awareness to be suppressed.

2. *Class shame* is the self-internalized oppression and self-blame based on racial, class, gender, or other social oppression. This is shame that is imposed chronically and repeatedly from the dominant culture, and results in the internalization of messages that one is bad because of artificially constructed labels of race, class, gender, or other social categories. Thandeka has convincingly described the psychological relationship between shame and racism in her book *Learning to Be White*.[84]

3. *Situational shame* is passing shame related to rejection, humiliation, allowing one's boundaries to be infringed, or violation of a social norm. This form of shame, according to Karen, functions to maintain the "civilizing process" but may harden into lasting social disgrace or stigma if one's situational shame feels irremedial, like a stain (e.g., Hester Prynne's "scarlet letter,"[85] or the shame of a man who ran from battle).

Nathanson has also identified two *phases* of shame. The first phase, the "cognitive phase," in which one becomes aware of feeling ashamed, may involve at least eight different themes or meanings that shame can take: (1) matters of size, shape, ability, skill (I am weak, incompetent, stupid); (2) dependence/independence (sense of helplessness); (3) competition (I am a loser); (4) sense of self (I am unique only to the extent that I am defective); (5) personal attractiveness (I am ugly or deformed;

the blush stains my features and makes me even more a target of contempt); (6) sexuality (There is something wrong with me sexually; I am undesirable); (7) issues of seeing and being seen (the urge to escape from the eyes before which we have been exposed; the wish for a hole to open up and swallow me); and (8) wishes and fears about closeness (the sense of being shorn from all humanity; a feeling that one is unlovable; the wish to be left alone forever).

The second phase, according to Nathanson, is a decision phase. In this phase, one can make a choice to adjust—in which one adjusts one's self-concept to fit whatever new information about oneself has been the source of the impediment. We can alter our self-view and take action to repair or reframe our identity. The alternative is defense. Defense can take one of four forms: (1) withdrawal (running away from the offending stimulus; becoming silent); (2) attacking oneself ("Yes, officer, of course I'll be more careful—thank you for the advice."); or (3) avoidance (turning to alcohol, drugs, or distracting the other with a source of pride; "Look at my new car! See something else besides what I can't stand to see about myself.); or (4) attacking the other (attempting to reduce shame by reducing the self-worth of the other—physical or sexual abuse, contempt, character assassination, banter, and put-downs).

Research on shame adds a helpful perspective to the assessment and treatment of pathology since shame is often involved in many of the forms of psychopathology—neurotic, psychotic, and characterological. Seeking any form of therapy can, in and of itself, be a shame-provoking experience, due both to the stigma against seeking psychological help as a sign of weakness and to the fear of exposure of one's innermost thoughts and secrets to a therapist. There is no specialized treatment for shame per se. (In cases involving chronic experiences of shame, Nathanson believes antidepressants can be helpful. Others, like Basch, have relied on the effectiveness of depth psychotherapy without medication.) What is most important is an appreciation for the pervasiveness and distress related to shame among those who come to us for help. Such an appreciation should strengthen our commitment to empathy and sensitivity in our therapeutic approach.

Pathology, Sin, and Evil: Human Beings Are Good; Human Beings Are Vulnerable

Finally, from a pastoral theological perspective, it is necessary to consider the relationship between pathology and sin and evil. The difficult paradoxical relationship between human beings' inherent goodness as created beings and our seemingly universal tendency toward alienation from God and one another is described in chapter 1. Some pastoral approaches of the late 1970s and earlier, like many secular therapeutic approaches, came to equate sin with pathology. In an effort to maintain a nonjudgmental therapeutic stance, "sin" was virtually explained away as sickness. Cure the sickness, and behaviors considered sinful would be eradicated. And yet, in the wake of such extremes of both despotic power and depravity as

seen in Adolf Hitler, Joseph Stalin, and Pol Pot, not to mention atrocities per-
petrated by both our declared enemies and our own government and its allies, a
naïvely psychologizing innocence is difficult to maintain. As Reinhold Niebuhr
was saying as early as the 1930s, it is necessary to face "the depth of evil to which
individuals and communities may sink, particularly when they try to play the role
of God to history."[86]

In 1973, Karl Menninger himself questioned this sidestep in his book *Whatever
Became of Sin?* Menninger, although a prominent psychiatrist, advocated against
losing sight of the moral nature of human behavior and the consequences of selfish-
ness and hate, "the behavior dictated by a *mens rea*, a wrong attitude, a hard heart,
a cold heart, an evil heart."[87] He called for clergy, including those he trained as
pastoral counselors in his clinic, not to abandon their prophetic role in confronting
moral failures. He advocated for traditional moral preaching as a form of preven-
tion, to be placed alongside the healing function of pastoral counseling rather than
being replaced by it: "Cry comfort, cry repentance, cry hope. Because recognition of
our part in the world['s] transgression is the only remaining hope."[88] Niebuhr, too,
in the appraisal of Arthur Schlesinger Jr.,

> emphasized the mixed and ambivalent character of human nature—creative
> impulses matched by destructive impulses, regard for others overruled by ex-
> cessive self-regard, the will to power, the individual under constant temptation
> to play God in history. This is what was known in the ancient vocabulary of
> Christianity as the doctrine of original sin. Niebuhr summed up his political
> argument in a single powerful sentence: "Man's [*sic*] capacity for justice makes
> democracy possible; but man's [*sic*] inclination to injustice makes democracy
> necessary."[89]

Much of contemporary pastoral counseling and psychotherapy continues, however, to avoid the ambiguous, difficult category of sin, for fear of losing its nonjudgmental therapeutic stance or conflating sin with pathology. But are pathology and
sin the same things? Is evil simply a by-product of neurosis, psychosis, and character
pathology? If we were able to heal everyone of their psychological wounds, would we
bring about a utopian world free of sin? My own view, after years of working with
victims of abuse and trauma, is that it is important to retain the distinction between
sin—as moral failure—and pathology, although there is a wide overlap between the
two. Illness and psychic injury can and do weaken a person's moral capacity. The
Western tradition of common law has always made room for compassionate treatment of those who are so psychologically impaired that they cannot distinguish right
from wrong—the legal definition of *insanity*. However, most pathology does not
totally eradicate a person's sense of right and wrong. We are still accountable for our
choices and our behaviors. Moreover, if sin is to be understood not simply in terms
of wrongful acts, but as the state of alienation we experience as human beings from

one another and from the divine, then sin goes beyond the therapeutic paradigm of illness or injury and cure.

A few years ago, I wrote a paper addressing the question of sin and evil in relation to the concept of splitting.[90] I began with the following question: is the Self psychological concept of the "vertical split" an adequate theoretical paradigm to account for good and evil (particularly evil) as understood in Christian theology? This exercise of "critical correlation"[91] takes us back one more time to theoretical considerations of pathology as splitting. In particular, the psychoanalytic concept here derived from Kohut's notion of the vertical split, and the theological conception being brought into dialogue with it, was the (rather enormous) conception of good and evil. To confine the latter category somewhat, I drew from my own Anglican tradition and limited this essay to a consideration of just two classic conceptions of evil and their appropriations into contemporary theology and postmodern philosophy, but clearly the dialogue could be extended much further.

KOHUT'S CONCEPT OF THE VERTICAL SPLIT

The vertical split was first introduced into self psychology by Kohut in his article "Two Analyses of Mr. Z"[92] and is conceived as a psychological mechanism of "disavowal."[93] Unlike the process of repression—in which mental contents are understood, as in Freudian theory, to be pushed downward out of consciousness into a deeper realm of the unconscious where they are entirely inaccessible to consciousness (except by analysis)—in the process of disavowal, certain aspects of oneself *are* accessible to consciousness, but they are so uncomfortable to one's own sense of self that they are normally kept out of awareness.

The difference between these two forms of splitting—repression and disavowal—are illustrated in Kohut's article (see Figure 8). The vertical split is so named because it divides consciousness into two areas, pictured on the same horizontal plane and not entirely inaccessible to each other, in contrast to the horizontal layers of the topographical model in which the deepest layer, the unconscious, is separated by a repression barrier that is normally impermeable.

The vertical split is usually identified with narcissistic pathology, and it is mainly manifested in behaviors, often compulsive acts that the person would ordinarily find completely alien. Thus, rather than splitting the personality into conscious and unconscious domains (as in classically defined neuroses), the vertical split is conceived to explain patterns of inconsistent behavior, in which different behavior patterns are governed by the two separate, different arenas of consciousness and corresponding inhibition or disinhibition. Individuals whose subjective experience resonates closely with this concept of the vertical split often describe it much in the same terms as Paul's self-description in Romans 7: "I do not understand my own actions . . . For I do not do the good I want, but the evil I do not want is what I do" (Rom. 7:15, 19).

The vertical split has its origins, according to self psychological theory, in the lack of parental provisions as reliable selfobjects, as described above. Inadequate or

THE CASE OF MR. Z - HIS PSYCHOPATHOLOGY AND THE COURSE OF HIS ANALYSIS

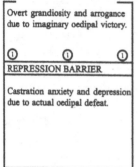

As Seen in Classical Dynamic-Structural Terms in the First Analysis

Overt grandiosity and arrogance due to imaginary oedipal victory.

①   ①   ①

REPRESSION BARRIER

Castration anxiety and depression due to actual oedipal defeat.

As Seen in Terms of the Psychology of the Self in the Narrow Sense in the Second Analysis

Overt arrogance, "superior" isolation on the basis of persisting merger with the (nondefinsively) idealized mother. Mother confirms patient's superiority over father provided patient remains an appendage of her. ① ① ① ①

Low self-esteem, depression, masochism, (defensive) idealization of mother.

②   ②   ②

REPRESSION BARRIER

(Non defensive) idealization of his father; rage against the mother; self-assertive male sexuality and exhibitionism.

VERTICAL SPLIT

The analytic work done on the basis of the classical dynamic-structural concept takes place throughout the analysis at the line indicated by ① ① ①.

The analytic work done on the basis of the self-psychological concept is carried out in two stages. The first stage is done at the line indicated by ① ① ①; Mr. Z confronts fears of losing the merger with the mother and thus losing his self as he knew it. The second stage is done at the line indicated by ② ② ②; Mr. Z confronts traumatic overstimulation and disintegration fear as he becomes conscious of the rage, assertiveness, sexuality, and exhibitionism of his independent self.

FIGURE 8. *The vertical split*

inconsistent parenting over a period of crucial early years results in weak or lacking internal psychological structure on both the mirroring and idealizing poles, resulting in narcissistic grandiosity and hypersensitivity.

With the phenomenon of the vertical split, the individual presents a "me" to the rest of the world with whom s/he can identify—typically quite successful in some arenas—but at the same time s/he is often unable to form genuine intimate bonds in relationships, and may be baffled by the reluctance of others in one's world to recognize his or her superiority. On this side of the split, the individual often finds him- or herself attempting to ward off depression and at times flying into inexplicable rages that are out of proportion to a perceived threat or criticism, but finally unable to soothe him- or herself or restore a sense of proportion and harmony. When productive activity and the release of tension through rages fails to soothe, then the individual slips over onto the other side of the split and engages in compulsive behaviors in a joyless attempt at filling the inner sense of emptiness or, in its most sociopathic form, the sense that "the world owes me" (which parallels Winnicott's "antisocial tendency"[94]). Sexual acting out, fetishes, alcohol and drug abuse, compulsive gambling, physical violence, and other behaviors destructive of self or others or both can often be understood dynamically as behavioral evidence of this vertical split borne of early narcissistic deficit or injury. The predominant affect associated with those moments in which the individual is aware of this "other side" of the vertical split is not guilt, as with neurotic behaviors, but shame: again, not "I *did* something bad," but "I *am* bad."

As an example, a prominent and respected pastor, "Pastor George" (a fictionalized composite case), used to engage in risky sexual behaviors when traveling on church business. Greatly admired for his ability to find financial resources to fund important church projects and an uncanny ability to match people with needed resources, this man had a highly developed "good" side. He enjoyed a position of considerable power and prestige in the world of his denomination. His marriage, however, was one characterized by emotional distance and subtly patronizing discourse, functioning mostly as a showcase to provide a traditional "happy marriage." When traveling, Pastor George hired prostitutes and became involved in a kind of "double life" sexually, in which he indulged masochistic fantasies he would never have wanted known publicly, nor would he ever have revealed to his wife. Pastor George was caught in this behavior when he charged a number of visits to an escort service to his church credit card. He denied that he had engaged in any behaviors the church would disapprove of so convincingly that he exuded moral outrage when accused. He felt genuinely indignant, and his wife joined him in vigorously accusing the church leaders of conspiring to hurt him out of jealousy. When the evidence came to light overwhelmingly enough that he could no longer deny it, his wife was devastated. Pastor George himself sank into a deep depression laden with intense shame, and he besieged church leaders to restore his former status and reputation as quickly as possible in a frantic effort to seal over the rupture in the wall of his disavowal and to restore his former delusion of superiority.

EVIL AS PRIVATION OF THE GOOD

How does the self psychological deficit model, which conceives psychological damage as a weakness of self-structure resulting from parental lack, correspond or correlate with Christian conceptions of good and evil? In Christianity, there have traditionally been two significantly different understandings of evil: *evil as negative* (in the sense of absence or lack) and *evil as positive* (in the sense of the presence of agency and/or ontological status)[95]—or, to use feminist theologian Kathleen Sands's terminology, *rationalistic* and *dualistic* interpretations of evil.[96]

The negative, or rationalistic, view of evil has its origins in Augustine's concept of evil as *privatio boni*, the privation of the good. For the mature Augustine, (who actually started out from an opposite, dualistic point of view, as a Manichean), evil could not be accorded an active status in the cosmos because that would elevate it to the level of divinity. As Augustine worked out his Christian theological doctrine, he came to insist upon the absolute original perfection and goodness of both God and creation. Evil, then, became, in Augustine's theology, not a countervailing force of badness but, rather, a *lack* or deficiency of good. For Augustine, evil had no place in God's original plan and was a human artifact. In the garden, Adam (we don't hear much about Eve in a positive light) was endowed with will, which was the perfect desire for God's perfect goodness and (borrowing from Plato) inexhaustible plenitude. The human creature was created to love God and with an innate capacity to apprehend the infinite. For Augustine, free will in its original, natural state meant the willing of, or desire for, the good.

For reasons Augustine could never fully explain (although he struggled with this in *De libero arbitrio* and elsewhere[97]), Adam perverted the will and invented what theologian John Milbank has termed the "fiction of choice,"[98] the illusion of self-governance in disregard for his created purpose—to love God. So after the Fall, human beings are prone to sin, which for Augustine meant the propensity to believe in the delusion of self-control and autonomous will.

After the Fall, human beings can no longer perfectly discern what is good and perfect—although we are still able to desire the good, however, now this desire is not automatic but mediated by God's reparative gift of grace. Evil in this conceptualization is not an active force but a delusory self-reliance and a deficit or lack of the originally intended capacity to desire only that which truly, that is, infinitely, exists: God and all things pertaining to God's perfection—peace, love, perfect harmony. In this way, sin means that human beings are prone to confuse lesser goods with greater goods (e.g., pertinent to the Pastor George case example above, able to choose a desperate act of risky behavior as the good of self-soothing, but at the same time to miss the destructive consequences of the same behavior to one's own and one's partner's health and security, and to tear at the fabric of community trust and accountability).

In this model, there is no positive—in the sense of active—force of evil. And unlike the ancient Greek view, the flesh was not a particular locus for evil. Both desire for the good and sin could originate in the passions of the flesh, depending largely on degree. Even something that is good—for example, the desire to procreate (as we know, a large stumbling block for Augustine!) or the desire for food—can, in excess, become idolatrous—what Augustine termed (in one piquant translation), "the birdlime of concupiscence."[99]

Evil "exists" in this model,[100] but not in an ontological sense. It exists as an absence, as a tear in the fabric of creation, or, as in the common explanation, as holes exist in Swiss cheese. Evil in the Augustinian model is emptiness, an absence or nothingness, in which the desire for good is confused with what turns out only to be an illusion, a chimera, of self-possession.

CORRESPONDENCES:
THE VERTICAL SPLIT AND EVIL AS PRIVATION

There are some ready points of correspondence between this theological conception and the psychological construct of the vertical split. Both are deficit models. That is, both conceive of the origins, or etiology, of "bad behavior" in terms of something that is missing, not something bad that is actively present (see Figure 9). In the narcissistic pathology described by the vertical split, "Me" (the aspects of my self that are congruent with my own self-perception and public identity) corresponds rather nicely with the desire for the good/God's perfection (still available since the Fall, but mediated now through grace).[101] The "Not-me" side of the vertical split (consisting of disavowed aspects of my self and behavior)—which has its origins in the lack of self-structure on poles of mirroring and idealization and the lack of early parental provisions—similarly corresponds with not an active desire to do bad things but, rather, the failure of the will to desire the good.

Me (aspects of self congruent with self-perception and public identity)	Not-me (disavowed aspect of self and behavior); lack of self-structure on poles of mirroring and idealization
Desire for the good/God's perfection (still available since the Fall, but mediated now through grace)	Failure of the will to desire the good (sin, first introduced by Adam's rebellion); evil = lack of good

FIGURE 9: *The vertical split with an Augustinian model of Good (Desire) and Evil* (Privatio Boni)

So, with the concept of the vertical split, "I do not do the good I want, but the evil I do not want is what I do" not because I am possessed by some active, external demon who is whispering naughty things to me from my left shoulder, or because my flesh has a mind of its own that does not "live up to" my lofty spiritual desires (the Platonic error), but because I am caught up in a desperate, shame-laden but disavowed effort to fill up the sense of emptiness inside me and soothe my painful feelings of fragmentation.

This never works, however, precisely because, from this point of view, evil *is* that emptiness, an absence or nothingness of which Augustine writes, in which the desire for good is confused with what turns out only to be an illusion of self-possession and "the craving for undue exaltation"[102]—in other words, narcissistic inflation!

The only remedy, then, is not more compulsive acts aimed at filling one's own internal void, because this is futile. We cannot fill ourselves up. The remedy, from the point of view of self psychology, is the process Kohut calls "transmuting internalization,"[103] whereby relationships with new selfobjects facilitate the process of structuralization. By surviving (usually over and over) the experience in this new relationship of empathic ruptures, being given an interpretation that allows "me" to see more clearly the nature and origins of my split self that caused me to be vulnerable to that empathic rupture, and, through this process, experiencing the growth or repair of the inner self-structure, the split can gradually be healed. In this way, my behavior can gradually change from shame-laden, compulsive, hidden activity driven by a need for grandiose self-inflation and self-soothing to behavior that is more integrated and genuinely relational.

In a sense, the original damage is done, but transmuting internalization functions in a way like grace—it does not replace the original goodness that was intended in creation, but it does mediate a restoration of the capacity, however imperfect, to desire the good once again. While this process of transmuting internalization may not *necessarily* require the services of an analyst, the aim of a self psychological analysis, as well as the potentially curative function of all loving relationships, is in the healing of the vertical split and the restoration of wholeness. This might be seen to correspond to the theological notion of the healing power of grace.

To the extent that Self psychologists increasingly view this conception of psychopathology as narcissistic deficit to be more or less true for everyone, this model even corresponds with the universality of the theological construct of original sin. No one gets out of childhood with a "perfect" self-structure, and so no one can escape the propensity toward self-inflation and narcissistic vulnerability of one form or another, although this may be acted out to varying degrees and may not enter into overtly destructive behaviors. In the same way, in this theological view, no one can escape the consequences of the Fall, and although some individuals will behave morally more badly than others, even the saints cannot any longer perfectly will the good without the mediating and redeeming power of God's grace.

The correspondence between the vertical split then, as a psychological construct, and the theological conception of evil as *privatio boni*, works rather neatly! And that's the problem. We have just explored a rather tidy heuristic correspondence between the deficit model in self psychology and the idea of evil as privation. But is this a sufficient model to understand evil in *all* its guises?

Evil as a Force

A second prominent strand in both Christian and post-Christian theology frames evil in a very different way—not as a negation, as a privation of the good, but as a positive (in the sense of active and ontological) force in the universe, competing directly against God's goodness and seeking to undo it.[104] Most opposite to that of Augustine, this is the *dualistic* view, which had its fullest flower in the Manichean doctrine of the patristic era and later reerupted in Catharism (the object of the Albigensian Crusade in the thirteenth century).[105] Dualism has always been labeled as heresy by the church but nevertheless is prominent in popular folk religion. Dualism sees God and the Devil as virtually equal cosmic forces competing for human souls.

For the medieval pietist, this view of an active devil as Adversary[106] was reconciled with the ultimate supremacy of God by saying that in the eschaton the Devil would finally be permanently subdued, but in this interim period of travail between the First and Second Coming of Christ, the Devil was still allowed to wreak havoc. So we have the story of Martin Luther hurling his inkwell at the Devil as he lurked in his study. Similarly, Ignatius of Loyola found it necessary to write *Rules for the Discernment of Spirits* (i.e., evil versus good spirits) to accompany his *Spiritual Exercises* because of his own experience of "the Evil Spirit," or Satan, who undermines the spiritual progress of maturing Christians through deception and seduction, resulting in spiritual desolation.[107] The idea of an active force of evil with sentience and agency is certainly biblical: "Be sober, be watchful. Your adversary the devil prowls around like a roaring lion, seeking some one to devour. Resist him, firm in your faith" (1 Pet. 5:8-9a).

A serious and scholarly contemporary conceptualization of evil as an active force has come from post-Holocaust theologians and modern and postmodern philosophers, who contend that in the wake of the mass horrors of the twentieth century, particularly the atrocities of Nazi Germany but also Stalinist Russia and the Pol Pot genocides in Cambodia, we can no longer subscribe to a view of evil as merely privation of the good. For many modern and postmodern philosophers, the category of "free will" is not a consequence of some primordial human error but, rather, intrinsic to the human condition. Paul Ricoeur's idea of "fallible man" opens the way toward viewing the capacity for sin and evil as inherent in human existence.[108] Traces appear in Ricoeur of the idea that evil is not simply a "nothing" but a "something." In his concluding sentence in the book *Fallible Man*, he states: "To say that man [*sic*] is fallible is to say that the limitation peculiar to a being who does not coincide with himself is the primordial weakness from which evil *arises*. And yet, evil arises from this weakness only because it is *posited*. This last paradox will be at the center of the symbolics of evil."[109] Elaborating further in *The Symbolism of Evil*, he states, within his framework of the "servile will:"

> Evil is not nothing; it is not a simple lack, a simple absence of order; it is the power of darkness; it is posited; in this sense it is something to be "taken away:" "I am the Lamb of God who takes away the sins of the world," says the interior Master . . . Evil comes to a [person] as the "outside" of freedom, as the other than itself in which freedom is taken captive . . . This is the schema of seduction; it signifies that evil, although it is something that is brought about, is already there, enticing . . . Evil is both something brought about now and something that is already there; to begin is to continue.[110]

Ricoeur's understanding is not strictly dualistic, however. Evil is always, for Ricoeur, subordinate to original goodness, neither symmetrical nor equal to it.[111] "However primordial badness may be, goodness is yet more primordial."[112]

Milbank locates the modern origins of dualistic interpretations of evil in the work of Immanuel Kant.[113] In a post-Kantian sense, Milbank has asserted, the capacity to will means the capacity to will *either* good *or* evil. The senses are amoral, and so tend toward self-preservation and pleasure (not unlike Freud's pleasure principle, but contrary to his idea of the death instinct). But because for Kant and the post-Kantians, there can be no access to the infinite through the senses, we are left with the dilemma of making moral choices based in the historical moment, with no recourse to such a thing as Augustine's desire for the good to guide us.

The problem of theodicy—justifying God's "allowing" evil to exist—gets resolved in this strand of thinking in one of several ways. Either God is dead, the nihilistic solution, or God has willingly limited God's own power in favor of the gift of free will (the process theology solution),[114] so that we might be made in God's own image, defined as being able to choose between good and evil for ourselves. The latter view preserves both human and divine agency while explaining how "genuine evil" is allowed to exist.[115] It has been popularized in books like Rabbi Harold Kushner's *When Bad Things Happen to Good People*,[116] and it is a view often cited in pastoral care.

The value of this positive view of evil is in its power to describe the way many people do experience evil in the contemporary world. The vast majority of survivors of trauma have not read Augustine and are unfamiliar with scholarly arguments about theodicy. They do, however, present themselves to us as legitimate experts on the experience of suffering and the sense of personal acquaintance with evil. One scholarly line of thought regarding theodicy is, in fact, that focusing on attempts to rationalize evil or justify God can serve as an intellectualizing distraction from the human reality of suffering as the proper focus for attention.[117] This may be especially true, or at least true in a distinctive way, for women's experience of evil and suffering. Nel Noddings, in her study of women and suffering, found that women experience evil as "relational and positively real."[118]

> Evil is a real presence, and moral evil is often the result of trying to do something either genuinely thought to be good or rationalized layer on layer in gross bad faith. Evil is thus intimately bound up in disputes over good . . . When we acknowledge that pain, separation, and helplessness are the basic states of consciousness associated with evil and that moral evil consists in inducing, sustaining, or failing to relieve these conditions, we can no longer ignore that we do think on and intend evil when we perform such acts. Just as disease is real and not just an illusion or absence of health, evil is real, and to control it we need to understand it and accept that the tendency toward it dwells in all of us.[119]

Noddings goes on to advocate for education as a means to understand evil, with the goal, in turn of combating mystification and informing moral action.

Sands has faulted classical, twentieth-century feminist, and postmodern theologians for not taking the existence of evil seriously enough, or for mystifying evil. She finds the distinction between a negative and a positive view of evil to be a dualism that is itself suspect.[120] Womanist theologians such as Emilie Townes, Frances Wood, and Delores Williams also point to the concreteness of the reality of the demonic as experienced in black women's suffering. They tend to locate evil not in abstraction or in "nature," but as institutionalized in the social, political, and economic realm.[121]

Peter Homans once commented that there are many forms of intelligence, including what he appreciatively termed "clinical intelligence."[122] In order to address this more active conceptualization of evil in relation to our psychological theories, we need to turn to our clinical intelligence and ask the question—what do *patients* experience? In my own clinical experience, individual's conceptualization of evil seems to depend on whether that person's perspective is one of being victimized or one of being a perpetrator (however unwittingly or disavowedly). Another way of putting this might be whether the predominant characteristics of the individual's suffering fall more into the pattern of post-traumatic symptomatology or narcissistic character pathology. The vertical split provides an excellent theoretical understanding of the problems experienced due to narcissistic injury, as already described above. But what about those patients whose injury falls more into the category of active traumatization than a deficit model of parental lack?

This is where, in my own clinical work and research, I have found the self psychological model somewhat lacking in explanatory power. I have found object relations theory, and particularly the relational-psychoanalytic school,[123] able to go further in explaining the complex intersubjective and mutual projective processes that are experienced in clinical work in general, but especially with trauma survivors.

ALTERNATIVE VIEWS OF EVIL
FROM CLINICAL EXPERIENCE

In this theory (see Figure 4 in chapter 1), the inner world is not characterized by one binary split as in the vertical split, nor is it adequately described by going back to Freud's repression model that divided consciousness into conscious and unconscious regions. The inner world, further, is filled with contradictory representations, based on the mechanism of splitting—operating out of the paranoid-schizoid position described above. External figures or events that are experienced as bad are unconsciously split off from good representations of the same figures in order to preserve those figures—especially those on whom the small child depends for survival. Both "me" and "others" are thus preserved in split-off forms. Persecutory objects may also be internalized as a survival mechanism of identifying with the oppressor. If the child is fortunate enough, there may also be alternative loving, soothing, and strengthening figures—pets, books, or even inanimate objects that carry symbolic healing power—that can be internalized as well.

In this model, behavior is not explained by the mechanism of disavowal but, rather, by *dissociation* and *fragmentation*. Persecutory inner objects and traumatic mental representations are not static inner images; they function as live introjects that can at times govern behavior. Although most trauma victims do not experience the degree of dissocation present in dissociative identity disorder (multiple personality disorder), in this model of mind all of us to varying degrees find ourselves in different affect states generated by associations between current circumstances and past state-dependent learnings and experiences. Because of the psychic necessity of splitting in an unconscious attempt to preserve the integrity of good objects, badness is projected "out there" onto other people and also "into" them through "projective identification" until new unconscious relationships are set in motion between people in an intersubjective co-construction of realities that, especially to the degree trauma has existed in the past, tend to reenact unhealed painful experiences. In this way, victims sometimes also become perpetrators of new evil, and the cycle continues.

In terms of religious faith, internalized representations of God also grow from these early inner objects, as Ana-Maria Rizzuto[124] and others have demonstrated. Theologian Jane Grovijahn, in her study of sexual abuse survivors' narratives, has identified ways in which the inner God imago may also be split by the traumatic experience into one or more versions of "Good God," "God gone wrong," and "No-God."[125] I would add to this the further splitting off, frequently, of an inner representation or figure opposing God as "Evil" or "the Devil," and some survivors have a rather large inner population of both avenging angels or helpers, *and* demonic figures that are fantasized or even actively experienced as something supernatural, or in some other realm beyond human form.

In this model, then, psychopathology is a result of *trauma*, not *deficit*. Suffering is a result not of emptiness and lack, but the insertion of active, persecutory "objects" into the child's inner landscape, and the splitting of good and bad aspects of others that cannot be held together and psychically survive. This model of personality *is* peopled, not structured, and pathology results not from insufficient structure or structural defects but from the felt *presence* of something, someone, or someones "bad" inside. The subjective experience of patients for whom this model holds the greatest explanatory power are those who report not only emptiness, although they do frequently describe something like a "hole" deep inside, but also suffering from continual, undifferentiated psychic *pain*, as described so poignantly by British analyst Betty Joseph.[126]

In this psychological model of trauma, it is hard to account for evil only as *privatio boni*—although a case could still be made, as Milbank does, that terrible, even catastrophic, things can be done as a result of absence of the good—and especially as a result of mistaking a lesser good for a greater one, a chilling explanation for how "good people" can be swept up in doing horrible things. The psychic experience of trauma survivors, however, calls forth depictions of demonic forces locked in battle with avenging angels, devils lurking on the rooftops of cathedrals, and so-called normal reality being more suspect and ephemeral than the certain knowledge of terror. Ask a trauma survivor about evil, and you will not likely get an abstract answer about privation of the good. Trauma survivors, especially if their trauma was one of human design and not a natural disaster, will say that they have seen evil, and they can give it a name and a face.

For many other trauma victims, internal representations of evil are not conscious and disavowed, but split off in the unconscious. Evil is located not in a known, though unwanted, part of the self, but most often, at least until healing integration begins to take place, located as in the unconscious, and experienced, through projection, as "out there" in another, whether this is an intimate partner, a publicly identified villain, or an entire nation labeled as "enemy." This model also has its claims to universality, since none of us not only do not leave our childhood with perfect self-structures, but most of us do not come through it unscathed. There have been numerous convincing arguments that much conflict at the level of groups and even nations is a result of our collective, mutually constructed reality based on splitting and projection of evil always somewhere outside ourselves.

THE AMBIGUITIES OF EVIL

So to return to the question: is the self psychological concept of the vertical split an adequate theoretical paradigm to account for good and evil (particularly evil) as understood in Christian theology? In good Anglican fashion, I think the answer to the question is "yes and no."

Yes—the vertical split offers a way of empathically understanding those whose suffering falls most prominently under the category of narcissistic pathology. From the narcissistically damaged individual's point of view, evil is most often experienced as an alien part of one's self-identity and character, corresponding well with the vertical split. Early experiences are predominantly of deficit and lack, specifically of appropriate mirroring and provision of reliable selfobjects for idealization. The process of removing contents from ordinary awareness is a conscious process of disavowal. Evil is experienced as lack, and one's own self-defeating behavior is experienced as both unintended and unwanted, or as necessary recompense. The classical theological doctrine of evil as privation of the good fits well with this psychological model, and the pain experienced by such individuals is the *pain of compulsion.*

But the answer is also no; the concept of the vertical split, in my view, is not sufficient to explain all conceptions of evil—with two objections. First, in the *experience of trauma victims,* and second, in the larger sense of *corporate, systemic evil.*

In the subjective experience of traumatized persons, evil is most often described as a malevolent attribute of someone else's identity and character, based on early experiences of injury and later life experiences born of projection of inner persecutory objects outward where they are then battled or feared. Early experiences are not predominantly of deficit and lack but of active trauma. The process of removing contents from ordinary awareness is an unconscious process of splitting and dissociation. Evil is experienced as "out there," and one's own self-defeating behaviors are understood, if at all, as righteous attacks on evil that is inflicted by others. The classical theological doctrine of evil as privation of the good fits less well with this psychological model, and it competes with views of evil as an active cosmic force battling the good. The pain experienced by these individuals is the pain of *expulsion* and the resulting experience of terror of what is out there—repeated, baffling experiences of intense attachment and rejection in relationships, internal fragmentation, and constant, undifferentiated psychic pain.

This is not a gender-neutral conclusion. While certainly both men and women experience trauma, the disproportionate number of women survivors of sexual abuse and assault in our culture may suggest that clinically, object-relational and intersubjective psychoanalytic theories—which can accommodate this experiential understanding of evil as something positive (i.e., active) within a framework of multiplicity—may be especially relevant to women's experience. The Augustinian notion of sin as pride or inordinate self-reliance (which I have correlated above with the self psychological understanding of narcissism) has been further challenged by feminist theologians as inappropriate when applied to women and other marginalized groups within patriarchal society. In the words of Elizabeth Johnson:

> If pride be the primary block on the path to God, then indeed decentering the rapacious self is the work of grace. But the situation is quite different when this language is applied to persons already relegated to the margins of significance and excluded from the exercise of self-definition. For such persons, language of conversion as loss of self, turning from *amor sui*, functions in an ideological way to rob them of power, maintaining them in a subordinate position to the benefit of those who rule . . . Analysis of women's experience is replete with the realization that within patriarchal systems women's primordial temptation is not to pride and self-assertion but rather to the lack of it.[127]

And what about corporate and long-term consequences flowing beyond individuals? Feminist and Womanist approaches to the subject of evil have tended to deemphasize classical arguments about the abstract nature of evil and individual sin and atonement, and to focus much more on what Noddings calls "cultural evil." Noddings highlights women's experience of suffering and participating in evil through complicity with the cultural conditions of poverty, racism, war, and sexism.[128] Womanist theologians especially have highlighted the systemic, institutionalized aspects of evil, as noted above.[129] Delores Williams redefines individual sin as participation in the larger social systems that devalue black women's humanity through a process of devaluation and "invisibilization."[130]

Neither psychoanalytic model described above has actually paid adequate attention to the larger systemic, cultural, and social forces that are implicated in human cruelty and human suffering. But at least one reason, and perhaps the most profound reason, that evil *is* evil is that it not only destroys individuals intrapsychically, but it tears at the fabric of human relationship and confounds the human capacity for community. In the words of David Tracy and Hermann Haring, "Evil has no center, but is everywhere. It does not send out its raiding parties, but spreads like moods and rampant growths."[131] The image here is not one of either of sheer nothingness nor of purposeful malevolent planning, but of *metastasis*. (The rejection of the image of "raiding parties" may be more debatable after September 11. However, in the larger sense, the image of metastasis still works: there is no precise beginning or end to contemporary terrorism, and there are no precise boundaries. Local, temporal acts are subsumed under larger movements and countermovements and cycles of retaliation across many centuries and continents.)

While few psychoanalytic theorists have yet adequately addressed this larger systemic and social dimension, (although there are a few exceptions, from both self psychology and object relations points of view), my sense is that an appreciation of the dynamics of projection not only by individuals but entire groups, and further application of theories of intersubjectivity, alterity, and social constructivism, may yield important understandings of the systemic dimension of evil than the vertical split, or indeed *any* theoretical conceptualization of intrapsychic pain, can do by itself, without the application of a wider social, political, and cultural lens.

CLINICAL IMPLICATIONS AND TRAGIC HOPE

What are the implications for clinical practice? From a Christian theological perspective, we probably cannot hope for a total eradication of evil this side of the eschaton. Final reconciliation of all beings is God's task and on God's time line, not ours. Nor will we ever, I think, entirely resolve the mystery of evil from an abstract theological perspective: if we take an eschatological perspective, the very question of theodicy, in the words of Todd Billings, "remains open and anomalous *rather* than answered and (hence) forgotten."[132] Such overpreoccupation with abstract questions of theodicy can undermine our very efforts to get about the business of addressing the *results* of evil and the suffering of the world.

My own theological leaning is finally toward the Augustinian view—not because I am necessarily convinced by any argumentation inherent in the doctrine itself, but because it makes the most sense from a *psychoanalytic* framework: All splitting, including a dualistic construct of good and evil, belongs to Klein's paranoid-schizoid worldview. Evil cannot finally be split off from human affairs, not our own, not anyone's. The depressive position acknowledges the tragic and poignant reality that all seeming opposites, including good and evil (mother, breast, father, me) are finally held together. When splitting begins to be healed and projections are withdrawn and reincorporated into the conscious life, to whatever extent that is fleetingly possible, evil can be understood as a tear in the very fabric of the good itself, and not apart from it. Especially in the form of the confusion of lesser for greater goods,[133] this integrated view of evil is a convincing and tragic explanation for the complexity of human life—including political life.

This view of the complexity of the moral life incorporates what feminist theologian Wendy Farley has identified as the classical tragic components to human suffering: finitude, conflict, and fragility.[134] This is not to abandon responsibility—on the contrary, to quote another feminist theologian, Kristine Rankka: "What a tragic view of reality and suffering might do, for example, is move one from self-blame or from the projection of responsibility to change things outside oneself to a more mature realization of one's own appropriate responsibility within a context of limitation and finitude."[135] The depressive position relinquishes, albeit with sadness, the possibility of perfection and acknowledges the seeming inextricability of evil from the very fabric of the good and the ever-present reality of suffering, at least from this side of the eschaton.

But our work is not, finally, abstract argumentation about the nature of good and evil, but compassionate solidarity with the suffering and concrete acts of healing. To quote Jürgen Moltmann again, "the question of theodicy is not a speculative question; it is a critical one . . . [the question] is the open wound of life in his world."[136]

However we decide abstractly to frame the existence of evil, healing is possible, and improvement in individuals' capacity to relate lovingly and productively is not unrealistic—if we do not confuse the mutual and intersubjective work of healing with a judgmental stance of trying to correct or perfect others who are in our care. Our work as clinicians is to facilitate the healing of splitting, whether the narcissistic splitting of emptiness; compulsive behavior and disavowal; or the post-traumatic splitting of projection, terror, and fragmentation—or our own countertransferential splitting in the form of trying to remove the speck from our patient's eye while ignoring the log in our own (Matt. 7:3). This work of therapy is not amoral or insensible of the reality of sin and evil in the world. On the contrary, because we could not begin to do therapy without believing in the hope of transformation, our work does contribute to the very mending of creation itself (*tikkun olam* in Jewish mystical tradition). By so doing, we can participate positively in the good—if not the "perfect," then at least the "good enough."[137] And for this human lifetime, that, perhaps, will be sufficient.

PART 2

Practicing Pastoral Psychotherapy

Chapter 4

The Therapeutic Process: Overview and Getting Started

Great is this power of memory, exceedingly great, O my God—a large and boundless inner hall! Who has plumbed the depths of it? Yet it is a power of my mind, and it belongs to my nature. But I do not myself grasp all that I am. Thus the mind is far too narrow to contain itself. But where can that part of it be which it does not contain? Is it outside and not in itself? How can it be, then, that the mind cannot grasp itself? A great marvel rises in me; astonishment seizes me. Men go forth to marvel at the heights of mountains and the huge waves of the sea, the broad flow of the rivers, the vastness of the ocean, the orbits of the stars, and yet they neglect to marvel at themselves.

—Augustine, *Confessions* 10.8.15[1]

Goals of Therapy and Overview of the Therapeutic Process

While psychotherapy as such did not exist prior to the nineteenth century, human beings have always sought wise companionship to help them strengthen relationships and to heal from emotional and spiritual distress. The "cure of souls" (*cura animarum*) and the "cure" or "care" of psyches belong to a long tradition, branches of which include (in Western culture) pastoral care, pastoral counseling, psychotherapy, and spiritual direction. *Pastoral psychotherapy* is defined in the introduction to this book as a mode of healing intervention that is specifically grounded in psychoanalytic theory and methods—that is, with a primary focus on *unconscious* mental and emotional processes—and held in a constructive, creation-affirming theology.

Its purpose is to help, accompany, and support others in recognizing and healing long-standing psychic wounds and/or patterns of self-defeating relationships to self and others. The psychological aspect of this definition does not differ significantly from a classic description given (in the medical language of the period in which she was writing) by Frieda Fromm-Reichmann in 1960:

> The goal of intensive psychotherapy . . . as I see it and as it is viewed by [my teachers] . . . is understood to be: alleviation of patients' emotional difficulties in living and elimination of the symptomatology, this goal to be reached by gaining insight into and understanding of the unconscious roots of patients'

problems, the genetics and dynamics, on the part of both patient and [psycho-analytic therapist[2]], whereby such understanding and insight may frequently promote changes in the dynamic structure of the patient's personality.[3]

What is added in pastoral psychotherapy is, of course, the ongoing process of theological as well as psychological reflection, and the conviction that healing is a sacred process desired and supported by God/the Holy, with a further ideal of free-ing and empowering persons to live out their unique giftedness and vocation from God as fully as possible. The main elements of the psychotherapeutic process, how-ever, and the methods involved remain largely the same. There is the initial phase, in which the patient and therapist explore the patient's hopes and fears for the therapy, begin to understand the contours of the patient's distress (pastoral/therapeutic as-sessment), and establish an initial sense of mutual trust and rapport. This initial phase begins in some sense in the patient's fantasy before the first phone call to schedule an appointment, and it blends gradually into the next phase until there is a shared sense that the therapy has "quickened."

Often the patient has unconsciously or consciously tested the therapist's reli-ability and safety in one or more ways and comes to at least a preliminary sense that there will be sufficient safe "holding" for the patient's deeper pains and anxieties. There is often also, at another unconscious level, a sense that there is some kind of unconscious match, in which the therapist's own psychological makeup—neuroses, character vulnerabilities, and all—will be a fertile enough ground for the necessary projective processes to take place in the transference in order for healing and change to occur. *Transference* is Sigmund Freud's term for the patient's projections, or trans-ferring, of experiences of parents and other authority figures from childhood onto the person of the therapist (or helping professional or authority figure). The thera-pist is also testing his or her own reactions and "gut" responses (countertransference) at this early stage, making sure that the coming psychic demands will be tolerable and that there is an early sense that the work to come will be genuinely fruitful. This is the early period in which the first diagnostic, psychodynamic formulations begin to emerge, although assessment does not end here but will continue (as discussed in the previous chapter), in collaboration with the patient, throughout the life of the treatment.

At this point, often about a month after the first session, but sometimes sooner and sometimes much later, a decision is reached by one or both partners to continue or discontinue the therapy. If the therapy is to be discontinued, this usually occurs very early in the process, after a session or two.[4] The patient either consciously or unconsciously recognizes that there is not a good match, or the process of therapy itself is emotionally too threatening for the patient to tolerate. The patient either notifies the therapist formally of the wish to discontinue or simply does not return. Occasionally such an early impasse can be repaired, launching an early investment into the real work of therapy itself.

It is important to respect a patient's sense of timing. Sometimes there may be a desire for change, but the circumstances of a person's life are too stressful to accommodate the additional stresses involved in deep self-exploration. The work of bringing the unconscious to consciousness is sometimes painful and frightening. Often there is an inner gatekeeper that knows when the conditions, both internal and external, are safe enough to engage in intensive work of self-discernment. If a patient announces a decision to terminate after one or a few sessions, it is important to convey an interest and openness to what this decision means to the patient, just as any other occurrence in the therapy, and to acknowledge truthfully whatever the therapist may have contributed wittingly or unwittingly to the patient's discomfort. Sometimes this exploration in itself may turn the decision around, and the patient will again feel safe enough to continue. If the patient remains determined to stop the therapy, barring unusual circumstances, the therapist should communicate that the door is open should the patient wish to return at a later date.

Once a decision to continue is firmly made, either explicitly (therapist and patient formally contract or agree that they want to work together) or implicitly (the therapy simply continues, and more hidden issues begin to surface), the long middle phase of therapy, called "working through," has begun. Both patient and therapist now commit themselves fully to the vicissitudes of the therapeutic process, to the realization of the challenges that are to come, and above all, to keeping their relationship with one another. Because human beings are multiple, mutable, and continually in process, the therapy will be guided by an appreciation and an intentional listening for all the many different parts of the patient, and of oneself, as they emerge in the intersubjective therapeutic relationship and as realizations and meanings continue to unfold and change through thoughtful exploration and reflection over time.

This middle phase includes a number of aspects of therapeutic work (to be described in more detail in the next chapter)—all of which involve mutual "interpretation" or exploration of the transference-countertransference dynamic and other manifestations of the patient's inner life—including dreams, fantasies, and memories; moments of impasse and resolution stemming from anxieties or "resistances" the patient may have to recognizing certain unconscious issues, feelings, or dynamics; nonverbal enactments and unconscious testing of boundaries and the therapist's safety and reliability; and the patient's growing sense of self-knowledge, self-containment, and acceptance of self and others, both in the therapy and in life in general.

The final stage of therapy, classically thought to last about six months but often abbreviated because of the pressures and changeability of contemporary life, is the "resolution," or "termination phase," in which the main issues uncovered and worked through in the middle phase of therapy are revisited. This revisiting usually occurs both consciously, through an intentional verbal review of all that has happened, and also unconsciously, through mini reenactments of some of the challenges and achievements of the therapeutic process that went before. If the working through is complete enough, the final session should occur with some formal leavetaking and mutual well-wishing. It is no longer thought necessary, however, that the door be closed to resuming therapy in the future if new issues (or new circumstances bringing new meanings to old problems) arise. This open-door policy was actually Freud's own recommendation,[5] and the rigid severing of all relationship was a later adaptation by classical "Freudians" who were more strict than Freud himself. Given the mobility of many people in North America, it is more likely in many cases that therapy will be ended by the patient's (or occasionally the therapist's) moving away rather than a fully resolved termination.

It is generally understood today (in contrast to the beliefs of earlier classical analysts) that there is no such thing as a "complete" therapy. The goal is a "good enough"[6] therapy, in which a good portion of the patient's unconscious issues and painful dynamics have been consciously faced, and the patient is able to use both the content of what has been brought to light and the process of therapeutic exploration itself. It is this internalization of the analytic *process*, more than anything, that is the sign of a fruitful therapy, a *habitus* of inner work and ongoing self-exploration that serves ongoing living—in Freud's words, to be able to "love and work"[7]—in a manner that is relatively unconflicted, free, and generative. In pastoral terms, moreover, a *pastoral* psychotherapy has met its goals if it has freed the patient "to do justice, to love kindness, and to walk humbly with his or her God" (Mic. 6:6-8)—or in more religiously pluralistic terms, being freed to live out his or her core values of purpose and meaning,[8] whatever his or her religious orientation might be.

The Initial Phase:
Committing to the Therapeutic Relationship

I dream that I am seeing a new patient in a clinic where I am a new therapist, although, strangely (but as in my waking life), I am also preparing to leave due to a professional move to another state far away. The patient, a young woman, offers me a choice of three gifts: a china horse, a cream pitcher, or a smaller horse. I choose the small horse but then say the horses want to stay together.

Our therapy patients bring us gifts that are tender, fragile, and sacred. The patient in the dream offers cream, an image of maternal richness and comfort, and horses, symbols of animal strength and energy. All are made of china—earthy (pottery) symbols, but in a delicate, fragile packaging. My associations are multilayered. The patient reminds me of a particular lovely, fragile young patient who is Chinese American. The china reminds me of her in a play on words that is not uncommon in the translation of verbal puns and symbols into nonverbal dream images—the "earthen vessels" of scripture as metaphors for the human being molded by God— but the delicacy of the china also reminds me of my mother's English bone china, which is transparent and pale, with a finely polished overglaze. All these elements were alive in the transference-countertransference dynamic with this patient, in which I identified variously as both mother and daughter, and in the internal relationship among my own inner objects at that moment in time.

We come new to each encounter with every patient, even when therapy has been lengthy or when termination is imminent. Both therapist and patient are always new, as each encounter in the realm of unconscious relationship is new.

I dream that I am sitting with an adolescent male patient. We are working together on some academic problem. I feel great tenderness toward him and touch his cheek with the palm of my hand. He leans forward, and our foreheads touch in a moment of great intimacy.

This dream patient is young. We are both thinkers. He is a younger version of my studious, self-critical self. We "put our heads together," but this "meeting of minds" is also a touch of great intimacy. In my compassion for the patient in the dream, I am able to touch and give care and compassion to my younger self that continues to live inside me.

These two dreams illustrate how the process of psychotherapy works deeply in the interior life of the therapist at least as much as the patient. In the intersubjective relationship between patient and therapist, a world is created in which new meanings can flow back and forth, drawing energy from the great fund of images, dreams, memories, thoughts, and feelings of both participants. What characterizes this process as therapy—in contrast to any other deeply intimate relationship—is that the center of attention is always on the patient. Both therapist and patient engage in a process that is mutually influential, but the focus is always on the patient's hopes for change, fears, and resistances to change (which are really security operations), and deepening explorations of the patient's growing understandings and sense of purpose for his or her life.

Bea's First Sessions

Bea (who was first described in the introduction to this book) lived with her mother, who spoke mostly Korean, and her four-and-a-half-year-old son, Sam. Her husband, Donny, had battered Bea physically twice, once when she was pregnant and once soon after the baby was born. Motivated by loneliness and longing for affection, Bea had had an affair early in the marriage, which Donny insisted must be "paid back." No physical violence had occurred toward Bea since the second incident, at which time Bea had Donny arrested, but Donny continued a daily pattern of grinding verbal abuse.

Bea initially called in crisis, in confusion and ambivalence about her inability to break off the relationship with Donny, although a divorce was already pending. She reported that Donny said he "did not want to be a parent to Sam," and that he thought Bea was too soft on Sam. Bea reported that Donny would spank Sam "too hard." It came out in only our second session that there was one recent episode in which Donny hit Sam on the face. I supported Bea in making a phone report to children's protective services during that therapy session—an action that came to have multiple significances for our therapeutic relationship: Would I waffle (as Bea felt she herself had done)? Side with Donny and condone his behavior (as his mother had done)? Condemn either him or Bea or both (as her mother had done)? Ignore the situation or abandon Bea (as her father had done)? Reject or abandon Sam (tapping Bea's own deeper history of neglect and abuse that would come out much later in the therapy)? I had passed a test. This shared enactment, which was tense and dramatic for both of us coming so early in the treatment, set the tone of safety, containment, and trust for the rest of the therapy.

As Bea's first two sessions illustrate, testing may occur throughout the therapy, particularly when new and tender material is bubbling to the surface, but the initial phase of psychotherapy can be particularly characterized by a testing of the therapist until a foundation of safety and reliability is established. Early stages of therapy often resemble supportive, and cognitive problem-oriented, counseling in the service of building rapport and helping the patient deal constructively with the immediate crises that may have precipitated her/his asking for help. Freud himself recommended such flexibility: "One can hardly master a phobia if one waits till the patient lets the analysis influence him to give it up . . . One succeeds only when one can induce [patients with agoraphobia] . . . to go into the street and to struggle with their anxiety while they make the attempt."[9]

Intensive psychotherapy, however, seeks to move beyond educative and supportive interventions. The therapist accompanies the patient on a journey toward the very particular wholeness and creativity that his or her innermost potential already knows—which, from a pastoral faith perspective, we might assert is God-given. "Insight" is not merely a matter of thinking more about oneself. True *insight* is intimate, feeling knowledge of the interior, a shifting of the powers of the unconscious into consciousness.

Such lasting insight and emotional transformation can best be achieved by "working in the transference," that is, focusing the primary attention of both partners on what unconscious dynamics are being played out in the intersubjective space between the patient and the therapist. Thus, awareness does not come second-hand, through "objective" speculation about why things happen or have happened to the patient. Instead, awareness comes holistically through the actual experience of relationship, in the immediate, here-and-now, embodied moment, attending to multiple registers of intellect, emotion, behavior, and bodily feeling. Only such an attentive, multifaceted, in-the-moment approach is adequate to the task of helping to heal the splits in a wounded psyche. The results of such therapy are described best in terms of *meaning* than *cure*. Existential therapist James Bugenthal has written:

> The person who explores life concerns in this fashion and utilizes the awareness
> that the search process yields, will emerge with a changed and enlarged sense

of identity and power. Take note that this postulate does not say, "all problems solved," "living more happily," "more friends," "greater success in work," "sexually a better lover," "able to influence people readily," or any other such desired and desirable outcomes, although most all of these are sought, consciously or not, by a lot of people who begin therapy. Intensive psychotherapy . . . *is not a problem-solving technique.* Not infrequently, the client at the end of several years of hard, costly, demanding work will recognize, "I still have the same hang-up I had when I came, but somehow it seems different now, smaller, less threatening. It's like it's remained the same, but I've grown much larger, so it doesn't seem so important or bothersome any more."[10]

This is not to say that problems are *not* solved in the course of therapy. The focus, however, is on the *person*, not just the immediate or presenting *problem*. Psychotherapy is a dialectical process in which seemingly irreconcilable parts can come to be held together to create a greater, richer harmonious diversity of self. C. G. Jung drew on the medieval art of alchemy as a metaphor for this transformative process of therapy.[11] In a hermetically sealed *vas*, or container, as described above, the king and the queen (therapist and patient) merge naked (without pretense) in the bath (immersion in suffering). In the flow of unconscious relationship, there is an experience of death and departure of the soul (old coping mechanisms, cognitive beliefs, and meanings of the ego that has held it all together). In the stage of *purificatio*, unhealth begins to be washed away. New meanings and symbols emerge, generating wholeness, a new birth. This alchemical marriage, the *coniunctio*, takes place in the symbol-rich realm of unconscious relationship, where distortions are perceived and unmasked, and a common human ground of suffering provides the rich soil for new life to grow.

Although there are technical aspects to the work—active listening skills, free-floating attention, recognizing and understanding transference-countertransference dynamics and enactments, management of the time and flow of sessions, crisis intervention skills, and so forth—the foundation of depth psychotherapy is not a matter of technique per se but, rather, an understanding and openness to *unconscious relationship*, and the multiplicity of both partners, as various inner parts of each person—but especially the patient—come to be known and to express themselves in the safety of the therapeutic "container."[12] In the flow of transference and countertransference, in the movement of projective identification, communication is opened at a deeper level than normal social discourse, and therapist and patient are able to touch a level that is better understood in symbols and feelings. There is *com*passion, deep feeling-with, that is healing and insight-bearing.

All psychodynamic work is indebted to Freud's basic belief that insight brings healing. The task of the depth therapeutic process is bringing the unconscious to consciousness. As I have told patients from time to time: "When you remember your childhood and allow yourself to know what you haven't known about the pain, *then* you will find that you can allow yourself to know what you need to know about the pain *now*. And when that happens, you will have the pain. The pain will no longer 'have' you. You will have freedom to decide what you want do to when you are feeling pain, rather than letting the pain automatically dictate what you do."

How is this work actually done? There are two kinds of answer to this question. The first involves the actual techniques that a therapist must learn and practice with increasing sensitivity and skill. The second involves a therapeutic philosophy or attitude, which goes beyond specific techniques to an overarching commitment to the quality of the therapeutic relationship itself. This attitude is one of openness—a therapeutic willingness to be confused for a while, to not-know—and the courage to allow room for chaos, which is often a necessary precursor to change.[13] This and the following chapter address therapeutic skills, techniques, and processes in more detail. In the conclusion, I will return to the question of a therapeutic philosophy: embracing chaos, silence, and the paradoxical dynamic of therapeutic love.

Human Beings Are Both Good and Vulnerable: Preconditions for Fruitful Therapeutic Work, and Providing a Safe Container

As described in chapter 1, *human beings are both good and vulnerable*. This complexity requires certain preconditions in order for a genuine therapeutic rapport to be established: unwavering respect for the patient as a human being, which transcends any particular frustrations or judgments that may arise from moment to moment; humility and a commitment to continuing to probe one's own inner dynamics, resistances, and blind spots; and the provision of a safe container for the therapy to proceed.

THE THERAPIST'S RELIABILITY

The therapist's reliability—devotion to empathic listening—is the foundation of trust upon which all fruitful therapy is built. Fromm-Reichmann once wrote, "What, then, are the basic requirements as to the personality and the professional abilities of a [therapist]? If I were asked to answer this question in one sentence, I would reply, *'The psychotherapist must be able to listen.'*"[14]

Some of the most fundamental ways in which safety is conveyed are through reliability and care in more concrete ways: maintaining confidentiality; consistent scheduling and billing practices; refraining from dividing one's attention by eating, note-taking,[15] or answering phone calls except in a true emergency; and refraining from enactments that begin to convey a social rather than professional relationship.[16] There are other ways in which the therapist conveys safety and reliability that are less quantifiable but no less crucial. They have to do with the therapist's overall attitude toward the patient and, at the deepest level, the therapist's own

sense of personal security—that is, not needing to seek unconscious personal fulfillment from patients.

Beyond the obvious prohibitions against exploiting patients sexually or finan-
cially, some guidelines for therapists set out by Fromm-Reichmann are still relevant
today:[17] Be self-aware enough to catch when we begin to fall into over-identification,
or envy, or voyeuristic satisfaction. Do not depend on any one client for income (thus
attempting to prolong a therapy for our own needs regardless of the patient's goals).
Do not indulge sexual fantasies about the patient; do not use patients to make up
for personal loneliness; and "be thrifty with the expression of any physical contact"
(more will be said specifically about touch below). Do not try to impress patients or
pump up our feelings of insecurity with "professional pompousness." While some
idealization of the therapist may be a necessary part of the therapeutic dynamic in
respect for the patient's selfobject needs,[18] do not overtly cultivate dependency and
admiration.

Bear in mind that a patient's progress is not a measure of our own worth or success; don't push a patient in some particular direction, following our own agenda or
timetable for "progress;" admit mistakes and limitations. Do not make false pretenses
about understanding what you don't; remember that displays of hostility generally
mask anxiety. Nurturing our own personal sense of security and sources of satisfaction outside our professional life and being open to our own feelings, fantasies, and
motives (whether we like them or not) are therefore the first and best safeguards of
the therapeutic process.

Confidentiality—and the ethical limits of confidentiality—is a particularly crucial matter that should be communicated in the first session. In every professional
therapeutic code of ethics, it is made clear that the patient's communications will
never be divulged without his or her written permission except as mandated by law,
with the one standard legally required exception involving imminent physical harm
to self or others.[19] The other professional exception to this rule is the sharing of case
material for purposes of supervision, in which case the patient's name is not revealed
and identifying details are disguised. Anonymity and disguise are similarly required
in professional case writing.[20] Even the most basic fact, that one is seeing a particular
person as a patient, should not be disclosed to anyone without written permission.
Even with the patient's permission, or upon his or her explicit request, the therapist
should be reluctant to disclose information about the patient outside the therapy
because part of the patient may have reason to want this but other parts may have
very different and much more negative reactions. What happens in the therapeutic
process belongs to the patient and should never be exposed to others, even with good
intentions, except in extreme necessity. This is one of the first ways in which the
container of the therapy will be safeguarded—in Jung's words, the therapeutic *vas*
remains hermetically sealed so that the alchemical reactions within it may become
fully active.

ADDRESSING PATIENTS' EXPECTATIONS

Time may also be needed in initial sessions to talk with the patient, even if s/he has been in therapy before, about the patient's expectations of therapy and the therapeutic process. The initial strangeness of the therapeutic dialogue often requires some explicit orientation.[21] Patients sometimes need some explanation for the absence of frank advice by the therapist, and the shedding of conventional social conversation in favor of more introspective discourse and sustained focus on the feelings emerging within and about the relationship itself. It is useful to know whether the patient ever had therapy before and how s/he perceived it. This not only will provide information about the issues s/he is dealing with but may offer some preliminary clues to how the transference-countertransference dynamic might unfold. Strong positive or negative transferences to a former therapist may need to be worked through explicitly, especially if there was a high degree of dependency and idealization or if there was exploitation or abuse. If the previous therapy was terminated by the therapist for any reason, issues of separation, loss, abandonment, even rage may need to be processed.

It is helpful to let the patient know early on that sometimes strong feelings will arise in the therapy, including feelings toward the therapist, and that you are not only willing but wanting to explore what those feelings might mean. The patient should be assured that s/he should not hesitate to bring them up, even if it doesn't feel polite to do so. One of the primary differences between therapy and ordinary social conversation is that what is happening in the here-and-now is a primary focus of exploration, and that all feelings are valid and allowed (although not all behaviors). Depending on the patient, particularly if there is a history of violence, it may be necessary to set some ground rules. A therapist I once knew, who worked with many seriously traumatized and sometimes volatile individuals, said, "There are only three basic rules here: (1) You can talk about anything. (2) You can't hurt me or trash anything in my office. And (3) we will not ever have sex or see each other outside of therapy." Not every patient and not every therapist would be comfortable with such a blunt pronouncement, but some version of ground rules and preparation of the patient for what is to come in terms of process creates a baseline that can be referred back to later in the therapy if things become more affectively intense. Making sure that the patient has consulted a primary-care physician to rule out physical causes for his or her complaint is also an important aspect of initial care that signals concern for the patient's overall well-being and safety.

Some therapists also recommend addressing patients' safety needs explicitly by asking them if they are feeling comfortable and encouraging them to voice ways in which the therapeutic environment might feel safer to them: "just as addressing breaches in the therapeutic alliance strengthens that alliance, negotiating about safety creates a safer atmosphere."[22] (Whether or not a patient's demands can be fully met, such a discussion in and of itself conveys to the patient that his or her safety is valued, and it also may provide preliminary clues for ways in which s/he felt unsafe as a child.)

BOUNDARIES AND THE THERAPEUTIC CONTAINER

Maintaining a strong container is fundamental, underlying all other transference work. Injuries from early childhood always involve some disruption of the developing child's sense of self, where she ends and the other begins. The therapist must therefore convey a strong sense of boundaries in order for the patient to feel safely "held" in the therapeutic process. This is akin to the secure holding provided by a "good-enough" parent for a small child, as described by D. W. Winnicott,[23] the British pediatrician and Kleinian analyst in the first generation after Freud. Thus, the therapeutic environment is akin to a healthy "facilitating environment"[24] for a child's growth, which allows space for creativity and spontaneity while maintaining rules and limits necessary for health and safety. As the patient learns that it is safe to engage in introspection in the presence of the therapist, his or her own inner sense of identity and agency is also strengthened—just as Winnicott observed how in healthy identity development an infant must first experience "being alone in the presence of the mother."[25]

At the most primal unconscious level, following Winnicott, the therapist must survive the patient's efforts to "destroy" him or her (i.e., the fantasied projection of the therapist that is being enacted), sometimes repeatedly, without either retaliating or abandoning the patient.[26] A careful attention to professional boundaries will create the safety that potentiates this inner, more threatening, and largely symbolic cycle of raising up and then destroying unconscious projections from early childhood.

By providing a strong and consistent framework for the therapy, the therapist is saying to the patient, in effect, "You are safe here, and I am strong enough to contain you." This is accomplished in a number of ways, for example: regular scheduling, a consistent length of time (whether a forty-five-, fifty-, or sixty-minute session), being reliable and available in true emergencies while modeling appropriate boundaries and self-care when the patient is making excessive demands, and taking decisive action when the patient is in danger of harming herself or others.[27] It should—although, sadly, perhaps does not—go without saying that the therapist must refrain from all grossly unethical behavior including financial exploitation and sexual boundary violations. This has been written about extensively elsewhere. Even seemingly benign boundary "crossings"[28] need to be examined in light of the therapist's own narcissistic needs[29] and the potential harm to the patient—especially in light of the multiplicity of subjectivities and possible meanings in any interaction beyond just surface, conscious representations.

TESTING THE THERAPIST

It has been documented that in order to feel safe, the patient will often unconsciously engage in some form of testing of the therapist's ability to keep the boundary secure.[30] This may either take the form of a "transference test," in which the patient unconsciously acts to elicit the same behavior from the therapist as was experienced from a parent, or a "passive-into-active test," in which s/he enacts toward the therapist what was done to him or her early in life.[31] Especially in cases involving childhood sexual abuse, this may include unconscious erotic pulls on the therapist. These function unconsciously to test the therapist's ability to refrain from touching or becoming sexually involved with the patient. It is in acknowledging the depth of the unconscious longing for union, honoring the need for a deep connection that remains safe, and *not* gratifying the expressed or enacted wish for physical connection, that the patient's multiple parts and deeper meanings will become known and transformation will take place.[32]

As the therapist is tested and proves able to maintain the boundary, in time the patient will relax, and more material will emerge from the unconscious. Excessive gratification, paradoxically, will not soothe the patient but often will "up the ante" psychodynamically, resulting in even more demands until the therapist is forced (it is the patient's need for secure boundaries that is unconsciously doing the forcing) to say "no." Nancy McWilliams, a seasoned analytic instructor, points out that this is true even regarding such basic boundaries as limits on one's own availability for phone calls and extra sessions.

> Because there are many clients—seemingly an increasing number over past decades—who need to go through a developmental process in which they rail against limits, let me stress again that the therapist is not going to preempt this difficult process by being generous. Excessive liberality with such patients only insures that their demands will escalate until a limit is finally reached and the developmental struggle can happen. It is better if this occurs before the therapist is in a stew of rancor and self-criticism. Most overtly clingy, dependent patients have an equally strong covert need to express anger and oppositionality. It is thus preferable to set reasonable limits on availability than to infantilize them by an overly caretaking response. Limits provide such clients the pleasures of indignation, and the consequent use of the angry energy to learn to meet their needs themselves, not to mention the lesson that the therapist sticks with them through their furious tirades, like parents who remain devoted after an adolescent rejects them in a rage.[33]

Safety, then, involves feeling comfortable with one's own boundaries, and is the opposite of "feeling cozy" with the patient, which actually may be a red flag that unexamined collusion is occurring in the countertransference.[34] Constance Goldberg, a well-known clinical supervisor, has pointed out that the more comfortable a therapist becomes with his or her own boundaries and limitations, the less patients even seem to push the envelope, because the therapist is nonverbally conveying a certain degree of healthy authority, and does not give unconscious signals of vulnerability to being easily manipulated.[35]

Therapeutic tact and kindness are very important, but these do not mean always agreeing with the patient's perceptions or demands. The therapist functions as a new and reparative object by being "good enough"[36] and—one hopes—not replicating the worst neglect, intrusion, or abuse the patient experienced early in life. The therapist also may function as a positive "new object"[37] by setting boundaries (which the patient may never have encountered in an empathic way) and by being an authentic and therefore separate person who is not subsumed entirely by the patient's projective processes. At the same time, the therapist will not be able to avoid at times saying and doing things that resonate with the old (and sometimes bad) objects. This, too, is part of the working-through that must take place in order for growth and healing to occur. As relational analyst Jay Greenberg has stated, "if the [therapist] cannot be experienced as a new object, analysis never gets underway; if [s/]he cannot be experienced as an old one, it never ends."[38]

PROMOTING VERBALIZATION

Safety is also established by a commitment to the primacy of verbal expression. This is not to retreat from the contemporary recognition of the power—and at times the inevitability—of unconsciously motivated enactments (which will be discussed further in the next chapter). Nevertheless, from Freud onward, the goal—and in some sense the ethos, even the ethic—of therapy has always been to transmute behaviors into words. The process of coming to understand the hidden, unconscious motivations of behavior that sabotages oneself or one's relationships reduces impulsivity and cultivates a value for self-restraint through self-reflection.[39] In Freud's famous saying, "Where id was, there ego shall be."[40] The practical wisdom of learning to pause and think before saying or doing something rash is an inherent value of the therapeutic process itself. Therapy gently works over time to uncover the most deeply imprinted impressions, memories, even bodily experiences, feelings, and unexplained behaviors,[41] and to transform them from the exclusively preverbal or nonverbal mode in which they were initially stored in the brain, through emergence in the form of symbols and images (where they first appear in dreams, artwork, sand tray, and other projective media), and finally into verbal interpretations by which they can be processed and given meaning through a mutual process of interpretation between therapist and patient.[42] More economically and more poetically, to quote Kim Chernin, there is a movement "from image to memory to curiosity."[43]

This process has been validated by contemporary neuroscience, as our understanding has increased regarding how the brain functions, both in recording experience and in emotional development and interpersonal relating.[44] Very early experiences, before the acquisition of language and the maturation of the brain's structure,[45] as well as traumatic experiences throughout the life span, are recorded mainly in the limbic system (midbrain),[46] where they are remembered, if at all, in a primary thought process—that is, through sensations and feelings.[47] The process of therapy makes such primary memories accessible, via symbols and images that are attached to the memories as they emerge into consciousness, and then the full powers of the prefrontal cortex can be applied to construct verbal descriptions and interpretations that were previously unavailable.[48]

THE PATIENT'S GOALS
AND THE THERAPIST'S FLEXIBILITY

Finally, safety is conveyed by respecting the patient's goals for therapy. The therapist must be attentive both to initially stated goals and to more unconscious hopes that may belong to other, more hidden parts of the patient that will emerge only over time—what Joseph Weiss and Harold Sampson have called the patient's "unconscious plan" for healing.[49] There is a line to be drawn here between waiting for further goals to emerge and believing there *should be* further goals, which one then attempts forcefully to elicit. Freud himself cautioned against "therapeutic ambition," in which the therapist is more highly invested in helping the patient make certain changes than is the patient him- or herself. Sometimes a patient simply wants to work on a focal issue. Sometimes there are practical issues of time and money that are not simply functioning as a form of resistance or a refuge from doing deeper work. Sometimes patients are not ready to open up certain avenues of exploration, and there is an inner sense of wisdom that functions within them as a gatekeeper, knowing when the time is right and both internal and external conditions feel safe enough. A therapist needs to respect the patient's goals and sense of pacing.

Not all patients will benefit from an intensive, relational-psychoanalytic approach in which exploration of the transference-countertransference dynamic is at the center of the therapeutic work. Therapy has sometimes been described in terms of an expressive-supportive continuum,[50] with interpretation/exploration and observation (particularly of what is happening in the here-and-now of the therapeutic relationship) on the "expressive" end of the spectrum, and affirmation, psychoeducation, and empathic validation (e.g., helping patients to name and accept their feelings, strengthen reality testing, clarify confused thinking, and contain impulsivity, while minimizing the regression and negative "transference neurosis" that is induced in psychoanalytic exploratory therapy) on the "supportive" end.[51] Basic listening skills and essential counseling interventions such as mirroring, clarification, encouragement for the patient to say more, and confrontation (which is not disputation, but noting discrepancies between what is being expressed verbally and nonverbally, or between what is being said now and what has been reported previously) fall somewhere in the middle and function to strengthen a patient's capacity for self-observation and reality testing. (Note that even affirmation is not simply agreeing with the patient but, rather, validating the patient's perceptions toward strengthening a sense of reality and identity formation.[52])

As mentioned in chapter 3, it was classically thought that only patients on the neurotic spectrum of pathology could benefit from the expressive realm of psycho-analytic therapy or analysis. Pioneering work by analysts from the 1940s, '50s, and '60s, such as Margaret Little,[53] Betty Joseph,[54] and Harold Searle,[55] showed that exploratory, or expressive, work could help many patients suffering from psycho-sis and severe borderline states. Heinz Kohut similarly extended the potential of psychodynamic work in treating narcissistic pathology,[56] and many contemporary practitioners' work with patients who show "borderline," post-traumatic, and nar-cissistic traits have further extended the potential of relationally oriented psycho-dynamic work.[57] The truth is that even the most rigorous psychoanalytic therapists at times will use interventions from the entire spectrum. It is a question of empha-sis. However, patients who tend to think more concretely than symbolically; have limited capacity, interest, or experience in introspection; or whose thinking falls on a spectrum of psychotic processes will not be helped by an insistently interpretive approach. This would be analogous to holding someone's head under water to force her to swim!

One theorist has recommended varying one's approach and listening for different theoretical themes according to four categories of patient personality organization: Freudian themes (sex, aggression, repression, inhibition) for patients with neurotic symptoms; self psychological themes (mirroring, idealizing, self-cohesion versus frag-mentation) with narcissistically wounded patients; object-relations themes (splitting, merger and abandonment, separation and individuation, recognition of differing af-fect states) with patients functioning in the borderline (post-traumatic) spectrum; and Kleinian themes (hunger, envy, aggression, hatred, paranoid-schizoid versus de-pressive organization) with disorganized patients (patients with severe regression and elements of psychotic process).[58] Attachment researchers have also suggested more interpretive therapies for patients who show evidence of secure attachment and more supportive therapies for patients with anxious or disorganized attachment patterns.[59] These suggestions may be useful in thinking about one's approaches to therapy with a variety of patients, and they offer a way to begin thinking in the abstract about how to apply the vast and burgeoning amount of theoretical literature that is now avail-able. In actual practice, however, I find it much too neat because patients are often too complex to categorize so definitively. A therapist is more likely to encounter several of these personality organizations or attachment styles in an intensive treatment over time, and different styles of relating will emerge as do different layers or parts of the self over time.

Brent—Freud, Winnicott, or Kohut?

Early in Brent's therapy, as he talked about his genogram, he described dynamics in his family that could be understood as classically oedipal. His relationship with his mother was profoundly enmeshed. Describing her as both "wonderful" and "cruel," he said she had been a fierce advocate for him in the school system when he began to struggle with learning disabilities as a child, and he grew up feeling an "us against the world" bond with her. He stated that on her deathbed she told him, "we're so much alike our shit smells the same."

At the same time, he felt rivalrous and at times contemptuous feelings for his father, saying, "I could pick him up like a toy." Brent also described a rivalry with his "Irish twin" brother that was conscious and fierce. Their mother's repeated suppression of expressions of anger and hate between the brothers, particularly by drawing Brent further into her confidence as "the boy I can trust to do the right thing" fostered a deep sense of guilt and intensified his attachment to their mother. This dynamic instilled classically "neurotic" defenses in Brent, including rationalization, intellectualization, and isolation of affect—in other words, Brent rationalized his reactions and kept his feelings deeply buried under the surface of his intellectual consciousness.

Brent's reaction to his job reassignment and feelings of disempowerment could also be understood classically in terms of a castration experience, and his depression as a result of suppressed rage. Brent deeply feared his own anger and aggression, related to guilt over surpassing his father's limited achievements. There was a buried fear of this oedipal victory catching up with him somehow, resulting in his own castration or death. This also caused him at times to feel anxious about being exposed as incompetent and a fraud. His relationships with women were greatly inhibited. He feared intimacy as dangerous and projected the harsh, judgmental side of his mother onto women who, "if they knew the real me," would reject him or punish him.

At the same time, Brent exhibited symptoms that were better understood pre-oedipally, in terms of object relations and self psychology. Winnicott's "true-self/false-self" dichotomy fit Brent well in many ways.[60] I have always found this terminology somewhat misleading and narrow, however, as was the case with Brent. Brent's "false self" was not so much a fake or phony self developed only for the sake of compliance with an overbearing socialization process—although Brent often doubted his genuine achievements and perceived himself as a fraud on the verge of being "found out." Brent's socially acceptable, high-performing "false self" had taken him a long way academically and professionally. The competencies Brent developed were real. I therefore prefer to call this the "ambulatory self," the part of a person that gets one around and takes care of business, often quite competently.

The problem was that Brent's competencies felt cut off from his own spontaneity and creativity. Performance was associated so long in Brent's life with obligation and demand in return for conditional love that he had withdrawn the lively part of himself from the parts that performed according to others' (including his mother's) expectations. Activities would lose their zest for him as soon as they moved out of the realm of avocation into occupation—for example, Brent was a talented soccer player, but when he was asked to coach a local high school team for pay, he suddenly found soccer an anxiety-producing obligation and burden.

Self psychology also contributed helpful understandings. Brent felt he came alive only with the attention and admiration of others. There were clear deficits on both the mirroring and the idealizing pole. On the mirroring pole, he had been given approval for performance, not just for being. And on the idealizing pole, there had been some structure from his no-nonsense mother, but there also had been disappointment and role reversal connected with his father, who had failed in his aspiration to become an attorney and whom Brent could "pick up like a toy." Brent frequently felt depleted and was painfully aware of his lack of confidence and self-esteem. He had little capacity to internalize and hold on to others' praise of him. He had somewhat grandiose dreams of success as a programmer, but he frequently sabotaged his actual success with reticence and obsessive, perfectionistic "dithering" (in his words) over details. The job transfer thus represented *both* castration *and* narcissistic injury. While Brent's anxiety appeared to relate most closely to his oedipal guilt, his depression seemed most connected to this primal area of narcissistic deficit and injury. Both areas were important foci of the therapy.

This dual theoretical formulation can be seen in the following interchange: Brent had been talking about the phoniness of the quasi-intimacy he experienced at a recent holiday family gathering. We reflected together how sentimentality of the "Hallmark card" variety was often a cover for hostility, and there was likely more anger and aggression throughout the family than had ever been allowed or tolerated. At this, Brent shed the somewhat chatty and formal quality he often came in with and began to access more feelings. He said that he felt he had surpassed his father in most ways: "I earn two or three times as much, I live in a bigger house, I'm totally self-sufficient." He felt that his father had been dependent on his mother and could not take care of himself without her. I commented that, "By society's standards, at least, that maybe makes you more of a man . . . Both you and your father may have been aware of this on some level?" Brent acknowledged this with some pain in his voice. He said he felt guilty, not so much for having his achievements as for his pride in having them. He quickly shifted to speaking, as he often had, of his rivalry with his brother and how he had always felt guilty for surpassing him, since he was the younger of the two. I said, "I wonder if it's not just in terms of success, but also being closer to your mom?" He said yes, especially since he was the one who won her approval most. "Mom taught me very well not to show pride in my accomplishments. She said, 'You'll rub your brother's nose in it.'" (More shit!) I said, "Sometimes it can be a real burden for a little boy to be told, 'You and I have a secret, and you're the better one, but no one can know about that.'" He nodded, looking sad and vulnerable.

After a pause, I asked, "Do you think that was true not just in relation to your brother, but also your dad?" He said this felt shocking but true, and began to cry. Weeping, he said, "This really strikes a true chord. I always knew it about my brother but I never thought about it about my dad. But it's true. And I didn't *want* it!" I said (hoping to hold opposites together at this point), "Well, I think you probably did and didn't. What's hard is that probably every little boy does want that, but it feels really unsafe to get it, and a tremendous burden that wasn't fair to you, and wasn't your fault." Time was up at this point, and Brent said "I have a lot to think about." He added he felt grateful that the session had helped him to return to "my whole self," after the time with his family that had thrown him back into a much more defensive, intellectualized place.

This example is on one level a clear illustration of the use of an expressive, and quite classical, interpretive technique. Yet it could also be argued that it was the provision of empathic understanding in itself, and not the oedipal interpretation, that caused Brent to feel more "whole" again after being with his family[61]—the more supportive aspect of this interaction provided Brent with nonjudgmental holding. It was my sense at the time that both the empathic understanding and the dimension of insight were equally valuable to Brent. Note that the timing of this "interpretation" was not unilaterally decided by me (as in a more classical approach) but collaborative, in that the themes we were exploring had been emerging slowly for a long time, and Brent himself was circling around the issues of rivalry and guilty conquest. In this regard, the work of reaccessing repressed affect and working through the anxiety and depression relating to Brent's guilt and unconscious hostility are fully in keeping with the more expressive end of the treatment continuum.

It may be most useful, then, to recognize that while some patients consistently need the therapist to be engaged mostly at one end of the expressive-supportive spectrum or the other, most patients have needs that shift with the inner and outer vicissitudes of their lives,[62] and some interventions actually can work at both levels simultaneously. In actual practice, most psychodynamic therapists, including analysts, move fluidly back and forth on this spectrum as the needs of the patient and the intersubjective climate change over time.[63] However one conceives of this, whether in terms of a supportive-expressive continuum, "elasticity of technique,"[64] maternal versus paternal approaches,[65] framing of the patient's wounds in terms of deficit versus conflict,[66] Kohut's poles of mirroring and idealizing, pediatrician T. Berry Brazelton's continuum of soothing and stimulation,[67] or McWilliams's thoughtful framing of therapeutic approaches in terms of both devotion and integrity,[68] most patients need the therapist to be fluently responsive at a variety of points along this spectrum.

Freud himself, in a letter to Séndor Ferenczi, clarified that he had emphasized "what one should not do" in order to prevent what he feared could devolve into "wild analysis."[69] He clarified, "The result was that docile analysts did not perceive the elasticity of the rules I laid down, and submitted to them as if they were taboos. Sometime all that must be revised, without, it is true, doing away with the obligations I had mentioned."[70] To quote Christopher Bollas,

A pluralist approach to psychoanalysis recognizes in the many differing theories—and the schools that teach them—important limited truths in the conceptualization of psychic life and the practice of psychoanalysis. To be sure, pluralism is no ideal—it is difficult to retain more than a few fundamentally different orientations in one's core practice. Pluralism as an ideal could easily collude with a superficial grasp of the differing models of mind. In fact, the only virtue one can find with pluralism is in what it is not. It is not a theory that embraces one total truth. One of the great problems in the psychoanalytic movement—as with all intellectual movements—is the effort to create totalistic theories, ones that all too often unavoidably aim to eliminate other points of view.[71]

The therapist's capacity for flexibility and responsiveness will, of course, also touch on—and at times challenge—his or her own preferred attachment styles, personality organization, and patterns of attachment.

Sensitivity to what is happening at the nonverbal level—for example, missed appointments or requests for more time—will often convey important clues as to when the therapy is moving uncomfortably too fast or too slow for the patient. If a therapist senses that s/he is working harder at the therapy than the patient, the reason for this should be explored. It may also signal a countertransference issue: why is the therapist so invested in seeing more "progress" than the patient seems willing or able to make?

The best approach with a patient who seems able and willing to engage in introspection, yet appears stuck at a surface level or reluctant to engage in exploration, is almost never direct confrontation and demand but exploration of what the therapist is noticing: "I've noticed, Eric, that there are times of late when it seems that we are talking about things that don't seem to connect with what's really important to you, or with what you might be feeling. Do you have any thoughts about that?" It is then up to the patient to control the flow of conversation and to decide (consciously or unconsciously) whether he is willing to explore what has been happening in the therapy and what might be suppressed, whether he agrees or disagrees with the therapist's observation, and if he agrees, whether it still feels safer to remain at a surface level for a while longer.

Human Beings Are Multiple: Meeting the Parts

So the therapy begins. A person calls, sets an appointment, and then walks through the door. From the first contact, it is crucial to remember that human beings are multiple, not unitary, and in some sense, the "one" who walks through the door is a crowd. As described in chapter 1, the metaphor for the inner life of the patient is not only that of the tree, with its "root causes" and vertical depths to be dug into; there is also the rhizomatic dimension of the patient's life, requiring attention to spatial, associational chains of meaning and the patient's experiences of belonging to a wide and complex web of relationships and cultures, past, present, and future. In the intersubjective matrix that begins to be created with the very first contact between patient and therapist, we meet the patient on both conscious and unconscious levels, as two multiple beings, whose many parts will meet, join, clash, and influence each other over the weeks and months to come.

The recognition of such multiplicity, and the resulting complexity of meaning(s) that are likely to emerge from the shared process of therapeutic exploration, has been a central feature of relational psychoanalytic therapy. To quote Greenberg again,

> As many of us have moved toward a two-person model of the psychoanalytic process, we become increasingly aware that there are always multiple perspectives on the participation of each party. This means that whatever is revealed is simply one person's understanding at a given moment—never (despite the patient's and sometimes the analyst's hopes) the last word on the subject.[72]

For this reason, it would be naïve to imagine that therapy will "go smoothly" from beginning to end. "A dynamic therapist is wise to remember that impasses or stalemates may often simply reveal the heart of the transference-countertransference work that needs to be examined."[73] The sheer numbers of selves and self-parts involved guarantee that the process will be more complicated than our initial hopes for a smooth ride. What both partners can expect is an infinite richness of experience, diving deep, and racing or crawling over a myriad of spatial planes where new meanings and insights can be discovered and rediscovered, all the while having our subjective perceptions and experiences being reworked and transformed.

So from the very beginning we are listening not only to what is communicated by the patient at the conscious, verbal level (which is the domain of counseling and coaching), but we are listening for the gaps, the breaches in consciousness that tickle our awareness, the parts of our multiple patient that have not yet spoken or even found a voice. This kind of psychoanalytic listening is akin to Jacques Derrida's deconstruction and perhaps in part gave rise to it. Postmodern therapist Susan Fairfield writes:

> One defining characteristic postmodernism shares with psychoanalysis is a suspicion of any attempt to cordon something off from scrutiny—to deny, or fail to see, that it can be put in question. Whenever it's claimed that some aspect of the way people behave or make meanings is simply the way things are, a fact about the world and not about the propounder of the claim, we're pretty sure that we're dealing with a fear of losing control, be it in a political regime, a culturally privileged group, or their intrapsychic analogues in a patient . . . Deconstruction joins Freudian psychoanalysis in examining the ways in which we are inhabited by what we attempt to put outside us.[74]

We listen for "unformulated experience"[75]—those preverbal or nonverbal, presymbolic aspects of the patient's history that have never been given narrative form, and, as well, the resonances of those wordless communications within ourselves.[76] We attend to knowledge that resides in the patient's body and nonverbal gestures. We attend to symbolic levels of communication. And we invite the possibility that what is being said is only a fraction of what all the parts of the patient know and might wish to express. As the therapeutic relationship quickens and we feel our own emotions, thoughts, and fantasies stirred by the patient's conscious and unconscious communications and projections onto and into us (the patient's transference to us), and by the intersubjective pool of experience in which we are both now swimming (like Jung's alchemical bath), we listen across all the same registers in our own multiple selves (our countertransference).

Thus, countertransference—our own thoughts, feelings, fantasies, and sensations in relation to the patient and the therapeutic relationship—becomes a primary tool for understanding what is happening both in the intersubjective dynamic of the therapeutic relationship and what has not been expressed or even known by the patient from within his or her own multiple inner world. The therapist's own multiply-constituted self becomes a key instrument for understanding the patient's many parts. (More will be said about transference and countertransference below.)

The mode of attention is, in Freud's terminology, an "evenly suspended" or "evenly hovering" attention or attentiveness (sometimes also called "free floating attention").[77] Freud used this expression to refer to the cultivated ability to attend, or "tune in," to several levels of communication going on in the therapeutic interaction simultaneously—in other words, to listen to all the parts of the person—without becoming bogged down in any one level of communication with the patient. Although multiplicity is now considered to be much more extensive than the three "institutions" of ego, id, and superego, Freud's structural model already recognized a degree of multiplicity in the human person. Given the multidimensionality we now are conceptualizing, evenly hovering attention becomes all the more important. It is always useful to wonder, "who's not getting a chance to speak right now?" and even, "what part of the patient's experience is so early, or so traumatic, that it has been stored in his or her memory without any words at all?"

Unlike a social conversation, then, the focus of attention is not only, or even primarily, on conscious content. The therapist "listens with a third ear,"[78] attending to the multiple messages from the unconscious that may be guessed at from the patient's flow of associations, slips of tongue, use of words that seem particularly charged or laden with symbolic content (including dream content), body language, and what is coming up in the countertransference.[79] While fully present with the patient, the therapist is at the same time scanning what s/he sees, feeling emotionally and in her body, and entertaining as many possible meanings as s/he can. Thus, the goal of therapy from the very outset is to create a climate of safety in which all the parts of the person are invited to speak, and those aspects of the patient's experience that could not be given words are transformed slowly from nonverbal to symbolic and finally to verbal expression and conscious reflection.

Practical Matters:
Particular Challenges for Pastoral Psychotherapists

One should always bear in mind that the seemingly most straightforward practical matters will become arenas in which some of the most strenuous testing of the therapist's reliability and pushing against boundaries may occur. The nuts and bolts of doing therapy, including placement of chairs, soundproofing, billing, informed consent and HIPAA (Health Insurance Portability and Accountability Act of 1996) regulations,[80] risk management and liability, dealing with insurance companies and HMOs (Health Maintenance Organizations), etc., have been well described in other recent sources.[81] However, there are some ways in which from the outset even the most seemingly ordinary practical matters may present particular psychodynamic challenges for pastoral psychotherapists.

Setting the Frame: Fees and Scheduling

Many if not most therapists, perhaps because we were called upon early in childhood to be emotionally superattuned or to care emotionally for others in the unconscious family dynamic, have a tendency, as Alice Miller pointed out,[82] to be supercarers and to suffer from guilt and anxiety when we have to say "no" or set limits. The pitfalls are well-known, of course—burnout, resentment for having overextended ourselves, and "compassion fatigue."[83] There is evidence that this general tendency of therapists may be even more burdensome for pastoral psychotherapists. Religious values of compassion and self-sacrificial love may make it even harder to set clear limits and boundaries.

One arena that is particularly fraught for religious therapists is the question of fees. Money has been so identified with greed, dirt, and sin, particularly in Christian piety, that it may seem selfish or heartless to demand anything other than a low fee. It is important, then, for pastoral psychotherapists to separate legitimate, reality-based reasons for providing therapy at a reduced fee to certain clients with genuine need, from a spurious, guilt-laden acquiescence to some other patients' transference-loaded demands for an unreasonably low fee. It becomes a question of balance. Pastoral psychotherapy as a profession has always prided itself on providing services not only to the wealthy, or the "worried well." At the same time, if they routinely work for below-market rates, pastoral psychotherapists do not model good boundaries and in the end may compromise their therapeutic work by tacitly devaluing their own labor and unconsciously conveying ambivalence about the value of therapy itself. Pastoral psychotherapists, because of their desire to be seen as nurturing (both by others and in their own self-image) may tend even more than other therapists to deny or split off their own resentment, anger, and even wants and needs. Over time, this can come back to haunt the therapy because the therapist may unconsciously begin to enact his or her resentment in a variety of subtle ways. Nothing can sour a therapist's unconditional positive regard for a patient faster than learning after agreeing to a very low fee that the patient just splurged on a luxury car or vacation!

There are two concrete ways in which pastoral psychotherapists generally deal with the matter of reducing fees. The most common is to have a sliding scale, based not on emotional pleas but on a straightforward chart listing various levels of income. A certain degree of trust is needed, of course, since we do not require patients to fill out a financial aid form or provide a bank statement! (Any gross violation of trust would certainly become grist for the mill of the therapeutic work over time.) The scale is then applied equally and consistently to all patients seen in the practice. Another method is to reserve a certain number or percentage of low-fee slots for patients who do not have insurance and cannot pay the full fee as a way of tithing a percentage of one's practice to care for those in need.

The need to raise fees is also often fraught with guilt and anxiety for pastoral psychotherapists. One reported method is to simply include a statement in one's orientation to therapy that the fee will be increased each year according to the rate of inflation.[84] Other therapists do not raise their fees for existing patients but incorporate increases as they bring new patients into their practice over time.

Patients' circumstances may also change, and fees may need to be renegotiated (upward or downward). The more matter-of-fact the therapist can be about such changes, the more the patient's own mature ego functioning is enlisted in considering what is fair. Once a therapy has been in progress for a while, all matters of frame, including fee, should be considered simultaneously as both reality-based needs assessments and potential enactments in the transference-countertransference dynamic that deserve thoughtful mutual exploration for underlying meanings. Most often both levels of relationship are at work simultaneously. Giving short shrift to either dimension, in the name of the "real relationship" or in the name of working only in the transference, runs the risk of infantilizing the patient by being too concrete or ignoring important unconscious communications about the therapy itself and how the patient is perceiving its value.

Scheduling is a similar issue. Patients will send a variety of unconscious signals about the way the therapy is going and their own internal desires and fears, in the form of coming late, failing to appear at all, or, on the other hand, requesting additional time both on the phone and in person. While there are many cultural variations on the relative strictness or fluidity of time-keeping, the important thing is that the therapist maintains consistency in his or her practice so that all patients will be given fair treatment, equal access, and equal limits. More fluid approaches may need to be modified in favor of being sure that no one has to wait an inordinate amount of time and no one's session is cut short. It is common practice when a patient arrives late to say kindly but matter-of-factly, "I'm sorry we won't have as much time to work together today, but we will still need to end on time."

The patient who is chronically late, the patient who is almost never late and then gets caught in a traffic jam, and the patient who is late for the session following a particularly intense emotional session, may be saying different things, but in every case, his or her behavior carries some message. Gentle exploration of what lateness might mean are as much a part of the therapy as the exploration of any other enactment—for example, were their own boundaries around time never respected as a child? Was the accident at the same time an unavoidable bad circumstance and also caused by the patient's rushing in order to counter an unconscious impulse to drag his or her feet, feeling distracted by thoughts about the therapy, etc.? Did something happen last time that somehow felt frightening or off-putting? Is the lateness trying to convey irritation, anger, disappointment, or even fear of too much closeness, which the patient is not yet able to verbalize? These are just a few of the possible meanings of lateness and should not be assumed as "the" meaning. There are also cultural differences regarding the relative fluidity or strictness of time-keeping. This, too, can simultaneously be both a reality-based matter and a refuge for a patient's unconscious communications. There is always value to exploration, and surface explanations of seemingly very reasonable excuses for lateness still deserve a gentle probing, since unconscious meanings can readily reside in seemingly straightforward realities. As one of my own professors put it, "Reality is the best defense."

With requests for extra time, as with requests for reduced fees, the meaning of a such a request deserves exploration, while the therapist also needs to maintain healthy boundaries for his or her own well-being. The best rubric for determining when too much is being demanded is how it feels. Is it out of the ordinary for the hours one usually maintains, does the request feel legitimate or manipulative, and does it simply feel like more than the therapist can give without becoming exhausted, angry, or resentful? Pastoral therapists in particular may need to be reminded again and again that it is not selfish to protect private and family time, and it is also important to maintain one's own health and rest in order to be effective as a therapist. Some patients who were never given any sense of boundaries in their own families of origin simply cannot distinguish and need to be gently educated about the difference between a genuine emergency—involving serious life or death issues—and an emotional crisis in which the patient longs for support and contact and feels unable to soothe or contain him- or herself. The therapist, again, should not over-extend him- or herself to the point of exhaustion or resentment because it will have negative effects on the therapy in the long run.

Further, patients who need to test limits in order to build their own internal sense of boundaries, will continue to push for more until even the most limit-avoidant therapist finally will find him- or herself forced to say "no." It is therefore more therapeutic, and more protective of the "therapeutic alliance"[85] from the outset, to set the limit that is real for the therapist, rather than trying to accommodate a patient unreasonably with the (impossible) goal of being seen as a special, inexhaustible nurturer.

Winnicott's observation that optimal frustration was necessary to promote growth, both in child-raising and in therapy, should be remembered in such situations.

Every therapist should have a regular system for handling emergencies, which may range from expecting that a patient should call 911 or a mental health hotline in a true emergency outside of session to accepting brief phone calls and redirecting the patient to appropriate help or scheduling an extra session. Even if practicing out of a home office, every therapist should have a separate office phone number and not give out his or her private home number. The office number should be equipped with an answering service or voice mail s/he checks regularly throughout the day and up to a designated time in the evening (of which the patient should be informed). Instructions to callers for emergencies during and after regular office hours should be included in the outgoing message. When returning calls to patients, it is best to keep phone communications very brief, and if the patient genuinely needs contact before the next regularly scheduled session, an additional session should be scheduled if possible.

Relational-psychoanalytic therapy cannot optimally be conducted over the phone because so much of the therapy depends on the face-to-face, embodied interaction in the room and the therapist's felt sense of what is happening. This tends to be diminished over the phone, when the therapist cannot see the patient's face and body language and may not be as able to interpret the emotional tone of the patient's voice. If there is simply no reasonable hour to offer before the next session, this should also be communicated kindly but matter-of-factly, and the issue of whether or not the patient needs to be seen more frequently on a regular basis should be addressed in the next regular session.

It may be helpful to remember that the first meaning of the original Greek word for martyr (μάρτυς, *mártys*) is not one who sacrifices his or her life, but one who *witnesses*. Our job as pastoral psychotherapists is not to die or make unreasonable sacrifices for our patients—in fact, at the level of unconscious relationship it is crucial that we survive, thus generating a new object relation.[86] Often when we strike the right balance, in which we are rationally generous but also taking care of ourselves so that we can be there for the long haul, we are (perhaps for the first time) modeling healthy assertiveness and self-care for our patients. Patients sometimes demand unreasonable arrangements as an unconscious "passive-into-active" test in the transference dynamic,[87] in which the surface demand represents what was unreasonably done to them when they were small, and what is most needed is our showing that by standing firm neither we nor the relationship is destroyed. This can then be internalized by the patient as growth, strengthening his or her own capacity for establishing healthy boundaries, and exercising appropriate assertiveness and self-care. Our job, then, as pastoral psychotherapists is not to sacrifice ourselves but to be witnesses—to stand alongside the patient and testify to the manifold moments of growth, changes, tests, and insights as the therapy proceeds.

Pastoral Practice Setting

Pastoral psychotherapists are often faced with another dilemma not common in other forms of psychotherapy—where to practice. Church-based offices often pose the most challenges with regard to privacy and boundaries. Church personnel are often accustomed to knocking on a pastor's closed door or buzzing on an intercom, so the therapist should make some explanation in advance that therapy sessions should not be disturbed, and have a prominent "do not disturb" sign that one can post when one is in session. This is true even when one is not on staff in that congregation, because other staff may not differentiate between a pastoral counselor and other professional staff unless the boundaries are clarified. Soundproofing is often a challenge as well, and certain physical modifications may need to be made to an office, such as a white noise machine or extra insulation, to protect patients' privacy. Entry and exit ways should be established to minimize patients' bumping into one another or into parishioners or staff. Waiting areas should be discreet and preferably separate from other common areas of the church; if this is not possible, patients may prefer to come close to their appointment times to minimize waiting, and in clement weather to wait in the privacy of their own car if they have one. If there is a receptionist, that person should be informed that the identity of patients is confidential.

The larger issue, of course, if one is practicing in a church setting, is whether or not to see one's own parishioners for therapy. While this might be conceivable with regard to very brief (three to five sessions), cognitive, problem-oriented counseling, which still falls basically under the rubric of pastoral care rather than psychotherapy,[88] parishioners should always be referred to another outside professional for any longer-term form of psychotherapy. Especially in the case of psychodynamic or relational-psychoanalytic therapy, it is crucial that the therapist not be in a dual role vis-à-vis the patient. The power of a psychoanalytically informed therapy is precisely in the exploration of the transference-countertransference dynamic between patient and therapist at conscious, unconscious, and fantasy levels, contained safely within a sealed dyadic container. If the therapist is simultaneously functioning in the patient's life outside the therapy, the "as-if" quality of the intersubjective dynamic, with all its ripeness of projection, fantasy, associative material, and symbolic interaction, will collapse. The quality of the therapeutic dialogue will become fused with everyday social and business discourse, while the supposedly extratherapeutic interactions may become laden with unconscious communications and enactments. One simply cannot sit in the consulting room with a patient one day and sit on a committee with him or her the next night.

Furthermore, if the therapist also has liturgical duties in the worship life of the congregation, the transference to the therapist as priest can complicate the therapeutic transference in ways that are not helpful to the therapy. Experiencing one's therapist also as one's priest is not only another form of dual relationship. It can have the effect of narrowing the transference-countertransference relationship into a particular, religiously loaded band of experience (whether this is a positive idealization or a negative transference) or flattening it—unduly inhibiting the patient from speaking freely about nonreligious or even antireligious feelings, thoughts, and fantasies, and/or heightening the feeling that all therapy is religious confession.

There is a fairly simple and clear-cut way of managing this boundary between one's role as priest/pastor/rabbi and one's role as pastoral psychotherapist. The therapist may see congregation members for home and hospital visitation, pastoral care, and crisis intervention, keeping this within the standard limits of three to five sessions, and for regular premarital counseling (which may extend to a few more than five sessions, depending on the method one uses). As a therapist, this minister will of course have a wealth of diagnostic training and experience, but this will be used in the service of assessing the parishioner's needs and making an appropriate referral to another professional in the community if those needs exceed the limits of ordinary pastoral care. At the same time, the therapist can be available to see patients who do not belong to his or her own congregation and can accept referrals of patients from other congregations from fellow clergy and from other colleagues in the community.

In very small rural communities, or in ethnic communities where seeking help outside one's own group is virtually taboo, exceptions to this general practice may need to be made. Over time, such taboos can be sensitively addressed in a congregation through education and personal introductions of "outside" helping professionals through adult education forums, guest sermons, or other means. If one absolutely has to see one's own parishioner for therapy, it is necessary to mutually negotiate ways to minimize contact between the therapist and the patient outside of therapy as much as possible and to decide in advance how to handle outside interactions. This can, in fact, mean that the therapist may need to restrict his or her voluntary involvements in the life of the congregation for the sake of the therapy and should find ways to meet his or her own spiritual and ecclesiastical needs elsewhere so that his or her self-care and spiritual nurture and need for community is not being neglected. As with all enactments, the patient's feelings, fantasies, thoughts, and experiences of any extratherapeutic contacts should be thoroughly, empathically explored in session.

This is occasionally true in even the most carefully protected therapeutic frameworks since chance meetings between therapist and patient do occur—even in large cities—and almost always have some kind of impact on the patient, and often on the therapist as well. An amusing example of this is seen in the television series "The Sopranos," in which the therapist, Dr. Melfi, is so disconcerted by running into her Mafia boss client Tony Soprano in a restaurant that she dissolves into giggles and leaves saying "Toodle-oo!"[89] This becomes grist for her next session with her own therapist/supervisor, as she recognizes the extent to which she has been pulled into an unconscious cat-and-mouse game of seduction by her at-times charming and boyish, but extremely dangerous, psychopathic patient.

A much more complicated example happened to me when a patient with a history of both sexual trauma and parental narcissism, and an ongoing struggle with dissociative episodes of self-injury, spotted me in a large downtown urban area. She believed that I had seen her too and, moreover, had met her eyes with a deep, meaningful look. She was thrown into a dissociative state on the spot, which was noted by friends who were with her and wondered aloud if she was OK. To make matters even more complicated, I was not, in fact, conscious of having seen her, preoccupied as I had been that day with my own business, but I was able to verify that I had, in fact, been there at the time she reported. I wrestled with the decision of whether, when, and how to disclose to her that I had not in fact seen her. Empathically processing how she had felt then, and how she felt subsequently upon hearing the truth that I hadn't seen her, was the subject of many sometimes quite painful sessions, where fantasy and reality became quite blurred at the intersection of an already intense transference-countertransference dynamic.

THIRD PARTY REQUESTS FOR INFORMATION
Legal Requirements

All therapists from time to time must deal with the requests by third parties that information about the patient be disclosed. In all therapies, but perhaps especially in psychodynamic therapy, where the seal of the container is so crucial to the fermenting of the transference-countertransference relationship, such requests can feel violating to the patient and always function as incursions into the therapeutic dynamic that need to be explored as with any other enactment or extratherapeutic occurrence.

Some such requests are unavoidable. Child abuse reporting, for example, is an absolute ethical and legal duty in all fifty states, as is the Tarasoff duty to warn. (Named for a landmark 1976 California Supreme Court case,[90] the Tarasoff duty requires a therapist to tell police if a patient presents a serious danger of violence to another person and also—the element that was established in the lawsuit—to warn that person directly). When treating a court-remanded criminal offender, reports may be legally required to probation officers or other legal entities. This ideally is done in consultation with the patient, but even without the patient's consent, reporting must be done as the law requires (e.g., if the patient ceases to cooperate with therapy) because of the potential for harm to others. The containment of behavior that such reporting represents can, if handled honestly and openly with the patient, enhance the patient's sense of safety. In extreme psychiatric emergencies where a patient's physical safety is at issue, disclosure of essential clinical facts may need to be presented in court in order to seek permission for hospitalization. Licensed therapists also must comply with all HIPAA regulations.[91]

Third-Party Payment

Beyond such mandatory reporting, however, there exists a broad category of more discretionary third-party disclosures, none of which should be made without consultation with the patient. Most common among these are requests for information from case managers at health-insurance companies and HMOs. Some pastoral counselors may belong to HMO or PPO (Preferred Provider Organization) panels and are expected to follow requirements for reporting on patients' progress in order to authorize beginning or continuing treatment. It is not uncommon for panels to limit treatment to twenty sessions per year and/or to require recertification every ten sessions. Obviously, such procedures are designed to encourage brief therapy models and are not conducive to longer-term intensive psychotherapy. Requests for disclosure should be discussed with the patient, not only practically, in terms of formal permission to disclose and compliance with legal regulations, but psychodynamically—that is, in terms of the anticipated effect of such disclosures on the dynamic of the therapy itself and the patient's sense of safety and confidentiality. Especially in situations where a considerable amount of disclosure of the actual content and process of the therapy is demanded of the therapist by an insurance company, some patients choose to "go off plan," that is, to forego third-party reimbursement, in order to preserve their privacy. It is the practice of many pastoral psychotherapists to renegotiate the patient's fee in order to accommodate this protection of privacy.

Referrals from Clergy Colleagues

The above examples are common to all practices of psychotherapy. Pastoral counselors, in addition, may be confronted with requests for information that are less common in other branches of psychotherapy. It is common to receive referrals of parishioners from clergy colleagues. Initially, the referring clergyperson may wish to tell the therapist a variety of details about his or her perceptions and experiences of the parishioner. It is best to try to limit such communications, as it is most helpful therapeutically to form one's own impressions from direct encounters with the patient. It matters little whether the patient reports various incidents or interpersonal issues that prompted the referral. The underlying issues and dynamics will appear soon enough. It is rare, in my experience, that whatever dynamics may be troubling the referring pastor do not emerge—and quickly—in the therapeutic relationship as well.

If the individual does come for a consultation, it is also important to limit communication about that patient to a cordial expression of thanks, as with any other collegial referral, and at most with a one-sentence indication that the therapy is or is not proceeding. Further communication with the referring clergyperson—even when this person is a friend and it would feel like a relief to share some aspects of the therapy—would need to be discussed with the patient, and written permission received. Unless critical issues of safety are involved, it is best not to engage in any ongoing discussion about the patient because it can severely compromise the patient's privacy and can complicate the therapeutic relationship with the insertion of a third party. (The same rubric applies with disclosures to patients' family members. Except in an emergency, the inclusion of any third party, even a spouse, into a therapy that is not a couples' or family therapy from the beginning is rife with potential for bias, triangulation, and/or shame at a conscious level, and violation of the patient's sense of safety and confidentiality at all levels of the relationship.)

Ordination Committees and Judicatories

Because of our relationships with religious institutions, pastoral counselors also frequently see patients for therapy who are candidates for ordination in their respective religious traditions. Especially when the patient has initiated therapy upon recommendation (or requirement) by his or her committee on ordination, the therapist may be requested by judicatory staff to verify the patient's compliance. Pastoral psychotherapists should know that while it is standard practice to verify attendance—with the patient's written consent—it is not standard practice to divulge any diagnostic or clinical information about the patient or the therapeutic process. Even when the patient requests such disclosure for the sake of expediting his or her ordination, such a rupture in the therapeutic container almost always does both the patient and the therapeutic alliance more harm than good. The patient will begin to censor his or her disclosures to the therapist for fear of being turned down for ordination. The net result of such a compromise to the therapeutic process is that no real therapy will actually be accomplished. Free association will be effectively blocked, and a third, nonbenign partner will be inserted into the unconscious transference-countertransference dynamic.

Ordination committees frequently refer individuals for therapy when they suspect that there are unresolved family-of-origin issues or entrenched characterological traits that might negatively influence the person's ability to function in ministry. It is helpful for the therapist to educate the patient, and the judicatory executive, at the outset about the limits of what can helpfully be disclosed—precisely in order to protect the effectiveness of the therapy. Especially when long-standing personality traits are at issue, the intensive therapeutic work that might actually have a healing effect on the patient will demand more than a brief cognitive therapy and should be protected with strict privacy. Judicatory bodies need to have sensitivity and respect for the potential shame that could result from exposing such a candidate's innermost fears and secret longings.

As I have discussed with a number of judicatory staff members, any suspected impairment of a candidate almost always has been observed at the level of behaviors and verbal interactions, including with members of a candidacy committee themselves.

This is likely how the need for referral manifested itself in the first place. For this reason, I encourage committees to continue to monitor behaviors and interactional patterns, which they themselves have already seen and which prompted the referral. Relevant information should also be sought from others who have a duty to report on a candidate's progress, such as seminary faculty, clergy supervisors, and lay committees in field education settings. Therapists should be aware that sometimes there is a temptation on the part of committees, clergy supervisors, and others to be "nice" to the candidate, and—often unconsciously—to try to make the therapist be "the heavy." The therapist's first responsibility, then, is not to share information that others can determine for themselves but, rather, to protect the sanctity of the therapeutic container so that actual therapy can take place.

Judicatories also makes referrals of ordained clergy who are discovered to have problems with drinking or addictions, who have violated sexual or other boundaries, or who have otherwise been found to be impaired in their ministry. Again, it is not the role of the therapist to divulge the actual process and content of the therapy to ecclesiastical authorities. The art of predicting future dangerousness is extremely imprecise at best, and the best single predictor of future behavior is a history of past behavior. As with an ordination process, the therapy will be most effective if the therapist limits his or her communications with the judicatory to a general statement verifying whether or not the patient has attended and cooperated with therapy.

Any communication, like all other disclosures to third parties, must be made with the patient's written consent. Most often, the goal of such reporting is to determine whether and when to reinstate the clergyperson in his or her practice of ministry, and there are numerous behavioral indicators upon which judicatory executives can rely to make such a determination without intruding into the details of the therapy, including genuine remorse and full acknowledgement of the offending behaviors; nondefensiveness; absence of blaming, excuse-making, minimization, or externalization of responsibility; and willingness not to rush back into ministry practice in the service of healing and better self-awareness and self-control.

SPIRITUAL DIRECTION

One additional outside factor that occasionally affects pastoral psychotherapy is spiritual direction. Patients occasionally begin psychotherapy after they are already engaged in a regular process of spiritual direction with another professional or come with the requirement by an ordination committee that they engage in both activities. Sometimes a patient will come to therapy because of a referral by a spiritual director. If a patient is already established with a director, it is important to determine the level of frequency and psychological intensity involved in the spiritual direction process. The danger is splitting. Patients who unconsciously have a strong resistance to probing more painful, frightening, or potentially shame-laden issues, or for whom splitting is a characteristic form of psychic functioning, may enlist two (or even more!) helping professionals in order to dilute the transference-countertransference intensity of any one relationship and to keep material "safely" compartmentalized. Things that are considered to be "spiritual" may be cordoned off and saved for spiritual direction, while important clues to the inner movement of the patient's spiritual life may be reserved for the therapist. Both processes suffer.

Spiritual direction and pastoral psychotherapy are not the same thing, and pastoral psychotherapists should not presume to be able to do both unless they are trained in both disciplines. However, a patient can be assured that pastoral psychotherapy by definition embraces the spiritual dimension of the patient's life, and that spiritual matters are welcome in the therapy just like any other concern the patient may want to explore.[92] The official recognition of "psychospiritual issues" as nonpathological, or V-Code, in the most recent DSM,[93] and the contemporaneous explosion of books from secular clinical publishers on the spiritual dimension of psychotherapy,[94] demonstrate the rising appreciation of the importance of spirituality among secular psychotherapists as well. The key is integration of whatever is of central concern to the patient, and a fundamentalist adherence to Freud's atheism (as discussed in the introduction to this book) is rapidly becoming anachronistic.

From the side of the therapy, at the very least, simultaneous therapy and spiritual direction may dilute the effectiveness of both processes because dual (if not dueling) transferences are actually at work. At its worst, it can set all the professionals involved in an unwitting position of being pitted against one another projectively as good and bad parental objects. Therapists and directors can even be induced through projective identification to begin competing and advocating against one another (in family systems terminology, "triangulated"), with little opportunity to understand what is happening because only the patient has access to the whole picture. Given these potential problems, my recommendation is that if spiritual direction is to continue during psychotherapy, it be limited to once a month to minimize the intensity of that transference formation, and that the potential for dividing up the energy of the treatment be explained to the patient. The patient then may periodically be invited to share insights or internal movements or changes s/he may be experiencing in spiritual direction in order to prevent a widening gap from occurring.

The patient should also be encouraged to inform his or her director that s/he is beginning therapy because that may also affect the process of spiritual direction. Some directors may prefer their directees to suspend direction for a period of time, either because therapy is needed before further spiritual movement can fruitfully occur or because the process of therapy may induce a period of fragility and regression in the directee that would make spiritual direction unproductive or even unsafe. More intensive experiences of spiritual direction, such as an Ignatian thirty-day retreat, or especially a Nineteenth Annotation "retreat in everyday life" that requires weekly meetings with a director, should be carefully thought through in relation to their potential effect on the therapy, and probably postponed at least until a solid therapeutic process is established (i.e., not in the first six months, and preferably not in the first year or even two, depending on the severity of the patient's presenting issues). If spiritual direction was recommended by an ordination committee, the therapist may want to suggest to the patient that s/he fulfill these requirements serially rather than simultaneously, using the therapy first to strengthen his or her capacity for self-observation, self-reflection, knowledge of the inner landscape, and wider self-acceptance, which can only enhance his or her ability to engage later in the introspective and contemplative aspects of spiritual direction.[95]

Projections onto the Pastoral Ministry Role

Whether or not a patient is affiliated with any formal religious tradition, a certain mana of spiritual power projectively accrues to any ordained clergyperson or vowed religious, as if by osmosis, from the culture at large. Pastoral psychotherapists need to be sensitive to the likelihood that, in addition to all the manifold ways in which any patient may project early childhood imagoes and other expectations onto a helping professional, a particular set of religious or spiritual projections are likely to hover over the pastoral psychotherapy and the person of the pastoral psychotherapy. Such projections will not always take overtly religious shape. Therefore, all influences, feelings, or occurrences in the transference should be considered not only in light of the patient's early parental experiences but also in light of the patient's possible fantasies about what it means to be sharing his or her innermost thoughts and feelings with a person who may appear to them as a "religious person," religious authority, or even representative of God.

A patient's earlier experiences of religious figures, whether positive or negative or a combination, can be a profound aspect of the patient's inner formation. Previous experiences may also condition the patient to expect or even fear certain kinds of responses from the therapist—often judgmental—simply because of the therapist's religious affiliation. Some patients will try to bait a religiously oriented therapist in order to test boundaries or disconfirm an unconscious belief that a "really good" person would reject them. In any therapy, a patient may test the therapist's tolerance for him or her as a way of expressing an unconscious need to find out, "if you knew how bad I really am, would you still care for me?" This projective dynamic may be heightened in pastoral psychotherapy because of the unconscious inflation of the pastoral psychotherapist's presumed goodness, even holiness.

If the patient is overtly religious, s/he may also expect complete agreement on certain religious practices or on theological or doctrinal points. This can pose ethical and emotional dilemmas in the countertransference, particularly if the therapist believes the patient is using religion defensively or in a self-defeating way, or is being exploited by a religious organization or group. The therapist may have difficulty in refraining from theological debate, advice-giving, or intrusive questioning into the patient's religious beliefs, practices, and affiliations. (This will be discussed further in the next sections on self-disclosure and on toxic religion.)

It is therefore helpful to engage in periodic exploration of the dynamic of religious projection by asking, "do you think the fact that I'm a [rabbi/priest/pastor] has any relevance to what you're [feeling/thinking/experiencing] here?" Conveying a nonjudgmental curiosity about whatever may be present at the level of fantasy can help diffuse unrealistic projections and also, like all other transference-countertransference explorations, may open up new dimensions of meaning and insight for the patient.

SELF-DISCLOSURE

Self-disclosure is another area that has been continually debated and reworked in contemporary psychoanalytic thinking—and may be particularly fraught with peril for pastoral psychotherapists. The classical idea of the therapist as an extremely private person, the details of whose life are kept entirely hidden from the patient, is seldom entirely practicable for any therapist, but particularly pastoral counselors. Freud's counsel that the therapist "be opaque to his patients and, like a mirror . . . show them nothing but what is shown to him"[96] was predicated on the idea that scientific objectivity was possible. And yet Freud himself was hardly opaque, at least to some of his own patients, whom he variously met on vacation, introduced to his family and to other patients, shared drafts of his writings, corresponded socially with their family members, offered puppies from his chow dog, Yofi, and disclosed many details of both his personal and his professional life, including his medical treatments.[97] Yofi was a frequent and even somewhat active companion in analytic sessions: Freud told one analysand that Yofi would leave the room in the presence of resistance and would also signal the end of the analytic hour by getting to her feet and yawning![98]

Sándor Ferenczi, the member of Freud's circle who most advocated an active technique (eventually leading to a rupture with Freud), believed that therapists reveal much more than they think or intend.[99] Theodor Reik similarly observed that "mortals are not made to keep a secret, and that self-betrayal oozes from all their pores."[100] Patients often know more about us than we perhaps prefer to think, and no matter how little we say, we are continually revealing ourselves nonverbally through facial expressions, body language, moments of intense interest and attention, and moments of inattention or even boredom. The reason intersubjectivity has replaced objectivity as our therapeutic perspective is precisely because so much of what "happens" in therapy occurs at the level of transference-countertransference interaction, enactment, and mutually disclosing yet unconscious relationship. Again, an awareness of multiplicity tends to temper the urge to disclose, since our motives as therapists are inevitably mixed (are we "sharing" truly for the benefit of the patient, or because we ourselves are feeling unseen in the therapeutic relationship, or lonely, or sad and in need of comfort, or exhibitionistic, or narcissistically undernourished?), and patients will not hear a therapist's disclosure with the ears of just one self-state. Jay Greenberg has noted in regard to self-disclosure, because of the multiplicity of subjectivities involved in therapy, "I am not necessarily in a privileged position to know, much less to reveal, everything that I think or feel."[101]

The shift from a more objectivist paradigm to a more intersubjective approach to therapy does not change the basic tenet that explicit sharing of details of the therapist's life are not generally beneficial for a patient.[102] They can serve to divert attention from the patient as the focus of the therapy. Especially for those who are ordained clergy, and therefore public figures, certain facts will be known about us—and many more may be assumed or fantasized by patients, both correctly and incorrectly! In an analytically oriented therapeutic framework, however, the generalities about the therapist's religious faith and moral and ethical convictions are best enacted in the quality of care and engagement s/he brings to the relationship, not disclosures of explicit details about one's own personal life and history—and never in proselytizing, which departs entirely from therapeutic neutrality and a nondirective, nonjudgmental therapeutic stance.

Disclosures of a therapist's personal faith may become a diversion from focusing on the patient's issues and, because of the privileged position of the therapist in the relationship, may even cause the patient to feel his or her own faith is less valid. Areas of common belief may be acknowledged briefly, but again, remembering that other parts of the patient may feel differently from the part who is having the discussion. Debates about areas of disagreement are fruitless—even when one believes that the patient's own religious convictions and practices are self-defeating. Such debates can easily devolve into situations in which the patient feels judged or harangued, or into intellectualizing digressions.

For example, a therapist would probably not bring up or discuss in any detail his or her particular involvements in social-justice work, unless a patient asked explicitly and the meaning of the patient's desire to know was fully explored first. The therapist's passion for justice will be present, however, in his or her appreciation for and sensitivity to real, external pressures on the patient such as racism, economic oppression, sexism, or other forms of objective societal subjugation. It may also influence his or her ability to join empathically with victims of injustice, whether political injustice or injustice that has occurred within the privacy of the patient's family. The specifics of the therapist's life—including religious beliefs, sexual orientation, personal health, and family matters—are better left undisclosed unless they have direct bearing on the therapy (e.g., if the therapist is pregnant and will be needing to plan for maternity leave). What has direct bearing in itself is sometimes a matter of discernment that will vary from patient to patient (e.g., the therapist's sexual orientation), and exploration of what should and should not be disclosed in the context of a particular therapy sometimes can become an important matter of both conscious negotiation and exploration of unconscious fears, hopes, and fantasies. While the therapist should respect a patient's "need to know"—or desire to know—s/he also should maintain healthy boundaries and not be pressured into revealing personal information that feels like a violation of his or her own privacy. This, too, becomes a matter of modeling healthy personal limits.

Personal details, whether shared explicitly or accidentally discovered, are less important in and of themselves or for what they mean to the therapist, but for what they mean to the patient and what feelings they evoke in him or her. For this reason, when asked a direct question about oneself by a patient, it is most helpful first to explore what the question means to the patient, what s/he may be fantasizing about the answer(s)—positive and negative—and what it might feel like actually to receive an answer. For example, a therapist might reply, "I will answer that question if you still want me to, but first, let's explore what might be behind it." Often the pressure behind a question will dissipate once the meaning of the question itself is fully explored. When the question still remains objectively, it is often most facilitative to give a brief, sincere answer, unless the question is felt by the therapist to be intrusive, assaultive, or otherwise inappropriate. In that case, it is wise to respond as nonreactively as possible: "I'm sorry, but I don't feel comfortable sharing details about [topic], but I am interested in exploring what you might be feeling that prompts the question." Similarly, it is my view that the explicit disclosure of overtly erotic or aggressive feelings about the patient are never advisable, since such disclosures, while ostensibly verbal, actually constitute verbal enactments and can quickly undermine the safety of the therapeutic container. Such strong feelings are best processed outside the therapy in consultation or supervision.

On the other hand, there may be times when, barring an obvious ethical breach or a sense of personal violation, a rigid refusal to self-disclose might be perceived as more harmful and distracting than giving an answer. Again, because of the multiplicity of perspectives that is always present in the room, it is important for the therapist to weigh the potential pros and cons of disclosure—considering both one's own countertransference feelings, positive and negative, and the perceived benefit to the patient. To quote Greenberg again, "These problems convince me that it is not particularly useful to attempt to come up with any sweeping statement about self-disclosure . . . Rather, our task requires coming to grips with an endless flow of decisions, each made by a particular [therapist], with a particular patient, in the context of a particular moment in their relationship."[103]

A helpful approach when being pressed by a patient for self-disclosure is to share the dilemma one is feeling about the possible ambiguous impact of such disclosure on the therapy. Gabbard advocates this approach particularly when sexual feelings are at issue,[104] but the rubric is useful at many crossroads in the therapy, as when there seems to be an impasse, however momentary. For example, in handling a lengthy silence, particularly when silence has not been a feature of the therapy previously, I have found it most empathic to offer something like, "I don't want to intrude on your thoughts, but I also don't want you to feel that I am not with you. Is there something you'd like to share about what you're thinking now, or would you rather we just sit here quietly together?" By offering the dilemma one feels in the countertransference about what to say or do next, the therapist invites the patient to join in shaping the direction of the therapy, and to share in the responsibility for what happens next.

TOUCH

Almost every therapist at one time or another is asked for a hug, or spontaneously hugged or grabbed by a patient. Different practitioners adhere to differing standards regarding whether or not to hug a patient. This can be a particular challenge for pastoral psychotherapists because, as clergy and vowed religious, giving hugs to parishioners and members of their religious communities may be a common, expected practice. As I have discussed extensively elsewhere,[105] touch, even when requested by a patient, never means just one thing.[106] Particularly in the heat of the transference-countertransference crucible, we always need to be watching and waiting for ambiguity and unconscious contradiction: "Gratification at any one level of reality leads to paradoxical frustration at another."[107] As we consider the implications of the multiplicity of both self and others, it becomes more evident that one part may be expressing a desire for touch, while other parts may be experiencing a variety of contrary, negative emotions. To act on the surface request or, even more perilously, to act impulsively out of one's own countertransferential hunches, may gratify parts of oneself and the patient, while invading, frightening, offending, or even retraumatizing other parts.

Even when a patient's desire for touching or hugging *appears* to be relatively unambivalent (which it rarely is upon further exploration), the decision to act rather than to explore collapses the "potential space"[108] in which the creative, imaginative, symbolic, and "as-if" dimensions of the therapy actually accomplish the alchemical process of healing. Metaphor collapses into concrete behavior, where it evades both the anxiety and the exploration of a multiplicity of potential meanings. No matter how much the patient may insist on his or her need for touch, there is virtually always ambivalence, and it is precisely this area of ambivalence and ambiguity that is the focus of therapy, not a quick fix. Such apparently quick fixes tend to fall back into the trap of attempting to "reparent" the patient, which may be temporarily satisfying to the patient—and almost always narcissistically gratifying to the therapist on some level ("I am seeing myself as a warm and nurturing special carer"), but which actually defeat the deeper movement of therapy from unformulated experience to symbolization to verbalization and ultimately a mature appreciation for the complexity of all human motivation and desire.

Physical touch, in particular, is an area in which therapists should maintain caution. Even when a patient asks for the therapist to hold his or her hand, to give a hug, or more, the multiplicity of each human being is a good reason to refrain. This is one of the key ways in which therapy differs from a friendship. While a friend may offer comfort in the form of a hug, it is the therapist's job to offer the possibility of understanding the impulse behind the desire.

Moreover, as Glen Gabbard, an expert in the area of boundaries in psychotherapy has written,

> Therapists can never be sure of their own intentions. We are unconsciously enacting various needs of our own when we relate to patients, and we can be masters of self-deception. We may think we are hugging a patient because he or she was deprived in childhood and therefore needs love in the present to make up for what was missed in the past. However, we may be unconsciously acting out our own sexual wishes or needs.[109]

Any departure from the norm of nonverbal sharing may signal the first step down a "slippery slope"[110] of enactments that may eventually become diversionary from the real work of therapy, or gratifying the needs of the therapist at the expense of the patient, or gratifying one part of the patient at the expense of another. Gabbard evaluates physical touch in two main ways: it should be "an extraordinary event under extraordinary circumstances" (such as a hug initiated by a patient in a moment of strong emotion), and, most important, "it should also be discussable."[111]

It is almost always most therapeutic to follow this sequence of responses: first, in a genuine and caring way, to acknowledge empathically the desire for more physical closeness and to validate and normalize the desire so that the patient does not feel shame for having expressed it; then to shift briefly into a psychoeducational mode and explain to the patient that enacting desires usually short-circuits the exploration of what they mean, and since they almost always mean more than what we can know consciously in the moment, it is better to refrain from the enactment in order to find out more about what the request really means to the patient; and finally, having signaled that many different meanings are possible, to engage in the exploration of the patient's hopes, desires, fears, fantasies, as well as to acknowledge more fully and to grieve whatever was not given to him or her when s/he was small.

Gifts and Invitations

Pastoral psychotherapists, again, may be used to receiving gifts from parishioners and others in the community and may find it particularly uncomfortable or rude to refuse a gift. On the other hand, religiously imbued shame about wanting or receiving may cause a pastoral counselor to be more conflicted than the average therapist about genuinely appreciating a patient's act of generosity. The classic stance toward gifts, predictably, was never to accept them and always to analyze their meaning without gratifying the underlying wish being expressed. This is an area that has been relaxed in modern psychoanalytic practice and probably has always been somewhat more relaxed in pastoral counseling practice. Clearly, extravagant gifts—similar to overt requests for a sexual or extratherapeutic intimate friendship—or gifts that feel like unexamined pleas for more or special contact, should be refused, as they can compromise the integrity of the professional relationship, and their meaning must be probed in as nonshaming a way as possible. A tactful way to decline a gift is to thank the patient but indicate that it is simply not part of one's therapy practice to accept gifts, or to take a psychoeducational approach of helping the patient to understand that accepting gifts might "affect the therapy in unforeseen ways."[112]

It is generally understood, on the other hand, that to refuse a small, nonsexualized gift would be likely to cause the patient unnecessary narcissistic injury and shame, especially when it is a rare occurrence (e.g., a small token of appreciation upon termination of the therapy). Nevertheless, it is important to bear in mind the classical recognition that every gift, like every enactment, expresses not only generosity but a wish—with multiple possible meanings.

It has been my own perception that gifts sometimes function as transitional objects[113] in reverse. Rather than needing to take something to remember the therapist by, some patients want to be sure the therapist will remember them. They like to give the therapist something in advance of a planned separation to feel secure that they will continue to be on the therapist's mind until they see each other again. Gifts may be signs of a patient's genuine gratitude and appreciation, but at the same time may also represent the defense of "undoing" after feeling they did something "bad" or after having had an intolerable angry or hostile thought toward the therapist. The important thing, as with all enactments, whether or not the therapist decides to accept the gift, is to explore its meaning. It is almost always the case that whatever the surface, stated meaning of the gift, there are underlying meanings that may be quite the opposite. Over time, the goal of therapy is to continue to convey the attitude that all feelings and meanings are allowable, and it is not necessary for any action to mean "just one thing." Keeping a psychoanalytic attitude means that one is always willing to entertain that any statement or action does not mean just one thing. A gift representing generosity or gratitude may also be enacting a wish to control—just as, in the reverse, a hostile attack may also convey a desire for connection and understanding.

Similarly, patients often invite therapists, and perhaps even more often pastoral psychotherapists, to special occasions in their lives such as weddings, graduations, and ordinations. It is standard practice to decline such invitations because when a therapist is present at an event outside the therapy, s/he enters into that outside life, blurring the distinction between the patient's everyday world and the uniquely separate container of the therapy. Invitations to perform weddings or take an active liturgical role in an ordination would represent even further incursions into this role confusion. I have written extensively elsewhere about the temptations of therapists to give in to such invitations out of a sense of strengthening rapport or supporting the client.[114] However, beneath such altruism often lurks a therapist's own latent narcissistic gratification at being chosen as special to the patient, and this temptation needs to be understood, like any other boundary crossing, within the context of the transference-countertransference dynamic rather than being enacted. Even apparently joyful events may hold some ambivalence for the patient (often going against his or her sense of what is socially acceptable), and by maintaining a respectful distance from the event itself, the therapist may be better able to invite further reflection that lifts up all the possible meanings of the event beyond the conscious celebratory feelings expressed in the moment.

PRAYER AND RITUAL

The domain of ritual, because of its overlap with religion, especially formal religion, may seem to be a comfort zone for pastoral psychotherapists. In my research on enactments in therapy, pastoral counselors were much more likely than nonreligiously trained therapists[115] to pray for and with patients, as well as to create or participate in rituals in therapy. In addition, approximately one-fourth of the pastoral counselors in my sample had invited patients to a lecture outside of the therapy and/or worship, and nearly half had offered a formal religious rite or sacrament such as baptism of a child or performing a wedding. While such practices fall technically into an ethical gray zone for pastoral counselors and may not be unduly harmful to the patient in the context of very brief, problem-oriented counseling, such extratherapeutic activities compromise psychodynamic therapy for all the reasons already discussed above. They constitute dual relationships that unworkably confound the transference-countertransference dynamic.

But what about the use of prayer and ritual within the context of the therapeutic container? As pastoral psychotherapists, we may be too ready to engage in ritual, especially religious or spiritual ritual, because we feel it is a dimension of our priestly domain, without fully considering all the multiple ramifications of such enactment.

Very experienced pastoral psychotherapists will disagree on the extent to which pastoral counselors should engage in explicit rituals in therapy, as my own research among diplomates in AAPC demonstrates.[116] Valerie DeMarinis, David Hogue, and others have argued thoughtfully for the incorporation of ritual into pastoral counseling.[117] Yet I would argue that especially in the context of psychoanalytically oriented therapy, the use of ritual—even in a seemingly consciously agreed upon, religiously sanctioned manner—can, like all other enactments and gratifications, collapse the symbolic and metaphorical domain of therapy into concrete action, thereby failing to maintain an open, exploratory stance.[118]

In addition, there are many rituals operating in psychotherapy that we may not readily identify as such because they do not have overt religious or spiritual content, and yet they are operative in our practices as psychotherapists. As Erik Erikson stated, "we must realize from the outset that ritualization is an aspect of everyday life which is more clearly seen in a different culture or class or even family than our own, where, in fact, ritualization is more often than not experienced simply as the proper way to do things; and the question is only why does not everybody do it our way."[119] How aware are we of rituals that are neither explicitly religious nor consciously intended?

Probably the most potent rituals in therapy are those that are unconscious, often for a time, for both participants. Some enactments occur not only once but repeatedly—for example, a patient develops a need to begin and end every session with a handshake; a patient brings the therapist a cup of coffee at every session; a therapist begins to pick up the same small figurine or object and turn it over in her hands when listening to a particular patient; a patient touches the doorframe in the same place each time upon entering the consulting room; a therapist sets out a glass of water for a particular patient each session; a patient clears his throat every time he brings up matters of scheduling. I have come to the conclusion that whenever an enactment becomes ritualized, that is, repetitive and conveying unconscious meaning, this is a call to pay attention because something new is trying to be said. Examining with the patient what possible meanings might be conveyed by habitual or repeated behaviors, however subtle, may open up new understandings.

Just as many enactments may be rituals, so many explicitly religiously motivated rituals when requested or enacted in a therapeutic context should be regarded as potentially meaning-laden enactments with multiple possible interpretations. In one of the more common examples of this, a patient may ask a pastoral counselor to pray with him or her. It is important to remember that praying is an enactment and, as such, should be explored just as any other enactment or potential enactment would be. A request for prayer will almost always mean more than what appears on the surface as a straightforward request for prayer and pastoral care among two religiously committed people. Such a request should be approached with great sensitivity and caution, since it is likely to bear multiple significances, although only a surface desire is consciously available in the interaction in the moment.

A request for prayer by a patient can convey, among many other possibilities, feelings of helplessness, dependency, closeness, a desire for greater intimacy with the therapist, a preconditioned cultural expectation, an erotic desire disguised as a more socially acceptable request, a wish to control the therapist or the hour, a means to avoid exploration of issues, or a cry of pain. Agreeing to such a request on the part of the therapist can also convey multiple meanings, not only the conscious desire to be caring, nurturing, and spiritually supportive, but less conscious motives such as the wish to control the patient or the hour; the narcissistic wish to *be seen* as caring, nurturing, and spiritually supportive; collusion with the patient around avoiding more painful issues; avoidance of the therapist's own difficult issues that current themes in the therapy may be stimulating in the countertransference; avoidance of overt conflict with the patient; or defense against feelings of hostility or hatred toward the patient.

Brent's Prayer Request

Brent spent a session sharing his shame and frustration about breaking up with a long-distance girlfriend, "Barb," with whom he had "never let the relationship go anywhere." In the previous session, he had noticed that he felt that she was in control, and he liked that. "In fact, she almost mothered me." He felt they were "very much alike." I observed that he was describing painful things, but there didn't seem to be much feeling in the room. He said, "I've got that cut off at the neck thing going on again." "What do you think the feeling might be, below the neck?" He paused for a bit, and then started to sweat, and said, "I'm really anxious." Going on my gut sense in the moment, I said, "Sometimes anxiety, like depression, is not so much a feeling as a defense against feeling something else. Do you think there is another feeling underneath the anxiety?" He said, suddenly, "I'm afraid of my own spontaneity!" We continued to explore the theme of control and his fear of losing control.

I began to notice that the heady quality of our conversation persisted. I said tentatively, "This may not fit for you, but if it were me, I might feel some real regret or sadness about breaking up with Barb." He teared up and said he did feel very sad that he had cut off the relationship before it had had a chance to go anywhere. He had used so many of the same words as he had used to describe his mother, I finally said, "I could be completely wrong about this, but it sounds a lot like the way you've described your mom." He looked struck between the eyes, and said "Oh, oh!" and began to wonder if the reason he had ended the relationship was because, while he enjoyed the feeling of being protected, he also feared her judgment, just as he had feared his mother's. In this session, we continued to explore his feelings of regret about losing Barb.

Toward the end of the session Brent began to tear up, and I noted that the end of the relationship coincided roughly with his mother's death. This led to further reflection on unresolved grief about his mother's death, and Brent began to cry in earnest, saying "You're right, too—I am so angry! I'm angry that for thirty-two years I haven't been able to feel joy, or other feelings either!" As he wiped the tears from his face, he said, "Here I go again, crying right at the end of the session. I need to work some more on why I do that."

It was time to stop, and he took quite a while writing his check, gathering his things, and getting up. He was going on a trip, and asked if I had any other times the following week so that we wouldn't have to skip a session (as he had earlier planned to do). I said I didn't have any other evening times, but could offer a late afternoon time if he could leave work a little early. He said, "No, evenings are really better for me because I like to get here once the rest of the day is over and leave it completely behind." At the door he paused and said, "Next time I'd like to talk about how prayer might be a part of our time here. That's what pastoral counseling means, right?" I responded that that sounded important for us to talk about next time.

As we processed this prayer request in subsequent sessions—without actually jumping in and praying—some underlying themes began to emerge, and the meanings of the request began to become more accessible. Prayer, as a socially acceptable way of sharing, came to represent yet another form of pseudointimacy, an enactment that could foreclose further emotional exploration. Brent elaborated that his fantasy about prayer was to be prayed over and prayed for *by me*. Brent's projections onto me as a woman priest factored into this—the desire for intimacy was again becoming blended with his fantasies of having me as a "better mother," one who again was powerful and perhaps even controlling, but without the frightening, judgmental aspect. (The fear of this, however, was of course lurking just beneath the surface request as well.)

His missing Barb, and his longing to be close to a woman, were being expressed, but again, at a safe distance, cloaked in a desire for prayer rather than explicit intimacy. At the same time, Brent was expressing a more aggressive urge—for control—on the heels of being denied the special concession he wanted. At a more unconscious level, he was turning the tables and pushing for something more, under the guise of a shared Christian practice.

As these fantasies began to emerge, I was able to say that I thought that our praying together carried the danger of important feelings being more and more subsumed under nice, Christian language, without being able to explore and know the more hostile and aggressive parts of him—toward his mother, his father, his brother, or me as "another one of those powerful women in your life." We never did end up praying together, because the wish to pray or be prayed for dissipated as we explored what it represented in the dynamic of the therapy. But the importance of Brent's desire, his longing to be loved and protected by a powerful mother/father—and perhaps even a powerful God—who would care for him without judging his performance or punishing him for either his inadequacies or his successes, was empathically held and valued in our shared exploration.

This example illustrates how prayer and spiritual ritual-making must be approached, as with all other enactments, with the utmost care. It is best to err on the side of being conservative, if only because once one has acted, the action cannot be undone. We cannot unring a bell. Action, even religious action, tends to concretize desire and dissipate the tension in which unconscious meanings live. But as long as the desire remains unenacted, it continues to belong to the realm of potential space, of fantasy, and of desire, where its multiple meanings can continue to be revisited. And when unexpected enactments and rituals do inevitably occur, the exploration of their meaning—far more than the gratification of desires of the moment, even those expressed in religious form—will contribute most fruitfully to the patient's long-term spiritual goals of expanded awareness, freedom, and peace.

TOXIC RELIGION

In keeping with the pastoral therapist's relative neutrality and restraint from self-disclosure about religion, it is also important to recognize that religion—like any other dimension of the patient's life—may be an arena in which unconscious conflicts and woundedness will play out over the course of a lifetime. Patients may not only be more likely to project religious memories, fantasies, idealizations, and fears onto pastoral psychotherapists. They may also be more likely to disclose particulars of their own religious experiences and practices. As Constance Goldberg has pointed out, religion is an area of particular sensitivity, requiring respect and therapeutic tact on the part of the therapist.[120] At the same time, it should not be assumed that the patient's religious thoughts and beliefs are somehow in a different category from other important aspects of his or her inner life, or off limits to therapeutic exploration. As Goldberg indicates, the foundations of a devoted believer's faith should not be questioned—to do so would be both disrespectful and countertherapeutic. How a patient uses religious language and metaphor, however, and especially how religion is *functioning* in the patient's life (i.e., in self psychological terminology, how its selfobject functions) can offer important information for exploration.[121] The patient's relationship to and use of religion and spirituality, like his or her use of sex, food, money, political values and activities, and a host of other important aspects of life, are potent areas of communication about the patient's inner world, both conscious and unconscious, and like all these other arenas, are also multiply-constituted and associated with multiple inner objects and object relations.

A patient's images of God, in particular, can convey important clues about parental imagoes, since authority figures internalized from earliest childhood are often writ large by the psyche onto the individual's impressions of the divine.[122] Several self psychologists interested in the intersection of religion and psychotherapy have recently explored the selfobject functions of God representations (including gender),[123] religious experience,[124] and experiences in congregational dynamics.[125] Relational analysts have also begun to explore the multiple potential meanings associated with patients' religious thoughts, conflicts, issues, and experiences.[126]

It is necessary, however, to recognize that because religion and spirituality exist at the very frontiers of an individual's hopes and dreads both about the meaning/meaninglessness of life and about mortality, they constitute one of the most fiercely protected domains of a patient's sense of identity and life purpose. We bring our own judgments of the patient's religiosity into the therapy at our own peril and the peril of the treatment. While secular therapists may be prone to carrying their own set of judgments about religion into the therapeutic relationship, religiously trained and pastoral psychotherapists are no less likely to carry our own biases when the religious beliefs of a patient differ significantly from our own. Pastoral therapists with advanced degrees in theology may be especially at risk of finding ourselves judging a patient's beliefs as rigid, dogmatic, sloppy, naïve, self-destructive, self-absorbed, or "just plain wrong!" Just as other attitudes we try to hide under a mask of therapeutic neutrality "ooze" into the therapeutic dynamic, so too will our judgments about religion. The more we try to hide our judgments especially from ourselves, the more this leakage is likely to occur in unconscious ways. This is not to advocate for self-disclosure about one's personal faith or for theological disputation but for a level of rigor and honesty regarding our religious feelings and reactions in the countertransference and maintaining consciousness about the ways in which our own attitudes might be a disservice to the therapy.

Jennifer's Tithe

I probably made some of my worst mistakes with "Jennifer." Both the setup of the therapy and my countertransferential resistances in supervision were problematic. Jennifer's case, however, illustrates well some of the perils of pastoral counseling with a religiously committed client of a different spiritual tradition.

My agency at the time had an arrangement to provide very low-fee therapy to residents of a shelter that provided comprehensive case management and job training for recently homeless women. As part of this arrangement, the shelter expected that therapists would be in communication with shelter case managers about the clients' progress in therapy and to participate in staffing meetings at the shelter, and clients were required to sign a release of confidentiality to that effect—in other words, they had no choice about giving up their privacy in this way, nor did the treating therapists. This was a matter of ongoing discussion and care among the staff. We were all aware of the pitfalls of the arrangement, but both the range of theoretical differences among staff and the practical benefits of being able to offer services to a desperately underserved population of women contributed to a consensus view that the advantages outweighed the disadvantages of this setup.

Each therapist navigated the parameters of the agreement with the shelter in his or her own way, with ongoing supervision and peer consultation to keep us honest about how our own issues and resistances might become entangled in the inherent triangulations of this arrangement. It was my practice to discuss the limits of confidentiality carefully with each client from the shelter, to be transparent with the client about what might need to be shared, and to respect clients' wishes about what should not be shared. I was very conservative about saying anything to the case managers, and I attempted to preserve the container of the therapy as well as possible.

Early in the therapy, Jennifer professed delight that I was an ordained minister. "It's so great that you are a minister! You can really understand how important faith is to me." She would frequently talk about her church involvement, and it became apparent that I was being cast in an all-or-nothing split as the good ally of her religious commitment, in contrast with the shelter staff, whom she experienced as negative, skeptical, and discouraging. In reality, the more she shared about her church life, the more I was inwardly squirming.

Jennifer initially remained reserved and somewhat mysterious about the breach between herself and her mother, indicating that her mother was always "very attentive" when she was growing up, and gave her a lot. Her father was mostly absent "working," or was verbally abusive, while her mother was "sweet, kind, and loving, the kind of parent I want to be." Over the course of the first year of therapy, however, a very different picture began to emerge. Her father was an active alcoholic during Jennifer's childhood, often absent on drinking binges, but when Jennifer started vocational school, he went into recovery and suddenly took on a mediating role as "the family communicator." Initially recounting details in a flat, unemotional voice,

Jennifer described how she had been physically abused by both parents—spanked hard and beaten in frustration, hair pulled, dragged by the hair, kicked in the chest. On one occasion, her mother put her fist through the wall immediately next to the place where Jennifer was standing, and then blamed Jennifer, forcing her to hang a poster over the hole to cover it up. One day when she was about six or seven years old, Jennifer decided to run away from home. She stole some food and cash and headed off down the street. She recalled her mother coming out to the front steps of the house and calling after her, "You can go, but if you do, that will be the last meal you'll ever eat!" Under her mother's stern gaze, Jennifer slowed her steps, then turned around and walked back into her house, where she was reprimanded harshly and refused food until the next day.

Much later in the therapy, when Jennifer was connecting feelings with her story, she realized that the worst part of that memory for her was not the punishment but the feeling that her mother had broken her will. This felt like a defining moment as she remembered it. Whether "it" was actually a single event, or more likely, an accumulation of similar moments in which she felt her will had been broken, this dynamic had shaped the adult she was to become—concerned with rules and obedience, operating with a surface persona of brittle dignity, but at the same time resenting authority and suppressing a simmering rage everywhere in her life—on the job, in her relationships with men, in her parenting, in her conflicts with her family members, and in her church.

Lying and covering things over became the family's favored mode of communication. Jennifer would frequently label one parent as the liar and the other as the one who "never lied to me," and then reverse the labels as different stories came out. "Truth" for Jennifer was either a rigid absolute or something that could be manipulated for the sake of survival—but this often backfired. During the first few months of therapy, she was fired from her job for stealing, and she spent many sessions protesting that her boss and a coworker had both lied about her. It emerged that another reason for the five-year rift with her mother was that she viewed her mother as a liar and had broken off with her, in spite of her father's pleas for family unity.

Jennifer's use of religion early in the therapy to shore up her defenses was a continual source of countertransference discomfort for me. I felt all the suppressed rage, outrage, as well as vicarious degradation and pain, as she flatly disclosed more and more stories of abuse. She once described their relationship as a "clash of the Titans," with her mother in the role of "Medusa." When I asked her who she was in the scenario, she retreated quickly, saying, "Oh, I don't really know Greek mythology. I just always try to be Jesus." I followed with one of my many early (and futile!) efforts to forcibly break down the splitting I was seeing, and to chip away at the defensive use of God, Jesus, and religion, by saying, "Medusa and Jesus, that's quite a combination." Not surprisingly, she responded defensively with, "Well, all Christians are supposed to pattern themselves after Jesus, aren't we?" During this time Jennifer also would frequently quote scripture to me, sometimes simply citing verse numbers, assuming that as a minister I would understand and agree with her interpretation. The conflict we began to enact, between the devout Christian disciple and the powerful but not-so-devout priest/counselor, began to feel very much like the same "clash of the Titans" she had described with her mother.

I came (somewhat reluctantly) to recognize that there was no way to soften Jennifer's religious defenses by arguing, convincing, or interpreting. Although I often bit my tongue, I challenged her often enough—and she was exquisitely attuned to empathic ruptures—so that religion became a kind of psychic battleground between us. I became the authority she felt a need to convert to "true" Christianity and the judgmental parent who once again was failing to meet her empathically. My best work with Jennifer would happen whenever I could let go of the need to somehow "fix" her approach to religion and was able to hear and give voice to her pain. Jennifer revealed that her mother as well as her father had been alcoholic. She remembered longing for her mother's attention and feeling jealous of the bond between her mother and her mother's mother. She held out her hand, and as she did, I shared an image that came to mind of holding out a fragile baby bird, hoping for it to be accepted but fearing it would be squashed. She was struck by this, associating that her mother's favorite animal was a cat. This opened a new level of acknowledgement of how much she had feared and even hated her mother, "and I even blamed God."

An important turning point in our work together came when Jennifer's defiance perhaps became lodged in me countertransferentially and was enacted not in direct relation to her but, rather, in relation to my own supervisors and to the shelter staff. Jennifer's case worker at the shelter, "Dorothy," called me and said that the shelter staff were opposed to Jennifer's continuing practice of tithing to her church. Dorothy wanted me to tell Jennifer that it was unhealthy, especially considering all her other expenses. Dorothy also expressed concern about a kind of pyramid scheme the church leadership had drawn Jennifer into, and I agreed with Dorothy that it seemed the church leaders were more concerned about their own goals than necessarily caring for Jennifer's welfare. However, I told Dorothy that it wasn't my style of therapy to advise clients what to do and that I also felt that Jennifer's religion was a source of strength and solace for her during this time of crisis. Dorothy and the staff had been considering "exiting" Jennifer from the program over this disagreement, and I strongly urged them not to do so.

When I reported this exchange to Jennifer in our next session, she expressed fervent gratitude for my advocacy, and some of the chronic, relentless feeling of anxiety in the room seemed to dissipate. She "vented" for a while about the unfair rules of the shelter, but by the end of the same session, to my surprise, she began to own that she herself had "a few major control issues, too." Clearly, on one level, I had joined with the rebellious part of her, siding with one half of the daughter-parent split, and this was deeply gratifying to her—though not necessarily therapeutic per se. On the other hand, by relinquishing my former territory as the parental authority, I unconsciously allowed her to pick up the adult role for herself, and she became more self-reflective.

My enactment also had the value of validating her self-determination vis-à-vis her very real circumstance with the shelter staff. In that sense, I also supported her claiming her personal authority (in the form of tithing, even if this might not have worked out well without my—or someone's—advocacy).

From that time forward, Jennifer began to express that therapy was "where I feel good." She brought her daughter, "Grace," to session frequently because she had no child care, and we both experienced a moment of hushed amazement when Grace, seemingly picking up on the more relaxed mood, playfully pulled up on my knee and rested her cheek there in a moment of intense intimacy. Jennifer expressed amazement and enjoyment watching Grace relax. Multiple levels of mother-daughter dynamics were being enacted in that moment. She was both receiving nurture vicariously and feeling supported as an adult mother; I was experiencing my own maternal feelings toward her, her daughter, myself as a daughter, and my own daughter (who was only a little older than Grace at the time).

As we continued to explore layers of understanding in the therapy over the next year, including not only the positive affects but also envy, competition, fear, hate, and aggression, Jennifer became more and more able to express a full range of feelings. She came to know about her abuse not only in split-off stories that lived mostly in her head but through her feelings. She was able to grieve. She began to talk with her mother again, sometimes still relying on the mediation of her father, but working toward a more honest and less mutually hostile and manipulative relationship. Most notably, she formed a new and more healthy relationship with a partner, Jake, who was kind to Grace and supportive of Jennifer's own growth. Deciding to challenge the church's rules, which she now increasingly saw as irrationally rigid and controlling, she defied church elders by moving in with Jake—but this time, her defiance was more consciously thought through. She made her decision with a fuller, more emotional sense of the possible consequences and appreciating the significance of taking her power into her own hands. After being threatened with removal as a Sunday school teacher for "living in sin," she left that church and, together with Jake, found a Baptist church in their neighborhood where there was a sense of acceptance and greater freedom—while Jennifer's core religious commitments as a "Bible-believing Christian," were still embraced there. Jennifer and Jake married after about six months, and at that time Jennifer decided to go back to school and to terminate therapy.

Astute readers, reading between the lines, will recognize that this "happy ending" was still a part of Jennifer's desire to have everything be fine and perfect, and that there would certainly be further conflicts in the future, further splitting and conflictual relations with authority, further irruptions of certain habitual defenses, and a tendency to idealize saviors while defying attackers. Jennifer's traumatic history would not be healed magically, either by religion, therapy, or by romantic love. But Jennifer did have some tools now to understand her own inner process better and to be more reflective in her relationships.

The paradoxical lesson Jennifer taught me was that a frontal attack on what may have all the earmarks of toxic religion, however diplomatically attempted, will not accomplish anything therapeutic. On the other hand, an empathical joining with the patient's hidden, even shame-laden needs, and offering nonjudgmental understanding of previously suppressed fears and traumatic memories can help to free the patient not only from the grip of a poisonous, disempowering religious community or practice but from the self-defeating parts of herself that once made such a religion so attractive.

Chapter 5

The Middle Phase and Termination: Multiplicity in Action

It is a very remarkable thing that the Unconscious of one human being can react upon that of another, without passing through the Conscious. This deserves closer investigation, especially with a view to finding out whether preconscious activity can be excluded as playing a part in it; but, descriptively speaking, the fact is incontestable.

—Sigmund Freud, "The Unconscious"[1]

Empathy: Human Beings Are Intrinsically Relational

The foundation for all effective therapeutic work is empathy.[2] Rather than a classical analytical "blank screen,"[3] it is important for the therapist to be warm and genuine and to have "unconditional positive regard" for the patient (though not necessarily for everything the patient says or does). The therapist offers an honest, deeply human presence. In this sense, Carl Rogers's view of empathic relationship is the basis for therapy: "It is the quality of the interpersonal encounter with the patient which is the most significant element in determining effectiveness."[4] This is echoed as a tenet of existential therapy as well: "It is the relationship that heals."[5] The therapist genuinely cares about the well-being of the patient as his or her first priority.

Therapeutic "neutrality" is important, but it is not the same thing as being a "blank screen." It does not mean coldness, aloofness, or lack of engagement. Sigmund Freud's famous recommendation that the therapist exercise surgical coldness[6] was written in the context of his anxiety about the dangers of erotic transference and countertransference, and there is ample evidence that he himself did not often adhere to it.[7] Neutrality *does* mean refraining from bringing a specific or judgment-laden agenda for the patient's life. In some sense, neutrality even resembles Rogers's "nonpossessive caring."[8] The therapist does not need the patient to be a certain way or to please him or her. The therapist's focus is on the patient's needs, not his or her own.

Neutrality also means reserving judgment about what one part of the patient may be expressing, recognizing that other parts may have very different views or experiences. Even when the "parts" of a person were conceived simply in terms of id, ego, and superego, Anna Freud defined neutrality as maintaining equidistance from these "institutions of the mind," and also external reality.[9] This is all the more crucial in light of contemporary formulations in which each self is even more multiply-conceived, and whatever is coming up in the present moment is more reflective of the particular interaction of the patient's inner objects with the therapist's, than a single, global "truth" that requires definitive interpretation.

Abstinence is a related principle, classically defined as "refraining from gratifying the patient's transference wishes"[10] or desires. There is obviously always going to be some gratification for both: for the patient, simply in being listened to empathically and nonjudgmentally, and for the therapist, in offering something of value. A complete absence of any expression of care for the patient would probably end in rapid termination! I understand abstinence not at all as withholding of warmth but as an attitude of quiet expectancy, in which one refrains from making too much noise or being too active in order to make room for whatever the many parts of the patient might want to come out and say or do. Especially with regard to enactments, abstinence suggests a value for reflection over action that can be very important when the multiple meanings of a potential pull to act are not yet even minimally understood psychodynamically. More will be said about enactments below. The important thing to remember is that genuine empathy usually does not mean more activity on the part of the therapist but, rather, more attunement to what is occurring in the transference-countertransference continuum.

Psychiatrist Howard E. Book has written:

> What one understands of a patient's internal experience and how one uses (or chooses not to use) that understanding are quite different. A test of successfully being this is the extent to which the therapist's responses stimulate and deepen the patient's narrative flow . . . Put another way, empathy is being able to finish a patient's sentence. Being empathic, though, is not finishing that sentence. Having one's sentence finished is seldom experienced as being understood or comforted, but, rather, is experienced as intrusive and infantilizing.[11]

There is some agreement between the use of the term *empathy* in psychoanalytic theory and Rogers's understanding of empathy as warmth and unconditional positive regard. Rogers's "client-centered" approach became popular in pastoral counseling from the 1960s onward, especially through the work of Howard Clinebell.[12] There are also significant differences, however, in the psychoanalytic understanding of empathy.[13] Because Rogers believed that clients would naturally grow if the right environment were provided,[14] his approach was nondirective, that is, refraining from leading the client toward a goal set by the therapist. Very little is said, although much is still conveyed nonverbally. "Following the client," that is, closely attending the patient's affect and content, and not taking the lead or setting one's own agenda in the course of a session, is central to all good therapy. For this reason, "Rogerian therapy" may appear rather passive, but this characterization of Rogers's own work is stereotyped and naïve. Working empathically with the patient as described by

Heinz Kohut, however, is a more active process, with the therapist taking more initiative, and involving intensive work in the transference-countertransference relationship.

Kohut defined empathy in an early paper as "vicarious introspection."[15] He later revisited this paper, stating that both critics and supporters had missed the points he was trying to make about empathy: it is not psychic activity or an association with a particular set of positive emotions (compassion or affection)—it can in fact be hostile or intuition.[16] Kohut himself viewed empathy as empirical, even scientific. He clarified that empathy is an "information-gathering mental activity," which as such does create a powerful emotional bond between people. Because of the beneficial action of empathy, he did view empathy as a precondition both for supportive, effective parenting and for therapy, and he regarded empathy as beneficial per se. Kohut believed that an empathic milieu was necessary to keep human beings alive and sane. Intersubjective theorists continue to affirm Kohut's contention that sustained empathy, or "empathic-introspective inquiry," is the primary tool of therapeutic observation and insight.[17]

Empathy works primarily through the medium of the countertransference, as the therapist experiences affects, resonances, fantasies, and images that are drawn from the pool of unconscious material and "shared wisdom" in the intersubjective dynamic of the therapy. As Christopher Bollas wrote in *The Shadow of the Object*, "it is a feature of our present-day understanding of the transference that the other source of the analysand's free association is the psychoanalyst's countertransference, so much so that *in order to find the patient, we must look for him [or her] within ourselves.*"[18] To quote Bollas further:

> By establishing a countertransference readiness I am creating an internal space which allows for a more complete and articulate expression of the patient's transference speech than if I were to close down this internal space and replace it with some ideal notion of absolute mental neutrality or scientific detachment ... What the analyst feels, imagines, and thinks to himself [or herself] while with the patient may at any one moment be a specific element of the patient's projectively-identified psychic life ... that creation of a total environment in which both patient and analyst pursue a "life" together.[19]

This requires a suspension of certainty, and a capacity to tolerate shared experience that is not yet verbalized or even symbolized, sometimes for prolonged periods in the therapy. Sometimes a therapist's not-knowing, or even a sense of being unable to think,[20] is in itself a countertransference reflection of the patient's own struggles with knowing what s/he knows and with symbolization. Bollas continues,

> For a very long period of time, and perhaps it never ends, we are being taken into the patient's environmental idiom, and for considerable stretches of time

we do not know who we are, what function we are meant to fulfill, or our fate as his [or her] object . . . The most ordinary countertransference state is a not-knowing-yet-experiencing one. I know that I am in the process of experiencing something, but I do not as yet know what it is, and I may have to sustain this not knowing for a long time . . . The capacity to bear and value this necessary uncertainty defines one of our most important clinical responsibilities to the patient; and it enhances our ability to become lost inside the patient's evolving environment . . . If our own sense of identity is certain, then its loss within the clinical space is essential to the patient's discovery of [him- or herself]."[21]

Therapy that seeks only to nurture (whether called "Rogerian" or "analytic"), and stops there, may feel supportive to the patient for a while, but it is not conducive to deep change. Construing empathy as warmth and nurture is actually a misreading of Rogers himself. Being empathic and being nice are not the same thing. Gratifying the conscious wish or demand of the patient is directly counter to her deeper need, her "unconscious plan for health."[22] Such direct gratification can even be retraumatizing if it reenacts a harmful childhood experience. This is especially true in the arena of touch. While a patient may consciously seem to wish, or ask directly, for nurturing touch, physical holding, or even sexual contact, any physical touching may be experienced at a deeper level by the patient as intrusive and retraumatizing.[23]

The therapist can also fall into the trap of trying to "reparent" the patient. This is a simplistic view of trying to provide the patient with a "corrective emotional experience,"[24] and in any case it is literally impossible.[25] Certain aspects of parenting must occur at the appropriate developmental age.[26] Alice Miller's understanding of the adult's task is one of *mourning* for what was lost and grieving the injuries of childhood.[27] This is quite different from trying to reexperience one's childhood in therapy and coming out a new person, as if the traumas never existed. I do not even see this as desirable. Our traumas, painful as they are, are also a source of richness and compassion in our lives and cannot be wiped away. Healing is not erasing the past but incorporating it into a living whole.

Therapy, then, cannot make up for the losses and devastations of the past. The work of healing is not finding some new perfection, or satisfying fantasies of revenge or retaliation, but, as Miller wrote, mourning what was not received in childhood and, through this process of grieving, being able to move on.[28] The therapist can facilitate this process not by trying to be the perfect parent the child never had, but by being an authentic human being who knows a thing or two about how to mourn, who tries sincerely to understand, who sometimes fails, and who is not afraid to explore such failures as a path to further understanding. In Glen Gabbard's words:

To some degree . . . therapists must ultimately fail their patients. In other words, patients must come to terms with the limitations of what another human being can do to gratify the longings that have been built up over a lifetime. Similarly, therapists who are beginning their practices need to mourn the loss of their cherished fantasies of healing others and shielding them from anxieties, stresses, period of dysphoria, and fundamental existential dilemmas. Therapists also need to mourn the limits of their profession while the patient mourns long-held fantasies.[29]

As the therapist remains nondefensive about moments of impasse or empathic rupture, s/he also models for the patient—who may have very exacting notions of perfection—an attitude of curiosity and self-acceptance that the patient can begin to internalize, replacing blame and self-criticism with curiosity and tolerance for ambiguity. In Kleinian terms, the paranoid-schizoid mode of all-or-nothing relating may begin to become less fixed as a tendency. The patient may begin to move internally toward the depressive position in which good and bad can be held together—including the good and bad moments of the therapy, the good and bad aspects of the therapist as internalized by the patient, and the patient's own tolerance of him- or herself.

In place of reparenting, Michael Basch proposes a better metaphor, that of midwife:

> The mobilization of the transference in dynamic psychotherapy permits the re-creation of a situation analogous to the traumatic one of the patient's childhood. But this time—since the patient now possesses adult faculties and experience, and the therapist is prepared to understand what is happening—the trauma is not so intense nor does it have the same consequences: arrest and regression. Instead, reliving it spurs maturation. By understanding what has happened to him [or her] the patient is prepared to face and resolve his [or her] difficulties. The therapist does not solve the patient's problems, nor does [s/]he supply what has been lacking in the patient's upbringing—only the patient can make up to [him- or herself] what he [or she] has missed. The therapist serves only as a midwife for the birth of a patient's self-esteem and for the development of a more adequate self-concept.[30]

Empathy, then, in and of itself is not enough to effect healing.[31] A psychodynamic approach requires the therapist to observe the process that is occurring between therapist and patient and to act as midwife to the patient's growing insights about why his or her relationship might be unfolding as it is. This leads to a direct engagement with the transference-countertransference dynamic, and the flow of associations, feelings, and meanings that emerge in the intersubjective space between the patient and the therapist. Because in relational psychotherapy it is understood that there is mutual influence in the therapeutic dynamic, it is not always possible or even desirable to try to isolate the transference from the countertransference. Some of the most meaningful emotional events will occur in the interaction *between* patient and therapist.

It is nevertheless helpful to survey the common techniques for understanding and working as a therapist with transference and countertransference, respectively, as separate concepts. Since they belong on the polar ends of a spectrum of shared subjectivity, there will still be times when one or the other seems more prominent, and in any case, the subjectivity of each partner in the therapeutic relationship deserves its own scrutiny. Exploration of the transference can help patients to begin to identify their own projective tendencies; exploration of the countertransference—whether or not disclosed to the patient—is an important foundation for maintaining safe boundaries and discerning what may be going on in the therapeutic relationship that is "my stuff" to deal with apart from the therapy. This clarity on both sides can further enhance the possibility of recognizing a more fluid interplay of subjectivities in the therapy as it becomes prominent.

Working in the Transference

Transference, as classically defined, is the *unconscious transferring* of expectations from the important figures in one's early childhood, particularly the parents/primary caretakers, onto other people in current-day life. Because infants and small children are literally at the mercy of these early figures, transference is especially intense in relation to authority figures in the patient's present life. Thus, transference is likely to be most evident in regressive life situations, such as a student in relation to a teacher, an employee in relation to a boss, or a patient in relation to a doctor—or a therapist! Because this dynamic is unconscious, it is often ignored or denied. In transient situations, such as a brief dentist's appointment, it may not manifest itself in any notable behaviors. In ongoing relationships where there is a power imbalance, however, transference may become a powerful unconscious force in the dynamic between two people. (Note that technically the term *transference* does not apply in marital/partnered relationships or friendships, which are supposedly equal and mutual. This is generally understood simply in terms of projection. However, a virtually indistinguishable process of projection and/or projective identification may occur and become chronic between partners, particularly whenever there is an unconsciously or consciously perceived imbalance of power, or the partners become locked in a chronic parent-child dynamic.)

Because the therapist represents power (however egalitarian his or her "style" of therapy on a conscious interpersonal level), psychoanalytic therapy works with a foundational assumption that the patient will bring into the therapeutic relationship a series of unconscious expectations and habitual responses that were laid down in earliest childhood.[32] The patient "transfers" her feelings toward intimate others in her childhood, especially her primary caretakers, onto the therapist. The less awareness there is of the quality of those original relationships, the more intensely it will be reenacted, or "acted out" in the therapeutic relationship. All forms of intensive or "depth" psychotherapy—from object relations, to self psychology, to "control mastery,"[33] to Jungian analysis, to contemporary psychoanalytic approaches, both relational and intersubjective—operate from some variation on this basic principle. Although most therapists find themselves most at home in a particular theoretical framework, the actual practice of psychoanalytic therapy tends to draw from a variety of psychoanalytic writers and resources, recognizing that most theories were derived from working with particular populations, and so may work better with one patient (or a particular phase of that patient's development) than another.[34] What distinguishes all analytic orientations from all other counseling approaches is that the *primary focus* of the work itself is on the various manifestations of this unconscious relationship, and the effect of the patient's inner objects on the therapeutic process.

This is why boundaries and safety, as described especially in chapter 4, are so crucial. There is a regressive dimension to being in the patient role and to the therapist's power—and responsibility—to maintain a safe container in which transferences can emerge in order to be understood and resolved. If the patient does not feel safe at a basic level, s/he will not be able to let go of the everyday conscious effort to control him- or herself, the environment, and, at times, the therapist. Without a fundamental sense of safety, the patient cannot let go and allow the flow of the irrational to emerge. Furthermore, if therapy is to attend the multiple parts of the patient and invite all parts to have voice, there must be safety not only for the "good" and compliant aspects of the patient's personality, but the guilty, the nasty, the hungry, and all the other parts that the person may have disavowed as unacceptable or repressed as intolerable. Without an immersion into and acceptance of the irrational, this kind of multiply-attuned therapeutic exploration cannot move forward.

The "Fundamental Rule": Free Association

Free association was Freud's term for the process involving both thought and speech, whereby the patient is encouraged to say whatever comes into his or her mind, without self-censorship.[35] This is not adhered to as a rigid rule, as once was observed in classical psychoanalysis. Nevertheless, the goal is to allow and create an environment of safety for the patient that encourages as unhindered a flow of associations as possible. Even more than dream material, the flow of associations is perhaps the most central evidence of what is happening in the patient's unconscious. Freud placed free association, together with the therapist's evenly suspended attentiveness, as the defining characteristics of psychoanalytic process. Thus, an intersubjective process lies at the center of Freud's own vision for the therapeutic enterprise, as freeing both participants from the constraints of ordinary, everyday social speaking and listening, in order that unconscious communication may become more available for shared examination.[36] The heart of psychoanalytic inquiry is to explore and foster a sense of nonjudgmental curiosity about what this flow of associations reveals: What is linked with what (people, ideas, events, feelings), however seemingly irrational? What gets mentioned, and, sometimes more significantly, what gets left out or passed over? This kind of free-flowing narrative of inner thoughts requires a loosening of everyday social, business, or intellectual discourse so that unconscious thoughts, feelings, fantasies, and memories can emerge and their meaning can be explored. In fact, a persistent clinging to social chatter, business issues, intellectualization, or even abstract "God talk" may be a sign of unconscious resistance on the part of the patient, therapist, or both to allowing more inward thoughts and feelings to spill out.

As Freud discovered early on in his own practice, one of the most significant aspects of fostering an atmosphere of free association is not what is allowed to flow forth from the patient but what becomes blocked. It is always a signal that an important issue has been touched when a patient struggles with saying aloud a thought that s/he feels too ashamed or afraid to express, or even with lapses in thinking in which s/he "goes blank," indicating that something is being blocked from consciousness altogether. This was for Freud the signal of the process of resistance at work, and even contemporary practitioners who prefer other models to the somewhat combative metaphor of "resistance" recognize that such impasses represent very important, and often very tender, issues for the patient, which, when allowed safely to be given voice, may lead to new levels of clarity and empowerment for the patient.

For the associational process to unfold, the therapist must also be available to his or her own inner thoughts and feelings, his or her own chain of associations. This requires a capacity to tune in to multiple channels of information, both spoken and unspoken, external and internal, simultaneously. This is Freud's "evenly suspended attention,"[37] as described in the previous chapter. It is also important to develop as much multicultural fluency as possible, so that one is more readily attuned to symbols, images, narratives, thought-processes, and beliefs that differ from one's own cultural upbringing.[38]

Interpretation/Exploration

Interpretation in its strictest sense is a verbal sharing by the therapist of a hypothesis about something the therapist perceives may be going on, either in the intersubjective field between him- or herself and the patient or—even more tentatively—in the internal dynamic of the patient. It is not, as it is sometimes caricatured, a flat-footed pronouncement from on high, such as "you are reacting negatively to your boss because as a child you unconsciously wished to kill your father" (although such a statement *might* emerge, in much more tentative language, in the course of shared examination of a particular troubling interaction in the patient's life!).

Nevertheless, without any hypothesizing at all on the part of the therapist, the patient could become caught in a repetitive loop of self-reflection that does not allow anything new to emerge into consciousness. Although some Rogerian therapists might disagree, the therapist's independent input is needed, at least from time to time, or when the patient reaches a point of impasse or frustration with his or her own limits of understanding. (As Rogers' own writings and videotapes reveal,[39] what the most nondirective therapist chooses to mirror and when have an interpretive function. Nondirective or "person-centered" therapy is a subtle art and should not be caricatured as total passivity on the part of the therapist.[40]) As Freud observed, "it is not the same thing to know a thing in one's own mind and to hear it from someone outside." Patients will also vary from one another, and among their own internal parts as well, as to how active they need or want the therapist to be at any given season in the therapy. Therapeutic tact and sensitivity also include, among other things, the capacity to discern when it may be most facilitative to venture a guess about what may be going on in the patient's inner world, and when it may be best to remain quiet and allow more time for meanings to emerge on their own.

Interpretation is most effective when it refers to something that is occurring within the context of the transference-countertransference dynamic itself.[41] There is power in noticing and verbalizing an emotional tone or a previously unnamed event happening between the patient and the therapist in the room, right in the very moment when it happens. Because it is potentially so exposing of hitherto hidden feelings, dynamics, or even patterns or relating, it can arouse tremendous shame—the affect associated with feeling exposed.[42] It is therefore a very powerful tool, and if misused, the patient can experience interpretation as retraumatizing and/or domineering. For this reason, it has been eliminated from many counseling methodologies. Nevertheless, well-timed and empathically attuned interpretation is still one of the primary tools of most analytically oriented therapy.

Interpretation well used is a hypothesis, not an authoritarian pronouncement about the patient's inner life. The therapist hazards a guess—humbly, in a spirit of curiosity—about a particular meaning of a patient's words or actions, which has the effect of inviting the patient to join the therapist in further exploration of possible meanings. In contemporary psychoanalytic practice, moreover, it is understood that interpretation is a mutual, shared enterprise, better described by the term *exploration*. The curiosity and awe that may initially be conveyed by the therapist's wonderings spill over into the shared enterprise of the therapy, to the point where the patient him- or herself is engaging in the process of interpretation.

Often, especially once the transference-countertransference dynamic is developing more fully, meanings and interpretations become more available after a session than while the therapist is immersed in the moment. Particularly when there has been an emotionally intense interaction, it is sometimes easier for both therapist and patient to engage in reflection after the fact rather than in the heat of the moment—in Fred Pine's words, to "strike while the iron is cold."[43] Particularly when the therapist realizes after a session that enactments have occurred, it is helpful for him or her to engage between sessions in a process of reverie by which one tries on various possible meanings and interpretations. By engaging empathically in a series of "trial identifications"[44] in which the therapist imagines what the recent interaction might have felt like to the patient, and what it might mean from the perspective of the patient's own inner world, the therapist develops fluency in the multiple possible meanings available. Patrick Casement describes how therapists come to rely on an "internal supervisor," an amalgam of accumulated wisdom and experience from one's own actual supervision, personal therapy, supervision of others and the learnings accumulated from one's own students, and a practiced capacity for reflection, improvisation, and play in the context of the Winnicottian "potential space"[45] of therapeutic exploration. Casement has drawn an analogy between this process of trial identification and a pianist practicing scales:

> In order that we can develop a more subliminal use of the internal supervisor when we are with a patient, it is valuable to use (or, in a Winnicott sense, to "play" with) clinical material outside of the session. A musician plays scales, or technical studies, in order that these can become a natural part of his [or her] technique. So too in psychotherapy: when a therapist is "making music" with a patient [s/]he should not be preoccupied with issues of technique. That technique can be developed by taking time, away from the consulting room, for practicing with clinical material. Then, when in the presence of a patient, the process of internal supervision is more readily available when it is most needed.[46]

The music will be made in the next session itself, when the patient's own subjectivity is available to play his or her part. But practicing can help the therapist to be more adept at picking up unverbalized clues to the patient's inner experience. Interpretation and exploration make use of the freedom of the potential space between patient and therapist to engage in a mode of play, "as-if," and improvisation.[47]

In my experience, patients often communicate powerful symbols of inner experience in the guise of superficial conversation or humor. For example, from several women patients I heard the mention of quite commonplace kitchen items ("my oven is dusty" and "my mother's cleaver is bigger than mine") as carrying enormous emotional freight and symbolic potential. Lifting such casual references up to the patient for further mutual exploration can be revelatory and can release pent-up emotion in poignant ways.

The patient is the final arbiter. Timing is important. The therapist's sensitivity, often referred to as "therapeutic tact," is particularly crucial in suggesting interpretations. Freud used the word *tact* to represent "almost everything positive that one *should* do,"[48] but also, as Beate Lohser and Peter Newton have pointed out, the German *Takt* also refers to timing in music—the therapist's "intuitive sense of what to do at any given time,"[49] and not mere politeness. As Freud himself observed, even an "accurate" interpretation given before the patient is ready to engage in exploring the themes involved can heighten "resistance"—the patient's natural self-protective function.[50] But in the context of a generally reliable, "good enough"[51] therapeutic relationship, an interpretation that is off-target or mistimed will sometimes just roll off the patient's back. "A mistaken interpretation will not destroy everything."[52]

If a suggested interpretation falls flat or is rejected by the patient, it is the task of the therapist to try to understand whether it was the timing or the accuracy of the interpretation itself (including countertransference), that was off the mark. It is further incumbent upon the therapist, then, to take responsibility for whatever hurt the patient may feel in relation to the therapist's ill-timed or incorrect hunch. More will be said below about this process of repairing the therapeutic relationship when, as inevitably happens from time to time, there is a failure of empathy on the therapist's part.

Interpretation and exploration are most powerful when they illuminate what is happening in the here-and-now. For this reason, they are most powerful when they concern what has just happened between the patient and the therapist. This is not to say that every therapy hour is concerned with a minute examination of what is happening between the patient and the therapist. Freud suggested interpreting the transference only when it became problematic.[53] But powerful insights sometimes become available to a patient when the transference is openly examined together. I have experienced this especially with *transference statements*, in which the patient is ostensibly talking about another situation but is unconsciously sending signals to the therapist about the therapeutic relationship. Sometimes if the therapist simply asks a question such as, "I wonder if that has anything to do with us?" or "I wonder if you ever feel that happening in here?" this can prompt an important breakthrough.

Other classically analyzable modes of unconscious communication include slips of the tongue or the pen, forgetting, being late or too early or mistaking the time of an appointment, stumbling, accidents, and the like, which Freud discussed in great detail in his essay on "Psychopathology of Every Day Life."[54] This dimension has been downplayed in contemporary therapy, particularly because it focuses on one-person enactments in a vacuum, and classic interpretations of these tended to become too formulaic ("You are late because you are resisting coming to therapy"). However, such nonverbal communications can be meaningful to the patient, as s/he becomes curious and self-observant about multiple modes of communication. They are also best considered contextually, in terms not only of what is going on in the isolated intrapsychic world of the patient but also, and perhaps primarily, of what is being signaled about the transference-countertransference relationship and the pressures the patient may be experiencing in the "outer" world—beyond the self and beyond the therapy room—as well.

In all the above situations, interpretation should be offered, not imposed. The most important thing the therapist can do is to proffer an interpretation or invite exploration of something that has occurred *tentatively*, with a spirit of *wondering*. Finally, this is important because there is never simply one meaning, one interpretation to any feeling or event. Just as symptoms are overdetermined, the multiplicity of one's self means that all insights are necessarily limited, partial, and contingent. There is always more meaning to be uncovered. The hope is that by wondering and caring about what the patient's words and behaviors mean, the patient will be roused to bring that same spirit of wondering and exploration to her own life.

Other Modes of Symbolic Communication

The patient's free association, the therapist's reverie, and the verbal exploration of meaning in both what is expressed and what is coming up that seems to defy expression constitute the primary material for psychodynamic psychotherapy. There are, however, some additional methods for accessing unconscious material—particularly material that is not yet known in any verbalizable form but may be emerging from the unconscious, particularly in the form of symbols, images, or physical sensations.

The first and best known of these additional methods is of course dream interpretation. Freud's discoveries about himself from his self-analysis largely depended upon his exploration of his dreams, and, notably, it was in his landmark work *The Interpretation of Dreams* in 1900[55] that he first formulated his topographical model of conscious, preconscious, and unconscious, and the concept of repression. Freud regarded dreams as the "royal road to the unconscious."[56] Although some contemporary neuroscientists have begun to question the psychodynamic significance of dreams, and in particular some of Freud's specific postulates about dreams as mechanisms of instinctual discharge,[57] a blanket dismissal of the potential for dreams to offer a meaningful glimpse into one's inner life has been challenged as overly materialist and reductionistic.[58] Of particular interest to pastoral psychotherapists, Kelly Bulkeley has probed the intersection of dream interpretation, neuroscience, and religious imagery in a number of published works.[59]

For many decades now, the consensus approach to dream interpretation has been to emphasize the patient's formulations over the therapist's.[60] While the therapist may offer possible symbolic references or associations, it is actually most helpful to refrain from doing so until the patient him- or herself has had ample time to associate to each element in the dream and to explore what each symbol and figure means to him or her. Dream interpretation is never as simple as looking up an image from the dream in a book. Whether the therapist's primary orientation is Freudian, Jungian, or some other branch of psychoanalysis in which dream work is considered important, there is no one meaning that can be applied to a particular symbol. The patient will discover what the dream means to him or her by associating to each of the elements of the dream, to probe the very personal and idiosyncratic meanings that symbol might hold for him or her. Further, quick or obvious interpretations—

those that may first come to mind—should be treated with caution, as Freud himself pointed out, because like any glib interpretation, they may be more defensive than illuminative at a more transformative level. There are always potentially multiple layers of any dream and subjectivities within the dream. As relational analyst James Grotstein has described, these "presences" lend clues about the patient's inner object world, including the characters in the dream who are viewed more or less in a third-person narrative way, "the dreamer who dreams the dream," "the dreamer who understands the dream," and a "Background Presence" that taps into the "Unconscious as a range of dimensions understandable in terms of nonlinear concepts of chaos, complexity, and emergence theory."[61] Of course the process of remembering and retelling the dream may further shape or focus on one band of meaning, while other elusive symbolizations and meanings may slip away or be stored away in the patient's psyche for future recollection.

Most important, in addition, is C. G. Jung's insight that every element in the dream, whether a human character, an animal, an object, or a landscape, represents an aspect of the dreamer's self.[62]

BRENT'S INITIAL DREAM

Jung believed that the patient's first dream during therapy, or "initial dream,"[63] might hold particular clues as to the central themes to be worked out in the course of therapy, as well as possibly some clues about the nature of the transference as it might develop. Brent did not share a dream immediately, but when he did, it seemed to represent almost literally the way Brent experienced himself, and possibly his fears about the therapy as well. In keeping with the theoretical fluidity that characterized Brent's therapy, as described in the preceding chapter, this dream could be understood both in terms of oedipal, phallic images and in self psychological terms as a "self state dream" and relational terms as a signal about the transference-countertransference dynamic as well.

Brent dreamed that he was exploring a rickety tower, something like a lighthouse, with a television set turned on in the top floor. There were construction workers milling around, but none of them seemed to be doing much work. At first he laughed, the phallic symbolism of the tower being "perfectly obvious" to him, but he couldn't go much beyond that pat interpretation, although he found the thought that the tower was rickety somewhat disconcerting as a Freudian symbol. Themes of impotence, castration, and his difficulties getting close to women came to mind and made sense, but remained somewhat disconnected emotionally for him. I then posed the Jungian question, "what if every element of the dream is some aspect of your self; does that help?" Brent then replied, "Oh, the tower *is* me." We explored what this might mean as he associated to various aspects of the image: under construction, lit up only by a cold, blue flickering light in his head, and dangerous to navigate. During the early stages of the therapy, as these dynamics were identified and incorporated into Brent's self-understanding, his depression and anxiety did lessen somewhat. He was able to "know," at least intellectually, about his use of intellectualization as a habitual defense.

Over time, as Brent identified his feelings more, especially the terror he had about his own anger and aggression, the dream also came to be linked with a statement he had made in his very first session, when he first shared his shame and anxiety about his suicidal fantasies erupting outward in homicidal insanity: "I'm so afraid of going crazy that I'm afraid I might end up like the guy in the tower with the gun" (a reference to the "Texas tower sniper"[64]). It was clear from the beginning that his depression was, in part, a way for him to push his hostile, angry, even violent feelings out of awareness, turning them instead on himself. He was reassured by the idea that the more aware he was becoming of his feelings, the less threatening they appeared to be, either to himself or to others. I relied heavily on my countertransference in this phase of the therapy as well—I never once felt personally threatened or afraid of Brent or of something he might do. I trusted his "ambulatory self" to continue working effectively on his behalf, even as other parts of him were allowed voice in the safety of the therapy.

The image of the tower was an important clue to the transference early in the therapy as well. Although Brent stuck with the therapy, old cultural prohibitions against seeking help perpetuated his sense of therapy as a stigma, and at times, especially at the beginning of the hour but often well into it, his conversation would stay at a rather chatty, superficial level. There was, of course, the issue of seeing therapy as a weakness, which fit the image of the rickety phallic tower. There was also that television set at the top of the tower—putting out cold blue light (his rational and at times rather obsessional musings that did not tap into feelings) and somewhat empty noise (like the chatter of commercials), but providing little real heat or illumination. The construction workers represented aspects of himself, unable to shore up his own sense of weakness, but also perhaps were a transference symbol, representing me, and his lack of confidence that I or therapy in general could really help him. I might just be—or together *we* might just be—like those construction workers, milling around the project but not really getting much done. The dream became one of many symbolic points of reference throughout the therapy and as such became useful as a point of contact with his buried feelings at times when his sense of confidence in himself, or in the process, faltered.

At the time of termination, Brent recalled this dream again. He reflected that "it's not all built yet, but it's definitely under construction." He reflected how he sensed that the internal presence of his mother had been growing and healing, so that he could incorporate her strength but without the constant dread of undermining—eroding the foundations of his self-esteem as once had been the case. He felt that he had internalized me as well. (In self psychological terms, I believe he had been able to use me successfully as both a mirroring and an idealizing selfobject). I was no longer just a construction worker milling around or a "consultant in the board room"—another of his images for me—but had joined with his mother's strength and his own internal strength, putting real "bricks and mortar" to his self-structure. He also stated, "the tower is lit up now, too." The TV—symbol of his intellectualization—was still on, he said, but "it's not the only light any more." The quality of this light was now incandescent and warm. He no longer feared that his anger would erupt unexpectedly with dangerous consequences, either for himself or others.

In keeping with the multiplicity of inner objects and the complexity of each person's inner world, a dream and its landscape may reveal parts of the self that had previously been kept out of conscious awareness. Dream analysis is thus probably the second most powerful tool, after free association, for accessing the unconscious, and should not be undertaken lightly. Because it allows the patient to travel into regions of his or her own unconscious that may not have been accessed before, the process of associating to the dream's images, and exploring what they might mean, can feel very threatening or frightening to the patient, especially at first. Over time, however, as the patient learns through experience, with the therapist as a guide who has made a similar journey of discovery in his or her own therapy, that the process is safe, and by exploring the most frightening images, the patient usually comes to recognize that they, too, have wisdom to offer. Often the most initially terrifying inner objects are those that once served a vital protective or survival function in infancy and early childhood, and their emergence signals that the unconscious is moving into aware-ness, enabling the patient to have an expanded sense of freedom from fear and free-dom of choice in his or her external life.

There are additional ways, beyond dream work, of bringing the patient's inner symbolic world into the therapy where it can be explored and put into words. Whether or not the patient is an artist in any formal sense, s/he can be encouraged to draw or paint (or even sculpt, if clay is available) whatever comes to mind in regard to feelings that are emerging in the therapy that do yet not seem conducive to verbalization. Some patients will not like this more active mode of work. They may feel embar-rassed by their own perceived lack of skill, or they may feel consciously or uncon-sciously afraid of being shamed for exposing parts of themselves whose meaning is not clear to them and therefore out of their conscious control. But for those patients who can tolerate this dimension of performance and exposure of unformulated mate-rial, the externalization of such inner symbolic material can give both patient and therapist more to examine together and explore for potential meaning(s).

KAREN—DREAM AND ART

The sources of Karen's depression were manifold, in all three domains of diagno-sis: biological, social/economic/cultural, and intrapsychic. Karen had grown up in an urban, blue-collar, Eastern European enclave where economic survival was the primary preoccupation of her parents' immigrant generation. Her parents, who were probably both dysthymic themselves, had a culturally reinforced stoicism, with a grim philosophy of life. Understandably, given their economic struggles, they regarded any expression of emotion or creativity as self-indulgent and an impediment to just getting by from day to day. Karen knew from early adolescence that she wanted to be an artist, but on the first day of high school her older brother accompanied her to registration for classes and signed her up as an engineering major so that she could "make a better life for herself." Karen had been raised never to question her parents, and her brother often served as an enforcer while her parents were out of the house working. Karen dutifully completed the engineering curriculum of her high school, completed a college degree in science and engineering, and went to work in a succession of laboratory jobs where she repeatedly sabotaged herself by working too slowly or making mistakes that got her fired.

Not surprisingly, when Karen began therapy she found it very difficult, even to the point of being painful, to put her feelings into words (a condition sometimes called "alexithymia"). She had been trained to keep quiet, to the point of not even allowing herself to know if she felt anything—particularly taboo emotions associated with anger, resentment, or rebellion. Her depression kept her in a kind of mental fog in which she could not think and did not have the energy to confront her mother or her boyfriend. It thus served a protective function but at a deeper level prevented her from finding satisfying relationships, satisfying work, and even from being herself.

Karen's therapy became a clear example of how, for many patients, the process of healing requires an invitation for what has been suppressed to emerge, first in purely symbolic form, and only gradually over time to be explored and given meaning in the shape of words. Brain function itself is involved in this process, as what has been "stored" in the lower portions of the brain is gradually shifted toward the prefrontal cortex where symbolization, and then verbalization and critical thinking, can be activated. Like many patients struggling with depression, there were many long pauses in her efforts to communicate, and the varying quality of each silence was important to attend, to feel with her, and to honor by not jumping in with too many words of my own.

To give an example of how the therapist's immersion in the patient's world can influence our own affect states, in my own countertransference reactions, I often found myself in a kind of sleepy fog during or after Karen's sessions, similar to her own frequent condition. I needed to take care of myself physically and emotionally so that I would not unwittingly fall into depression myself, especially when working with her more frequently than once a week. I sometimes needed a cup of strong caffeinated tea before seeing the next patient. Dogged persistence, which interestingly enough was a trait and a value that Karen had also imbibed from her parents with a certain degree of functionality, was needed for a long time in order to stay with the slow pace and depressive atmosphere of Karen's therapy. I stayed alive and awake, especially in Karen's early therapy, the same way she survived—by sheer determination. So early on I came to experience how she managed, without any joy, to get from one day to the next.

Karen's first real breakthrough in therapy came when she reported a dream she had of being in an old, crumbling house that resembled her parents' home but was more decrepit. She heard rustling sounds beneath some rotting floorboards and realized some kind of animal was trapped there. She ripped up the floorboards with her hands and discovered a nest of kittens, curled up with their eyes closed. She sorrowfully reported that when she went to lift them out of their hole, all but one of the kittens were dead. She gently raised that one up, and it began to mew pitifully and opened its eyes.

Karen initially had no idea what the dream might mean, but it aroused powerful feelings in her, including both grief and hope. She initially associated the sadness with her grief over her father's death, and we sat together quietly holding the feeling of loss. Eventually, as it seemed to me (partly from the shift I was feeling in the atmosphere and in my own mental state) that she was moving back from an alive feeling of sadness into her more depressive not-thinking fog, I asked her what it might mean if everything in the dream was somehow a part of herself; her eyes grew wide, and she said, "Oh, my God."

A brief silence ensued, in which a tear silently rolled down her cheek, and a tiny squeal—almost like a mew—came from her throat. She then said, "They are me. A whole lot of me—me's—are already dead . . . killed before they could live I guess . . ." She wept more freely than she had ever done previously. (In some other situation I might have said something like, "yes, a part of you was kept from living, maybe even from the time you were born," but in this instance it was clear that she got it, and there was no need to add my own interpretation, which in the moment might have taken the authority to interpret away from her, more than it would have added anything to her already dawning awareness. So I simply remained quiet and sat with her tears.) When she became calmer, I asked, "And the other kitten, the one that was still alive?" She said, "I saved it . . . I rescued it . . . didn't I?"

We sat in silence again for a period of time, but this time the silence had a different, slightly more energetic quality. In my own reverie I found myself liking that the dream animals were kittens—small and vulnerable, but also sharp. They were not Hallmark puppies. These little neonates had teeth and claws! "And if that kitten is also a part of yourself?" I eventually prompted. "Does that mean there is still hope for me?" She looked me in the eye and laughed—nervously, it seemed to me. Later in the therapy I might have explored the question itself, and what it meant in the transference that she might be seeking permission for hope from me as the parental authority. At that time, I simply gave the authority back to her by asking, "What do your feelings tell you?" Another pause ensued, and then she said, "I think so. I think maybe there is hope . . . " We both smiled. "What does it mean, do you think, that it's a kitten and not a cat?" "Oh, that it's a part of me that's still a baby . . . no, that's not quite right . . . it *is* that, it's a part of me that got pushed away from the time I was little, but it's also a part of me that is just being born now—like the artist me!?" "Could be," I said. She smiled again rather shyly, and I smiled back. We lapsed into a kind of quiet but now expectant reverie in which we simply sat companionably for a bit. We further explored how the house itself simultaneously represented her parents' house (which she experienced as lifeless and stifling), her own house (which she experienced as run down because she didn't have the energy to clean or the assertiveness to demand that her boyfriend pick up after himself), and most of all her self—her sense of how she barely held herself together. She experienced herself, especially at her most depressed, as crumbling and decrepit, yet the dream had revealed to her that under the floorboards (the repression barrier?) there were both losses to be grieved and fragile new life to be discovered, brought up into the air and allowed to breathe. Finally, just before the close of the hour, she asked, "Do you think I could bring in some pictures of my paintings to show you?" There was no time to explore the meaning of the request itself, but I felt it was not the time to say, "Let's talk about what that means to you next time," because to do so would possibly replicate her family's own hesitance and skepticism about her art. So I agreed, and expressed interest in seeing the pictures.

Over time, we did explore (working in the transference) how it had felt to ask to bring in her pictures (terrifying and exposing), how my initial positive response had felt (a deeply surprising relief, an unexpected contrast from her family even though she "rationally" knew I didn't have the same attitudes), and how it felt over the ensuing weeks and months to share them with me (initially very frightening, afraid of judgment both on the art itself and on her, but then freeing as she came to trust that the process would not expose her to ridicule, shame, or punishment). But the art itself also turned out to be highly symbolic, and, like the exploration of the dream, we found it very fruitful to explore each painting as if it were also a dream, in which each symbol or figure represented some aspect of herself that had previously been denied expression. Because Karen had had to suppress words for virtually her entire life, the symbolic realm of her paintings gave voice for the first time to the parts of herself that had felt unacceptable, and as she slowly and haltingly became more able to play with alternative meanings to the images in her art, she also found herself more able to stand up to her mother and her boyfriend and to find the energy to work more productively. She even found a way to become more playful with her boyfriend, and he responded by being more willing to devote time to simple pleasures like playing Frisbee in the park, sharing in the cooking, and taking walks together.

Like all such therapies, this one was not a smooth upward ride. Other parts of Karen's inner world that were more identified with her parents and her brother also manifested themselves in periodic severe depressive and self-persecutory behavior. Karen found that she needed antidepressant medication and light-box therapy to contend with the periodic recurrences of depression. It became evident that these medical treatments facilitated the therapy work by making it possible for her to have enough energy to do the work, and it also enhanced her ability to think and reflect more clearly. Feelings of anger continued to be difficult for her to access (as is very common with depressive patients), and it was extremely difficult for her to express anger directly to me, instead of collapsing back into a kind of frustrated whine or complaint. This was an important focus in our work in the transference-countertransference dynamic. But the overall trajectory during her time in therapy, which lasted a little over two years, was one in which she felt increasing benefits as she became stronger, more assertive, more spontaneous, and more self-aware.

One additional method by which inner symbolic material may be made available in therapy is a Jungian technique called "sandplay," created by Margaret Lowenfeld in the 1920s and further developed by Dora Kalff in the 1950s and '60s.[65] Sandplay drew upon Jung's own spontaneous return to childhood self-healing games after feeling devastated by his break with Freud. Jung began playing with stones and earth, eventually creating an entire miniature world on the side of a secluded creek, which he understood to be a process of externalizing his inner world and its conflicts.[66] In sand tray work, the therapist has a wooden box specified by Dora Kalff to 19½ inches by 28½ inches by 3½ inches deep, half filled with sand, and an abundant collection of small figures that may readily represent a patient's inner objects and inner symbolic life. In Jungian practice in particular, figures are also made available that resonate with archetypal figures and symbols. There is an obvious parallel between Kalff's descriptions of a "free and protected space" and the use of play and imagination in sandplay, and Winnicott's discussions of playing and reality, and potential space.

Some therapists use the sand tray only when particularly strong, imagistic material is being presented, while others use it more regularly as part of the therapeutic process. In either case, the patient is invited to enter a state of reverie or uncensored play in which s/he may select whatever figures s/he likes from the collection, and place them wherever s/he chooses in the sand tray. When the process feels complete, the therapist and patient then examine the resulting scene in the sand and explore possible meanings—again, with the assumption that every image represents in some way an aspect of the patient him- or herself. Some therapists conclude a sand tray session by taking a photograph of the scene before the figures are put away, and over time the succession of scenes, similar to a series of dreams, may yield further insights about what is happening in the patient's inner world.

Human Beings Are Multiple: Working with the Parts

The therapy patients described above all show how individuals are not monolithic. Some of the most valuable work that occurred in both cases was when each person was able to recognize that she or he was not simply one thing—whether it was a negative persona that had been assigned to her by her parents, or some aspect of himself that he most valued or most disliked. Both people benefited by coming to terms with their own inner complexity and by accepting and valuing their many different moods and self-states. They came to understand that even the parts of themselves that they most feared or hated were parts that had developed under duress in childhood and often had served a protective function either by identifying with an oppressive parent for the sake of psychic survival or by carrying the fierceness to fight back or the grief and sorrow that knew forbidden truths.

I have therefore found it helpful to think of doing therapy, in addition to the aspects of the work described above, as working with "parts"—including "your" parts (i.e., the patient's), "my" parts (the therapist's), and "ours" (what is multiply-shared, consciously and unconsciously, in the intersubjective field between us—termed by Thomas Ogden the "analytic third"[67]), as the therapeutic relationship continues to unfold. Some of our own and our patients' parts are conscious nearly all the time. The easiest way to grasp this is to think about how different dimensions of ourselves are more prominent in different settings—for example, imagine how different parts of yourself would emerge in the following situations:

- sitting in a classroom as a student
- standing at a blackboard, teaching a class
- standing on the pitcher's mound in the ninth inning of a close game
- standing in the pulpit delivering a sermon
- playing with a large, happy, muddy dog
- filing an insurance claim for the dent a hit-and-run driver put in your car
- reading a story to a four-year-old
- attending a peace march
- paddling a canoe with a teenager
- in bed making love
- solving a complicated math problem
- being so angry that you want to hurt someone badly
- performing in a concert or play
- reprimanding a kid for breaking a window
- negotiating a loan
- sitting with a therapy patient who is sharing a harrowing story of abuse
- sharing intimate feelings in a mixed-race group in an antiracism workshop
- reading a book that really makes you think
- attending the funeral of a close family member
- dancing at a club where no one but your date knows you
- dancing at a church social where everybody knows you and two-thirds of the people there are members of your congregation

The writer Anne Lamott gives a wonderful example of the multiplicity of conscious selves:

> The day after Sam turned thirteen, we were going through our usual hormonal transformations together, which is to say, sometimes the house gets crowded. There was Sam at thirteen—usually mellow, funny, slightly nuts. But when the plates of the earth shifted, there was the Visitor, the Other. I called him Phil. Phil was tense. Also sullen and contemptuous. There was me at forty-eight— usually mellow, funny, and slightly nuts—and there was the Menopausal Death Crone. Some days were great, because Sam and I at these ages were wild and hilarious and full of our best stuff; but other days, when Phil and the Death Crone dropped by, we were awful.[68]

This crowd of selves we know about is also, of course, just the tip of the iceberg of all the parts that make up all of who we are. Referring back to Figure 4, "An Object Relational View of Self" in chapter 1, both patient and therapist are populated internally with figures and part-figures from the past, including good father, bad father, good mother, bad mother, good breast, bad breast, good sibling, bad sibling, good grandparent, good teacher, other alternative soothing adult, bad grandparent, bad teacher, other alternative frightening adult, friends (potential sources of soothing), abuser(s) (persecutory inner objects), internalized resources (for pleasure, soothing, stimulation, etc.—pets, books, plays, or movies, achievements), transitional objects, self-representations (including good me, bad me, happy me, sad me, scared me, scary me, etc.), and representations of God (good God, bad God, "God gone wrong").[69] Early object relations theorists W. R. D. Fairbairn[70] and Harry Guntrip[71] among others have described in compelling detail how parents' affect states from earliest childhood also live on as quasi-independent internal figures, such as depressed parent, alive and spontaneous parent, tantalizing and seductive parent, withholding and depriving parent, punitive and scary parent, even dead parent.

These parts may be invited into the therapy and allowed a forum to give voice to previously unvoiced dimensions of the patient's self. Jody Messler Davies describes this process as "therapeutic dissociation."

> Therapeutic dissociation is . . . an invitation we make to the patient, a way of saying, "Let us suppose that I could have a moment with this part of you; that we can assume for the present that this is the only part of you; that this part of you does not need to compromise itself in any way to get along with the other parts of you; that we can invite her into our therapy together, and allow her in the most playful spirit imaginable, to be with us, all of the many things she cannot be anywhere else. Such an invitation presumes the temporary suspension of more overarching, cohesive levels of psychic organization, in order to permit

such an unfolding of unconscious process that oftentimes exaggerated transference processes; the belief that together patient and [therapist] can manage such
transitory regressive enactments of otherwise unavailable aspects of self-other
experience.[72]

This can stimulate what Davies calls

a temporary but necessary iatrogenic [therapy-induced] intensification of a
kind of "crisis of multiplicity"; an experience of increased discontinuity and
disintegration, which can often accompany working within a predominantly
interactive mode and is often accompanied by heightened anxiety and disori-
entation. It seems to represent the emergence of those aspects of self that have
been defensively foreclosed, sacrificed to a more fluid systemic flow, abandoned
in pursuit of an enhanced cooperative compromise among separately organized
self-states.[73]

As Davies has rightly cautioned, because of the inherent anxiety and potential
destabilization such "parts work" can entail, even temporarily, working in this way
cannot be undertaken lightly, or with patients who are already struggling with severe,
pathological dissociation or fragmentation.

An appreciation of multiple self-organizations and association-dissociation as
the predominant dynamic forces of mind must not be confused with the crip-
pling fragmentation of experience that accompanies traumatic dissociation in
its most extreme forms. Multiplicity and fragmentation exist at opposite ends
of the clinical spectrum, and, as we begin to replace the concept of repression
with that of dissociation, I believe we need to clarify this distinction . . . Such
distinctions often become essential at moments of clinical choice in determining whether one wants to move in a direction of enhanced integration or invite
the kind of therapeutic dissociation described.[74]

Multiplicity, then, is not the same thing as fragmentation. Often, naming and
working with a patient's many different parts and self-states has the paradoxical effect
of strengthening the sense of self-cohesion. This is because, at least in my experience, many patients—especially those who have been traumatized in the past—will,
when in a crisis or state of distress, fall into a kind of tunnel vision where their present self-state is the only one they can experience, imagine, or ever remember having.
In such situations, it is often helpful to remind (re-mind!) them that their whole
being encompasses more than the current state of mind they are experiencing: "So
before the holiday you were feeling warm and excited about having your parents
come to visit. What do you think happened to the voice inside of you that was trying
to remind you to be prepared for the ways in which they sometimes hurt you?" "You

feel very sad right now, feeling so hurt by your partner, but there is also a part of you that feels very angry about what he said to you, and another part that maybe wants to protect him from your anger." "You are feeling so bad right now, that all you can think of is killing yourself, but there is another part of you that wants to live, the part that brought you here today." As Philip Bromberg has said,

> Used judiciously, I have found that an approach which addresses the multiplicity of self is so experience-near to most patients' subjective reality that only rarely does someone even comment on why I am talking about them in "that way." It leads to a greater feeling of wholeness (not *dis*-integration) because each self-state comes to attain a clarity and personal significance that gradually alleviates the patient's previously held sense of who [s/]he "really" is and how [s/]he came, historically, to be this person.[75]

Bea Gets Angry

Not surprisingly, given both Bea's personal history and her cultural upbringing, anger was a taboo emotion, one that she disavowed and essentially feared. Because Bea could not even know about her anger, she was unable to assert herself successfully with Donny. On one occasion, she described being scathingly insulted and denigrated by Donny and then immediately agreeing to going to bed with him. She consciously understood her desire to have sex as a way of eliciting care and love from him. She was able to know to some extent about how hurt she felt by his contempt and derision, but her anger and disgust at being verbally brutalized were inaccessible to her. As she described "letting him have sex" on the heels of this verbal abuse, I found myself actually wincing. As we talked about my visible reaction, she acknowledged that the sex had been actually painful and felt degrading under such circumstances. Still, she did not express any anger (although I could feel my own countertransference outrage boiling up within me).

We eventually traced Bea's reluctance to know about or express her anger, as described above, back to her mother, whose controlling and at times deliberately neglectful, withholding behavior was—she thought as she examined it from the perspective of now being a mother herself—"pretty bad." She was able to recognize that she would be angry if someone treated her own child that way, but it was still hard to summon anger toward either her parent or her husband.

Finally, we were able to explore Bea's anger through the transference. I needed to reschedule an appointment, for which I apologized, but I could see that Bea's face was reddening with something that looked like a combination of shame and anger. Bea felt ashamed for wanting something from me that I could not give—again, resonating with her feelings toward her mother—and she was able to recognize this as we explored her reaction. But also, there had been that flash of rage in her eyes that she quickly covered over by looking down. The veil of hair once again fell across her face.

"Bea," I prompted, "I may be wrong, but I think I saw something else just now. I wonder if maybe you are feeling not just ashamed of wanting something from me, but also a little angry with me." "No, no, that's not it," she demurred. "OK," I said. "Well, what if we pretended just for a moment that you *were* angry with me, even though you're not . . . What do you think you would say if you were angry?" At first, looking down at her feet, Bea began, "Well, I would say . . . It doesn't feel fair that you, you know, get to call the shots. I mean, there are times when I want to reschedule and you can't . . . or don't . . . and this is really not a good time for me to have to rearrange my schedule . . . " She looked up at me and continued, raising her voice, "and I'm always here on time, and this is really important to me, and it feels like you don't care!" I let her last words ring in the room, and then said, "It sounds like maybe there is a part of you that *is* a little angry after all?" She smiled sheepishly then, and I smiled back. I acknowledged that I knew the schedule change was hard for her, and repeated my apology. "At the same time, I think it's important for you to know that it's OK for you still to be angry. A part of you wants to be understanding and caring, and that's who you are. But another part of you is feeling angry, and that's a real part of you, too, a part that is equally OK and equally important."

Needless to say, this was not a dramatic, once-and-for-all cathartic release of her anger. But it did provide a kind of benchmark in the therapy, after which it was possible to refer back to the part of Bea that could be angry. As Bea was able to allow her angry self to emerge in the safety of the therapy, she found it more possible over time to become assertive with her spouse, her mother, and her boss. And she discovered to her great surprise that her anger destroyed neither her relationships nor herself. She found herself gaining confidence and respect in the eyes of others. She was finding the full range of her feelings, and thus finding her voice.

Multiplicity can take a variety of specific forms, in addition to the many idiosyncratic, individual dynamics within each person. For example, as therapy deepens and trust builds, parts of a person that fall on a continuum of personal, familial, and socially formed internal objects may emerge—including multiple gender, sexual, racial, cultural, and class selves.

Gender and Sexual Multiplicity

There is also considerable fluidity of gender identity and sexual orientation among an individual's many parts.[76] Theories of gender fluidity, going back to Freud's discussions of infantile bisexuality,[77] have been discussed at length in recent postmodern and psychoanalytic literature.[78] One of my most severely traumatized patients contained many conflicting identities and self-states, including seemingly rather androgynous babies, girls and women of all ages, a rebellious teenage boy who represented her self-sufficiency and self-protectiveness, and a viciously sadistic internal persecutor built on the foundation of the male neighbor who kidnapped and tortured her. Therefore, although a patient and a therapist may appear to be of the same or opposite gender at the surface, conscious level, the inherent multiplicity of each individual's gender construction, and the increasing porousness of the unconscious relationship as the therapy progresses, means that the therapist may represent any of the internal parts of the patient, regardless of their ostensible gender, as they are extruded onto or into the therapist through projection and projective identification.

Patients may initially have a preference for a therapist of one gender,[79] especially if they associate safety with one gender over another, but as the therapy evolves, given this multiplicity, the work that needs to be done in relation to the other gender will usually still be able to occur at the level of unconscious relationship. Similarly, regardless of the conscious sexual orientations of patient and therapist (whether disclosed or not), homoerotic, heterosexual, and homosexual wishes, fantasies, dreams, and unconscious interactions may occur in virtually all therapeutic dyads, particularly if the therapy continues long enough for more hidden parts of the patient to feel safe to emerge.

Split-Off Aggression

Equally important as sexual multiplicity is multiplicity along a spectrum of kindness and aggression. Pastoral psychotherapists may be especially leery of the most aggressive, hungry, greedy, envious, vengeful, and sadistic parts of ourselves. Most clergy and vowed religious have internalized strong and sometimes harsh internal prohibitions against having, knowing, and expressing these aspects of ourselves. All patients, except perhaps for those who are sociopathic, will also bring varying degrees of shame and denial about the extent of their own inner aggression. Inner objects that were formed as early as infancy through identification with one's parents in the crucible of neglect, abuse, abandonment, or more subtle forms of parental inattention stemming from narcissistic preoccupation, depression, or illness, frequently carry some of our most intolerable wishes and impulses. In this light, the "seven deadly sins" are nothing more and nothing less than a part of the human condition. It is much of the task of therapy to allow these wishes into consciousness, to recognize the tragic reality of our own brokenness, violence, and avarice, to accept or at least to tolerate the needs they represent, and to develop a more mature capacity for self-control without splitting off these parts of ourselves we dislike onto or into other people, groups, cultures, or nations. There are, therefore, also clear social and political implications to the healing of these split-off parts of ourselves that we have repressed as intolerable.

Racial and Cultural Diversity

Until recently, issues of race, racism, and cultural diversity have been notably absent from both pastoral and psychoanalytic literature. The pastoral field has made important inroads in understanding racial dynamics in both counseling and care of communities as well as individuals.[80] In the psychoanalytic literature, the most sophisticated considerations of race, culture, and the effects of oppression—both overtly and as it is internalized—have emerged from the various object-relations and relational schools. In the words of analyst Kimberlyn Leary,

> despite the public rhetoric of diversity and multiculturalism, race remains one of the most vulnerable social discourses in America today . . . The dynamics of race center on the dialectics of deprivation and domination, powerlessness and control, and privilege and rejection. This is the "deep structure" of our cultural conversations about race. In this sense, racial experience may have something in common with what Stern called unformulated experience—that is, experience that is not yet reflected on or linguistically encoded but that nevertheless remains a part of our everyday psychic grammar.[81]

Most contemporary analytic theorists of race and culture agree that—contrary to traditional approaches to psychoanalysis, which focused primarily on the intrapsychic and the individual,[82] or social-psychological theories, which emphasized the social over the intrapsychic[83]—a both-and approach, seeking a "thick description"[84] of both interior and exterior social realities, will yield the richest understandings.[85] Adding gender and class to the mix of race oppression and the world of inner object relations, Adrienne Harris writes:

> Adding gender and class to the analytic mix with race and psychodynamics raises a sensitive matter. Gender cannot subsume race, and class cannot explain race and/or gender. Dynamic explanations cannot be the final determinative explanation, and they cannot be ignored or minimized. Social forces and intrapsychic forces interpenetrate, and all must be held in creative tension.[86]

One of the only in-depth studies of the way race is consciously and unconsciously depicted in psychoanalysis was written in 2003 by a self psychologist who is also a pastoral counselor, Celia Brickman.[87] Brickman has explored the racial overtones in psychoanalytic theory both historically, in Freud's equation of the unconscious with dark continents to be discovered, and in more recent and contemporary strands of theory concerned with "primitivity," both in normal human development and in clinical states of regression.[88]

Because psychoanalysis was a European import that quickly came to be controlled by the medical-psychiatric establishment in America, both psychoanalysis and its many psychological offspring, including pastoral care and counseling, continued to be theoretically shaped and practiced by white people. However, the individual model of care and counseling is now increasingly being recognized as a cultural preference of the northern and western hemispheres, and group and communal practices of care are being revalued. Pastoral theologian Emmanuel Lartey, originally from Ghana, has written cogently about drawing the best from Euro-American models of psychiatrically informed counseling and from African (and by extension Asian, Latin American, and other non-Eurocentric) models of community-based care and healing practices. At the same time, psychoanalyst Neil Altman has worked for several decades to bring psychoanalytic methods into urban settings and across racial lines where, primarily because of economic factors, psychoanalytic therapy was largely unavailable.[89] Psychoanalytic theory, particularly object-relations theory focusing on shame and narcissistic wounding, has been used to explore the internal dynamics of whiteness and white racism; see for example, Thandeka's book *Learning to Be White: Money, Race, and God in America*.[90]

Psychoanalytically informed pastoral psychotherapy, I would argue, still has a place at the table among various forms of psychospiritual healing—particularly from a relational, constructivist framework. The psychoanalytic attitude—with its valuing of curiosity about multiple layers of meaning beyond surface impressions; the conviction that the implicit, the unspoken, and the as-yet unknown are as important as what is made explicit; and the search for understanding how projective processes shape relationships both between individuals and in groups—still has relevance and value not only for psychotherapy but also for cross-cultural understanding, group dynamics (as in congregations and community organizations), and relations between and among groups (including local community, national and international relations, and interfaith dialogue).

Further, although Freud himself, and particularly the American ego psychologists who followed him in the mid-twentieth century, labored to show how psychoanalysis was a science, psychoanalysis as a hermeneutic has always been a mode of cultural inquiry as well, beginning with Freud's own cultural works, which, though time-bound and limited by a colonialist impression of other cultures, opened the door for psychoanalytic investigation of cultural phenomena. As Diane Jonte-Pace recently argued, psychoanalysis is not merely or simplistically a product of nineteenth-century colonial society; it is—or at least offers the tools for—an analysis of colonialism.[91] Jonte-Pace offers Franz Fanon's 1950s analysis of the conscious and unconscious effects of white racism on both blacks and whites in *Black Skin, White Masks*; Juliet Mitchell's use of psychoanalysis in 1974 to analyze patriarchal social structures in *Psychoanalysis and Feminism*; and Anne Anlin Cheng's more recent analysis of race, culture, and psychology in *The Melancholy of Race* as examples of this use of psychoanalytic methods of inquiry to reveal discourses of oppression.[92]

Freud's own experience of oppression and marginalization as a Jew in Vienna further infuses psychoanalytic theory with a sensitivity to power, powerlessness, the liminality involved in efforts at assimilation into the dominant culture, and the ways in which oppression is not only enacted but also internalized.[93] Jews were labeled "blacks" by the Viennese in Freud's time.[94] It might even be argued that oedipal theory, with its themes of power and powerlessness, castration, and desire for what is denied, was formed at least in part not only in the crucible of family life but in the crucible of anti-Semitism in the decades immediately following the Holocaust. From Freud's formative experience as a child of watching his father humiliated on the street for being a Jew to his own reluctant flight to London with his daughter Anna after she was detained and interrogated by the Gestapo, the arc of Freud's own experience is one of a life of brilliance always under siege. The more subtle effects of his parents' own subjugation, and simultaneous denial of oppression that was common among Viennese Jews of their generation, may also have played a role in Freud's own sense of himself as a persecuted and lonely pioneer, with frequent reenactment of this dynamic in his demand of absolute loyalty from his followers and the many dramatic ruptures that ensued.

Therapist and patient meet, then, as multiple and multiply-constituted beings, "gendered, raced, sexed and classed, formed in the crucible of power hierarchies."[95] Our multiple parts are not gender-neutral, nor are they color-, race-, or class-blind. The society exists as yet another "third" in the therapy room.[96]

BEA'S CULTURAL HERITAGE

Bea's life, and our work in therapy together, was profoundly shaped both by her Korean cultural heritage and the intertwined cultural expectations about the proper roles of girls and boys, women and men. The stoicism and lack of emotional expressiveness of Bea's parents were described by her as commonplace among the parents of her first-generation Korean-American peers. Political events also made their mark on Bea's family history. Bea eventually learned that much of the way her mother had treated her was a direct result of her mother's own experiences of being abandoned, not once, but twice as a small child—by her mother and then by an aunt—literally left by the side of the road on the way out of North Korea during a time of political turmoil and oppression.

Bea's relationship to authority, including my role as therapist, was also shaped by her upbringing to be deferential to elders and authority figures, which made it at times even harder for her to confront me or express certain negative feelings that were taboo not only as a familial rule but also as a cultural one. "We don't tell our business to people outside the family." My social work experience for many years with Asian clients, as well as my ethnographic research as a doctoral student specializing in Asian music, had sensitized me to many of the dynamics in Bea's life, but I could never begin to shed all of my white, middle-class assumptions about how and what might be communicated between us. To the extent that this became accessible for us to talk about together, trust and permission to be honest together increased, and the therapy was enriched. But our cultural differences could not be glossed over or disappear, nor should they have.

As Altman has written,

Psychoanalysis ... teaches that no one's unconscious, including the best analyzed [therapist's] will ever disappear. Racism, then, will not be dealt with by any finite list of its manifestations against which we can attempt to immunize or guard ourselves. It is better that we take the attitude that racism is always there and that vigilance is always required . . . Social learning approaches to racism, I believe, underestimate both the subtlety and insidiousness of the social (and psychic) forces that promote racism. As [therapists], we can help round out the picture with our sensitivity to unconscious factors.[97]

Leary agrees:

Rather than try to transcend differences . . . patient and [therapist] endeavor to live with them subject them to careful consideration, and give them their full weight. To live in this way is to accept that racial enactments encompass considerably more than "mistakes of the head" (e.g., inattention to knowledge about other cultures). They also emanate from the sore spots in the heart that are the legacy of the social history of race in the United States (cf. Toni Morrison). It is a history to which each of us is heir.[98]

KEEPING MULTIPLICITY IN MIND

The same might be said as well of sexism, heterosexism, classism,[99] and other forms of deeply ingrained institutional oppression and prejudice. Our task, then, as therapists committed to speaking the unspeakable, is to make the effort to overcome our own shame—whether it takes the shape of the shame of internalized oppression or the shame of being part of an oppressive group[100] (both historically and as we are granted privilege in the present power arrangements of the society in which we live), or (as is most often the case) some of each—at least enough to give voice to these issues as they arise in the intersubjective therapeutic relationship. To the extent that race, class, gender, and sexual orientation remain as a socially conditioned backdrop, as an "unspeakable" in therapy, we will miss crucial interactions and significant opportunities for further collaborative exploration and understanding.

Considering the multiple potential interactions among all these parts, then—sexual, aggressive, racial and cultural, and idiosyncratic to each individual, both internally within the patient and the therapist and projectively in the intersubjectivity of the therapeutic dyad—it is easy to see how every moment of the therapeutic encounter represents a multilayered kaleidoscope of shifting interactions and potential meanings. There is no better explanation for the exponential determination of symptoms, the convolution of motives, and the complexity of every statement, every enactment that occurs in therapy, as well as in life outside the consulting room. Every therapeutic pair is really a crowd. Time, compassion, and imagination are needed to explore the multiple dimensions of meaning involved, but the potential for healing through this more multiple approach is amplified exponentially as well.

BRENT

Close to two years into Brent's therapy, a curious phenomenon arose in the transference-countertransference dynamic at the level of fantasy and images. For several
weeks, as Brent talked about his siblings, and particularly how his sister had become
increasingly estranged from the rest of the family, I experienced an intrusive thought,
from studies decades earlier as a graduate student, about Chinese opera and legends.
The phrase "hungry ghost" kept popping into my head. The thought at first seemed
irrelevant, and I kept brushing it away, but it became more persistent when I realized
that it kept coming up only in sessions with Brent, and particularly in relation to
his siblings. The "hungry ghost," it turns out, is a cross-cultural symbol—perhaps in
Jungian terms it could be understood as an archetype—depicted in Buddhism as a
type of being with its own region on the Wheel of Life. Hungry ghosts are pathetic
figures, depicted as "teardrop shaped with bloated stomachs and necks too thin to
pass food such that attempting to eat is also incredibly painful. This is a metaphor
for people futilely attempting to fulfill their illusory physical desires."[101] In Chinese
legend, the hungry ghost also was associated with a monk, MuNian, who saved his
mother from being devoured in flames in the mouth of a hungry ghost by observing
a set of ancestral rules of piety.[102] A festival of hungry ghosts is observed in many
Asian cultures, similar to the Mexican *día de los muertos* ("day of the dead"), at which
time ancestors are honored with remembrances and offerings of food. In Hindu tradition as well, the hungry ghost is described in the Garuda Purana as "spirit-beings
driven by the passionate objects of their desire."[103] In some traditions, hungry ghosts
are also seen as powerful and terrifying beings who will devour the living if their
hunger is not satiated. All these resonances were present in the therapy but not yet
at a conscious level for either one of us.

Finally one evening, this hungry ghost came to mind so strongly that I decided
to mention it. We had just been reflecting curiously about the fact that Brent was
the only sibling whose name did not begin with the letter combination J-O, after
his father, John. It felt like another uncomfortable sign of Brent's somehow being
singled out for a special role in the family. "Brent" was also a favorite name of his
mother's. At this point, the "hungry ghost" almost seemed to be wailing for attention
inside my mind. I said, feeling very odd because it felt like such a non sequitur, "This
is probably going to sound really strange, because it's so out of the blue, but I've
noticed that for several weeks now when you talk about your brother and sister, I get
this idea popping into my head, from an old Chinese legend, the idea of a 'hungry
ghost.' Does that thought mean anything at all to you?"

Brent visibly started, which in turn startled me. It felt as though a chill had suddenly settled in the room.

"There is one," he whispered.

"What?!"

"There is one—a ghost, at least. It's the baby."

"What baby?"

"The baby who died before my brother and I were born."

As we talked further, it became clear that there had been a stillbirth between his sister and his brother, and this had been hushed up by both parents until it was virtually forgotten in the family history. Pulling out Brent's genogram, we discovered that he had not even put this sibling—an unnamed boy—on the chart. His parents bought their own grave site shortly after this baby's death and had had him interred there without any marker. His mother had been buried beside the dead baby, but Brent had made no mention of this in all his descriptions of the funeral or the family's bereavement after her death.

As we explored this revelation in many subsequent sessions, the effect of this little ghost in the family dynamics and on Brent's own development gradually began to emerge, as if from a fog. On one level, Brent's mother, it appeared, had suffered a profound sense of loss and grief when the baby died, which were quickly silenced by the family's "everything is great with us" mythology. When his brother Josh was born, postpartum depression merged with suppressed grief to sink their mother further into depression. Unconsciously, mother and father planned one more pregnancy, and this baby was to be the one who would save them from the mother's sadness and the father's sense of failure. He was to be given the name "Brent," which his mother had hoped to name her firstborn son—in other words, he had the dead baby's name. Brent's mother continued to suffer from depression through his toddler years, and it seemed, at least as reconstructed from Brent's childhood memories, that it was precisely her rising up as a "mother tiger" to defend him when his school difficulties began that her depression began to fade and a distant, sad affect came to be replaced with a powerful, controlling, and irritable one.

Thus, in his earliest years of life, Brent's mother was not the all-powerful mother of his more conscious memory but, rather, an absent, even "dead" mother, whose lack of affect and attachment were frightening in a quite different way. Both Harry Guntrip and more recently André Green have written of the continuing depressive, deadening after-effects of having a mother who was physically alive yet emotionally absent or dead.[104] The guilt of possessing his mother as an oedipal victor had been long preceded by a sense of abandonment and confusion, that a mother who was present in the flesh was nevertheless unresponsive, even dead emotionally.

At the same time, Brent's role as a replacement for the dead baby was also at work in Brent's narcissistic vulnerability as the "chosen one." Brent literally was carrying the dead baby Brent as another internal part of himself, where this baby had been placed—entombed—by his parents' extrusion of the baby and their intolerable grief from their own consciousness. Canadian analyst Louise Demers well describes this projective dynamic as "ectopic mourning," defined as "relying upon different forms of distancing, encapsulating or displacing the lost object" both within and outside of the parents' psyches:

> These aforementioned masking strategies of the traces of the lost object [baby] are processed through projective substitutions rendering a child a "cryptophore," meaning a designated carrier of a crypt, imposed by the unattended grief of the immediately concerned parent. The latter benefits from this strategy by the fact that his crypt, a rejected and unmanageable part of his ego, is dealt with by someone else.[105]

This explanation spoke volumes about Brent's performance anxiety and inner conflicts about fulfilling his mother's need for him to be a star, a savior of the family. To quote Demers again,

> the patient absorbs an unending parental grief. By definition, a "cryptophore" is an individual unknowingly struggling with unmourned griefs, transferred to him by the preceding generation. The "cryptophores," through an occult incorporative process, become hosts to these unmourned deceased, the latter having developed a parasitical relationship to them . . . Basically "cryptophores," constantly struggling with a "ghost effect," are the unconscious carriers, or carry in their unconscious, the crypts of their parents.[106]

These psychodynamic considerations helped to move the therapy, and to open Brent's own self-understanding, into vast new areas of exploration, and they had great explanatory power for much of what Brent had gone through in his childhood and adolescence. In Chinese legend, "When our ancestors die, the living must take care of them . . . But some ghosts die with no one to bury them. Some die at sea, some have no family, some die in childhood, and hence they wander the underworld as the uncared-for dead."[107] The "hungry ghost," long buried inside Brent, finally was given a voice, and in the therapeutic process finally began to be mourned in ways that restored this first "Brent" to his own identity and began to free the adult Brent to discern his own life's purpose, apart from serving as the replacement for the long-dead child.

Countertransference and the Use of the Therapist's Self

Perhaps the most important contribution of contemporary psychoanalytic theory is the recognition that therapy is not a one-way process in which the flow of unconscious material is entirely coming from the patient toward the therapist or that all interpretation is flowing from the therapist toward the patient. In contemporary psychoanalysis (but with roots in much earlier psychoanalytic theorists, sometimes regarded as mavericks in their time, such as Sándor Ferenczi[108]), countertransference is recognized not only as an impediment to a therapist's perceptions—although unconscious distortions of the patient are always still a possibility—but also as a valuable tool for understanding what the patient's inner life is like.[109] How does this work?

In contemporary psychoanalytic psychotherapy, the therapist's self, as it is multiply-constituted, becomes a central tool—some would say even the most important tool.[110] Countertransference as it is being used by contemporary psychoanalytic therapists of many schools (object relations, self psychology, Jungian analysis, relational analysis) is not only those unconscious aspects in the therapist's own psyche that may be pathological or blocking the therapeutic relationship as Freud described.[111] It is not only the therapist's own "neurotic baggage," or unresolved issues, as it was classically defined, but in contemporary psychoanalytic understandings more broadly includes *whatever* is coming up in the therapist's psyche-soma in response to what the patient is communicating, both consciously and unconsciously. It is therefore one of the several fields of information that the therapist is continually scanning.

This use of the therapist's countertransference is especially important in addressing the deep childhood wounds that have resulted in splits in consciousness in the patient. The split-off parts will be literally evacuated into the therapist as the relationship deepens.[112] Attending to the process of projective identification requires working in the transference with particular emphasis on using the body and emotions as an instrument.

Especially as the therapist has her own corresponding life experiences, feelings, and wounds, or "valencies,"[113] these introjects from the patient can be sorted out into what is "my stuff" as the therapist and what is likely to be the patient's. Several types of destructive (i.e. unconscious and acted out) countertransference have been identified as common pitfalls: being overprotective; trying to be friends, over-disclosing, and over-gratifying; rejecting (usually arising out of fear of the patient's demands); or hostility (usually a sign of fear of being infected by the patient's pathology).[114] The most valuable corrective to these unconscious enactments out of the countertransference are continual self-examination, supervision, and personal therapy.

When the therapist is honestly engaging in the process of sorting out her own vulnerabilities, countertransference can become one of the primary channels of information about the patient. Through careful and tentative exploration, the split-off parts of the patient can be gradually handed back to her and incorporated with greater consciousness. This can be a deeply transformative process.

BEA'S HEADACHE

Bea's divorce from Donny was finalized in January, a year and a half after we first began working together. She had grown in her ability to assert herself. She continued, however, to see Donny and to sleep with him several times a week. Bea told him he did not need to pay her child support as long as they stayed together. In February, Bea began moving herself and her son, Sam, back into Donny's apartment, although she still kept legal residency and some of her belongings at her mother's. At the end of March, she moved back to her mother's again. This cycle of staying, leaving, and returning, a not uncommon aspect of many battered women's patterns of coping and survival,[115] had characterized her relationship with Donny since before the divorce.

Around this time, Bea's headaches and neckaches, which had improved somewhat in the past months, began to come back. We had the following exchange, involving an unusual degree of somatic communication. Bea began the session saying she had gone on her lunch hour to care for an elderly uncle in the hospital rather than to go to lunch with Donny. Then she described at some length her newfound resistance to Donny's belief in punishing Sam. She made the connection: "Donny treats Sam exactly like me. He sets him up." She had assertively insisted on Sam's safety with Donny. She described overhearing parents yelling at their children at a store and feeling deeply sad for the children. She was able to recognize that this touched her own life story, although she did not have any concrete memories. This led to the segment that follows. At the very end of the session, she came back to her uncle, describing why her visits are more than duty and even more than just cultural expectation. She said, "It's 'do unto others as you'd have them do unto you . . .'" (sheepish laugh, then teary again). "I don't think anyone should be left alone."

BEA: Yeah, well, Donny makes things worse. It might be bad, but he'll say something and make it worse. And I guess something else I'm more attuned in to now are kids, and how other kids are being disciplined and how I feel sorry for them when I'm at the store and I'll hear kids getting yelled at. And I go "poor kid . . . (very softly) God! Him and Donny think the same music." I mean you hear kids, you know, you can hear them, "You have to go to the bathroom, are you sure? OK, OK, so let's go look for it," and then the next minute you hear the guy yelling at the poor kid and it's like night and day. The kids were good, and all of a sudden the kid did something wrong, and it's like "No! no!" and you hear the kid yelling and crying and screaming, and I think "poor kid, you know, the things they put the kid through." And you know, so I'm real tuned in to kids now. And I read in an article once about someone who saw some other kid and . . . saying, "Hurry up or I'm going to leave you" and the kid was walking out of the store and the person said just to comfort the kid, saying, "You know, dads say lots of things that they don't mean. You can catch up to him. He really didn't mean to leave you," and just to help the kid along, you know. Um, and so I think about things like that, but I think it's not my place to try to do anything like that, and I'm afraid they'll go, "Who are you to parent my kid," you know? Um.

ME: But it hurts to watch it.

BEA: Yeah.

Me: I wonder if you wish somebody had said that to you as a kid.

BEA: Maybe. (*sad smile*) I don't know. I really don't remember anything. I really can't. (*sniff*)

ME: I was thinking of the time you said you were home and your dad left for some reason and you were there, with your head just peeking up over windows of the door, crying.

BEA: Yeah, um . . . [She dissociates.] My brother Philip says that.

ME: It was your brother who actually witnessed that scene?

BEA: (*takes a tissue*) I think so. [She's back.] Philip, Philip would . . . it's Philip's story so Philip is the one that remembers . . . so I don't know whether Philip is jealous of me or if he really cares about me.

ME: Philip? [The suspicion of jealousy took me by surprise.]

BEA: Yeah. I mean I think he cares about me, but I don't know whether there was any jealousy because I know he got really mad when I got a skateboard, like you raised all of us kids and you never got us anything that was one bit dangerous, and there she is in sixth grade with a skateboard. (*laugh*) So, you know, it was like, no way did he ever get anything like that.

ME: What made you think about that?

BEA: Jealous? Whether he was jealous or not? What my brother missed out on and what he knows . . .

ME: But he knows things about your childhood that you can't remember or don't know.

BEA: Probably. (*tears*)

ME: What made you tear up?

BEA: Um . . . I think all of us had a rough childhood. Or all of us were missing something. Um, definitely the affection, and closeness. And I don't know whether I actually would ask him. I mean, I wrote him when he had left one time, after he'd come up and left, and, um, then I thanked him for doing something. He fixed something or did something, and I, you know, I sent him a card, kind of a joke like, "Job well done. Mom would be proud of you too" on the inside or something like that, and I told him that I appreciated the time talking with him on the way to the airport and hoped that we could talk again, but you know he's never said anything or brought anything up again. So I don't know whether it would be just as hard on him as it is on me to find out or to know about stuff in the past.

ME: Like maybe he has big holes in his memory too?

BEA: Probably. Um . . . let's see . . . thinking back, you know, Mom always says this, the same thing that this kid, that I'm telling you about this story, Mom says in Korean, "You better hurry up or your Mom's going to leave you." (*mimicking a sadistic tone*) And she says "Your mom's gone," like when my nephew doesn't put on his shoes quick enough and he's gone to the bathroom and my sister is putting the kids in the car, (*sniff*) "Your mom left!" [She's identifying with the abandonment.]

ME: Oh. [I felt sad.]

BEA: (*blows nose*) Thinking about the things that my mom says now, that's one.

ME: It's pretty scary, huh?

BEA: And, um, she does this with the twins. Like today she picked up the boy first, well, first she said she looked at the little girl, and they're both in their car seats, and, I don't know, just to make her jealous or what, but she says (*slow, creepy, almost "psycho" voice*) [imitating] "I'm going to take your brother out first." And the little girl's watching, and my mother goes, "What are you watching? Are you watching? I have your brother!" Right. And I'm sitting at the table watching, and I'm like OK, so she puts down . . . I get up, and I go get the little girl; I go, "Hey, Christina, it's me, I'll take care of you, I'll pick you up. I'll take you, I'll play with you, you know?"

ME: Mmm . . . [appreciating her]

BEA: I tell her, like, if I was that little kid and I understood what Mom . . . boy, that wouldn't have, you know, that wasn't real nice. So you know I picked her up and you know, played with her (*inaudible*)

ME: Playing mind games or something almost?

BEA: I don't know. [She can't know it yet.]

ME: Why do you think she said that?

BEA: I don't know. I tried to think about it as I was watching it because it was more like, OK, I'll just pick up the girl. (*a little more animated now*) Because it's like ever since the two of them were born . . . I'll never say it again, but my sister says she likes the boy better. I'd never tell her kid that, but, you know, and so (*sniff*), um, he used to always cry a lot and she was real good so they never had to pick her up because she never cried, and now she's becoming, [correction:] beginning to cry a little bit more where he's beginning to more play by himself, so I think, "That's not fair, you're always carrying the boy," you know? And I've said all along, "That's not fair, she needs to be carried a lot." I carry the girl and never the boy. I don't know . . .

ME: Mm hmm. What does it do inside of you when you're taking care of her?

BEA: Umm . . . It's kind of just like "I'll take care of you," you know? "I'll play with you. I'll be there for you. I'll be there when you're older too." Cause even Sam plays with the boy more. He smiles more . . . goos and gahs a lot more . . . bigger because he was the first one born and everything. So everyone seems to favor the boy. And so I just check on the girl and see if she's OK.

ME: You are so faithful. [Completely unconsciously at this point, I was drawing on the theme of her guilt about being "*un*faithful" to Donny and his insistence upon how unfaithful she is.]

BEA: (*sniff*) What do you mean by that? [She can't believe anyone could see her as faithful.]

ME: I'm not sure. (*laugh*) It's what came up when you said, "I'm here for you now and I'll be here for you when you're older too."

BEA: Yeah, I don't know. (*takes a tissue*) I guess I'm trying to just, like with my uncle, I know he has needs, and I know that if I was sick I think I'd like someone to visit me, and so I try to, you know, tune in with him and try to think what he would like, and like on Sunday I went during my lunch, I felt kind of bad too on Sunday, because on Saturday, Saturday after the phone call, I says OK, Donny, so OK, well, I'll call you tomorrow cause we were going to, supposed to, have lunch anyway, so I called him on my break, and he was already out, and so I says, well I don't know whether we're having lunch, so give me a call if you're not still not mad at me. So I called him again and he still wasn't there, so finally right when I punched out and was ready to walk out the door and I get a call and it was him, and I'm like, "Well, where are you?" and he said "I'm at my friend's." "Well how long would it take you to get here?" He goes,

"Oh, ten or fifteen minutes," and I go, "Well, I already punched out so I don't know. I'll meet you somewhere." And he goes "Well, I don't know," so I go, "OK well," (*sniff*) I said "I'll just go visit my uncle, so I'll talk to you later." So, you know, I felt I didn't know whether I did the right thing or the wrong, or whether I should have just sat there and waited to spend time with Donny, and that might have been bothering me too because I haven't seem him since then. Maybe I did the wrong thing, maybe I should have waited for Donny to come by. So that was that and so . . .

So back to my uncle's, and it was like "I think he could use his face washed," so I asked for a towel, and I asked him, "Would you like me to wash your face?" And he goes, "Yeah," so, you know, like, he had crusty eyes a little, so I washed him down, and he said, "That's enough." I thought, you know, I just thought it would be a little refreshing to wash his face.

ME: You're really there, there for him.

BEA: Yeah, so . . .

ME: And there for your niece.

BEA: Yeah, so like for her, I talk to her. I don't know, I just know that everyone picks up the boy, my mom too, I mean she does have to feed her and change her, she does take care her. Um, you know, just watching what she did, um, you know.

[We sat in silence for a moment.]

ME: It really touched something inside of you that you wish for too.

BEA: Yeah. Yeah, I don't know whether I, you know, tuned in and said you know that that was what mom did to me, and you know . . . I don't know . . . (*pause*) . . . (*very small voice*) My headache's gone! (*smile*)

ME: Mm.

BEA: I mean I'm relaxed, I don't have to keep giving it any more . . .

ME: I'm glad.

BEA: You got rid of it. Or I got rid of it, or we got rid of it! (*laughing, sniffing*)

ME: (*smiling, staying with the feeling . . . after a pause . . .*) You know, something else I wondered, going back to Sunday with Donny, you punched out at work . . . [I want to see if she can touch any of her anger, the passive-aggressive aspect of her decision to see her uncle instead of Donny.]

BEA: Yeah.

ME: Yeah . . .

BEA: I called him, and I says I'm just double checking, I guess I'm punching out now cause I'm going to lunch, and I was in the bathroom and I heard a page and I didn't know who it was for, and it was like "Who was that for?" and it says "Bea, line 1," oh, OK, so I picked it up, and it was Donny, so, you know, I talked.

Me: When you said, "Well, I guess I'll go visit my uncle," and he said "OK," what were your feelings toward him right when you said that?

BEA: My feelings toward . . . ?

ME: Donny.

BEA: I don't know exactly, but I know that I was thinking I was uncertain about where we were because of what I did last night with Sam, "spoiling" him, so to speak, that he might still be mad at me and went out and didn't want to have lunch with me any more, and I didn't know.

ME: And he was calling because he did want to have lunch?

BEA: Yeah.

ME: And he would have come over.

BEA: Yeah, but calling me at 2 when he knows that 2 is when I have my lunch! (*skeptical laugh*)

ME: So there was a double message in that?

BEA: Yeah, well, he might have lost track of the time, that's possible, because he ended up spending the whole day with this guy and sold his speakers and sold a CD, and I don't know *what* else he did . . . (*laugh*)

ME: Well, what was crossing my mind was, I was wondering if you weren't still possibly mad at him? At least partly mad?

BEA: Well, I definitely still wanted to go see my uncle . . .

ME: Mm hm.

BEA: Um . . . and even contemplated going back after work that night too. But I didn't. Um, I mean he hadn't called, and I figured he wasn't, so I started making plans anyway, so I says, well, OK, I'll go see my uncle. He's like five minutes away from my work, so that would be really good.

And was I mad at Donny? Mmm . . . mmm, I don't think I was mad at him. I just didn't know where things were. I mean I understand, I guess I kind of understand why he was mad, he thought that I was spoiling Sam, so you know I didn't . . . and if I'm mad at Donny, it's never for long. I mean . . .

ME: Maybe you were mad that he wasn't there when you were ready to go? You wanted him to be there for you and have lunch.

BEA: Sometimes I do, but sometimes going out to lunch with him ruins my day. (*laughs*) It turns out to be, you know, either like yeah, this happened like two weeks ago: he had to go to work on a weekend that I have to work, so he calls me up and he says, "Oh, I'm only working four hours, so I could meet you," so I said, "OK, well, lunch is at this time," and he says OK, and he comes over and he's in a bad mood, (*sigh*) and I go, "What's wrong?" and he says nothing, and he mentioned that he was, "Oh, I drove by _____ and I saw this Porsche, and I thought it was your *boyfriend's*." [She is angry now.]

ME: Where did *that* come from?

BEA: Well, that's just it. I mean, I'll be OK, I mean I'll be fine, I won't be mad at him, and then he'll bring things up; he always brings things up from the past that'll *make* it bad. So it's like, you know, if I don't have lunch with him, that's OK, I'll go walk around, and I'll go do something, and sometimes it's like maybe it's better if I don't see him. It won't ruin my day. (*laugh, sniff*) It's not often that happens, but one time we went to lunch, and I got my order because I got like a soup, and it comes from the front, and the cook, like, cooks from the back and somehow they forgot his order, so he's like, "Forget it! Let's just finish your food and pay for your order, and I don't want mine." And so then you know he got mad, you know, he got mad like that. (*sniff*)

ME: I got . . . I got a twinge in my neck, just as you were describing that, that whole thing about the two lunches, those two stories?

BEA: Mm hmm.

ME: There's something in there, I don't know what it is.

BEA: Um, I don't know.

ME: Let me see what it feels like . . . boy, being in a . . . being in a collar! . . . not this kind! [I was wearing my clerical collar, and she smiled.] Uh, like a leash, a collar. Hmm. Just like I'm expecting to be . . . *erk*! (*pulling motion*)

BEA: Yeah, I mean, like, I don't, I mean *I* didn't do anything wrong!

ME: Unh uh.

BEA: But something will *make* it wrong. You know? I mean how am I supposed to know he drove down 77 instead of 90, and saw a Porsche on the road and thought of, you know? You know, he's so, um, what's a good word? (*pause*) Um, what's the word I'm looking for? Obsessed? with what I had done and everything that everything bothers him. I don't know . . . (*laugh, sniff*)

ME: Um, you'll be just kind of going along and all of a sudden he yanks your chain. Kind of like . . . (*pulling motion again*)

BEA: Yeah . . . I mean that happens when I say something, and I don't know I said it you know, or said it in the text that he understood it?! [She is fully touching her anger now.]

ME: Mm hm.

BEA: Um, you know, I'll say something, and it wasn't personal and it wasn't "How's the best way to hurt Donny, how could I word it that way?" but if I say it, then I guess that way it was my fault, but like I'm not aware of it (*laugh*) that I did it!

In this excerpt, it was striking how Bea's allowing herself to know her need for care, and her vicarious receiving of care by giving it—to her uncle, her niece, her compassion for strangers' children—released something psychosomatic in Bea so that her headache disappeared. And then, in the same session, when her anger began to rise and she pressed it down at first, the neck discomfort recurred, but this time in me, through the intersubjective medium of the transference-countertransference relationship. The neck pain was an embodied form of projective identification that I could literally, physically feel. By naming it, it was my intent to help bring it from a nonverbalized, embodied experience to one that could be known and processed.

As the therapy progressed, I received such physical projections from her on several occasions, particularly in the form of neck pain. I received and "held" headaches, neck aches, and stomachaches (symptoms that are all quite rare in my own physical health), commented upon them, wondered what they might mean for Bea, and in effect, handed them back to her in somewhat metabolized form to be integrated more fully into her own consciousness. Later in the therapy, I learned that I could bypass some of these steps and simply notice and hold the physical sensations. I learned that this often carried just as good a therapeutic effect. This process of holding and metabolizing, even without comment, began to create a process of change in which Bea began to have memories of her childhood where the "hole in my memory" once was.

Bea remembered having been kept in a crib until she was five years old and her legs had to stick out of the slats because she no longer fit. More disturbingly, she remembered eating the tassels off a bedspread, also when she was around five, because she had not yet been given any solid food. She was literally starving. Her parents' response had been to punish her by gathering the family and cutting off the remaining tassels. She loved going to school because "the bread and butter they gave us at snack time tasted so good." She remembered feeling abandoned by her father, but then one session she also began to wonder if she had been sexually abused as well. Moments before she disclosed the question whether she had been molested, I experienced a sensation of pins and needles in my legs and thought, "That's a new one . . . feels dissociative . . . I wonder what it means." Without framing any question, I simply sat with her as she struggled to remember something that was slowly coming up, first as a question and then, over the next many months, as new information of abuse by an adult cousin, both physical and sexual, and the lack of protection by her parents, was subsequently disclosed.

Repetition, "Resistance," and "Working Through"

Freud first identified that much of what causes people pain in their adult lives is the unconscious attempt to repeat, and thereby resolve, childhood traumatic experiences.[116] As feminist critics of Freud and psychoanalysis have rightly pointed out, this principle of the "repetition compulsion" has become oversimplified and misused. Therapists have wrongly invoked the repetition compulsion to blame women for situations in which they are victimized, focusing on the intrapsychic dimensions of assault and abuse while ignoring the larger social and political context. Nevertheless, Freud understood something true about the nature of early psychic wounding and the harm that can result in adult life by continuing to enact outmoded patterns of psychic survival. Many of these patterns will arise in the transference as blockages to self-knowledge and healing. Freud considered that the working-through of these so-called resistances is the hallmark of analytic treatment.[117] Resistances have a protective function, however. They signal defenses that the psyche has used to protect the core integrity of the self. Such defenses as denial, projection, displacement, repression,[118] and deeper manifestations of pathology including dissociation and projective identification must be understood as having been critical for the child's survival. Problems may have arisen for the patient, not because of the mobilization of defenses per se, but because those defenses have become habitual. For this reason, defenses must be befriended, not subjected to frontal attack.

Especially with regard to repressed memories, a careful and patient approach is needed. In the current climate of debate about the validity of repressed memories, it is extremely important to be open to whatever memories of trauma the patient may bring. The therapist must validate the patient's own experience of reality, without passing judgment on what did or did not *factually* occur. Even when facts can be more or less objectively verified, there will be, as noted above, multiple meanings associated with every event. While in the past most therapists (following Freud[119]), embedded in a social and political climate of repression, denied the reality of women's childhood sexual abuse and often interpreted it as something else, there is now at times, in some therapy circles, a tendency perhaps to overcorrect for this problem. In cases of known or suspected abuse, it is not helpful, and can even be harmful, to go "prospecting" for repressed memories. This is not to argue for a skeptical stance. On the contrary, as Freud himself originally believed,[120] sexual abuse is widespread. A climate of safety, an ability to hold and contain the split-off parts of the patient's self until s/he is ready to own them, and careful attention to what is happening in the transference here and now will create an environment in which memories will surface as the patient is ready.

Enactments

Because of its emphasis on the co-constructed reality that develops over time in the intersubjective relationship of patient and therapist, contemporary psychoanalysis has paid particularly close attention to *enactments* in therapy.[121] *Enactment* is used as a technical term by relational analysts, beginning with Theodore Jacobs,[122] to refer to the important but often overlooked nonverbal cues and communications that occur in a helping interaction. In the relational model, knowledge is understood as not only rational thought but involving affect, sensation, and behavior. Classical psychoanalysis, and most forms of psychotherapy, including pastoral counseling, traditionally have privileged words over behavior. Thoughts, fantasies, the flow of associations, talking about life events and dreams were what constituted the "talking cure." This serves a protective purpose, especially in long-term therapeutic relationships, in which unconscious material was intentionally elicited, admitting irrational, preposterous, and even dangerous contents of the unconscious into investigation without the threat of reenactments that could exploit and harm the patient.

Relational theorists now argue, however, that some form of unconsciously motivated enactment is inevitable in all therapeutic relationships, and that this privileging of the verbal has led in psychotherapy to an unintended ignoring of nonverbal communication.[123] Freud himself recognized early on that unconscious material that is not expressed will be communicated in action in the therapy.[124] Relational analysts have also recognized that words and actions are not so distinct as previously conceptualized. Enactments, following Jacobs,[125] are not equivalent to the more pejorative term *acting out*, which is traditionally considered as a failure of the process of reflection and verbalization. Many actions are more subtle than the types of behavior labeled as "acting out." They may be as nuanced as a glance, a tone of voice, or the momentary slight tremor of a foot.

Enactments are inevitable, continual, part of the nonverbal behavior of both patient and therapist, and therefore they are part of an ongoing dance of mutual influence—the intersubjective relationship—between therapist and patient. When regarded in this light, *virtually every action* may have meaning, and often some of the most powerful work of the therapy may be carried—at least for a time—on a nonverbal level. Further, while even the most minute behaviors are meaningful ("ordinary, quotidian enactments that form the daily ebb and flow of ordinary analytic process"[126]), there are certain enactments that "grab hold" of both therapist and patient, that come packaged with a distinctive affective atmosphere, and that may hold sway for a period of time—what Anthony Bass has termed "E," enactments with a capital E.

> [These] forms of enactment seem to up the ante of the analytic work; they raise the stakes in certain phases to the point that the [therapy] itself may be at risk. At such times, the [therapist] is especially challenged to locate in herself or himself personal forms of creative responsiveness to the complex subtleties of an analytic moment, and the fate of the analytic process itself often hinges on the patient's and the [therapist's] both coming to new, expanded modes of self-awareness. In other words, these are phases of both unusually high risk and high-potential growth for [therapist] and patient alike. These extremely personal, unique forms of creative participation push the [therapist] far beyond the conventional roles of listening and framing interpretations. These methods rely on the fullest possible range of interpersonal and intrapsychic resources that [a therapist] can bring to bear on the work with a patient. Enactments often rest on mistakes, slips, and blind spots that serve as doors through which the [therapist] and patient are transported into realms of personal encounter and self-experience that might otherwise remain accessible.[127]

Awareness of countertransference, as a continual openness to the movements within one's own subjectivity, is key to the therapist's being able to maintain a thinking function, somewhat like continuing to paddle a kayak—with, around, and above the tides of nonverbal interaction. To resist entirely would mean to be overturned, but to cease to paddle would also mean becoming swamped. And, as Bass, among others, has pointed out, no two therapists will respond in exactly the same way.

Of course, no two [therapists] bring the same inner resources to bear. We rely on different instruments (as each of us is strung a bit differently) for the reception of stimuli, inside and out. Each of us favors a different mode of experience and calls on a unique cognitive apparatus for processing what is being received. And Enactments provide opportunities for each of us to discover new inner resources, new levels of self-awareness, which come to life for the first time as latent personal potentials are newly evoked in interplay with a given patient.[128]

As I have written elsewhere,[129] some ethical reformulation is necessary in light of this new appreciation for the power of enactment. It is not an open invitation to helping professionals to become more intentionally "active," or personally involved on a social level with individuals who come to them for help. A new (or renewed, following Ferenczi[130]) appreciation of the role of the nonverbal in therapy and the inevitable involvement of the therapist in dynamics that are enacted first before they are discussed is not an open license for the therapist to do whatever "feels right" in the moment. It does mean that there is even more to attend to, and to explore, within the shared interactive field of patient and therapist. Judith Chused has written:

> One of the problems in our field that followed the recognition that enactments could be useful was that enactments began to be glorified. Some analysts even went so far as to insist that there is no movement in an analysis except following an enactment. I see enactments as only one of the multitude of interactions that occur in an analysis. I have found that most often it is the exploration of the enactment, rather than the enactment itself, that is mutative, just as it is the use of the analytic relationship, not simply the fact of a relationship, that is therapeutic.[131]

Refraining from overactivity, and a commitment to seeking understanding of what is not yet put into words, is still our baseline. It is awareness, and not enactment for its own sake, that becomes therapeutic. New appreciation for the potentially multiple meanings any action can represent, at multiple levels of consciousness and unconsciousness, and the fluidity and revisability of meaning over time, constitute a good argument for continuing to be conservative about one's level of activity. To quote Chused again:

> Of considerable value are those moments when [a therapist] catches herself about to participate in an enactment and, rather than enact, subjects her affects and thoughts to scrutiny, and then pursues some other course of behavior rather than enacting. *Awareness of our inevitable subjectivity, not just acting on that subjectivity, is our goal.*[132]

It is the rationale, then, not the rule about refraining from overactivity or overinvolvement, that has shifted. One no longer refrains from overinvolvement and overactivity because of a classical adherence to neutrality and objectivity but, rather, out of an appreciation of the inherent *complexity* of all interactions, and the need within the helping relationship to focus as much as possible on the immediate presenting needs of the patient. Because enactments are inevitable in any case, there is always more than enough occurring at multiple levels of consciousness and unconsciousness for the therapist and patient to process for the patient's benefit. Therapists do not need to "muddy the waters" by introducing, or allowing themselves to be pulled into, a greater level of activity than already exists. If one is feeling pulled toward a nonverbal action, it should signal a time to step back and reflect rather than to act (as much as this is possible). The motto Freud is said to have put on his own desk is still good advice: "When in doubt, don't." A nonverbal action can always remain as a tension or possibility for a future session, but once enacted, it cannot be erased or undone. To enact is to foreclose exploration.

In my own research among pastoral counselors and clinical social workers,[133] I found that a substantial number of therapists from both disciplines reported having engaged at least once in a number of behaviors deemed unethical by an independent ethics panel. A statistically significant association was found, especially among religiously ordained male therapists, between the report of experiencing erotic feelings in psychotherapy and nonerotic but unethical enactments. Enactments, including unethical enactments, were often rationalized by therapists under the rubric of the "real relationship," or for the purposes of nurturing, creating rapport, or bolstering the patient's sense of holding and security. However, an unconscious narcissistic need to be needed, or to see oneself as a "special helper," often underlies such seemingly caring intentions.

Psychodynamic consideration of therapists' need (perhaps universal, to some degree[134]) to be seen as warm, caring, and special helpers has led me to make three recommendations for pastoral psychotherapists:[135] (1) claiming (or reclaiming) a more exploratory stance, including a renewed clinical focus on interpretation of transference and countertransference dynamics in the context of an intersubjective relationship operating at conscious and unconscious levels; (2) greater use by therapists of in-depth clinical consultation and supervision with particular focus on countertransference and the intersubjective relationship; and (3) a deromanticization of the term *empathy* and a recuperation (following Kohut[136]) of its diagnostic usefulness.

Because of the fluidity of subjectivities in the helping relationship as understood in the relational paradigm, it might be construed that therefore traditional norms concerning boundaries, and what constitutes ethical behavior by helping professionals, should also be revised.[137] Relational theorists, however, virtually unanimously stress that ethical rigor is not diminished by the new paradigm. If anything, the new appreciation of intersubjectivity requires an even greater attention to ethical integrity on the part of the helper.[138] Irwin Hoffman has written, "The kind of authenticity that I have been talking about should not be confused with . . . damaging actions. On the contrary, that authenticity actually incorporates the special kind of discipline that the analytic situation requires."[139] Exceptions should be rare and spontaneous,[140] not staged or contrived. A good example is Winnicott's description of a moment in which a patient actually hit him, and through his immediate, unpublishable reaction, "got a little bit of the real me."[141] In fact, the power of such enactments largely resides in the contrast they represent to the normal therapeutic process, which is characterized by reliability, thoughtful verbal exploration, and restraint.

Empathic Failures and Transmuting Internalization: Human Beings Are Mutable, Fluid, and in Process

Even when ethics and matters concerning the safety of the therapeutic framework are well cared for, patients may frequently feel that the therapist has been insufficiently caring, attuned, or effective. One of the most poignant surprises for beginning therapists is the frequency with which patients reject, distort, or fail to see the therapist's caring intentions, because as the transference develops, projective processes come into play in which old expectations become more powerful than present reality. In addition, there are instances in which the therapist is insensitive, fails to understand, or because of countertransference dynamics unconsciously retaliates or psychically abandons the patient. Patients do not only imagine a therapist's slights or inattention because of transference distortions; patients also perceive, both consciously and at times unconsciously, aspects of the therapist's own countertransference attitudes and feelings that may be unempathic, even hurtful.

Kohut made a unique contribution to psychodynamic work in his understanding of the role of empathic failure on the part of the therapist. No matter how empathically attuned the therapist is, lapses in perfect empathy are as inevitable in therapy as they are in parenting. In "good enough" parenting,[142] the general climate of reliability allows the occasional lapses to actually be used by the child to grow. Occasional lapses provide "optimal frustration."[143] However, when failures and unreliability are the rule and not the exception, the patient is likely to bring expectations of similar failures to the therapeutic relationship. When the therapist does anything, however subtle, to reactivate the patients' original wound, or is perceived in a distorted way by the patient as retraumatizing, this will likely result in the patient's returning, or "regressing," to the corresponding childhood coping mechanisms. It is Kohut's conviction that the healing response is to recognize such enactments as a message of pain from the wounded psyche, to acknowledge the patient's perception of the therapist's empathic failure as real, and to explore together with the patient the possible meanings of the entire interaction.

Using Kohut's conceptualization of therapy as a process of building structure in the self, it is precisely the empathic exploration and interpretation of disruptions and failures in the therapeutic process that effect healing.[144] Kohut used the term *transmuting internalization* to refer to this transformation of inner structure via the integration of experiences of empathic failure and loss. This is a different use of empathy than Rogers's. Rogers believed that if the right environment was provided (i.e., unconditional positive regard) repression would lift by itself. Rogers understood this as naturally arising from an innate, internally derived movement toward growth. Because Kohut believed that structure is formed from the outside, via selfobjects, he viewed the therapeutic process as a more active process of building structure—the process of transmuting internalization.[145]

Thus, psychodynamic treatment is an active, at times even strenuous, process for both therapist and patient. It is important, therefore, to stress that the process is also delicate and subtle. One interpretation or important insight in an hour—or a month!—may be all that can be thoroughly assimilated. To the extent that Freud's metaphor of archaeology is still relevant, in light of the horizontal extensity of all that is being shared and uncovered, the image that comes to mind is one delicate archaeological work with a tiny brush. More aggressive excavation is likely to be invasive and retraumatizing. Exposing the patient's unconscious motivations, whatever the therapist's conscious good intentions, may evoke shame or rage and may even be an unconscious expression of the therapist's own sadism or issues of control. Sensitivity and tact are always needed because there are always more parts in each person in the therapeutic dyad than are communicating in any given moment.

For some patients, especially those whose boundaries were invaded in childhood, and who experienced empathy used in the service of abusing them, being understood can even be experienced as threatening and frightening. As Book suggests:

> Therapists should consider whether they may have misused empathy whenever a patient responds with withdrawal or rage. In this situation, it is ultimately very helpful to the patient for the therapist to respond to a misuse of empathy by focusing on what just transpired between him or her and this patient and attempting to respond to this misuse in a more accurate, empathic, and therefore reparative, manner.[146]

In conclusion, because human beings are multiple, the sense of unity and seamless self-coherence is more a necessary illusion about the way the human mind works than a hard reality. And because human beings are continually mutable and in flux, the process of internalization is an ongoing one, not closed off sometime in childhood. Even as experiences of lack, trauma, and intrusion were taken in and incorporated into the patient's early life, so the hope of therapy is that structure can be built or rebuilt through the internalization of the healing process. If human multiplicity and changeability are to deeply inform the way we do psychotherapy, then all the aspects of doing psychotherapy described above become more complex, and more multiply determined, than in a traditional model that assumed one person—the therapist—sitting with one person—the patient—in an essentially bipolar process of communication. A hallmark of contemporary psychoanalysis is, then, an appreciation of the great complexity and diversity of "minds" and "voices" in the room at any given time and an attentiveness to the idea that whatever is being spoken aloud by either partner in the therapeutic enterprise is merely one of many possible voices, expressing one of many possible meanings that may have emerged in the past and may yet emerge in future dialogue.

The "Analytic Third"

In addition to the parts that may eventually be identified as belonging to the patient and given voice in the therapeutic process, and those belonging to the therapist (whether or not disclosed aloud in the therapy), over time in the therapy there comes to be a constellation of parts that do not belong exclusively to the patient or to the therapist, or even to the two of them together, but to the therapy itself. Thomas Ogden identified this as the "analytic third" that emerges over time in the therapy.

> I use the term *analytic third* to refer to a third subject, unconsciously co-created by analyst and analysand, which seems to take on a life of its own in the interpersonal field between analyst and patient. This third subject stands in dialectical tension with the separate, individual subjectivities of analyst and analysand in such a way that the individual subjectivities and the third create, negate, and preserve one another. In an analytic relationship, the notion of individual subjectivity and the idea of a co-created third subject are devoid of meaning except in relation to one another, just as the idea of the conscious mind is meaningless except in relation to the unconscious.[147]

As I have described elsewhere,[148] there is a shared pool of conscious and especially unconscious wisdom that exists from the beginning of the therapeutic relationship but is increasingly filled with images, fantasies, thoughts, feelings, and sensations as the intersubjective relationship grows. This pool itself, then, may in some ways take on a life of its own as a third subjectivity in the room—neither the therapist's, nor the patient's, and not experienced in the same way by either, but something that is perhaps greater than the sum of the many multiple parts that constitute both partners.

Ogden clarifies that the analytic third is both explored and experienced asymmetrically:

> The relationship of roles of analyst and analysand in an analysis strongly privileges the exploration of the analysand's unconscious internal object world and forms of relatedness to external objects. This is a consequence of the fact that the analytic enterprise is most fundamentally a therapeutic relationship designed to facilitate the patient's efforts to make psychological changes that will enable him [or her] to live his [or her] life in a more fully human way . . .

It is also asymmetrical in the way it is experienced by analyst and analysand: each experiences the analytic third in the context of his own separate personality system, his own particular ways of layering and linking conscious and unconscious aspects of experience, his own ways of experiencing and integrating bodily sensations, the unique history and development of his external and internal object relations, and so on. In short, the analytic third is not a single event experienced identically by two people; it is an unconscious, asymmetrical co-creation of analyst and analysand which has a powerful structuring influence on the analytic relationship.[149]

It is therefore incumbent upon the therapist not to get lost—much less to drown—in the pool! When the waters become deep or shark infested, it is the therapist who must keep one hand on the side of the pool at all times. The therapist must, above all, survive, as Winnicott knew. In this way, the therapist's reverie can involve an immersion in the memories and meanings that are being generated by the patient and therapist together but at the same time keep his or her own contact with reality, or ego-functioning, intact. By keeping one hand on the side of the pool (that is, always keeping one part of oneself in touch with some sense of reality and with one's own thinking function), the therapist is also able to fish the patient out of the water if the patient is at risk of being overwhelmed.

Eventually, by finding and modeling a way to swim without drowning, and even to pace the level of immersion by treading water some of the time, the therapist can help the patient to learn how to trust that his or her own deep waters are safe to navigate. This is another way of expressing the goal of therapy itself. At the end of therapy, the patient's issues will probably not all be perfectly resolved. But s/he will have had enough repetition of a new object experience with the therapist to transform the most problematic inner object relations, and enough practice at swimming (immersing, exploring, and learning to express what is discovered), that s/he will be able to go on swimming on his or her own with newfound freedom. Finally, even joy becomes more accessible, as all feelings are allowed and more choices are available.

The Termination Phase

Of all the odd features of the [therapeutic] relationship, the ending of it is the oddest of all. It is a very strange good-bye, for both [therapist and patient].

—Stephen A. Mitchell[150]

As noted in the previous chapter, the idea of a formal termination is often impractical in contemporary practice. The idea of a "complete" therapy is increasingly being called into question,[151] recognizing that therapy is not a mechanistic procedure with a standardized, predictable product. Nevertheless, even therapies that are interrupted by a move, an illness, or other apparently external cause, do undergo a termination phase in which old themes are reconsidered, sometimes reenacted, and the patient has an opportunity to reflect on what has been gained in the process. The most important aspect of termination, even when it is relatively sudden, is to encourage the patient to engage in some review of the whole process, so that the gains of therapy can be consolidated and internalized.

Optimally, termination occurs when the patient feels that important goals have been met, and there is a felt sense of completion. But these elements are useful even when the ending is initiated by some external situation in the patient's life, and even more so if the interruption is caused by some event in the life of the therapist—in which case themes of abandonment and deprivation may be even more important to address, since remembered and fantasied feelings are being reinforced by an actual abandonment in the patient's current experience.

Termination is therefore a special time in the course of therapy, and although the relationship is about to change radically, it is not simply a summary or a wrap-up. From a multiple, relational perspective, quoting Jody Messler Davies, termination involves all

> the self-states of patient and [therapist], all the developmentally organized systems of identification and counteridentifications, concordant and complementary . . . that have engaged, disengaged, fought, loved, struggled, and survived to tell their story, a story of the patient's unique internal self-organizations, the meanings created by these organizations, and the varieties of engagement with significant others that have the potential to emerge and solidify from within them . . . The termination process, seen from such a [relational] vantage point, is not, then, just a long good-bye. Termination so conceived involves a multitude of good-byes—many, many good-byes—between the self-states of patient and [therapist], good-byes that emanate from a multitude of developmental epochs and from different centers of developmental trauma, conflict, and meaning making. From my own perspective, each good-bye deserves its own attention; each one is different; each one holds the potential not only for growth, emergence, and liberation, but also for grief, despair, and narcissistic collapse. Termination is not a unitary and linear process, but one that is contradictory and complex, containing many, often irreconcilable, experiences of the same separation and ending. Each good-bye between [therapist] and patient holds the potential to define the entire experience of the [therapy] and to determine how that experience is remembered and held over time.[152]

Therapy continues through the last goodbye, and even beyond, as the relationship itself—the "analytic third"—continues to live on in the memory and the imagination of both therapist and patient.

As with any intensely intimate relationship, if the ending is marked by emotional honesty, respect for the feelings of the other, and a gentleness that speaks to the vulnerability of the moment, the relationship can be jointly grieved and may yet be remembered with warmth and a preponderance of loving feeling that supports the narcissistic injury imposed by the loss and separation.[153]

Therefore, one's commitment to remaining therapeutic is as critical at the end of therapy as it was at the very beginning. Gabbard describes the process of termination, including some of the potential pitfalls, as follows:

Termination is a time when boundaries may become a little more permeable. Patients may feel they have the right to ask the therapist personal questions. Therapists who feel guilty may feel the need to take a more personal approach and reveal more about themselves. Both patients and therapists have difficulty with losing a significant relationship, and there is an ever-present risk of colluding with a denial of the loss. This collusion may take the form of planning posttermination meetings or imagining a social relationship together. Therapists should be particularly alert to a compromise of professional boundaries during the termination phase.[154]

There are a number of helpful things to remember when entering the final weeks of the termination phase. First, the goal of termination is to "stay on subject"—the need to navigate the separation and to say good-bye.[155] Review of the therapy continues, but now in the context of the question: what is it like to have to say good-bye? What would help this process? It can be helpful to share with the patient the idea that sometimes the last hour or few hours may recapitulate the whole course of the therapy, as a way of anticipating and making room for some of the more negative feelings that may come up—especially since the temptation of both patient and therapist at the time of termination is to wrap things up in a warm, cozy feeling of gratitude and mutual consolation. The therapist's observations are important to the process of review as well as the patient's: What is the patient now choosing to do or to say, instead of simply acting on unrecognized inner impulses? How has the patient become more able to self-observe? Sometimes examples can be given and can become shared stories as a record of important moments of change that occurred in the therapy. The therapist can recall together with the patient the memory of what s/he was like at the beginning and how far s/he has come. And finally, some questions can be explored to help keep feelings about the process of termination present for both partners: What will you miss the most about us? What do you wish we could have done/you could have gotten that you didn't? Where do you think the path of growth is leading you now?

BEA—VOICES FOUND

As the end of Bea's therapy approached, we talked about our work together and what she might like to have happen at a final session. She stated "I feel fed . . . that's the thought that comes to mind." I thought immediately of the bedspread tassels, the lack of solid food for years. To complicate things further, I was moving away, so there really was no possibility of an "open door" for further therapy in the future between us. I had made a referral in case she felt such a need, and she said that helped her feel less abandoned by knowing that I was leaving the city. She added, "I still wish I had more of a life. Donny and I don't really have a life, either one of us." I asked, "Do you have a life by yourself? If you were standing in the middle of a desert, would you know who you are?" "I'm a person who wants a lot," she said. We explored the themes again of self-sacrifice, deprivation, and giving to others as a way of giving to herself. I validated her beginning to learn to give herself the kindness and appreciation she didn't get earlier in her life. We talked about what she would like to have happen in our last session, and she replied, "I already have it, I think—that you won't forget me." (Again, the importance of knowing herself to be held in mind by another who cared for her was a crucial piece in her being able to draw on her own inner strength now.)

In the final session, she cried about missing me and saying good-bye, but then was able to talk about her hopes for applying for a better job soon. Some of the old patterns were still present—she was able to know she was sad about terminating, and sad that I was moving away, but not able to express anger about it. She did complain angrily for a bit about Donny (which I read at two levels—recapitulating an important theme of the therapy, allowing Bea's anger to emerge in their relationship, and also some transference anger toward me for moving away). She reflected on having learned to stand up for herself better and to be stronger, at first by practicing this part of herself in the therapy, and then eventually with Donny, at work, and finally with her mom. She felt clear that she would not live with Donny again, but felt that she had to try to make the relationship work because she wanted him to be a better father to Sam, so she would not sever ties with him completely. I validated that it had been important and healing for her to be aware of more parts of herself, including the angry parts, and to learn that she could express her negative feelings honestly and still survive.

She also reflected that she was finally talking with her mother, including talking about her childhood. They were even now able to talk about the abuse, a little bit at a time. She had taken a trip back to Korea with her mother in the last months preceding the termination of therapy, and although the trip stimulated traumatic memories for her mother and "she got very mean again for a while," she felt it had opened new avenues for truth-telling between them. Bea came to understand more deeply that due to her mother's own trauma, there were things she literally could not see—including when Bea was molested. While Bea never used the word *forgiveness*, and this was not something I would ever push as an agenda,[156] there was a sense that Bea's understanding of her mother's lack of protection had a new quality of empathy that went beyond simply retreating into her earlier pattern of denying her anger. We acknowledged that we had still only barely touched upon many things, but she also felt she was ready to "live her life now," making use of the things she had learned and her newfound strengths.

I still think of Bea. After a lengthy period of time, she had not returned to Donny, was working at a management-level position, felt that Sam was growing up to be a "normal, healthy kid," and had met a man she thought might "have some potential." As of her last letter to me, she was happily engaged to him, and although she was disappointed because her mother did not like her new husband-to-be and continued to say hurtful things, she had felt strong enough not to rush into this decision simply out of loneliness. Without denying the pain of her life, Bea was finally beginning to allow many different parts of herself to speak and choose and act. This newfound freedom carried with it considerable hope for her future as well as that of her son.

Bea's story illustrates that one of the primary goals of therapy, finally, is self-acceptance. To quote McWilliams,

> Self-knowledge is one goal of psychoanalytic treatment, but a more profound goal is self-acceptance. The more one accepts aspects of the self that have been seen as shameful, the less one is controlled by them. Psychoanalysis as a field has tried to name one after another propensity that comes with the territory of being human, including all the seven deadly sins, with the assumption that acknowledging these tendencies allows us to find better ways to deal with them.[157]

In Christian terms, this is genuine self-love. It is the opposite of narcissistic self-absorption, Martin Luther's definition of sin as the "self curved in upon self." On the contrary, it is the love of self with which one "loves the neighbor as oneself" (Lev. 19:18; Matt. 22:39). Such self-acceptance, in all our multiple, moveable parts, leads to what is perhaps the most pastoral goal of therapy—in Irenaeus's words, "the glory of God is a human being fully alive."[158] The ideal image of the fully human person, as exemplified for Christians in the life and witness of Jesus of Nazareth, is a person freed from the shackles of both sociopolitical and psychological oppression, who enters freely and generously in the dance of creation, receiving and giving abundant love in communion with the Holy and with all other created beings.

Chapter 6

The Therapeutic Sensibility:
Chaos, Silence, Love

Nel mezzo del cammin di nostra vita
mi ritrovai per una selva oscura,
ché la diritta via era smarrita.
Ahi quanto a dir qual era è cosa dura
esta selva selvaggia e aspra e forte
che nel pensier rinova la paura!

Midway upon the journey of our life
I found myself within a forest dark,
For the straightforward pathway had been lost.
Ah me! how hard a thing it is to say
What was this forest savage, rough and stern,
Which in the very thought renews the fear!

—Dante, *Inferno*, I:1–6[1]

TOWARD THE BEGINNING of chapter 4, I suggested that there are two kinds of answer to the question of how pastoral psychotherapy is actually done. The first involves the actual techniques that a therapist must learn and practice with increasing sensitivity and skill, as described in the previous two chapters. But the second, and perhaps most important, answer involves a therapeutic philosophy or attitude, which goes beyond specific techniques to an overarching commitment to the quality of the therapeutic relationship itself. This attitude is one of openness, a therapeutic willingness to be confused for a while, to not-know, and the courage to allow room for chaos, which is often a necessary precursor to change. In this conclusion, we return to the question of a therapeutic philosophy or sensibility, which involves embracing chaos, silence, and therapeutic love.

Chaos

Paradoxically, given the reams of psychotherapeutic publications over the last one hundred years, and the tooth-and-claw fights among therapists of differing theoretical persuasions, perhaps the most important capacity of a therapist is "the moral

"Midway upon the journey . . . a forest dark"

courage not to understand."[2] A favorite quotation among relational analysts is Wilfred Bion's statement that therapists should approach the work of therapy "without
memory or desire."[3] Bion cited the poet John Keats's term *negative capability*[4] to
explain this crucial quality of the therapeutic attitude. The therapist, like the poet,
should be "capable of being in uncertainties, mysteries, doubts, without any irritable

reaching after fact and reason."[5] It is ironic that Bion, of all possible theorists, wrote so much toward the end of his life about therapy as an "act of faith,"[6] when one of his greatest concerns was laboriously categorizing modes of cognition, including an elaborate grid of algebraic symbols. Yet Bion's own symbol for the ineffable, "O,"[7] literally went "off the charts"—it does not appear on Bion's complicated grid.[8] This referred to the reality beyond what can be grasped, "represented by such "O" as ultimate reality, absolute truth, the godhead, the infinite, the thing-in-itself."[9] While Bion retains a Platonic, essentialist conception of ultimate reality, the implicit tolerance, even appetite for chaos and uncertainty, resonates also with a postmodern psychoanalytic sensibility.

This is perhaps the paradoxical value of deeply critical, theoretical thinking—that it finally leads to the recognition of its own limits and a lifting of one's gaze past books and papers and theories toward the horizon of that which, inevitably, appears in the distance as a shimmering Unknown. Moreover, Bion's own slipping into theological language shows how thin the membrane finally is between the "faith" of secular therapy and religious faith. Bion's words begin to sound very much like Catherine Keller's tehomic theology of creation itself (as described in chapter 2): "O . . . can 'become,' but it cannot be 'known.' It is darkness and formlessness, but it enters the domain K [knowledge] when it has evolved to a point where it can be known, through knowledge gained by experience, and formulated in terms derived from sensuous experience; its existence is conjured phenomenologically."[10] So chaos breaks into even the most seemingly rational of therapeutic theories, and again turns the hubris of any supposedly scientific knowledge upside down.

The best time for making use of theory and considering technique is before and after sessions with patients. As my own labor in the previous chapters shows, I am certainly committed to making a place for disciplined, critical reflection, informed by one's training and one's searching of therapeutic literature! But finally, the knowledge of theory and practical skills must dissolve into the immediacy of the therapeutic encounter. One does not theorize as a primary activity in the presence of a patient. Theoretical speculations are precisely that—they are *speculi*, mirrors, or, more aptly, prisms, by which one facet of theory after another can be held up to our experience with a patient, to see what lights and patterns may be reflected—always with the benefit of the patient and not merely the brilliance of the therapist as the aim.

Sometimes, of course, theoretical ideas will arise in the flow of the countertransference, just like other associations, and they are to be treated in the same way—as grist for the mill, possible matters for discussion with the patient, but just as often, hints and clues not meant to be spoken, but to further open us up to the patient's own inner, lived experience. Theory in this way does not provide us with "information" about the patient but, rather, a sensitivity to multiple meanings that arise in the intersubjective matrix of the therapeutic relationship. It does not provide us with answers, but over time it may provide us with more complex and sophisticated questions.

In his *Letters to a Young Poet*, Rainer Maria Rilke wrote,

> I would like to beg you dear Sir, as well as I can, to have patience with every-thing unresolved in your heart and to try to love the questions themselves as if they were locked rooms or books written in a very foreign language. Don't search for the answers, which could not be given to you now, because you would not be able to live them. And the point is to live everything. Live the questions now. Perhaps then, someday far in the future, you will gradually, without even noticing it, live your way into the answer.[11]

We are called as pastoral psychotherapists to embrace the chaos of creation, including the chaos of both our own and our patients' "ring-streaked, specked and spotted"[12] inner worlds. Like Anselm, we embrace the mystery of God and ourselves as a multiplicity of "*nescio quids*," or "I know not whats," even as we discern certain cloudlike forms in the motion of the dance itself. These forms are the "truths" that emerge from pastoral psychotherapy—not *the* truth, but approximations and move-ments pointing toward a horizon where understandings of selves and others shim-mer ever more complexly.

Therapy itself is finally a process of *kenosis*. We empty ourselves of all pre-sumptions and presumptuousness, in order to enter a Trinitarian "third space" of metaphorical play and imagination. Empathy itself is *kenosis*. It is the self-emptying that relinquishes the need to "grasp" wisdom or show off one's knowledge, invit-ing both therapist and patient into an intersubjective realm of exploration. In this intersubjective space, encapsulated and at times harmful fantasies and projections can be recognized and put in perspective, as mutual understanding can be tried on, practiced, and finally internalized as a *habitus* that is at once psychological, spiritual, and deeply ethical.

Silence

All of this requires a tolerance, even a deep reverence, for silence. Above all, as quoted above in chapter 4, "*The psychotherapist must be able to listen.*"[13] Sheldon Roth put this sensitivity beautifully into words when he wrote, "we want to behave as if excessive movement puts all of living nature into hiding, as it does at a woodland pond."[14] Even with all the many revisions to psychoanalytic theory in the century since Sigmund Freud, there is a primary quality of psychoanalytic therapy that is one of refraining and restraint. Freud's little motto, "when in doubt, don't," applies not only to unconsidered enactments but to words as well.

Far from being a cold and aloof "blank screen," silence is the ground out of which much therapeutic work is allowed to grow. This is the therapist's discipline: to refrain from consciously adding anything extraneous, anything unconsidered, anything born of his or her own need. Enough will be added unconsciously—which is one of the best arguments for sitting still as much as possible. This stillness in analytically oriented practice is not unlike Zen sitting. We wait, with complete attention.

We also wait with humility. The patient is not an "It" to be acted on, but a "Thou,"[15] a precious subject, as multiply and wonderfully constituted as we ourselves and all living beings. This is the heart of the theological task: to be with the patient not as the expert who will tell him or her who s/he is, but as a respectful guide to his or her own winding journey into the *selva oscura*, the forest full of shadows. At the place of primordial silence, the therapist and the patient share a common humanity filled with both joy and suffering. The therapist receives the gifts from the patient's psyche and enters, if only vicariously, a little way into the patient's own inner world. On the journey, both are transformed.

Therapeutic Love

Finally, then, with our embracing of the *chaosmos*, we journey with each patient in an attitude of therapeutic love. As a pastoral theologian, I find it sometimes interesting to observe how secular therapeutic writers squirm and wrestle with this concept, and yet few in the end can entirely avoid it.[16] Perhaps especially in our society, which has so reduced love to a purely sexualized phenomenon, North American psychology has had a difficult time extricating itself from this association of all love with *eros* in the narrowest sense. The importance of many other forms of love, so subtly differentiated in ancient Hellenic culture, seems to have become muted in our sexualized consumer culture—*philía* (φιλία, "friendship/loyalty"), *storgé* (στοργή, "natural" or "parental love"), *philoxenía* (φιλοξενία, "hospitality/love" shown toward the stranger), *philanthropía* (φιλανθρωπία, "love of humanity/kindness"), *philadelphía* (φιλαδελφία, "brotherly love"), and the familiar biblical word *agápe* (ἀγάπη, "compassion," or "nonpossessive love"). The cultural association of love with sex infuses therapeutic relationships as well, and perhaps (without in any way disregarding necessary cautions about observing sexual boundaries), we have therefore become too squeamish to acknowledge the nonsexual intimacy—the bond of genuine love and care—that does exist between therapist and patient.

This is not to say that we simply "cure" our patients by loving them well enough. Our loving intentions do not in and of themselves constitute effective therapy, nor does a patient's idealization of us represent a complete picture of what we have accomplished. Such idealizations are usually transient, as anyone who has practiced enough longer-term psychotherapy knows well, and they will oscillate over time with a variety of other feelings toward the therapist until a more genuine, complex, "good-and-bad" relationship is allowed to come into being. Freud did not consider a patient's good feelings that stemmed from a positive and often idealized erotic transference, that is, "a cure through love," to constitute a lasting therapeutic result.[17]

Nevertheless—especially when he was not anxiously reprimanding his followers about not sexually exploiting their patients—Freud himself seemed to give credence to a different, and perhaps more generalized, form of love—often in the form of the love of family and friends—as therapeutic: "Side by side with the exigencies of life, love is the great educator; and it is by the love of those nearest him [or her] that the incomplete human being is induced to respect the decrees of necessity."[18]

This is perhaps where the pastoral psychotherapist has an advantage. The language of nonpossessive, compassionate love permeates the Judeo-Christian scriptures—as *rachamim* ("womb love") and *agape* ("compassion")—and in the ancient church's tradition, both *caritas* ("care/charity") and *amor* ("love"). "We love because God first loved us" (1 John 4:19). The temptation for pastoral psychotherapists, unlike many secularly trained therapists, lies not in the trap of skepticism about love but, rather, in the trap of sentimentality. We love to see ourselves as loving, and we are heavily socialized to be kind and nice. But niceness is not therapeutic love.

To return to the theme of multiplicity one last time, therapeutic love is therapeutic precisely because it allows room for *all* the parts of both patient and therapist to be present to one another, to be given expression, and over time to be recognized and accepted. As discussed above, this is not license to act out in either overtly sexual or aggressive ways. But therapeutic love is not simply an aspect of therapeutic tact. It encompasses not only the "nice" feelings, thoughts, and attitudes but also their opposites. To love therapeutically, we must love not only the friendly parts of ourselves and our patients; we must "love the enemy" as well, including the enemy within ourselves and within our patients.

So, paradoxically, therapeutic love encompasses hate, envy, hunger, need, desire, sex, and aggression. It encompasses all that has been denied, repressed, or disavowed. In this sense, as quoted in the previous chapter, it *is* "the relationship that heals"[19]— not because the therapist is nicer and more loving than anyone has ever been before (although sometimes, sadly, this is true), but because the therapist is committed to hearing out all the parts of the patient—lovable and unlovable—and joining with the patient in coming to understand and to accept the needs, desires, fears, fantasies, and feelings (including the taboo ones, like envy, rage, and hate) that those parts have represented, often unconsciously, for years.

Part of the therapeutic sensibility, then, is to recognize that love and hate are always co-present, in therapy and in life. Even in the most passionately romantic loving relationships, an element of aggression, even hostility, is present.[20] The recognition that human beings are multiple, fluid, and in process includes the recognition that we are never "just one thing," nor are our feelings, nor are the fantasies, thoughts, and meanings attached to them. In his famous article "Hate in the Countertransference," D. W. Winnicott asserted that love cannot exist without hate, and one cannot really love if one has not been able (i.e., if one's spontaneous "true self" has been suppressed) to allow oneself to hate[21] and feel hate.[22] He even went so far as to state that "the mother hates the infant from the word go" and enumerated a list of reasons.[23] In contrast to all who might want to sentimentalize Winnicott as the cuddly, understanding pediatrician, classicist Mary Jacobus has this important word to say:

> In an essay called "Hate in the Countertransference," D. W. Winnicott asserts baldly that "the mother hates the infant from the word go." The inventor of the good-enough-mother offers a surprisingly bleak account of the psychic and physical threat posed by the tyrannical baby, who represents a drastic interference to the mother's private life, while at the same time demanding her unstinting love. Winnicott's list of all the reasons the mother has to hate her child includes this grim warning: "If she fails him at the start she knows he will pay her out for ever." Perhaps the Electra complex should be renamed the Clytemnestra complex when viewed from the perspective of this never-good-enough mother who lurks in the wings of Winnicott's holding environment.[24]

Thus, the therapeutic sensibility incorporates the tragic dimension, as described at the end of chapter 3, in relation to sin, evil, and human vulnerability. We, too, sometimes feel tyrannized or drained by our patients, and we sometimes feel that we will never be "good enough"[25] even to survive, much less to "hold" all the chaos that roils in the therapeutic container. Sometimes our love is simply manifested in our sheer, dogged persistence, which is strengthened as we survive and continue to practice over the years. Experience helps us to remember, even in the worst moments of impasse, the principle of multiplicity, which assures that things cannot but change as the therapy unfolds.

Our role is a complex one,[26] involving all the training and technical knowledge we have gained, alongside the capacity to suspend it all for the sake of being present and listening, and with an appreciation of the both-and, love-hate, good-bad messiness of the human condition. Nancy McWilliams states it well:

> I want to make it clear that psychoanalytic love includes respect and is anything but infantilizing. It is not incompatible with all the negative feelings toward patients that get stirred up in therapy, nor is it incompatible with setting limits, interpreting defenses, confronting self-destructiveness, and inflicting inevitable pain—both by accurate observations that are hard on a patient's self-esteem and by inaccurate ones that disappoint because the therapist has again demonstrated fallibility. Like any kind of love worth the name it is not based on distortion; that is, therapists do not idealize clients in order to feel loving toward them. We try to love them as they are and have faith that they can grow in the ways they need to grow. I doubt that anyone can feel truly

loved unless he or she has been truly recognized as a combination of positive and negative qualities, good and evil.[27]

McWilliams relates this love to a commitment to being honest: "In supporting the effort to pursue and name what feels true, no matter how unattractive, the therapist creates the conditions under which clients can feel loved for who they really are. In the context of this love, they can begin to expand, to experiment, to hope, to change."[28]

The therapeutic sensibility is one that, among other things, stands for resistance to splitting. We help people feel who only want to think, and vice versa. We help people who only want to know about their niceness to feel the opposite, and we help the hardest of wounded and cynical people to rediscover within themselves areas of softness and compassion. We do this by remembering (or at least trying) to hold opposites together, including the splits within our own psyches, whenever we ourselves are tempted to become too hard or too soft, too rational or too emotional, too much of anything at the expense of all the other parts and conditions that exist in our own and others' very human existence.

Therapeutic love is therefore not a feeling. We may feel, at times, quite angry or exasperated or envious or frightened or even disgusted by something a patient has said or done, and if we are true to our own range of experiences and affects, we will sometimes hate the patient. At times, then, therapeutic love may not "feel" like love at all, but it is nevertheless present on the part of the therapist in the form of faith in the process itself and acting as carefully as possible to safeguard the therapeutic relationship so that transformation can eventually occur.[29] Sometimes it is precisely the hope, the faith, and even the fascination with the therapeutic process itself—in a sense, the love of the "analytic third" that is the therapy—that carries forward the therapist's care and compassion until more warm, positive feelings are again accessible. As Hans Loewald wrote,

> It is impossible to love the truth of psychic reality, to be moved by this love as Freud was in his life work, and not to love and care for the object [the patient] whose truth we want to discover . . . In our work it can truly be said that in our best moments of dispassionate and objective analyzing, we love our object, the patient, more than at any other time and are compassionate with his [or her] whole being.[30]

Finally, then, therapeutic love is also an ethic. We try as therapists to meet the patient face to face, as openly as possible. We do not succeed in every moment in achieving an "I-Thou" encounter, which Martin Buber himself acknowledged was only possible as a fleeting moment. But in the effort to be present to whatever parts of the other are being presented, moment by moment, we are conveying our commitment to the integrity of the process and to an attitude of honesty and curiosity.

We further convey our commitment by being willing to dive into the messiness and the chaos, sometimes without having any idea where the path through the forest is leading, but on sheer trust that the journey is worth it, and the patient deserves our taking the risk. Like the analytic third, which is the therapeutic relationship, Jessica Benjamin calls this dimension, this commitment, the "moral third" in psychotherapy: "The moral third, as I define it, is based on a principle of witnessing compassion, rather than moralistic judgment. It is the compass for analytic practice."[31] This compassionate stance extends reflexively to the therapist's self as well:

> I used to wonder, when I first began this work and struggled to stand under the weight of my own self-judgment how . . . other analysts lived up to those ideals: correct interpretation (which I can't seem to find right now), neutrality (which I can't embody in this moment), the well-analyzed analyst (who doesn't feel shame as I do), who knows what is going on here (which I don't). Eventually, with the help of my colleagues, I came to see the futility of such judgment and instead began to hope that we could change our analytic norms from "ought" to "is." I came to think that our moral third needed to expand to include the ideas of reality, which means accepting the dialectic of repetition and repair; of honesty, which is always tempered by awareness of our unconsciousness; of freedom, which would be our desire; and of compassion, which we sometimes attain. I imagined that our community as a whole could take some of the heat . . . and widen that space of moral thirdness that acknowledges our human fragility in a way that helps us to be honest and responsible at the same time.[32]

Conclusion

Dante had a guide on his journey—the poet Virgil. While none of us would presume to aspire to Virgil's wisdom, we share his role. When we meet a new patient, we do not yet know the landscape through which s/he will need to travel. But having traveled into the realms of our own shadows, through personal therapy and a continuing commitment to introspection, we do understand something about the way the road can twist and turn, and the many strange and sometimes disguised beings—even those that look like demons—that are to be encountered along the way. We have gotten messy before, up to our necks in the muck of our own existence, and we have survived the knowledge of at least some of our pain. We have been afraid before, and we have survived. And we have read and studied with others who have traveled the way before us. We have studied their maps (theories) and kept many of them for reference. We have even learned not to trust maps entirely but to be alert to new, rhizomatic tracings that lead off the map and into new territories, toward new horizons. These, then, are gifts that we bring to our meetings with patients. They are not unlike the gifts we receive again from our patients in return, as we discover new roads and new forests as we accompany them on their unique journeys.

Finally, as pastoral psychotherapists, we also do bring faith—not only as secularly defined, but faith in the Holy. In our practice/praxis of psychotherapy, we try daily to live out our faith in the God of creative profusion, of incarnational desire, and of living inspiration, who joins us on the journey and who turns the journey into a dance. Just as the indwelling Spirit prays in us when we pray, interceding for us "with sighs too deep for words" (Rom. 8:26), I believe that the power of the Holy, which is Love, not only guides the process of therapy but *is* the process. And therefore the trajectory of therapy is not merely toward "self-actualization," in a solipsistic sense, but one of continual growth, healing, and renewal. Pastoral psychotherapy is therefore a sacred process, in which increasing empathy for the Other, both within and without, empowers both our patients and ourselves to respond more and more fully to Love, living more and more closely to God's own desire for the creation: "to do justice, to love kindness, and to walk humbly with our God" (Mic. 6:8).

We learn new roads with each new patient as we enter again into all the fragility, the pain, and the good that they bring into our lives. There are no fixed positions, no final resting places, either of certain theological construction or of psychological "once and for all" insight, but through the flux of all of these, through the multiplicity of metaphor, of desire and shifting memory, we continue to move in and out of different internal and external states of pressure, desire, conflict, and union. As we do so, we may, in relationship, continue to "divine" both ourselves and our patients. In such "divination," we find new potential for growth, healing, and empowerment for emancipatory witness and liberative practice in the world.

> *Lo duca e io per quel cammino ascoso*
> *intrammo a ritornar nel chiaro mondo;*
> *e sanza cura aver d'alcun riposo,*
> *salimmo sù, el primo e io secondo,*
> *tanto ch'i' vidi de le cose belle*
> *che porta 'l ciel, per un pertugio tondo,*
> *E quindi uscimmo a riveder le stelle.*

> *The Guide and I into that hidden road*
> *Now entered, to return to the bright world;*
> *And without care of having any rest*
> *We mounted up, he first and I the second,*
> *Till I beheld through a round aperture*
> *Some of the beauteous things that Heaven doth bear;*
> *Thence we came forth to rebehold the stars.*[33]

Abbreviations

AACC	American Association of Christian Counselors
AAPC	American Association of Pastoral Counselors
AJP	*American Journal of Psychiatry*
AJPC	*American Journal of Pastoral Counseling*
CP	*Contemporary Psychoanalysis*
CW	*The Collected Works of C. G. Jung*, trans. R. F. C. Hull, Bollingen Series XX (Princeton: Princeton University Press, 2000).
DPCC	*The Dictionary of Pastoral Care and Counseling*, ed. Rodney J. Hunter (Nashville: Abingdon, 1990).
DSM	*Diagnostic and Statistical Manual* (various editions), (Washington, D.C.: American Psychiatric Association, I [1952], II [1968], III [1980], III-R [1987], IV-TR [2000]
ICD-10	World Health Organization, *International Statistical Classification of Diseases and Related Health Problems*, 10th revision, 2nd ed. (Geneva, Switzerland: World Health Organization, 2004).
IJPA	*International Journal of Psycho-Analysis*
IRPA	*International Review of Psycho-Analysis*
JAMA	*Journal of the American Medical Association*
JAPA	*Journal of the American Psychoanalytic Association*
JPC	*Journal of Pastoral Care and Counseling* (in former years, *Journal of Pastoral Care*)
JPT	*Journal of Pastoral Theology*
JSTM	*Journal of Supervision and Training in Ministry*
PD	*Psychoanalytic Dialogues*
PP	*Pastoral Psychology*
PR	*Psychoanalytic Review*
PsP	*Psychoanalytic Psychology*
PQ	*Psychoanalytic Quarterly*
SE	*The Standard Edition of the Complete Psychological Works of Sigmund Freud*, ed. and trans. J. Strachey (London: Hogarth Press, 1966).

Notes

Preface

1. Sigmund Freud, *The Interpretation of Dreams* (1900), in *SE* 5:541ff.
2. Ibid., vols. 4–5.
3. Pamela Cooper-White, *Shared Wisdom: Use of the Self in Pastoral Care and Counseling* (Minneapolis: Fortress Press, 2004).
4. Pamela Cooper-White, "The Therapist's Use of the Self: Countertransference in Pastoral Counseling and Clinical Social Work," PhD dissertation, Institute for Clinical Social Work, Chicago, 2000; summarized in Cooper-White, "The Use of the Self in Psychotherapy: A Comparative Study of Pastoral Counselors and Clinical Social Workers," *AJPC* 4, no. 4 (2001): 5–35; also summarized in idem, *Shared Wisdom*, 155–80.

Introduction

1. All the patients described in this book are fictional composites based on real therapeutic interactions—that is, as they exist in my own subjective memory. Identifying details have been altered for the sake of confidentiality (American Association of Pastoral Counselors Code of Ethics IV.G.; American Counseling Association Code of Ethics B.5.a and G.3.d).
2. Robert Kegan, *In Over Our Heads: The Mental Demands of Modern Life* (Cambridge, Mass.: Harvard University Press, 1994).
3. Catherine Mowry LaCugna, *God for Us: The Trinity and Christian Life* (San Francisco: HarperSanFrancisco, 1991), 383; also citing J. Zizioulas, *Being as Communion* (Crestwood, N.J.: St. Vladimir's Seminary Press, 1985). The term *praxis* has been used in numerous liberation theologies, adapting the Marxist insistence that theory and practice are mutually constitutive; praxis signifies liberative theory in particular, as it is put into action. See also Chung Hyun Kyung's "God Praxis, Not Just God Talk," in *Struggle to Be the Sun Again: Introducing Asian Women's Theology* (Maryknoll, N.Y.: Orbis, 1990), 100.
4. Early movements toward a more narrative, or hermeneutical, approach in pastoral care and counseling appeared in Charles Gerkin's *The Living Human Document* (Nashville: Abingdon, 1984), and Donald Capps's *Pastoral Care and Hermeneutics*

(Philadelphia: Fortress Press, 1984). Narrative theology has been a parallel movement in systematic theology, e.g., George Loughlin, *Telling God's Story: Bible, Church, and Narrative Theology*, rev. ed. (Cambridge: Cambridge University Press, 1999); George Stroup, *The Promise of Narrative Theology: Recovering the Gospel in the Church* (Atlanta: John Knox, 1981); and Stanley Hauerwas and Gregory Jones, eds., *Why Narrative? Readings in Narrative Theology* (Grand Rapids, Mich.: Eerdmans, 1989). For an overview and detailed bibliography of narrative theory in theology and religious studies, see Vincent W. Hevern SJ, ed., "Narrative in Other Disciplines: Theology and Religious Studies; Moral Development," Narrativepsych.com, Narrative Psychology Internet and Resource Guide (June 10, 2003), http://web.lemoyne.edu/~hevern/nr-theol.html. More recently, explicit use of narrative theory has been applied to pastoral care and counseling, e.g., Carolyn Bohler, "The Use of Storytelling in the Practice of Pastoral Counseling," *JPC* 41 (1987): 63–71; Paul Vitz, "Narratives and Counseling, Part 1: From Analysis of the Past to Stories about It," *Journal of Psychology and Theology 20* (1992): 11–19; and idem, "Narratives and Counseling, Part 2: From Stories of the Past to Stories for the Future," *Journal of Psychology and Theology 20* (1992): 20–27; Andrew Lester, *Hope in Pastoral Care and Counseling* (Louisville: Westminster John Knox, 1995); R. Ruard Ganzevoort, ed., *De praxis als verhaal: Narrativiteit en praktische theologie [Praxis as Story: Narrative and Practical Theology.]* (Kampen, Netherlands: Kok, 1998); Gordon Lynch, "Telling Tales: The Narrative Dimension of Pastoral Care and Counselling," in *Spiritual Dimensions of Pastoral Care*, ed. J. Swinton and D. Willows (London: Kingsley, 2000), 181–87; Christie Cozad Neuger, *Counseling Women: A Narrative, Pastoral Approach* (Minneapolis: Fortress Press, 2001); R. Ruard Ganzevoort, "Investigating Life-Stories: Personal Narrative in Pastoral Psychology," *Journal of Psychology and Theology 21*, no. 4 (2005): 277–87. The importance of narrative in African American pastoral care has been highlighted in particular: Edward Wimberly, *African American Pastoral Care* (Nashville: Abingdon, 1991); Archie Smith Jr., *Navigating the Deep River: Spirituality in African American Families* (Cleveland: United Church Press, 1997). Several foundational texts in narrative psychology include Theodore R. Sarbin, ed., *Narrative Psychology: The Storied Nature of Human Conduct* (New York: Praeger 1986); Joseph de Rivera and Theodore R. Sarbin, eds., *Believed-In Imaginings: The Narrative Construction of Reality* (Washington, D.C.: American Psychological Press, 1998); and Roy Shafer, *Retelling a Life: Narration and Dialogue in Psychoanalysis* (New York: Basic, 1992).

    5. E.g., Blanton-Peale Institute, 3 West 29th Street, New York, NY 10001-4597; www.blantonpeale.org.

    6. E.g., the Center for Religion and Psychotherapy, 30 N. Michigan, Ste. 1920, Chicago, IL 60602. In the pastoral literature, see, for example, Chris Schlauch, *Faithful Companioning: How Pastoral Counseling Heals* (Minneapolis: Fortress Press, 1995).

    7. In spite of Freud's own dream of a "Project for a Scientific Psychology" (1895), *SE* 283–398, psychoanalysis has been repeatedly critiqued as unscientific (most scathingly by Thomas Szasz in *The Myth of Psychotherapy: Mental Healing as Religion, Rhetoric, and Repression* (Syracuse: Syracuse University Press, 1988). Freud's single-case studies and

self-analysis lack rigor according to a pure modernist scientific method. The rigor of psychoanalysis as a hermeneutic, however, and the eloquence and resonance of Freud's use of language and symbol, testify to Freud's genius and to the ongoing usefulness and adaptability of his method, not only in therapeutic application, but also in social research, literature, philosophy, and other disciplines. For discussions on the dialectic between hermeneutics and science in psychoanalysis, see Stanley Messer, Louis Sass, and Robert Woolfolk, eds., *Hermeneutics and Psychological Theory: Interpretive Perspectives on Personality, Psychotherapy, and Psychopathology* (New Brunswick, N.J.: Rutgers University Press, 1988); Carlo Strenger, *Between Hermeneutics and Science: An Essay on the Epistemology of Psychoanalysis* (Madison, Conn.: International Universities Press, 1991); Donald Spence, "The Hermeneutic Turn: Soft Science or Loyal Opposition?" *PD* 3, no. 1 (1993): 1–10; Mauricio Cortina, "Causality, Adaptation, and Meaning: A Perspective from Attachment Theory and Research," Doris Silverman, "Bridging Natural Science and Hermeneutics: An Oxymoron or a Conjunction?: Commentary on Paper by Mauricio Cortina," and Carlo Strenger, "Why Constructivism Will Not Go Away: Commentary on Paper by Mauricio Cortina," *PD* 9, no. 5 (1999): 557–616.

8. Tracy Chevalier, *Girl with a Pearl Earring* (New York: Plume, 1999), 100–101.

9. For further discussion of these distinctions see Pamela Cooper-White, *Shared Wisdom: Use of the Self in Pastoral Care and Counseling* (Minneapolis: Fortress Press, 2004), 131–33.

10. The term *Christian counseling*, of course, actually signals a discipline that differs in some significant ways from the field of pastoral counseling. Christian counseling, also sometimes called "biblical counseling," has only recently begun drawing in a systematic way from the secular knowledge base of psychology, and focuses on finding scriptural help, advice, and moral admonition as its primary mode of helping. Its method, then, tends to be authoritative, directive, and largely behavioral in orientation, and its practitioners are largely non-state-licensed counselors in evangelical church settings. The most representative textbook of Christian counseling is Gary Collins's *Christian Counseling: A Comprehensive Guide*, rev. ed. (Nashville: Word, 1988), and its organization, the American Association of Christian Counselors (AACC) may be found at www.aacc.net. Pastoral counseling as a discipline is not only Christian (although the vast majority of actual practitioners to date are Christian, mostly mainline Protestant in affiliation), and it represents an effort to value and integrate a broadly defined spiritual and theological perspective with nondirective, psychologically and clinically grounded therapeutic theory and practice. Its practitioners are mostly state-licensed counselors who practice in a variety of church-based, agency, and private practice settings. Its organization, the American Association of Pastoral Counselors (AAPC), may be found at www.aapc.org.

11. E. Brooks Holifield, "Psychology and Psychotherapy," in *A History of Pastoral Care in America: From Salvation to Self-Realization* (Nashville: Abingdon, 1983), 184–95, 201–9; Orlo Strunk Jr., "Counseling and Psychotherapy," in *The Dictionary of Pastoral Care and Counseling*, ed. Rodney Hunter (Nashville: Abingdon, 1990), 236–37.

12. Carroll Wise, *Pastoral Psychotherapy: Theory and Practice* (New York and London: Aronson, 1980), 3.

13. E.g., David E. Scharff and Jill S. Scharff, *Object Relations Family Therapy* (Northvale, N.J.: Aronson, 1987); idem, *Object Relations Couple Therapy* (Northvale, N.J.: Aronson, 1991); Samuel Slipp, *The Technique and Practice of Object Relations Family Therapy* (Northvale, N.J.: Aronson, 1988); and idem, *Healing the Gender Wars: Therapy with Men and Couples* (Northvale, N.J.: Aronson, 1996).

14. Adapted from Vincent D'Andrea and Peter Salovey, *Peer Counseling: Skills and Perspectives* (Palo Alto, Calif.: Science and Behavior Books, 1983), 63, citing Joseph Luft, *Group Processes: An Introduction to Group Dynamics*, 3rd ed. (New York: McGraw-Hill, 1984). See also Cooper-White, *Shared Wisdom*, 133.

15. On gentle confrontation as proclamation in pastoral care, see Charles Taylor, *The Skilled Pastor: Counseling as the Practice of Theology* (Minneapolis: Fortress Press, 1991).

16. Margaret Kornfeld, "Change Supported by the Solution-Focused Method," in *Cultivating Wholeness: A Guide to Care and Counseling in Faith Communities* (New York: Continuum, 1998). See also http://sfbta.org.

17. Taylor, *The Skilled Pastor*, esp. 65–80. See also http://www.rebt.org.

18. E.g., Bohler, "The Use of Storytelling"; Vitz, "Narratives and Counseling," parts 1 and 2; Lester, *Hope in Pastoral Care and Counseling*; Neuger, *Counseling Women*; Ganzevoort, "Investigating Life-Stories;" Wimberly, *African American Pastoral Care*; and Smith, *Navigating the Deep River*. For more detail on narrative therapy, see n4 above.

19. The shift in terminology from *patient* to *client* is generally attributed to Carl Rogers, *Client-Centered Therapy: Its Current Practice, Implications, and Theory* (Boston: Houghton Mifflin, 1951); see also Q. L. Hand, "Counselee/Client/Parishioner," and "Counselor," s.v., *DPCC*, 233–34, 237–39.

20. Sigmund Freud as quoted in Joseph Wortis, *Fragments of an Analysis with Freud* (New York: Aronson, 1984 [1954]), 64, cited in Beate Lohser and Peter Newton, *Unorthodox Freud: The View from the Couch* (New York: Guilford, 1996), 149.

21. Sigmund Freud, "Dynamics of the Transference," trans. Joan Riviere, in Steven J. Ellman, *Freud's Technique Papers: A Contemporary Perspective* (Northvale, N.J.: Aronson, 1991 [1912]), 50, emphasis added. This paper also appears in English in *SE* 12:99ff.

22. What further distinguishes psychoanalytic psychotherapy from psychoanalysis proper is almost daily contact (four to five times per week), an atmosphere that encourages "the fundamental rule" of free association as the primary mode of communication by the patient, and, in most practices of psychoanalysis, if the patient's basic psychic structure is strong enough, the use of the couch, which further facilitates the loosening of the flow of the patient's associations. For this reason, psychoanalysis is not indicated for everyone and can even be dangerous to the psychic stability of certain individuals. Psychoanalysts are certified by recognized psychoanalytic training institutes after an average of four to six years of postdoctoral training involving a personal training analysis and intensive supervision of upwards of five psychoanalytic "control cases."

23. This and other definitions of Greek words used here are based on W. J. Hickie, *Greek-English Lexicon to the New Testament* (Grand Rapids, Mich.: Baker, 1977), and George Henry Liddell and Robert Scott, *A Greek-English Lexicon*, 9th ed. (Oxford: Oxford University Press, 1996).

24. René Descartes (1596–1650), "Second Meditation," *Meditations on First Philosophy*, ed. and trans. John Cottingham (Cambridge: Cambridge University Press, 1996 [1641]). For a concise summary of this famous phrase, see http://en.wikipedia.org/wiki/Cogito_ergo_sum.

25. E.g., Roy Herndon SteinhoffSmith, *The Mutuality of Care* (St. Louis: Chalice, 1999). For a critical discussion of SteinhoffSmith's work, see Judith Orr, "Review of *The Mutuality of Care*, by Roy SteinhoffSmith," *JPT* 10 (2000): 126–29. For a recent review of the issue of mutuality in pastoral care, see also Bonnie Miller-McLemore, "Sloppy Mutuality: Just Love for Children and Adults," in *Mutuality Matters: Family, Faith, and Just Love*, ed. Herbert Anderson, Edward Foley, Bonnie Miller-McLemore, and Robert Schreiter (Lanham, Md.: Rowman & Littlefield, 2004), 121–36.

26. Virginia Beane Rutter, *Woman Changing Woman: Feminine Psychology Re-Conceived through Myth and Experience* (San Francisco: HarperSanFrancisco, 1993), xv–xvi.

27. For a helpful essay on the eschatological role of hope in pastoral counseling, see Lester, *Hope in Pastoral Care and Counseling*.

28. Rutter, *Woman Changing Woman*, xiii.

29. Eda Goldstein, "Psychoanalysis and Social Work: Historical Perspectives," *Psychoanalytic Social Work* 9, no. 2 (2002): 34, also citing F. Hollis, "Contemporary Issues for Caseworkers," in *Ego-oriented Casework*, ed. Howard J. Parad and Roger R. Miller (New York: Family Service Association of America, 1963), 7–26.

30. Freud, "Wild Psycho-Analysis" (1910), in *SE* 11:225.

31. Pastoral diagnosis has seldom been addressed as a topic. The two major exceptions to this are Paul Pruyser's now classic text, *The Minister as Diagnostician* (Philadelphia: Westminster, 1976), and Nancy Ramsay, *Pastoral Diagnosis: A Resource for Ministries of Care and Counseling* (Minneapolis: Fortress Press, 1998).

32. Irvin Yalom, *Love's Executioner and Other Tales of Psychotherapy* (New York: Basic, 1989), 89, 232.

33. World Health Organization, *International Statistical Classification of Diseases and Related Health Problems*, 10th revision, 2nd ed. (Geneva, Switzerland: World Health Organization, 2004) (hereafter ICD-10).

34. The one obvious exception to this is post-traumatic stress disorder and its related brief form, acute stress disorder, which by definition require a trauma to have occurred as the origin of the disorder.

35. E.g., Robert Spitzer, introduction, DSM-III, 5-6.

36. DSM-I, coordinated with ICD-6, the first ICD to include mental disorders (see Allen Frances et al., introduction, DSM-IV, xvii, and DSM-II) were less influential, and problems with reliability and psychoanalytic bias were cited. As director of DSM-III,

(1980) and DSM-III-R (1987) (and special advisor to DSM-IV), Robert Spitzer inaugurated the current process of classification based on extensive clinical observation, field trials, and committee work. For a lively history of this process, see Alix Spiegel, "The Dictionary of Disorder: How One Man Revolutionized Psychiatry," *The New Yorker*, (January 3, 2005): 56–63.

37. Allen Frances et al., introduction, DSM-IV, xv.

38. E.g., Stuart Kirk and Herb Kutchins, professors of public policy and social work, respectively, have written a diatribe against the DSM called *Making Us Crazy: DSM—The Psychiatric Bible and the Creation of Mental Disorders* (New York: Free Press, 1997).

39. Ibid., xxii, xxiv. See also David Lukoff, Francis Lu, and Robert Turner, "Toward a More Culturally Sensitive DSM-IV: Psychoreligious and Psychospiritual Problems," *Journal of Nervous and Mental Disease* 180, no. 11 (1992): 673–82.

40. Ramsay, *Pastoral Diagnosis*, 9.

41. For more detail on the developmental aspects of woundedness on behavior, see Pamela Cooper-White, "Human Development in Relational and Cultural Context," in *Human Development and Faith: Life-Cycle Changes in Body, Mind, and Spirit*, ed. Felicity Kelcourse (St. Louis: Chalice, 2004), 91–110, and idem, "Opening the Eyes: Understanding the Impact of Trauma on Development," in *In Her Own Time: Women and Developmental Issues in Pastoral Care*, ed. Jeanne Stevenson-Moessner (Minneapolis: Fortress Press, 2000), 87–101.

42. Several texts detail the rationale and practice of brief psychoanalytic/psychodynamic therapy, e.g., James Groves, ed., *Essential Papers on Short-Term Dynamic Therapy* (New York: New York University Press, 1996); James Mann, *Time-Limited Psychotherapy* (Cambridge, Mass.: Harvard University Press, 1973); Peter Sifneos, *Short-Term Dynamic Psychotherapy: Evaluation and Technique* (New York: Plenum, 1979); and Stanley B. Messer and C. Seth Warren, *Models of Brief Psychodynamic Therapy: A Comparative Approach* (New York: Guilford, 1995). From a contemporary relational perspective that focuses particularly on the use of countertransference in brief therapy, see Jeremy Safran, "Brief Relational Psychoanalytic Treatment," *PD* 12, no. 2 (2002): 171–95.

43. For a more detailed discussion of this "Cartesian anxiety" and its implications for pastoral theology, see Cooper-White, *Shared Wisdom*, 36–37.

44. Thomas Kuhn, *The Structure of Scientific Revolutions*, 3rd ed. (Chicago: University of Chicago Press, 1996).

45. Werner Heisenberg's uncertainty principle, based on the study of atoms, is that if one sets out to measure one property of a subatomic particle, such as its position, other properties, such as momentum, become uncertain. For more detail see Cooper-White, *Shared Wisdom*, 42.

46. Egon Guba, "The Alternative Paradigm Dialog," in *The Paradigm Dialog*, ed. Egon Guba (Newbury Park, Calif.: Sage, 1990), 19–20.

47. Emmanuel Lartey, "Global Views for Pastoral Care and Counselling: Post-modern, Post-colonial, Post-Christian, Post-human, Post-pastoral," address given at the Seventh Asia-Pacific Congress on Pastoral Care and Counselling, Perth, Western Australia,

July 15, 2001, http://www.icpcc.net/materials/globalvi_1.htm. Lartey gives a brief survey in this address of the impact of these "posts" for pastoral care and counseling in "Embracing the Collage: Pastoral Theology in an Era of 'Post-Phenomena,'" *JPT* 12, no. 2 (2002): 1–10. For a review of some influences of postmodernism on the field of pastoral theology since 1990, see also Pamela Couture, "The Effect of the Postmodern on Pastoral/Practical Theology and Care and Counseling," *JPT* 13, no. 1 (2003): 85–104.

48. There are multiple schools of thought that come to similar conclusions regarding this idea of reality as constructed rather than known *in se*. The three main positions regarding reality may be summarized as *positivism*, the scientific view in which reality exists "out there" and may be positively discovered or known; *constructivism*, the most radical postmodern view in which no reality "out there" is given credence, and all supposed reality is understood as continually constructed through mental and social processes; and *postpositivism*, a position in between, which holds that reality does exist "out there" but it cannot be positively known through the senses because of bias and the ongoing influence of one's environmental and social context. For more detailed discussions of these categories, see Guba, *The Paradigm Dialog*. A related concept is *social constructionism*, a term coined by Kenneth Gergen in "The Social Constructionist Movement in Modern Psychology," *American Psychologist* 40, no. 3 (1985): 266–75; idem, "Psychological Science in a Post-Modern Context," *American Psychologist* 56, no. 10 (2001): 803–13; John Shotter and Kenneth Gergen, eds., *Texts of Identity* (Newbury Park, Calif.: Sage, 1989). Social constructionism emphasizes in psychology the social influences and structuring of what we understand to be reality. See also sociologists Peter L. Berger and Thomas Luckmann, *The Social Construction of Reality: A Treatise in the Sociology of Knowledge* (New York: Anchor, 1967). For more detail, including a graphic representation of positivism, postpositivism, and constructivism, and their relationship to intersubjectivity and relational psychology, see Cooper-White, *Shared Wisdom*, 35–56.

49. Jacques Derrida, *Of Grammatology*, trans. Gayatri Chakravorty Spivak (Baltimore: Johns Hopkins University Press, 1976 [1967]).

50. Michel Foucault showed how professional jargon institutionalized and reinforced sociopolitical power structures in such landmark works as *Madness and Civilization: A History of Insanity in the Age of Reason*, trans. Richard Howard (New York: Pantheon, 1965 [1961]); *The Birth of the Clinic: An Archaeology of Medical Perception*, trans. A. M. Sheridan Smith (New York: Vintage, 1994 [1963]); *The Archaeology of Knowledge and The Discourse on Language*, trans. Rupert Swyer (New York: Pantheon, 1972 [1969 and 1971]); *Discipline and Punish: The Birth of the Prison*, trans. Alan Sheridan (New York: Panthon, 1977 [1975]); and *The History of Sexuality: An Introduction*, trans. Robert Hurley (New York: Vintage, 1985 [1976]). See also idem, *Power/Knowledge: Selected Interviews and Other Writings, 1972–1977*, ed. and trans. Colin Gordon (New York: Pantheon, 1980).

51. George Orwell, "As I Please," *Tribune*, 4 February 1944, http://whitewolf.newcastle.edu.au/words/authors/O/OrwellGeorge/essay/tribune/AsIPlease19440204.html.

52. Considerable research has shown that race is a political, social, and historical construction, e.g., Audrey Smedley, *Race in North America: Origin and Evolution of a*

Worldview (Boulder, Colo.: Westview, 1999); Nancy Stepan, *The Idea of Race in Science* (London: Macmillan, 1982); and George Fredrickson, *The Black Image in the White Mind* (Middletown: Wesleyan University Press, 1987). Scientists have shown that there is no biological basis for dividing human beings into separate genetic groups. See Stephen Jay Gould, *The Mismeasure of Man*, rev. ed. (New York: Norton, 1996); and Richard Lewontin, *Human Diversity* (New York: Scientific American, 1982). An excellent educational tool summarizing this material is the video series "Race: The Power of an Illusion" (San Francisco: California Newsreel, 2003), http://www.pbs.org/race/000_General/000_00-Home.htm.

53. Popular paraphrase of a key question posed by Karl Marx in *Capital*, vol. 1. Trans. Ben Fowkes (New York: Penguin, 1992).

54. Summarized in Guba, "The Alternative Paradigm Dialog," 20–23. See also Denis Phillips, "Postpositivistic Science: Myths and Realities," in *The Paradigm Dialog*, ed. Egon Guba (Newbury Park, Calif.: Sage, 1990), 31–45.

55. For more detail on the ontological debate within this "paradigm dialog," particularly as it relates to qualitative vs. quantitative/statistical approaches to research see, e.g., Yvonne Lincoln and Egon Guba, "Paradigmatic Controversies, Contradictions, and Emerging Confluences," in *The Handbook of Qualitative Research*, ed. Norman Denzin and Yvonne Lincoln, 2nd ed. (Newbury Park, Calif.: Sage, 2000), 163–99.

56. Lincoln and Guba, "Paradigmatic Controversies, Contradictions, and Emerging Confluences," 165.

57. Irving Greenberg, "Cloud of Smoke, Pillar of Fire: Judaism, Christianity, and Modernity after the Holocaust," in *Auschwitz: Beginning of a New Era?* ed. Eva Fleischner (New York: KTAV, 1977), 23, quoted in Kenneth Cauthen, *The Many Faces of Evil: Reflections on the Sinful, the Tragic, the Demonic, and the Ambiguous* (Lima, Ohio: CSS, 1997), 13.

58. Berger and Luckmann, *Social Construction of Reality*; Gergen, "The Social Constructionist Movement."

59. Vinay Samuel and Christopher Sudgen, *Lambeth: A View from the Two Thirds World* (Harrisburg, Pa.: Morehouse, 1990).

60. Pamela Cooper-White, "The Relational Paradigm: Postmodern Concepts of Countertransference and Intersubjectivity," in *Shared Wisdom*, 35–60.

61. Susan Fairfield, "Analyzing Multiplicity: A Postmodern Perspective on Some Current Psychoanalytic Theories of Subjectivity," *PD* 11, no. 2 (2001): 242.

62. The foundational text for this school of thought is Stephen A. Mitchell, *Relational Concepts in Psychoanalysis: An Integration* (Cambridge, Mass.: Harvard University Press, 1988); see also Jay Greenberg, *Oedipus and Beyond: A Clinical Theory* (Cambridge, Mass.: Harvard University Press, 1991); and Lewis Aron, *A Meeting of Minds: Mutuality in Psychoanalysis* (Hillsdale, N.J.: Analytic Press, 1996). The development of relational theory can be traced through the journal *Psychoanalytic Dialogues* beginning with vol. 1 in 1991, and in Stephen A. Mitchell and Lewis Aron, eds., *Relational Psychoanalysis: The Emergence of a Tradition* (Hillsdale, N.J.: Analytic Press, 1999). For more on the history

of relational psychoanalysis, see Mitchell and Aron, *Relational Psychoanalysis*, ix ff.; Jay R. Greenberg and Stephen A. Mitchell, "Object Relations and Psychoanalytic Models," in *Object Relations in Psychoanalytic Theory* (Cambridge, Mass.: Harvard University Press, 1983), 9–20; and Stephen A. Mitchell, *Relationality: From Attachment to Subjectivity* (Hillsdale, N.J.: Analytic Press, 2004).

63. This bias in classical analysis is in part an artifact of Freud's own fin-de-siècle battles to be respected as sufficiently scientific, which began with his *Project for a Scientific Psychology* (1895), in *SE* 1:283–398.

64. "Object relations theory" began with the work of Melanie Klein, *"Envy and Gratitude" and Other Works* (New York: Delacorte, 1975), and was further extended by W. R. D. Fairbairn, *Psychoanalytic Studies of the Personality* (Boston: Routledge, 1952); D. W. Winnicott, *Maturational Processes and the Facilitating Environment* (London: Hogarth, 1965); idem, *Playing and Reality* (New York: Basic, 1971); and Harry Guntrip, *Schizoid Phenomena, Object-Relations, and the Self* (New York: International Universities Press, 1961. More recent exponents of an object relations perspective would include Thomas Ogden, *The Primitive Edge of Experience* (Northvale, N.J.: Aronson, 1989), and Christopher Bollas, *The Shadow of the Object: Psychoanalysis of the Unthought Known* (New York: Columbia University Press, 1987). See also Gregorio Kohon, ed., *The British School of Psychoanalysis: The Independent Tradition* (New Haven: Yale University Press, 1986).

65. Also called "Sullivanian," interpersonal psychoanalysis was founded by Harry Stack Sullivan (author of *The Interpersonal Theory of Psychiatry* [New York: Norton, 1978 (1953)]), Erich Fromm, Frieda Fromm-Reichmann, Mabel Blake Cohen, Clara Thompson, and others. This school of thought was developed at the Washington School of Psychiatry and the William Alanson White Institute, New York City.

66. The concept of a shift from a one-person to a two-person psychology is generally attributed to Merton Gill, *Psychoanalysis in Transition* (Hillsdale, N.J.: Analytic Press, 1994) and Irvin Hoffman, "Some Practical Implications of a Social-Constructivist View of the Psychoanalytical Situation," *PD* 2 (1992): 287–304. It has been much discussed in the relational literature (see n62 above).

67. Carrie Doehring, "The Challenges of Bridging Pastoral Care Experiences and Post-Modern Approaches to Knowledge," *JPT* 14, no. 1 (2004): 6, citing Paul Lakeland, *Postmodernity: Christian Identity in a Fragmented Age* (Minneapolis: Fortress Press, 1997), 48. Lakeland includes among these "radical postmodern theologians" Mark C. Taylor, Thomas Altizer, Carol Christ, and Sharon Welch.

68. Lartey, "Embracing the Collage."

69. Theodore Jennings, "Pastoral Theological Method," in *DPCC*, 862ff

70. "Transcendence and Beyond," Conference on Religion and Postmodernism, Villanova University, 18–20 September 2003.

71. Catherine Keller, *Face of the Deep: A Theology of Becoming* (London and New York: Routledge, 2003), xviii.

72. Lakeland, *Postmodernity*, distinguishes among three types of contemporary theological construction: "radical postmodern," (see n62), "late modern" (in which he includes

David Tracy, Sallie McFague, Jürgen Moltmann, and Peter Hodgson), and "nostalgic postmodern" (in which he includes both George Lindbeck, Hans Frei, and the "postliberals," and John Milbank and the "radical orthodox" school). To be specific, in this book I am drawing mainly from Catherine LaCugna and other Trinitarian theologians, e.g., Catherine Keller, Gordon D. Kaufman, John Milbank, and Elizabeth Johnson.

73. For a discussion of recent trends and efforts at bringing theology, theory, and practice into dialogue in pastoral care and counseling, see Nancy Ramsay, ed., *Pastoral Care and Counseling: Redefining the Paradigms* (Nashville: Abingdon, 2004).

74. C. G. Jung, "The Practical Use of Dream-Analysis" (1934), in *CW*, 16.

75. This integration is not unusual. The separation of Jungian and classical psychoanalysis is less pronounced in Britain, for example, in the work of Michael Fordham (e.g., *Freud, Jung, Klein—The Fenceless Field: Essays on Psychoanalysis and Analytical Psychology*, ed. Roger Hobdell [London: Routledge, 1998]), and this integration was a strong aspect of Jungian training in the C. G. Jung Institute of San Francisco. More recently, an entire issue of *Psychoanalytic Dialogues* was devoted to reflections by Jungian analysts on contemporary questions in psychoanalysis: James Fosshage, Jody M. Davies, Beverley Zabriskis, Andrew Samuels, Polly Young-Eisendrath, JoAnn Culbert-Koehn, David Sedgwick, Donald Kalsched, Mario Jacoby, and Stephen Mitchell, "Analytical Psychology after Jung . . .," *PD* 10, no. 3 (2000): 377–512.

76. For a recent survey of some of the intellectual debates in the field of religion and psychology, see Diane Jonte-Pace and William Parsons, eds., *Religion and Psychology: Mapping the Terrain—Contemporary Dialogues, Future Prospects* (London and New York: Routledge, 2001).

77. E.g., see Ivan Ward, ed., *Is Psychoanalysis Another Religion? Contemporary Essays on Spirit, Faith, and Morality in Psychoanalysis* (London: Freud Museum Publications, 1993); Diane Jonte-Pace, "In Defense of an Unfriendly Freud: Psychoanalysis, Feminism, and Theology," *PP* 47, no. 3 (1999): 175–81; Kirk Bingaman, *Freud and Faith: Living in Tension* (Albany: State University of New York Press, 2003); Don Browning and Terry D. Cooper, "Metaphors, Models, and Morality in Freud," in *Religious Thought and the Modern Psychologies*, 2nd ed. (Minneapolis: Fortress Press, 2004), 33–56. See also Diane Jonte-Pace, *Teaching Freud*, AAR Teaching Religious Studies Series (London and New York: Oxford University Press, 2003). For a more critical evaluation of Freud, see Browning and Cooper, "Metaphors, Models, and Morality in Freud."

78. Freud, *Civilization and Its Discontents* (1930), in *SE* 21:64.

79. Freud, *Moses and Monotheism* (1939), in *SE* 23:3–140.

80. Bruno Bettelheim, *Freud and Man's Soul* (New York: Knopf, 1982).

81. Freud, *Project for a Scientific Psychology* (1985), in *SE* 1:283–398.

82. Peter Homans explores the implications of Freud's cultural theories for theology in *Theology after Freud: An Interpretive Inquiry* (New York: Bobbs-Merrill, 1970).

83. Peter Gay, *Freud; A Life for Our Time* (New York: Norton, 1998), 354–55, 394, et passim; Felicity Kelcourse, *"Intersubjectivity, Infantile Helplessness, and Occultism: Non-Ordinary Experience in the Dialogue between Freud and Jung,"* paper presented to

the Person, Culture, and Religion group, American Academy of Religion, Philadelphia, November 2005.

84. There are five published first-hand accounts of Freud's analyses: Smiley Blanton, *Diary of My Analysis with Sigmund Freud* (New York: Hawthorn, 1971); Hilda Doolittle (the poet "H. D."), *Tribute to Freud* (New York: New Directions, 1956); J. M. Dorsey, *An American Psychiatrist in Vienna, 1935–1937, and His Sigmund Freud* (Detroit: Center for Health Education, 1980); Abraham Kardiner, *My Analysis with Freud: Reminiscences* (New York: Norton, 1977); Joseph Wortis, *My Analysis with Freud* (Northvale, N.J.: Aronson, 1994). For interesting contemporary analyses of these accounts, see Johann Cremerius, "Freud bei der Arbeit über die Schulter geschaut: Seine Technik im Spegel vom Schulern und Patienten," *Jahrbuch der Psychoanalyse* 6 (1981): 123–58; Luciana Momigliano, "A Spell in Vienna: But Was Freud a Freudian? An Investigation into Freud's Technique between 1920 and 1938, Based on the Published Testimony of Former Analysands," *IRPA* 14 (1987): 373–89; and especially Beate Lohser and Peter Newton, *Unorthodox Freud: The View from the Couch* (New York: Guilford, 1996).

85. Ernest Jones, *Sigmund Freud: Life and Work*, 3 vols. (London: Hogarth, 1957); R. G. Clark, *Freud: The Man and the Cause* (New York: Random House, 1980); Richard Wollheim, *Sigmund Freud* (Cambridge: Cambridge University Press, 1981); Paul Roazen, *Freud and His Followers* (New York: Random House, 1975); Louis Breger, *Freud: Darkness in the Midst of Vision: An Analytical Biography* (New York: Wiley, 2000); and Madelon Sprengnether, "Reading Freud's Life," in *Freud 2000*, ed. Anthony Elliott (New York: Routledge, 1999), 139–68. See also Lilli Freud-Marle, *In My Uncle's House: Memoirs of Lilli Freud-Marle* (New York: Basic, 1980); Stephen Applebaum, "Is the 'Impossible Profession' Possible?" *PsP* 4, no. 1 (1987): 81–88; Hans Küng, *Freud and the Problem of God*, trans. E. Quinn (New Haven: Yale University Press, 1979); Ana-Maria Rizzuto, *Why Did Freud Reject God? A Psychodynamic Interpretation* (New Haven: Yale University Press, 1998).

86. See especially Freud's respectful, even admiring thirty-year correspondence with the Swiss pastor Oskar Pfister in Heinrich Meng and Ernst L. Freud, eds., *Psychoanalysis and Faith: The Letters of Sigmund Freud and Oskar Pfister* (New York: Vintage, 1975 [1963]). See also other correspondence of Freud, e.g., *The Letters of Sigmund Freud*, ed. Ernst Freud, trans. Tania Stern and James Stern, with introduction by Steven Marcus (New York: Basic, 1960; also available in the Dover reprint edition, 1992); William McGuire, ed., *The Freud/Jung Letters*, trans. Ralph Manheim and R. F. C. Hull (Princeton: Princeton University Press, 1974).

87. Ernest Wallwork, "Thou Shalt Love Thy Neighbor as Thyself: The Freudian Critique," *Journal of Religious Ethics* 10 (1982): 266, also discussed in Browning and Cooper, "Metaphors, Models, and Morality in Freud," 47–50.

88. Phillip Rieff, *Freud: The Mind of a Moralist* (Chicago: University of Chicago Press, 1979).

89. On Freud's hermeneutics in particular, see Susan Handelman, "Interpretation as Devotion: Freud's Relation to Rabbinical Hermeneutics," *PR* 68 (1981): 2ff.; on Freud

and midrash, see Jerry Jennings and Jane Peterson Jennings, "'I Knew the Method': The Unseen Midrashic Origins of Freud's Psychoanalysis," *Journal of Psychology and Judaism* 17, no. 1 (1993): 53–75.

90. E.g., David Bakan, *Sigmund Freud and the Jewish Mystical Tradition* (Princeton: Van Nostrand, 1958); Marthe Robert, *From Oedipus to Moses: Freud's Jewish Identity* (Garden City: Anchor, 1976); and Moshe Gresser, *Dual Allegiance: Freud as Modern Jew* (Albany: State University of New York Press, 1994). Note that Freud biographer Peter Gay has taken a somewhat contrasting view, emphasizing Freud's departure from religious Judaism, in *A Godless Jew: Freud, Atheism, and the Making of Psychoanalysis* (New Haven: Yale University Press, 1987).

91. Edward Said, *Freud and the Non-European* (London: Verso, 2004), 53, also citing Isaac Deutscher, *The Non-Jewish Jew and Other Essays* (New York: Hill and Wang, 1968), 35, 40.

92. Freud, *The Future of an Illusion* (1927), in *SE* 21:3–58. See also Joachim Scharfenberg, *Sigmund Freud and His Critique of Religion* (Philadelphia: Fortress Press, 1988); Gregory Zilboorg, *Freud and Religion: A Restatement of an Old Controversy* (Westminster: Newman, 1958).

93. E.g., Freud, *Totem and Taboo* (1913), in *SE* 13:1–164; *New Introductory Lectures on Psycho-Analysis* (1932–33), in *SE* 22:67; *Moses and Monotheism: Three Essays* (1939), in *SE* 23:1–140.

94. Reinhold Niebuhr, "Human Creativity and Self-Concern in Freud's Thought," in *Freud and the Twentieth Century*, ed. Benjamin Nelson (Gloucester, Mass.: Smith, 1974), 260ff.; also discussed in Browning and Cooper, "Metaphors, Models, and Morality in Freud," 50–56.

95. Freud, *The "Uncanny"* (1919), in *SE* 17:219–56.

96. Ibid., 252.

97. Ibid., 243.

98. Freud, "Beyond the Pleasure Principle" (1920), in *SE* 18: esp. 7–17.

99. Kirk Bingaman, *Freud and Faith: Living in the Tension* (Albany: State University of New York Press, 2003), 60, also citing Paul Ricoeur, *The Conflict of Interpretations* (Evanston, Ill.: Northwestern University Press, 1974), 339.

100. Freud, "The Question of Lay Analysis" (1926), in *SE* 20:183–250.

101. Judith Van Herik, *Freud on Feminity and Faith* (Berkeley: University of California Press, 1982); Rizzuto, *Why Did Freud Reject God?*; Diane Jonte-Pace, *Speaking the Unspeakable: Religion, Misogyny, and the Uncanny Mother in Freud's Cultural Texts* (Berkeley: University of California Press, 2001).

102. Critiques of Jung's attitudes toward God and religion have been advanced beginning with writers in his own lifetime, such as Martin Buber (*Eclipse of God: Studies in the Relation Between Religion and Philosophy* [London: Gollancz, 1953]) and Victor White, who broke with Jung over Jung's *Answer to Job* in *Soul and Psyche: An Enquiry into the Relationship of Psychology and Religion* (London: Collins, 1960). For more recent critique, see Browning and Cooper, "Creation and Self-Realization in Jung," 144–81. For a review

of critiques, see Michael Palmer, *Freud and Jung on Religion* (London: Routledge, 1997), 166–96.

103. E.g., Morton Kelsey, *Christo-Psychology* (New York: Crossroad, 1983); Ann Belford Ulanov and Barry Ulanov, *The Healing Imagination: The Meeting of Psyche and Soul* (New York: Paulist, 1991); Urban T. Holmes, *The Priest in Community: Exploring the Roots of Ministry* (New York: Seabury, 1978); Thomas Hart, *Hidden Spring: The Spiritual Dimension of Therapy* (Minneapolis: Fortress Press, 2002), 23–24.

104. Abraham Maslow, *Toward a Psychology of Being* (New York: Wiley, 1968).

105. Robert Hutchins, "What Is Transpersonal Psychology," Institute of Transpersonal Psychology, http://www.itp.edu/about/tp.cfm.

106. C. G. Jung, *Memories, Dreams, and Reflections*, rev. ed., ed. A. Jaffe, trans. R. and C. Winston (New York: Vintage, 1989 [1961]).

107. E.g., C. G. Jung, "Christ, a Symbol of the Self," in *Aion: Researches into the Phenomenology of the Self* (1934), in *CW* 9, part 2:36–71; and idem, "A Psychological Approach to the Dogma of the Trinity," in *CW* 11:152–57.

108. Victor White, "The Frontiers of Theology and Psychology," Guild Lecture No. 19 (London: The Guild of Pastoral Psychology, 1942); and idem, *God and the Unconscious* (Cleveland: World, 1952). For a discussion of White's relationship with Jung, see Murray Stein, *Jung's Treatment of Christianity: The Psychology of a Religious Tradition* (Wilmette, Ill.: Chiron, 1985), 5–8.

109. E.g., John A. Sanford, *The Kingdom Within: The Inner Meaning of Jesus' Sayings* (San Francisco: HarperSanFrancisco, 1987); and idem, *Mystical Christianity: A Psychological Commentary on the Gospel of John* (New York: Crossroad, 1993).

110. Jung, and H. G. Baynes, *Psychological Types, or, The Psychology of Individuation* (1921), in *CW* 6.

111. Jung, *Aion*, in *CW* 9, part 2:8–10; and *The Archetypes and the Collective Unconscious* (1934, 1954), in *CW* 9, no. 1:20ff.

112. Jung, *Answer to Job* (1952), in *CW* 11:369, 372 et passim.

113. Jung, *Memories, Dreams and Reflections*, 39.

114. Ibid., 56.

115. For a concise history of body-soul dualism in Christian theology, see F. LeRon Shults, *Reforming Theological Anthropology: After the Philosophical Turn to Relationality* (Grand Rapids, Mich.: Eerdmans, 2003).

116. E.g., John Wesley, "A Plain Account of Christian Perfection" (London: Epworth Press, 1968 [1872]), 366–446; Jonathan Edwards, "The Importance and Advantage of a Thorough Knowledge of Divine Truth" (1739), in *The Sermons of Jonathan Edwards: A Reader*, ed. Wilson Kimnach, Kenneth Minkema, and Douglas Sweeney (New Haven: Yale University Press, 1999), 26–48.

117. Jung, prefatory note, in *Answer to Job*, in *CW* 11:358. For a discussion of the tension in Jung's writings between "suspicion and affirmation" of religion, see Peter Homans, "C. G. Jung: Christian or Post-Christian Psychologist?" and "Psychology and Hermeneutics: Jung's Contribution," in *Jung and Christianity in Dialogue: Faith,*

Feminism, and Hermeneutics, ed. Robert Moore and Daniel Meckel (New York: Paulist, 1990), 21–37 and 170–95. Homans views hermeneutics as the bridge between Jungian psychology and theology, using religious imagery to create interplay between "the archetypal dimensions of theological doctrine, religious myth, and the individuation process" (177).

118. Jung, *Psychology and Religion* (1937, 1940), in *CW* 11:59.

119. Jung, *Answer to Job*, in *CW* 11:469.

120. Jung, *On the Psychology of the Unconscious* (1943), in *CW* 7:9–122; idem, "The Relations between the Ego and the Unconscious," in *Two Essays on Analytical Psychology* (1928, 1935), in *CW* 7:123–244.

121. First defined in *Two Essays on Analytical Psychology*, in *CW* 7:64–79, 127–38; see also *The Archetypes and the Collective Unconscious* (1954), in *CW* 9, no. 1:3–53.

122. Jung, "Christ, a Symbol of the Self," in *CW* 9, no. 2:36–71; "A Psychological Approach to the Dogma of the Trinity," in *CW* 11:152–57.

123. Jung, *The Archetypes and the Collective Unconscious*, in *CW* 9, no. 1:142.

124. Jung, "Concerning Mandala Symbolism" (1950), in *CW* 9, no. 1:357.

125. Jung, *Transformation Symbolism in the Mass* (1954), in *CW* 11:201–98.

126. Jung, *Psychology and Religion*, in *CW* 11, esp. 64–105.

127. Melanie Klein, "A Contribution to the Psychogenesis of Manic-Depressive States," in *Contributions to Psycho-Analysis 1921–1945* (London: Hogarth, 1935), 282–311; and idem, "Notes on Some Schizoid Mechanisms" in *"Envy and Gratitude" and Other Works* (New York: Delacorte, 1975 [1946]), 1–24.

128. For further discussion of this point, see Palmer, *Freud and Jung on Religion*, 123–28.

129. Jung, *The Symbolic Life* (1976), in *CW* 18:707.

130. W. McGuire and R. F. C. Hull, *C. G. Jung Speaking* (Princeton: Princeton University Press, 1977), 251.

131. Martin Buber, *Eclipse of God* (New York: Harper, 1957), 83–84, cited in Stein, *Jung's Treatment of Christianity*, 9.

132. Stein, *Jung's Treatment of Christianity*, 9.

133. Browning and Cooper, "Metaphors, Models, and Morality in Freud," 180.

134. Elizabeth Ann Danto, *Freud's Free Clinics: Psychoanalysis and Social Justice, 1918–1938* (New York: Columbia University Press, 2005); Robert Coles, *Anna Freud and the Dream of Psychoanalysis* (Cambridge, Mass.: Addison-Wesley, 1993).

135. Jung, *Memories, Dreams and Reflections*.

136. Stein, *Jung's Treatment of Christianity*, 193.

137. Ibid.

138. Jung, "Psychotherapists or the Clergy?" (1932), in *CW* 11:347, emphasis added.

139. D. W. Winnicott, "Transitional Objects and Transitional Phenomena" in *Collected Papers: Through Paediatrics to Psycho-Analysis* (London: Tavistock, 1958 [1951]), 229–42; idem, "Morals and Education," in *The Maturational Processes and the Facilitating*

Environment (London: Hogarth, 1965), 94; see also idem, *Playing and Reality* (New York: Basic, 1971).

140. Ibid., 230.

141. Winnicott, "Ego Distortion in Terms of True and False Self" (1960), in *The Maturational Processes and the Facilitating Environment*, 145.

142. Ibid.

143. Winnicott, "The Use of an Object and Relating through Identifications" (1969), in *Playing and Reality*, 86–94.

144. Ibid., 91–92.

145. Paraphrasing from Winnicott, "The Location of Cultural Experience" (1967), *Playing and Reality*, 103.

146. Ana-Maria Rizzuto, *The Birth of the Living God: A Psychoanalytic Study* (Chicago: University of Chicago Press, 1979).

147. James Jones, *Religion and Psychology in Transition* (New Haven: Yale University Press, 1996), 144, citing Winnicott, "Transitional Objects and Transitional Phenomena" and *Playing and Reality*. See also James Jones, *Contemporary Psychoanalysis and Religion: Transference and Transcendence* (New Haven: Yale University Press, 1993), and *Terror and Transformation: The Ambiguity of Religion in Psychoanalytic Perspective* (New York: Brunner-Routledge, 2002), esp. 82–105; Ann Belford Ulanov, *Finding Space: Winnicott, God, and Psychic Reality* (Louisville: Westminster John Knox, 2001); Marie Hoffman, "From Enemy Combatant to Strange Bedfellow: The Role of Religious Narratives in the Work of W. R. D. Fairbairn and D. W. Winnicott," *PD* 14, no. 6 (2004): 769–804.

148. Winnicott, "The Location of Cultural Experience," 100.

149. W[illiam] W. Meissner, "Transitional Phenomena in Religion," in *Psychoanalysis and Religious Experience* (New Haven: Yale University Press, 1984), 177–83, reprinted in Donald Capps, ed., *Freud and Freudians on Religion: A Reader* (New Haven: Yale University Press, 2001), 220–25.

150. Capps, *Freud and Freudians on Religion*, 223.

151. Term borrowed from Philip Bromberg, *Standing in the Spaces: Clinical Process, Trauma, and Dissociation* (Hillsdale, N.J.: Analytic Press, 2001).

152. E.g., Brooke Hopkins, "Jesus and Object Use: A Winnicottian Account of the Resurrection Myth," *IRPA* 16 (1989): 93–100, reprinted in Donald Capps, ed., *Freud and Freudians on Religion: A Reader* (New Haven: Yale University Press, 2001), 231–39; and Marie Hoffman, "From Enemy Combatant to Strange Bedfellow."

153. Dodi Goldman, *In Search of the Real: The Origins and Originality of D. W. Winnicott* (Northvale, N.J.: Aronson, 1993), 123; also cited in Hoffman, "From Enemy Combatant to Strange Bedfellow," 787.

154. Rudolf Otto, *The Idea of the Holy: An Inquiry into the Non-Rational Factor in the Idea of the Divine and Its Relation to the Rational*, 2nd ed., trans. John Harvey (Oxford: Oxford University Press, 1958 [1923]).

155. For a reflection on Freud's "uncanny" and the uncanny as the "foreigner" in ourselves, see Julia Kristeva, *Strangers to Ourselves*, trans. Leon Roudiez (New York: Columbia University Press, 1991), esp. 181–92, reprinted in Donald Capps, ed., *Freud and Freudians on Religion: A Reader* (New Haven: Yale University Press, 2001), 327–34.

156. Wilfred Bion, *Attention and Interpretation* (London: Karnac, 1984 [1970]). See also Carlo Strenger, *Between Hermeneutics and Science: An Essay on the Epistemology of Psychoanalysis* (New York; International Universities Press, 1992).

157. Bion identified this ineffable dimension of reality as a region of thought, which he labeled "O," resonating with eastern meditative vowels and intimations of eternity (see Wilfred Bion, *Attention and Reality* [London: Tavistock, 1970]).

158. E.g., William Meissner, *Psychoanalysis and Religious Experience* (New Haven: Yale University Press, 1984). For an excellent bibliography on religion and psychoanalysis, see Ward, *Is Psychoanalysis Another Religion?* 79–93.

159. Anton Boisen, *The Exploration of the Inner World: A Study of Mental Disorder and Religious Experience* (New York: Harper, 1952).

160. Michael Eigen, *The Psychotic Core* (Northvale, N.J.: Aronson, 1986); idem, *The Electrified Tightrope*, ed. Adam Phillips (Northvale, N.J.: Aronson, 1993); idem, *Ecstasy* (Middletown, Conn.: Wesleyan University Press, 2001); and idem, *Rage* (Wesleyan University Press, 2002)

161. Michael Eigen, "The Area of Faith in Winnicott, Lacan, and Bion," *IJPA* 62 (1981): 413–33, reprinted in *The Electrified Tightrope*, 109–38.

162. Mary Lou Randour, ed., *Exploring Sacred Landscapes: Religious and Spiritual Experiences in Psychotherapy* (New York: Columbia University Press, 1993); Kerry Gordon, "The Tiger's Stripe: Some Thoughts on Psychoanalysis, Gnosis, and the Experience of Wonderment," *CP* 40 (2004): 5–45; Peter Lawner, "Spiritual Implications of Psychodynamic Therapy: Immaterial Psyche, Ideality, and the 'Area of Faith,'" *PR* 99 (2001): 525–48; and Alan Roland, "The Spiritual Self and Psychopathology: Theoretical Reflections and Clinical Observations," *PsP* 16 (1999): 211–33.

163. E.g., Salman Akhtar and Henri Parens, *Does God Help? Developmental and Clinical Aspects of Religious Belief* (Northvale, N.J.: Aronson, 2001). See also Benoni Reyes Silva-Netto, "Cultural Symbols and Images in the Counseling Process," *PP* 42, no. 4 (1994): 277–84.

164. Heinz Kohut, "On Courage" (1985), in *Self Psychology and the Humanities: Reflections on a New Psychoanalytic Approach*, ed. Charles Strozier (New York: Norton, 1985), 5–50. Kohut also explicitly drew a connection between the idealized parent-imago and images of God in *Analysis of the Self: A Systematic Approach to the Psychoanalytic Treatment of Narcissistic Personality Disorders* (New York: International Universities Press, 1971), 27.

165. Joachim Scharfenberg, "The Psychology of the Self and Religion, in *Advances in Self Psychology*, ed. Arnold Goldberg (New York: International Universities Press, 1980), 434, citing David M. Moss, "Narcissism, Empathy, and the Fragmentation of the Self: An Interview with Heinz Kohut," *Pilgrimage* 4, no. 1 (1976): 26–42.

166. Nancy McWilliams, *Psychoanalytic Psychotherapy: A Practitioner's Guide* (New York: Guilford, 2004), 4.

167. McWilliams, *Psychoanalytic Psychotherapy*, 45, also citing Louis A. Sass, *Madness and Modernism: Insanity in the Light of Modern Art, Literature, and Thought* (New York: Basic, 1992).

168. Freud, *Analysis Terminable and Interminable* (1937), in *SE* 23:211–53.

169. John McDargh, "Concluding Clinical Postscript: On Developing a Psychotheological Perspective," in *Exploring Sacred Landscapes: Religious and Spiritual Experiences in Psychotherapy*, ed. Mary Lou Randour (New York: Columbia University Press, 1993) 172–93.

170. J. Jones, *Religion and Psythotherapy in Transition*, 83.

Chapter 1: A Relational Understanding of Persons

1. This tradition runs deep in pastoral theology, including Anton Boisen's concept of "the living human document" in *The Exploration of the Inner World* (New York: Harper, 1952); see also Bonnie Miller-McLemore, "The Living Human Web: Theology at the Turn of the Century," in *Through the Eyes of Women: Insights for Pastoral Care*, ed. Jeanne Stevenson Moessner (Minneapolis: Fortress Press, 1996), 9–26. It is also part of a larger trend of correlational theology that is attributed to Paul Tillich, *Systematic Theology*, introduction to vol. 1, and vol. 3 (Chicago: University of Chicago Press, 1973); David Tracy, *Blessed Rage for Order: The New Pluralism in Theology* (New York: Seabury, 1975); and Mark Kline Taylor, *Remembering Esperanza: A Cultural-Political Theology for North American Praxis* (Maryknoll: Orbis, 1989).

2. Jürgen Moltmann, *The Trinity and the Kingdom* (Minneapolis: Fortress Press, 1993), 49, also cited in Todd Billings, "Theodicy as a 'Lived Question': Moving Beyond a Theoretical Approach to Theodicy," *Journal for Christian Theological Research* 5, no. 2 (2000): 1.

3. The first four functions were articulated in William Clebsch and Charles Jaekle, *Pastoral Care in Historical Perspective* (Englewood Cliffs, N.J.: Prentice-Hall, 1964), drawing the first three from Seward Hiltner, *Preface to Pastoral Theology* (New York: Abingdon, 1958), 89–172; the last three were elaborated in Carroll Watkins Ali, *Survival and Liberation: Pastoral Theology in African American Context* (St. Louis: Chalice Press, 1999), 9.

4. Emmanuel Lartey, *In Living Color: An Intercultural Approach to Pastoral Care and Counseling*, 2nd ed. (London and Philadelphia: Jessica Kingsley, 2003), 26.

5. Carrie Doehring, "The Challenges of Bridging Pastoral Care Experiences and Post-Modern Approaches to Knowlededge," *JPT* 14, no. 1 (2004): 10–11; see also idem, *The Practice of Pastoral Care: A Postmodern Approach* (Louisville: Westminster John Knox, 2006).

6. Also citing Keneth Gergen, "Psychological Science in a Post-Modern Context," *American Psychologist* 56, no. 10 (2001): 807.

7. Gordon D. Kaufman, *An Essay on Theological Method*, 3rd ed. (Oxford: Oxford University Press, 1995 [1975]). Kaufman has advocated a theological method that is explicit about the humanness of its conception, which he terms "imaginative construction." Kaufman is influenced by the more skeptical, atheist version of this assertion, that all theology is simply projection by human beings of their situation onto a transcendent being, proposed in 1841 by Ludwig Feuerbach (*The Essence of Christianity*, trans. George Eliot [Buffalo: Prometheus Books, 1989]). Kaufman describes this trajectory in his own thinking, while rejecting its nihilist implications, in his epilogue to *In the Beginning . . . Creativity* (Minneapolis: Fortress Press, 2004), 111.

8. Kaufman, *In the Beginning . . . Creativity*, 116, following H. Richard Niebuhr, *The Meaning of Revelation* (New York: Macmillan, 1941. See also Gordon D. Kaufman, *Systematic Theology: A Historicist Perspective* (New York: Scribner, 1968), and Benoni Reyes Silva-Netto, "Cultural Symbols and Images in the Counseling Process," *Pastoral Psychology* 42, no. 4 (1994), 277–84.

9. Wayne Proudfoot, *Religious Experience* (Berkeley: University of Berkeley Press, 1985).

10. Emmanuel Lévinas, *Totality and Infinity*, trans. Alphonso Lingis (Pittsburgh: Duquesne University Press, 1969).

11. E.g., Jacques Derrida, *Acts of Religion*, ed. Gil Anidjar (New York: Routledge, 2002), and idem, "How to Avoid Speaking: Denials," in *Derrida and Negative Theology*, ed. Harold Coward and Toby Foshay, trans. Ken Frieden (New York: State University of New York Press, 1992); and John Caputo and Michael Scanlon, *God, the Gift, and Postmodernism* (Bloomington: Indiana University Press, 1999).

12. Julia Kristeva, "The True/Real," in *The Kristeva Reader*, ed. Toril Moi (New York: Columbia University Press, 1986), and idem, *In the Beginning Was Love: Psychoanalysis and Faith*, trans. Arthur Goldhammer (New York: Columbia University Press, 1987). The correspondence between Kristeva and Catherine Clément, reflecting on religion and the sacred in relation to women, is also of interest: Clément and Kristeva, *The Feminine and the Sacred*, trans. Jane Marie Todd (New York: Columbia University Press, 2001).

13. Luce Irigaray began by identifying "God" with the phallic logic of the one/the "Same," but she began early on to suspect a different kind of (experience of) God, particularly for women, in her essay on feminine mysticism/hysteria, "La Mystérique," in *Speculum of the Other Woman*, trans. Gillian Gill (Ithaca, N.Y.: Cornell University Press, 1985), 191–202. Irigaray later elaborated her theological speculations in *Divine Women*, trans. Stephen Muecke (Sydney: Local Consumption, 1986), and *Sexes and Genealogies*, trans. Gillian Gill (New York: Columbia University Press, 1993).

14. Jean-Luc Marion, *God Without Being*, trans. Thomas A. Carlson (Chicago: University of Chicago Press, 1991).

15. Grace Jantzen, *Becoming Divine: Towards a Feminist Philosophy of Religion* (Bloomington: Indiana University Press, 1999).

16. A term from Martin Heidegger, developed most fully in "The Onto-Theological Constitution of Metaphysics," in *Identity and Difference*, trans. Joan Stambaugh (Chicago:

University of Chicago Press, 2002 [1957]). Heidegger's earlier, seminal work critiquing the ontology of metaphysics is *Being and Time*, trans. Joan Stambaugh (New York: State University of New York Press, 1996 [1927]).

17. One theory of how readers engage with and absorb texts is known as "reception theory" and has been widely applied in literary, biblical, cultural, and African American studies, etc. For an overview, see Robert C. Holub, *Reception Theory. A Critical Introduction* (London: Methuen, 1984), and *Crossing Borders: Reception Theory, Poststructuralism, and Deconstruction* (Madison: University of Wisconsin Press, 1992); James Malchor and Philip Goldstein, eds., *Reception Theory from Literary Theory to Cultural Studies* (New York: Routledge, 2001). For an example of its use in biblical studies, see Eugene Ulrich, "Multiple Literary Editions: Reflections toward a Theory of the History of the Biblical Text," in *The Dead Sea Scrolls and the Origins of the Bible* (Grand Rapids, Mich.: Eerdmans, 1999), 99–120. "Reader response" is another approach in biblical studies; see Edgar V. McKnight, "Reader-Reponse Criticism," in *To Each Its Own Meaning: An Introduction to Biblical Criticisms and Their Application*, ed. Steven L. McKenzie and Stephen R. Haynes (Louisville: Westminster John Knox, 1999), 230–52.

18. See also Sallie McFague's argument for a metaphorical theological method in *Metaphorical Theology: Models of God in Religious Language* (Philadelphia: Fortress Press, 1982), and *Models of God: Theology for an Ecological, Nuclear Age* (Philadelphia: Fortress Press, 1987).

19. Ana-Maria Rizzuto, *The Birth of the Living God: A Psychoanalytic Study* (Chicago: University of Chicago Press, 1981); Valerie DeMarinis, *Critical Caring: A Feminist Model for Pastoral Psychology* (Louisville: Westminster John Knox, 1993), esp. "The Case of Heather," 67–81; Antoine Vergote and Alvara Tamayo, eds., *Parental Figures and the Representation of God: A Psychological and Cross-Cultural Study*, Louvain Psychology Series Studia Psychiologicia (New York: Mouton de Gruyter, 1981).

20. Augustine, "The Trinity" [*De Trinitate*], in *The Fathers of the Church*, vol. 45, trans. Stephen McKenna (Washington, D.C.: Catholic University of America Press, 1963), 400–416, as cited in Kaufman, *In the Beginning . . . Creativity*, 15. See also Catherine Mowry LaCugna's discussion of Augustine's "theo-psychology of the soul created in the image of the trinity and longing to return to God" (82), in "Augustine and the Trinitarian Economy of the Soul," in *God for Us: The Trinity and the Christian Life* (San Francisco: HarperSanFrancisco, 1991), 81–110.

21. Friedrich Schleiermacher, *On Religion: Speeches to Its Cultured Despisers* (1799), cited in Kaufman, *In the Beginning . . . Creativity*, 17.

22. Karl Jaspers, *Philosophy of Existence*, trans. Richard Grabay (Philadelphia: University of Pennsylvania Press, 1971). Jaspers contrasts the human experience of limit with the transcendent, which he terms "The Being of the Encompassing" (15). For Jaspers, this is the realm of absolute unknowability; philosophical symbols are the product of humanity's self-transcending impulse, attempting to make the finite infinite.

23. Heidegger, "The Onto-Theological Constitution of Metaphysics," in *Identity and Difference*.

24. For a good anthology of Celtic sources with a helpful introduction, see Oliver Davies and Thomas O'Loughlin, eds., *Celtic Spirituality*, trans. Oliver Davies, Classics of Western Spirituality (Mahwah, N.J.: Paulist, 2000).

25. Julian of Norwich, *Showings*, ed. and trans. Edmund Colledge and James Walsh, Classics of Western Spirituality (Mahwah, N.J.: Paulist, 1978), 130.

26. My own social location is basically that I am a white, married, "professional class," middle-aged woman, with a teenage daughter and two grown stepsons. As an Episcopal priest and former United Church of Christ ordained minister, my theology has been formed both as an Anglican pastoral theologian, and ecumenically through a wide variety of experiences and contexts, including my theological training at Harvard Divinity School (largely in reformed, process, feminist, and liberation theologies) and at Holy Names College (Roman Catholic), time spent on missions of accompaniment in El Salvador, and three decades living among Lutherans, both as a spouse of a Lutheran pastor and more recently as an ELCA seminary professor. As a woman born in 1955, educated in the nontraditional professions of ordained ministry and psychoanalytic therapy, I have experienced gender discrimination and both the oppression and the empowerment of women through movements for social change in the radical decades of the 1960s and '70s. My class background presents a mixed-class picture.

The home in which I grew up was much like Tex Sample's "respectables" in *Blue Collar Ministry: Facing Economic and Social Realities of Working People* (Valley Forge, Pa: Judson, 1984), 74. The population of my hometown, a seaside bedroom suburb of both Boston and the closer industrial city of Lynn, Massachusetts, was all white, with strong religious and white-ethnic enclaves, most predominantly Italian Catholics, white Anglo-Saxon Protestants (our family's religious and ethnic identity), and a large population of both Conservative and Reform Jews. There were many first- and second-generation Holocaust survivors. Through my father's rising economic and social status, and my own private university and Ivy League graduate education, I moved at some point during my teenage years into what Barbara Ehrenreich identifies as the "professional middle class" (*Fear of Falling: The Inner Life of the Middle Class*, New York: Pantheon, 1989). As a professional opera singer in the 1980s, I have also been a union member, and inhabited the worlds of classical music and the professional theater, each with its own diverse and category-defying subcultures. I currently live on two seminary campuses, one in an intentionally diverse, urban residential neighborhood of Philadelphia, and one in the small, rural, historically and culturally rich town of Gettysburg.

Like many academics and therapists, my present-day life best fits a blend of Paul Fussell's upper-middle and "X" classes, in *Class: A Guide through the American Status System* (New York: Summit, 1983), 146–74, 212–23, defined more by education and the conscious adoption of certain social values than by income. Like most of my white peers, I am simultaneously privileged, distressed by privilege, ashamed and angered by the atrocity of white racism (for more on this, see Thandeka, *Learning to Be White: Money, Race, and God in America* (New York: Continuum, 1999), and anxious (in both senses of the word) to work for social change and justice.

27. Lartey, *In Living Color*, 34, citing anthropologists Clyde Kluckholn and Henry Alexander Murray, *Personality in Nature, Society and Culture* (New York: Knopf, 1948).

28. Miller-McLemore's play on Boisen's "living human document" (in "The Living Human Web").

29. Paul Ricoeur, *The Symbolism of Evil* (Boston: Beacon Press, 1967), 232–78.

30. Ibid., 25–150.

31. Paul Tillich, *Systematic Theology*, vol. 2, 68, cited in Bonnie Miller-McLemore, Hein-Fry Lecture.

32. Miller-McLemore, Hein-Fry Lecture.

33. For example, as John Meyendorff has shown, Eastern Orthodoxy shared the West's belief in the inheritance of the moral knowledge of right and wrong from Adam, but not Adam's sin as something that rendered each human individual "hateful to God and condemned . . . to eternal damnation prior to any independent, willful act," cited in David Weaver, "From Paul to Augustine: Romans 5:12 in Early Christian Exegesis," *St. Vladimir's Theological Quarterly* 27, no. 3 (1983): 187. See also John Meyendorff, *Byzantine Theology: Historical Trends and Doctrinal Themes* (New York: Fordham University Press, 1974), 145. Both are cited in F. LeRon Shults, *Reforming Theological Anthropology: After the Philosophical Turn to Relationality* (Grand Rapids, Mich.: Eerdmans, 2003), 192. Shults goes on to document that Augustine's exegesis of Genesis and of the meaning of Paul's words "in Adam" in Romans 5:12 were not universally shared by patristic theologians, such as Cyril of Alexandria and John Chrysostom (204–5). Shults summarizes New Testament scholars' (Henri Blocher, Mark Rapinchuk, Douglas Moo, and David Parker) suggestions that Paul's view of the universality of sin is not necessarily that it is inherited from Adam, but that it affects all peoples (204).

34. Shults, *Reforming Theological Anthropology*, 207.

35. Ibid., 213.

36. Gustavo Gutiérrez, *A Theology of Liberation* (Maryknoll, N.Y.: Orbis, 1988); and Andrew Sun Park, *The Wounded Heart of God: The Asian Concept of Han and the Christian Doctrine of Sin* (Nashville: Abingdon, 1993), also cited in Shults, *Reforming Theological Anthropology*, 214.

37. In broad strokes, historically, this spectrum might be depicted with the Reform tradition (Calvinism and its offshoots) representing the absolute otherness, separateness, transcendence, and sovereignty of God and the depravity of human beings on one pole, and Christian humanism (Christian Unitarian Universalist, churches descended from the Transcendentalist movement, and others) representing a belief in divinity within humanity, the immanence of God, and inherent goodness of human beings on the other. The Catholic, Eastern Orthodox, Anglican, and Lutheran traditions might be seen, then, as points along the middle of that spectrum, with differing degrees of belief in the capacity of human beings to effect good on their own and the world's behalf, and including a spectrum of different views *within* each tradition as well.

38. Matthew Fox, *Original Blessing: A Primer in Creation Spirituality* (New York: Tarcher/Putnam, 2000 [1983]).

39. http://en.wikipedia.org/wiki/Namaste.

40. For a concise summary of this history of body-soul dualism, see Shults, *Reforming Theological Anthropology*.

41. Calvin, *Institutes* I.15.16, cited in Shults, *Reforming Theological Anthropology*, 169.

42. Shults, *Reforming Theological Anthropology*, 174.

43. Carolyn Merchant has made the link between the subjugation of woman, sex, and nature in *The Death of Nature: Women, Ecology, and the Scientific Revolution* (San Francisco: HarperSanFrancisco, 1990). For a more detailed discussion of this separation, and its reinforcement of misogyny, see Pamela Cooper-White, *The Cry of Tamar: Violence against Women and the Church's Response* (Minneapolis: Fortress Press, 1995), 46–49.

44. Naomi Goldenberg, *Returning Words to Flesh: Feminism, Psychoanalysis, and the Resurrection of the Body* (Boston: Beacon, 1990).

45. Antonio R. Damasio, *Descartes' Error: Emotion, Reason, and the Human Brain* (New York: Avon, 1994). See also idem, *The Feeling of What Happens: Body and Emotion in the Making of Consciousness* (New York: Harcourt Brace, 1999).

46. Vilayanur S. Ramachandran et al., "Neural Basis of Religious Experience," *Society for Neuroscience Conference Abstracts*, 1997): 1316, summarized in "God and the Limbic System," in Ramachandran and Sandra Blakeslee, *Phantoms in the Brain: Probing the Mysteries of the Human Mind* (New York: Harper Perennial, 1999).

47. Nancey Murphy, "Darwin, Social Theory, and the Sociology of Scientific Knowledge," *Zygon* 34, no. 4 (1999): 596; Eugene d'Aquili and Andrew Newberg, *The Mystical Mind: Probing the Biology of Religious Experience* (Minneapolis: Fortress Press, 1999); idem, "The Neuropsychological Basis of Religions, or Why God Won't Go Away," *Zygon* 33, no. 2 (1998): 187–202; and James Ashbrook and Carol Rausch Albright, *The Humanizing Brain* (Cledveland: Pilgrim, 1997).

48. Nancey Murphy, *Bodies and Souls, or Spirited Bodies?* (Cambridge: Cambridge University Press, 2006).

49. Shults, *Reforming Theological Anthropology*, 178.

50. E. Earle Ellis, *Christ and the Future in New Testament History* (Leiden: Brill, 2000), 177, cited in Shults, *Reforming Theological Anthropology*, 178.

51. Anthony Thistelton, "Human Being, Relationality and Time in Hebrews, I Corinthins and the Western Tradition," *Ex Auditu* 13 (1997): 77, cited in Shults, *Reforming Theological Anthropology*, 178.

52. See for example, Elisabeth Moltmann-Wendel, *I Am My Body: A Theology of Embodiment* (New York: Continuum, 1995).

53. Sallie McFague, *Models of God: Theology for an Ecological, Nuclear Age* (Minneapolis: Fortress Press, 1989).

54. See for example, Delores Williams, *Sisters in the Wilderness: The Challenge of Womanist God-Talk* (Maryknoll, N.Y.: Orbis, 1993); and Emilie Townes, ed., *Embracing the*

Spirit: Womanist Perspectives on Hope, Salvation and Transformation (Maryknoll, N.Y.: Orbis, 1997).

55. Ntozake Shange, *For Colored Girls Who Have Considered Suicide/When the Rainbow Is Enuf: A Choreopoem* (New York: Macmillan, 1977), 63.

56. Lartey, *In Living Color*, 34, citing Kluckholn and Murray, *Personality in Nature, Society and Culture*.

57. John Hoffmeyer (via personal communication) points out that this standard modern account of Plato, in which forms are thought to have separate ontological status, is suspect. In Plato, the eternal forms are always told as myths, which creates a certain ironic distancing at the end of his works.

58. The term *the Same* (*tauton*) comes from Plato's *Sophist* and is linked in Lévinas with "the traditional subject, the Ego or the Consciousness of modern philosophy"; it is also identified with "totality"—"the way in which the Ego inhabits the world" (Adriaan T. Peperzak, Simon Critchley, and Robert Bernasconi, eds., introduction, *Emmanuel Lévinas: Basic Philosophical Writings* [Bloomington: Indiana University Press, 1996], x), that is, subsuming or attempting to subsume everything to its own perspective, needs, and way of being. Plato's Sophist argues against the Parmenidean "logic of the Same," in favor of the ontological possibility of difference, which Parmenides denies.

59. Elizabeth Castelli, "Interpretations of Power in 1 Corinthians," in *Michel Foucault and Theology: The Politics of Religious Experience*, ed. James Bernauer and Jeremy Carrette (Hampshire, U.K., and Burlington, Vt.: Ashgate, 2004), 34.

60. Harry Stack Sullivan, *The Interpersonal Theory of Psychiatry* (New York: Norton, 1953).

61. Neil Altman, "Black and White Thinking: A Psychoanalyst Reconsiders Race," *PD* 10, no. 4 (2000): 590.

62. Lévinas, *Totality and Infinity*; Peperzak, Critchley, and Bernasconi, *Emmanuel Lévinas: Basic Philosophical Writings*.

63. Jacques Derrida, *Of Grammatology*, trans. Gayatri Chakravorty Spivak (Baltimore: Johns Hopkins University Press, 1976 [1967]).

64. E.g., the following works of Michel Foucault: *Madness and Civilization: A History of Insanity in the Age of Reason*, trans. Richard Howard (New York: Pantheon, 1965 [1961]); *The Birth of the Clinic: An Archaeology of Medical Perception* (New York: Vintage, 1994 [1963]); *The Archaeology of Knowledge and The Discourse on Language*, trans. Rupert Swyer (New York: Pantheon, 1972 [1969 and 1971]); *Discipline and Punish: The Birth of the Prison*, trans. Alan Sheridan (New York: Panthon, 1977 [1975]); *The History of Sexuality: An Introduction*, trans. Robert Hurley (New York: Vintage, 1985 [1976]). See also *Power/Knowledge: Selected Interviews and Other Writings, 1972–1977*, ed. and trans. Colin Gordon, (New York: Pantheon, 1980).

65. E.g., Luce Irigaray, *Speculum of the Other Woman*—see especially "Any Theory of the 'Subject' Has Always Been Appropriated by the 'Masculine,'" 133–46; and *This Sex*

Which Is Not One, trans. Catherine Porter with Carolyn Burke (Ithaca: Cornell University Press, 1985 [1977]). "One, oneness (*le un*)" is defined in this edition of *This Sex Which Is Not One* as

> the universal standard and privileged form in our systems of representation, oneness expresses the requirements for unitary representations of signification and identity. Within such a system, in which the masculine standard takes itself as a universal, it would be impossible to represent the duality or plurality of the female sex and of a possible language in analogy with it. (221)

Similarly, the "other/same (*autre/même*)" is translated as "a related tendency in Western discourse which privileges masculine "sameness-unto-itself" as the basis of signification and identity and, as a consequence, posits the feminine as other only in relation to masculine sameness, that is, not as a different mode of signification" (221).

66. Gayatri Chakravorty Spivak, "Can the Subaltern Speak? Speculations on Widow Sacrifice," *Wedge* 7, no. 8 (1985): 120–30; see also idem, *A Critique of Postcolonial Reason: Toward a History of the Vanishing Present* (Cambridge, Mass.: Harvard University Press, 1999); and idem, *The Spivak Reader: Selected Works of Gayatri Chakravorty Spivak*, ed. Donna Landry and Gerald MacLean (New York: Routledge, 1996).

67. Martin Buber, *I and Thou*, trans. Walter Kaufmann (New York: Free Press, 1971).

68. For an interesting essay on the face and the mirror in psychoanalytic theory, including considerations of Kohut, Winnicott, Bion, Spitz, Lévinas, Lacan, and others, see Michael Eigen, "The Significance of the Face," in *The Electrified Tightrope*, ed. Adam Phillips (Northvale, N.J.: Aronson, 1993), 49–60.

69. Jacques Lacan, "The Mirror Stage as Formative of the Function of the I as Revealed in Psychoanalytic Experience" (1949), in *Écrits: A Selection*, trans. Bruce Fink, Heloise Fink, and Russell Grigg (New York: Norton, 2004), 3–9.

70. Cooper-White, *Shared Wisdom*. See especially chapter 3, "The Relational Paradigm: Postmodern Concepts of Countertransference and Intersubjectivity," 35–60.

71. Homi Bhabha, *The Location of Culture* (New York: Routledge, 1994). See also Bhabha, "The Third Space," an interview by Jonathan Rutherford, in Jonathan Rutherford, ed., *Identity: Community, Culture, Difference* (London: Lawrence and Wishart, 1990), 207–21.

72. Bhabha, *Location of Culture*, 37. For a glossary of terms used in postcolonial studies see Bill Ashcroft, Gareth Griffiths, and Helen Tiffin, *Post-Colonial Studies: The Key Concepts* (New York: Routledge, 2000).

73. Bhabha, *Location of Culture*, 114.

74. Ibid., 120.

75. Ibid., 218.

76. Bhabha, "The Third Space," 208.

77. Ibid.

78. Dwight Hopkins, *Being Human: Race, Culture, and Religion* (Minneapolis: Fortress Press, 2005).

79. Robert Bellah, *Habits of the Heart: Individualism and Commitment in American Life* (Berkeley: University of California Press, 1996).

80. Hopkins, *Being Human*, 5.

81. E.g., Jacques Derrida, *Writing and Difference*, trans. Alan Bass (Chicago: University of Chicago Press, 1978 [1967]). For further discussion, see Cooper-White, *Shared Wisdom*, 40.

82. Spivak, *Critique of Postcolonial Reason*.

83. Lévinas, *Alterity and Transcendence*, trans. Michael B. Smith (New York: Columbia University Press, 1999), 169–82.

84. Ibid., 170.

85. Gregorio Kohon, "Objects Are Not People," *Free Associations* 2 (1985): 19–30.

86. Eigen, "The Area of Faith in Winnicott, Lacan, and Bion," in *The Electrified Tightrope*, 113.

87. D. W. Winnicott, *Playing and Reality* (New York: Basic, 1971).

88. Jessica Benjamin makes this distinction in "Commentary on Paper by Gerhardt, Sweetnam, and Borton," *PD* 10, no. 1 (2000): 45.

89. Jessica Benjamin, *Shadow of the Other* (New York: Routledge, 1998).

90. Benjamin, "Commentary on Paper by Gerhardt, Sweetnam, and Borton," 45.

91. Ibid., 87. For further discussion of difference and mutual recognition from a relational psychoanalytic perspective, see Julie Gerhardt, Annie Sweetnam, and Leeann Borton, "The Intersubjective Turn in Psychoanalysis: A Comparison of Contemporary Theorists: Part 1: Jessica Benjamin," with a response by Benjamin and further reply by Gerhardt, *PD* 10, no. 1 (2000): 1–63.

92. Hopkins, "Culture: Labor, Aesthetic, and Spirit," in *Being Human*, 53–80.

93. For a thoughtful exposition of this interplay of self and communal identity, see Hopkins, "Selves and the Self: I Am Because We Are," in *Being Human*, 81–117.

94. Richard Schweder and Robert LeVine, eds., *Culture Theory: Essays on Mind, Self, and Emotion* (Cambridge: Cambridge University Press, 1984).

95. Freud, "Group Psychology and the Analysis of the Ego" (1920), in *SE* 18:67–143.

96. Clifford Geertz, "Thick Description: Toward an Interpretative Theory of Culture," in *The Interpretation of Cultures* (New York: Basic, 1973), 3–32.

97. Benedict Anderson, *Imagined Communities: Reflections on the Origin and Spread of Nationalism* (London: Verso, 1983), cited in Seyla Benhabib, "Complexity, Interdependence, Community," in *Women, Culture, and Development: A Study of Human Capabilities*, ed. Martha C. Nussbaum and Jonathan Glover (Oxford: Clarendon, 1995), 235–55.

98. Benhabib, "Complexity, Interdependence, Community," 244.

99. Charlotte Towle, *Common Human Needs*, rev. ed. (Washington, D.C.: National Association of Social Workers, 1987 [1955]).

100. First published in Abraham Maslow, "A Theory of Human Motivation," *Psychological Review* 50 (1943): 370–96, and elaborated in idem, *Motivation and Personality*,

2nd ed. (New York: Harper & Row, 1970). For a more current view, see also Joseph Lichtenberg, Frank Lachmann, and James Fosshage, *Self and Motivational Systems* (Hillsdale, N.J.: Analytic Press, 1992).

101. Silvan Tomkins, *Affect, Imagery, Consciousness*, 4 vols. (New York: Springer, 1962–1992); and Tomkins and E. Virginia Demos, eds., *Exploring Affect: The Selected Writings of Silvan Tomkins*, Studies in Emotion and Social Interaction (Cambridge: Cambridge University Press, 1995). Tomkins's research found evidence of nine innate or primary affects, identified by distinct facial expressions beginning in infancy, including interest/excitement, enjoyment/joy, surprise/startle, distress/anguish, fear/terror, anger/rage, shame/humiliation, dissmell (reaction to bad smell), and disgust. As this theory is applied in psychotherapy, with a particular emphasis on the effects of shame, see also Donald Nathanson, *Knowing Feeling: Affect, Script and Psychotherapy* (New York: Norton, 1996); Eve Kosofsky Sedgwick and Adam Frank, eds., *Shame and Its Sisters: A Silvan Tomkins Reader* (Durham: Duke University Press, 1995); and Melvin Lansky and Andrew Morrison, *The Widening Scope of Shame* (New York: Analytic Press, 1997).

102. Richard Lewontin, *Human Diversity* (New York: Scientific American, 1982).

103. Demaris Wehr, *Jung and Feminism: Liberating Archetypes* (Boston: Beacon, 1987); and Polly Young-Eisendrath and Florence Wiedemann, *Female Authority: Empowering Women through Psychotherapy* (New York: Guilford, 1987). These authors argue that anima and animus are not necessarily archetypes at all, but cultural phenomena functioning as archetypes.

104. For a general introduction to C. G. Jung's theory of archetypes, see Jung, *Man and His Symbols* (New York: Doubleday, 1969); for a more technical discussion, see Jung, "The Archetypes and the Collective Unconscious" (1934), in *CW* 9, Part I.

105. For more on this, see Janice Gump, "Commentary on Paper by Neil Altman," *PD* 10, no. 4 (2000): 630–31.

106. Barbara Johnson, "Thresholds of Difference: Structure of Address in Zora Neale Hurston," in *"Race," Writing, and Difference*, ed. Henry Louis Gates Jr. (Chicago: University of Chicago Press, 1986), 322, quoted in Patricia Elliot, "Working through Racism: Confronting the Strangely Familiar," *Journal for the Psychoanalysis of Culture and Society* 1 (1996): 68, and Gump, "Commentary on Paper by Neil Altman," 631.

107. One of the earliest studies of interrupted attachment was René Spitz, "Hospitalism: An Inquiry into the Genesis of Psychiatric Conditions in Early Childhood," *Psychoanalytic Study of the Child* 1 (1945): 53–74; John Bowlby's work on attachment is summarized in *Attachment*, 2nd ed. (New York: Basic, 2000 [1982]); see also Mary Ainsworth, *Patterns of Attachment: A Psychological Study of the Strange Situation* (New York: Lawrence Erlbaum Associates, 1978). More recent attachment theorists have also examined the role of culture and research into cross-cultural aspects of attachment, for example, Robert Karen, *Becoming Attached: First Relationships and How They Shape Our Capacity to Love* (Oxford: Oxford University Press, 1998).

108. Daniel Stern, *The Interpersonal World of the Infant: A View from Psychoanalysis and Developmental Psychology* (New York: Basic, 2000); Allen Schore, *Affect Regulation*

and the Origin of the Self: The Neurobiology of Emotional Development (New York: Lawrence Erlbaum Associates, 1999); and Michael Basch, "Affect: The Gateway to Action," in *Understanding Psychotherapy: The Science behind the Art* (New York: Basic, 1988).

109. D. W. Winnicott, "Further Thoughts on Babies as Persons" (1964), in *The Child, the Family, and the Outside World* (Reading, Mass.: Addison-Wesley, 1987), 88.

110. Buber, *I and Thou*, 69.

111. Ibid.

112. Ibid., 78.

113. John MacMurray, "The Form of the Personal," Gifford Lectures 1953–54, published as *The Self as Agent* (New York: Harper & Brothers, 1957), and *Persons in Relation* (New York: Harper & Brothers, 1961); discussed in LaCugna, "Augustine and the Trinitarian Economy of the Soul," 255–60. The influence of Winnicott and Fairbairn on this Scottish philosopher seem evident.

114. MacMurray, *Persons in Relation*, 27–29, cited in LaCugna, "Augustine and the Trinitarian Economy of the Soul," 257.

115. MacMurray, *Self as Agent*, 11, cited in LaCugna, "Augustine and the Trinitarian Economy of the Soul," 256. See also Paul Sponheim, "To Be Related: This Is the Empowering," in *The Pulse of Creation: Transformation of the World* (Minneapolis: Fortress Press, 1999), 88–113.

116. E.g., Ramachandran and Blakeslee, *Phantoms in the Brain*; and James Ashbrook and Carol Rusch Albright, *The Humanizing Brain: Where Religion and Neuroscience Meet* (Cleveland: Pilgrim, 1997).

117. Augustine, *Confessions*, trans. Henry Chadwick (Oxford: Oxford University Press, 1998), 183.

118. Gilles Deleuze and Félix Guattari, *A Thousand Plateaus: Capitalism and Schizophrenia*, trans. Brian Massumi (Minneapolis: University of Minnesota Press, 1987), 3.

119. Freud, *The Interpretation of Dreams* (1900), in *SE* 5:541ff.

120. E. Brooks Holifield, *A History of Pastoral Care in America: From Salvation to Self-Realization* (Nashville: Abingdon, 1983); see also Orlo Strunk, "Emmanuel Movement," s.v., *Dictionary of Pastoral Care and Counseling*, ed. Rodney Hunter (Nashville: Abingdon, 1990), 350–51.

121. The terms "God gone wrong" and "No-God" are from Jane Grovijahn, "A Theology of Survival" (PhD dissertation, Graduate Theological Union, 1997).

122. James Hilman, *Re-Visioning Psychology* (New York: Harper & Row, 1975), 228, cited in Louis Sass, "The Self and Its Vicissitudes: An 'Archaeological' Study of the Psychoanalytic Avant-Garde," *Social Research* 55, no. 4 (1988): 595.

123. Philip Bromberg, "'Speak! That I May See You': Some Reflections on Dissociation, Reality, and Psychoanalytic Listening," *PD* 4, no. 4 (1994): 529. See also Stephen Mitchell, "Multiple Selves, Singular Self," in *Hope and Dread in Psychoanalysis* (New York: Basic, 1993), 95–122.

124. In an offshoot of self psychology itself, intersubjectivity theorists Robert Stolorow, and George Atwood have proposed three interrelated forms of unconsciousness:

[1] the prereflective unconscious—the organizing principles that unconsciously shape and thematize a person's experiences; [2] the dynamic unconscious—experiences that were denied articulation because they were perceived to threaten needed ties; and [3] the unvalidated unconscious—experiences that could not be articulated because they never evoked the requisite validating responsiveness from the surround. All three forms of uncoinsciouess, we have emphasized, derived from specific, formative intersubjective contexts. (*Contexts of Being: The Intersubjective Foundations of Psychological Life* [Hillsdale, N.J.: Analytic Press, 1992], 33)

For the sake of brevity, I have omitted a detailed examination of this contemporary movement in psychoanalysis since most of its contributions are similar to those of the relational school, whose appropriation of object relations and constructivist paradigms in my view carry more explanatory power.

125. Jody Messler Davies, "Multiple Perspectives on Multiplicity," *PD* 8, no. 2 (1998): 195. The relational-psychoanalytic understanding of "dissociation" as potentially non-pathological, and the distancing from the automatic equation of dissocation with trauma, is also discussed in Cooper-White, *Shared Wisdom*, 48–50, in relation to intersubjectivity.

126. Jody Messler Davies, "Dissociation, Repression, and Reality Testing in the Countertransference: False Memory in the Psychoanalytic Treatment of Adult Survivors of Childhood Sexual Abuse," *PD* 6, no. 2 (1996): 197. See also Adrienne Harris: "This model of consciousness is less archaeologically organized and more a set of surfaces or representations with boundaries of varying permeability" ("False Memory? False Memory Syndrome? The So-Called False Memory Syndrome?" *PD* 6, no. 2 (1996): 159n2.

127. Lacan, *Écrits*, 3–7.

128. Bromberg, "Speak! That I May See You'," 517–47, cited in Cooper-White, *Shared Wisdom*, 49. See also Philip Bromberg, "Standing in the Spaces: The Multiplicity of Self and the Psychoanalytic Relationship," *CP* 32 (1996): 509–35, and *Standing in the Spaces: Clinical Process, Trauma, and Dissociation* (Hillsdale, N.J.: Analytic Press, 2001).

129. E.g., Alan Roland, *In Search of Self in India and Japan: Toward a Cross Cultural Psychology* (Princeton: Princeton University Press, 1988).

130. Clifford Geertz, "'From the Native's Point of View': On the Nature of Anthropological Understanding," in *Local Knowledge: Further Essays in Interpretive Anthropology* (New York: Basic, 1983), 59.

131. Stephen A. Mitchell, *Hope and Dread in Psychoanalysis* (New York: Basic, 1991), 105.

132. This may be close to what Jung referred to as the "Self" archetype, which is greater than the executive ego who does the conscious knowing, and incorporates all the disavowed and unknown parts of oneself. But there is a distinction from Jung's concept as well. For Jung, the Self was conceived of as a whole, or potentially whole, and desiring the archetype of Wholeness. There is still one unitive self, or being, implied, and the direction of the unconscious is still imagined largely in terms of downward "depth."

133. Steven Stern, "The Self as a Relational Structure: A Dialogue with Multiple-Self Theory," *PD* 12, no. 5 (2002): 698.

134. Ibid., 702, also citing Freud's views on identification in "Beyond the Pleasure Principle" (1920), in *SE* 18:1–64; W. R. D. Fairbairn, *An Object-Relations Theory of the Personality* (New York: Basic, 1952); and Hans Loewald, "Instinct Theory Object Relations, and Psychic Structure Formation" (1978), in *Papers on Psychoanalysis* (New Haven: Yale University Press, 1980), 207–18.

135. Anna Freud, "The Concept of Developmental Lines," *Psychoanalytic Study of the Child* 18 (1963), 245–65.

136. Ken Corbett, "More Life: Centrality and Marginality in Human Development," *PD* 11, no. 3 (2001): 328.

137. The doctrine of panentheism, articulated by early church theologians such as Nicholas of Cusa (1401–1464), *Nicholas of Cusa: Selected Spiritual Writings* (Mahwah, N.J.: Paulist, 1997), was a view of God in all things and all things in God; for a contemporary view, see Philip Clayton and Arthur Peacocke, eds., *In Whom We Live and Move and Have Our Being: Panentheistic Reflections on God's Presence in a Scientific World* (Grand Rapids, Mich.: Eerdmans, 2004); see also "Pantheism in Time," *Science and Theology News*, http://www.stnews.org/articles.php?category=guide&guide=Panentheism&article _id=418.

138. Corbett, "More Life," 328.

139. Robert Emde, "The Affective Self: Continuities and Transformation from Infancy," in *Frontiers of Infant Psychiatry*, vol. 2, ed. J. D. Call et al. (New York: Basic, 1984), 38–54; and idem, "The Prerepresentational Self and Its Affective Core, *Psychoanalytic Study of the Child* 38 (1983): 165–92.

140. Daniel Stern, *The Interpersonal World of the Infant* (New York: Basic, 1985).

141. Beatrice Beebe and Frank M. Lachmann, "The Contribution of Mother-Infant Mutual Influence to the Origins of Self- and Object Representations," in *Relational Perspectives in Psychoanalysis*, ed. N. J. Skolnick and S. C. Warshaw (Hillsdale, N.J.: Analytic Press, 1992), 83–117. Note that Lachmann himself is somewhat skeptical of a multiple-self construct; he is in favor of a fluid, complex but ingrated, singular self in process: "How Many Selves Make a Person?" *CP* 32, no. 4 (1996): 595–614; see also the response by Malcolm Owen Slavin, "Is One Self Enough? Multiplicity in Self-Organization and the Capacity to Negotiate Relational Conflict," *CP* 32, no. 4 (1996): 615–25.

142. Stern's "representations of interactive experience as generalized," or "RIGs," in *The Interpersonal World of the Infant*.

143. First discussed in Heinz Kohut, *The Analysis of the Self: A Systematic Approach to the Psychoanalytic Treatment of Narcissistic Personality Disorders* (New York: International Universities Press, 1971).

144. *American Heritage Dictionary*, 4th ed., 2000, http://dictionary.reference.com /search?q=rhizome.

145. Deleuze and Guattari, *A Thousand Plateaus*, 3–25 et passim. An excerpt from 7–13 outlining the principles of the rhizome is also reproduced online at www.gseis.ucla .edu/courses/ed253a/kellner/deleuze.html.

146. Deleuze and Guattari, *A Thousand Plateaus*, 16–17.

147. Ibid., 7.

148. Deleuze and Guattari, in *A Thousand Plateaus*, are refuting Noam Chomsky's theory of "generative grammar," in which he posits a universal grammatical "hierarchy." They do not cite his works specifically, but the origins of the theory may be found in Chomsky, "Three Models for the Description of Language," *IRE Transactions on Information Theory* 2 (1956): 113–24, and "On Certain Formal Properties of Grammars," *Information and Control* 1 (1959): 91–112. For an overview, also see "Noam Chomsky" at http://en.wikipedia.org/wiki/Noam_Chomsky#Chomsky_hierarchy and "Generative Grammar" at http://en.wikipedia.org/wiki/Generative_grammar.

149. Deleuze and Guattari, *A Thousand Plateaus*, 7, citing Catherine Backès-Clément, "Sur capitalisme et schizophrénie," an interview with Deleuze and Guattari in *L'Arc* 49 (rev. ed., 1980): 99.

150. Deleuze and Guattari, *A Thousand Plateaus*, 8–9.

151. Ibid., 9.

152. This term is used frequently in the survivor literature. It was originally used by Ernest Hemingway in *A Farewell to Arms*: "The world breaks everyone, and afterward many are strong at the broken places. But those that will not break it kills" (New York: Scribners, 1995), 249.

153. Deleuze and Guattari, *A Thousand Plateaus*, 12; Jean Baudrillard works with a similar image in *Simulation and Simulacra*, trans. Sheila Faria Glaser (Ann Arbor: University of Michigan Press, 1995 [1981])—"the cartographer's made project of the ideal coextensivity of map and territory" (2).

154. Deleuze and Guattari, *A Thousand Plateaus*, 12.

155. See *American Heritage Dictionary*, s.v. "décalcomanie," http://dictionary.reference.com/search?q=decalcomania.

156. Deleuze and Guattari, *A Thousand Plateaus*, 13.

157. Ibid.

158. Deleuze and Guattari's work should not be taken uncritically. For example, their image of the "body without organs" (*A Thousand Plateaus*, 149–66) is troubling in relation to a feminist insistence on embodiment. While they are not referring literally to the individual human body, but rather to a corporate communal body, the image calls for some careful critique and qualification.

159. Deleuze and Guattari anticipate this critique directly and assert that "it is a question of method: the tracing should always be put back on the map" (*A Thousand Plateaus*, 13). While continuing to privilege maps over the rootlike metaphor of "tracings," they insist that as soon as any theorist pursues a genetic line of thinking, "whenever desire climbs a tree, internal repercussions trip it up and it falls to its death" (14). While still

arguing dichotomously, they are showing the rhizome as a continually necessary corrective to the universalizing tendency of root-and-tree thinking.

160. "Where the potato is the hero of this story, the tree becomes the villain," Dan Clinton, "Deleuze and Guattari, 'Rhizome,' Annotation," http://www.chicagoschoolmediatheory.net/annotations/deleuzerhizome.htm.

161. Gilles Deleuze, *Difference and Repetition*, trans. Paul Patton (New York: Columbia University Press, 1968), 229; also described in Catherine Keller, *Face of the Deep: A Theology of Becoming* (London and New York: Routledge, 2003), 168.

162. Graham Ward, "Introduction, or, A Guide to Theological Thinking in Cyberspace," in *The Postmodern God: A Theological Reader* (Malden, Mass.: Blackwell, 1997), xv.

163. Freud, "Analysis Terminable and Interminable" (1937), in *SE* 23:211–53.

164. Freud, "Civilization and Its Discontents" (1930), in *SE* 21:59–145.

165. Deleuze and Guattari, *A Thousand Plateaus*, 25.

166. Jean-Michel Oughourlian, *The Puppet of Desire,: The Psychology of Hysteria, Possession, and Hypnosis*, trans. E. Webb (Palo Alto: Stanford University Press, 1991), 11–12 (emphasis original), cited in Sponheim, *The Pulse of Creation*, 91.

167. Freud, "Civilization and Its Discontents," 59–145.

168. Winnicott, "Ego Distortions in Terms of True and False Self" (1960), in *The Maturational Processes and the Facilitating Environment* (London: Hogarth, 1965), 140–52.

169. This term is from Irigaray, "The Mechanics of Fluids," in *This Sex Which Is Not One*, 106–18.

170. Jane Flax, "Multiples: On the Contemporary Politics of Subjectivity," in *Disputed Subjects: Essays on Psychoanalysis, Politics, and Philosophy* (New York: Routledge, 1993), 93 (emphasis added), also cited in Cooper-White, *Shared Wisdom*, 53.

171. Elizabeth Castelli, "Interpretations of Power in 1 Corinthians," in *Michel Foucault and Theology: The Politics of Religious Experience*, ed. James Bernauer and Jeremy Carrette (Hampshire, U.K., and Burlington, Vt.: Ashgate, 2004), 22–23, also citing Foucault, *Power/Knowledge*, 198–99.

172. Irigaray, "'Frenchwomen,' Stop Trying," in *This Sex Which Is Not One*, 203–4.

173. For further elaboration of the relationship between postmodernism and justice, including an appropriation of Winnicott's *Playing and Reality*, see Jane Flax, "The Play of Justice," in *Disputed Subjects*, 111–28.

174. This, admittedly, is an idealistic vision. In practical terms, not all persons are capable of such an egalitarian sharing and balance. The issue of pathology and its relation to sin and evil will be developed further in chapter 3.

175. Note that "divine dance," while popular as a translation for *perichoresis*, is not technically correct, although it is a good image for the relationality of trinitarian energy. *Perichoreo* means "to encompass"; *perichoreuo* means "to dance around" (Catherine Mowry LaCugna, *God for Us: The Trinity and Christian Life* [San Francisco: HarperSanFrancisco, 1973], 312n94). This will be discussed further in chapter 2.

176. Donnel Stern, *Unformulated Experience: From Dissociation to Imagination in Psychoanalysis* (Hillsdale, N.J.: Analytic Press, 1997). On creativity, see esp. chap. 4, "Creative Disorder and Unbidden Perceptions: Unformulated Experience as Possibility," 65–82.

177. Christopher Bollas, *The Shadow of the Object: Psychoanalysis of the Unthought Known* (New York: Columbia University Press, 1987).

178. Phillip Bennett, *Let Yourself Be Loved* (Mahwah, N.J.: Paulist, 1997), 74.

179. See LaCugna, *God for Us* 15, 335–68. This theme will be taken up again in more detail in chapter 2.

180. Melanie Klein, *The Writings of Melanie Klein*, vol. 1, *Love, Guilt, and Reparation and Other Works, 1921–1945* (New York: Free Press, 2002).

181. Harry Harlow's experiments in the late 1950s with monkeys receiving sustenance from wire mother-substitutes demonstrated that even when fed, primates fail to thrive without cuddling and responsive affection from primary caretakers (Harlow, "The Nature of Love," Address of the President, American Psychological Association, Washington, D.C., 31 August 31 1958; first published in *American Psychologist* 13 [1958]: 573–685.

182. Irenaeus, Bishop of Lyon, *Against Heresies* 4.20.7, trans. Dominic Unger (New York: Paulist, 1992).

Chapter 2: A Relational Understanding of God

1. Gordon D. Kaufman and Francis Schüssler Fiorenza, "God," in *Critical Terms for Religious Studies*, ed. Mark C. Taylor (Chicago: University of Chicago Press, 1998), 136–59 as summarized in Gordon D. Kaufman, *In the Beginning . . . Creativity* (Minneapolis: Fortress Press, 2004), xi. Kaufman and Schüssler Fiorenza identify three strands of language about God that further historicizes and relativizes any single meaning for "God" as ultimately normative: (1) the tension between popular, anthropomorphic depictions of God and more abstract, philosophical formulations (both of which are found in biblical and later Christian liturgical, conciliar, and theological sources); (2) the role of subjectivity and human creativity in relation to the word "God" and the human awareness of infinity; and (3) the strand of negative theology—"the awareness and articulation of the inadequacy of all human language and ideas about God" (7).

2. Ibid., 120. See also Gordon D. Kaufman, *An Essay on Theological Method*, 3rd ed. (Atlanta: Scholars Press, 1995 [1975]).

3. James Ashbrook and Carol Rausch Albright, *The Humanizing Brain: Where Religion and Neuroscience Meet* (Cleveland: Pilgrim, 1997).

4. Frank Lynn Meshberger, "An Interpretation of Michelangelo's 'Creation of Adam' Based on Neuroanatomy," *JAMA* 264, no. 14 (1990), 1837–41, cited in Ashbrook and Albright, *The Humanizing Brain*, 44–47.

5. Friedrich Nietzsche, *Thus Spoke Zarathustra: A Book for None and All*, trans. Walter Kaufmann (New York: Penguin, 1966 [1891]).

6. Martin Heidegger, "The Onto-Theological Constitution of Metaphysics," in *Identity and Difference*, trans. Joan Stambaugh (Chicago: University of Chicago Press, 2002 [1957]). Heidegger's earlier, seminal work critiquing the ontology of metaphysics is *Being and Time*, trans. Joan Stambaugh (New York: State University Of New York Press, 1996 [1927]).

7. Kaufman, *In the Beginning . . . Creativity*, 24. Kaufman provides a very helpful, brief summary of modern and postmodern trends in theology, particularly the strand of negative theology or not-knowing about God on 22–26.

8. Thomas J. J. Altizer, *Radical Theology and the Death of God* (Indianapolis: Bobbs-Merrill, 1966). Note that Altizer's radical theology was not, strictly speaking, as nihilistic as his provocative title suggested. Drawing on Nietzsche, Kierkegaard, and others, Altizer's proposal was a shattering of the traditional Christian transcendent God in favor of a radical "Being in every Now."

9. See http://en.wikipedia.org/wiki/Image:Timeisgoddead.jpg.

10. Merold Westphal, "Overcoming Onto-Theology," in *God, the Gift, and Postmodernism*, ed. John Caputo and Michael Scanlon (Bloomington: Indiana University Press, 1999), 146–69.

11. Ibid., 164.

12. Catherine Mowry LaCugna, *God for Us: The Trinity and Christian Life* (San Francisco: HarperSanFrancisco, 1973), 15; this theme is elaborated on 335–68.

13. Caputo and Scanlon, *God, the Gift, and Postmodernism*, 4. See also John Caputo, *Prayers and Tears of Jacques Derrida* (Bloomington: Indiana University Press, 1997).

14. The first and last lines of Jacques Derrida, *Memoirs of the Blind: The Self-Portrait and Other Ruins*, trans. Pascale-Anne Brault and Michael Naas (Chicago: University of Chicago Press, 1993), as cited in Caputo and Scanlon, *God, the Gift, and Postmodernism*.

15. Westphal, "Overcoming Onto-Theology," 148.

16. Ibid., 150.

17. LaCugna, *God for Us*, 368.

18. Ludwig Wittgenstein, *Culture and Value*, ed. G. H. von Wright and Heikki Nyman, trans. Peter Winch (Chicago: University of Chicago Press, 1980 [1977]), 85. Wittgenstein wrote this sentence in the course of refuting doctrine (he gives belief in the Trinity as his example) if it is only "a theology which insists on the use of certain particular words and phrases, and outlaws others, does not make anything clearer (Karl Barth). It gesticulates with words, as one might say, because it wants to say something and does not know how to express it. *Practice* gives the words their sense."

19. Religion and Postmodernism 4 Conference, "Transcendence and Beyond," Villanova University, 18–20 September 2003.

20. Jean-Luc Marion, "The Impossible to Man: God," opening address at Religion and Postmodernism 4 Conference; see also idem, *God without Being*, trans. Thomas A. Carlson (Chicago: University of Chicago Press, 1991).

21. Jean-Luc Marion, "In the Name: How to Avoid Speaking of 'Negative Theology,'" in *God, the Gift, and Postmodernism*, 39.

22. Ibid., 40.

23. John Caputo and Michael Scanlon, "Apology for the Impossible: Religion and Postmodernism," in *God, the Gift, and Postmodernism*, 2.

24. Freud's term for the multiple factors leading to the development of a symptom, first described in *The Interpretation of Dreams* (1900), in *SE* 5: chap. 7.

25. Caputo and Scanlon, "Apology for the Impossible," 3.

26. Ibid., 2, also citing Jacques Derrida, *Points . . . : Interviews, 1974–1994*, ed. Elisabeth Weber, trans. Peggy Kamuf et al. (Stanford: Stanford University Press, 1995), 428.

27. For further discussion of this, see Pamela Cooper-White, *Shared Wisdom: Use of the Self in Pastoral Care and Counseling* (Minneapolis: Fortress Press, 2004), 38–40, also citing Zygmunt Bauman, *Modernity and the Holocaust* (Ithaca, N.Y.: Cornell University Press, 1989), and Thomas Docherty, "Postmodernism: An Introduction," in *Postmodernism: A Reader*, ed. Thomas Docherty (New York: Columbia University Press, 1993). Details of the death toll from the Holocaust can be found at http://en.wikipedia.org/wiki/Holocaust#Death_toll.

28. Jacques Derrida, *The Specters of Marx: The State of the Debt and the New International*, trans. Peggy Kamuf (New York: Routledge, 1994), cited in Gayatri Chakravorty Spivak, *A Critique of Postcolonial Reason: Toward a History of the Vanishing Present* (Cambridge, Mass.: Harvard University Press), 431. For a discussion of Derrida and deconstruction in relation to globalization, see Spivak, *A Critique of Postcolonial Reason*, 423–31.

29. Luce Irigaray, *Speculum of the Other Woman*, trans. Gillian Gill (Ithaca, N.Y.: Cornell University Press, 1985 [1974]), see especially "Any Theory of the 'Subject' Has Always Been Appropriated by the 'Masculine,'" 133-46; and idem, *This Sex Which Is Not One*, trans. Catherine Porter with Carolyn Burke (Ithaca: Cornell University Press, 1985 [1977]).

30. Spivak, *A Critique of Postcolonial Reason*; idem, *The Spivak Reader: Selected Works of Gayatri Chakravorty Spivak*, ed. Donna Landry and Gerald MacLean (New York: Routledge, 1996); and Homi Bhabha, *The Location of Culture* (New York: Routledge, 1994).

31. Bhabha, *The Location of Culture*.

32. Trinh T. Minh-ha, *When the Moon Waxes Red: Representation, Gender, and Cultural Politics* (New York: Routledge, 1991), 234, 232 (emphasis original), cited in Catherine Keller, *Face of the Deep: A Theology of Becoming* (London and New York: Routledge, 2003), 204.

33. D. W. Winnicott, *Playing and Reality* (New York: Basic, 1971).

34. Thomas H. Ogden, "The Analytic Third: An Overview," *fort da: The Journal of the Northern California Society for Psychoanalytic Psychology* 5, no. 1 (1999), http://psychematters.com/papers/ogden.htm. See also idem, "The Analytic Third: Working with Intersubjective Clinical Facts," *IJPA* 75 (1994): 3–20; and idem, *Conversations at the Frontier of Dreaming* (Northvale, N.J.: Aronson, 2001), 19–21 et passim.

35. Daniel Crane Roberts, "God of Our Fathers" (national hymn), in *The Hymnal 1982* (New York: Church Hymnal Corporation, 1985), #718.

36. Jacques Derrida, "Sauf le Nom," in *On the Name*, ed. Thomas Dutoit, trans. David Wood, John P. Leavey Jr., and Ian McLeod (Stanford, Calif.: Stanford University Press, 1993), 71, also cited in Caputo, *Prayers and Tears of Jacques Derrida*, 1–68; Marion, "In the Name," 20–47; and Keller's discussion of negative theology in *Face of the Deep*, 208.

37. Keller, *Face of the Deep*, 208.

38. Jacques Derrida, "White Mythology," in *Margins of Philosophy*, trans. Alan Bass (Chicago: University of Chicago Press, 1982), 207–72.

39. Ellen Armour, *Deconstruction, Feminist Theory and the Problem of Difference: Subverting the Race/Gender Divide* (Chicago: University of Chicago Press, 1999), also drawing from Irigaray's writings on the "*Other*" in *Speculum of the Other Woman*.

40. Dwight Hopkins, *Down, Up, and Over: Slave Religion and Black Theology* (Minneapolis: Fortress Press, 2000), 89.

41. Edward Said, *Orientalism* (New York: Vintage, 1979).

42. Babha, *The Location of Culture*.

43. Keller, "Docta Ignorantia: Darkness on the Face *pne choshekh*," in *Face of the Deep*, 200–212.

44. E.g., C. W. Maggie Kim, Susan M. St. Ville, and Susan M. Simonaitis in *Transfigurations: Theology and the French Feminists* (Minneapolis: Fortress Press, 1993); and Grace Jantzen in *Becoming Divine: Towards a Feminist Philosophy of Religion* (Bloomington: Indiana University Press, 1999).

45. For an introduction to the writings of Karl Marx and Friedrich Engels, see *The Marx-Engels Reader*, ed. Robert Tucker, 2nd ed. (New York: Norton, 1978).

46. Adriaan T. Peperzak, Simon Critchley, and Robert Bernasconi, eds., introduction, *Emmanuel Lévinas: Basic Philosophical Writings* (Bloomington: Indiana University Press, 1996), xii.

47. Gilles Deleuze and Félix Guattari, *A Thousand Plateaus: Capitalism and Schizophrenia*, trans. Brian Massumi (Minneapolis: University of Minnesota Press, 1987).

48. John Milbank, *Theology and Social Theory: Beyond Secular Reasons* (Oxford: Blackwell, 1990), 267, 306, 309.

49. Paul Tillich, *Systematic Theology*, vol. 1, (Chicago: University of Chicago Press, 1951), 155–57, drawing on his acquaintance with Eastern religious sources, and resonating with the biblical passage "God, in whom we live and move and have our being" (Acts 17:28).

50. Gilles Deleuze, *Difference and Repetition*, trans. Paul Patton (New York: Columbia University Press, 1968), 229; also described in Keller, *Face of the Deep*, 168. I do not find that, for my own theological thinking, Deleuze can be incorporated "whole." (See also the critique of Deleuze in chapter 1 above, n158). His strong dependence on Nietzsche in "radical horizontal thought"—including his refusal to stand in a lineage of philosophical thought but tending to repudiate all genealogy (for a summary of these constructs, see John Lechte, *Fifty Key Contemporary Thinkers: From Structuralism to Postmodernism* [London and New York: Routledge, 1994]); his absolute rejection with Félix Guattari of Freud (notably, as read via Lacan, in *Anti-Oedipus*, trans. Robert Hurley, Mark Seem, and

Helen Lane [Minneapolis: University of Minnesota Press, 1983 [1972]); his strangely unreconstituted oedipal meditations on masochism (in *Masochism: An Interpretation of Coldness and Cruelty*, trans. Jean McNeil (New York: Braziller, 1971 [1967]); and his disembodied notion of the "body without organs" (Deleuze and Guattari, *A Thousand Plateaus*, 149–66)—are all troubling to my own feminist psychoanalytic sensibilities. Irigaray uses the same term precisely in critique of the relegation of women's sexuality to otherness in relation to a phallocentric norm in French Freudian analysis (see "Così Fan Tutti," in *This Sex Which Is Not One*, 90). Nevertheless, Deleuze's reframing of existence in phenomenological terms, using horizontal rather than vertical images and metaphors—such as conceiving of depth as "extensity" (229); his intricate discussions of repetition as distinct from "Identity" as in the pure realm of Platonic Ideas, as being a slavish reiteration of unity or the "Same" (*Difference and Repetition*); and his image of the "Rhizome" (*A Thousand Plateaus*, 3–25 et passim, as discussed in detail above in chapter 1)—contribute to both theological and psychological ways of thinking that avoid monolithic vertical plumbing for a single universal truth. See also Pamela Cooper-White, "Higher Powers and Infernal Regions: Models of Mind in Freud's Interpretation of Dreams and Contemporary Psychoanalysis, and Their Implications for Pastoral Care," *Pastoral Psychology* 50, no. 5 (2002): 319–43.

51. Cooper-White, "Higher Powers and Infernal Regions."

52. Deleuze, *Difference and Repetition*, 229. Also cited in Keller, *Face of the Deep*, in connection with the chaotic depths of "tehom," in *Face of the Deep*, 168.

53. Gilles Deleuze and Félix Guattari, *What Is Philosophy?* trans. Hugh Tomlinson and Graham Burchell (New York: Columbia University Press, 1994 [1991]), 205, cited in Keller, *Face of the Deep*, 171. For a further discussion of Deleuze's concept of "chaosmos" in comparison to process theology, particularly Whitehead, see also Keller, "Process and Chaosmos," in *Process and Difference: Between Cosmological and Poststructuralist Postmodernisms*, ed. Catherine Keller and Anne Daniell (New York: State University of New York Press, 2002), 55–57.

54. Umberto Eco, *The Aesthetics of Chaosmos: The Middle Ages of James Joyce*, trans. Ellen Esrock (Cambridge, Mass.: Harvard University Press, 1989), also excerpted at http://www.noteaccess.com/APPROACHES/Chaosmos.htm.

55. Annie Dillard, *Pilgrim at Tinker Creek* (New York: Harper's Magazine Press, 1974), 144.

56. Ibid.

57. Deleuze and Guattari, *A Thousand Plateaus*, 313, cited in Keller, *Face of the Deep*, 169.

58. Keller, *Face of the Deep*. For a similar discussion of chaos theory and creation theology, and a critique of the doctrine of *creatio ex nihilo* from a scientific perspective, see also Sjoerd Bonting, *Creation and Double Chaos: Science and Theology in Discussion* (Minneapolis: Fortress Press, 2005), esp. 52–125.

59. Keller, *Face of the Deep*, frontispiece: "*Face of the Deep* is the first full theology of creation from the primal chaos. It proposes a *creatio ex profundis*—creation out of the

water depths—both as an alternative to the orthodox power discourse of creation from nothingness, and as a figure of both bottomless process of becoming." Lévinas worked in similar images in his early writings, grappling with Heidegger's critique of onto-theology. In a fragment "Il y a," he posits a "dark and chaotic indeterminacy that precedes all creativity and goodness." Lévinas's work from the beginning focused on the ethical, however: in his first book, *De l'existence à l'existent* [*Existence and Existents*], the Good transcends Being, even as for Heidegger, Being transcends the "'metaphysics' of beings" (Peperzak, Critchley, and Bernasconi, *Emmanuel Lévinas*, ix).

60. Gilles Deleuze, *The Fold: Leibniz and the Baroque*, trans. Tom Conley (Minneapolis: University of Minnesota Press, 1998), 211–19, drawing from Nicholas of Cusa's terms *implicatio, expicatio,* and *complicatio* as a way of understanding the inextricable relation and mutual enfolding between God and the created universe. Cusa's terms are summarized by Keller in a discussion of panentheism as "the 'dynamic contracting, or *complicatio* ('enfolding') and *explicatio* ('unfolding') of God and universe into each other; and that of the radical interrelatedness of creatures," *Face of the Deep*, 206.

61. The doctrine of panentheism, articulated by theologians as early as Nicholas of Cusa (1401–1464), *Nicholas of Cusa: Selected Spiritual Writings* (Mahwah, N.J.: Paulist, 1997) was a view of God in all things and all things in God; for a contemporary view, see also Philip Clayton and Arthur Peacocke, eds., *In Whom We Live and Move and Have Our Being: Panentheistic Reflections on God's Presence in a Scientific World* (Grand Rapids, Mich.: Eerdmans, 2004); see also "Pantheism in Time," *Science and Theology News*, http://www.stnews.org/articles.php?category=guide&guide=Panentheism&article_id=418.

62. Keller, *Face of the Deep*, 172–82.

63. Translation from Danna Nolan Fewell and David M. Gunn, *Gender, Power, and Promise: The Subject of the Bible's First Story* (Nashville: Abingdon, 193), 23, quoted in Keller, *Face of the Deep*, 281n6.

64. Fewell and Gunn, *Gender, Power, and Promise*, 23, quoted in Keller, *Face of the Deep*, 173.

65. Keller, *Face of the Deep*, 173.

66. Fewell and Gunn, *Gender, Power, and Promise*, 23, quoted in Keller, *Face of the Deep*, 173.

67. Fewell and Gunn, *Gender, Power, and Promise*, 23, quoted in Keller, *Face of the Deep*, 281n6 (emphasis added).

68. Keller, *Face of the Deep*, 174, citing Rashi in Avivah Gottlieb Zornberg, *The Beginnings of Desire: Reflections on Genesis* (New York: Doubleday, 1995), 4ff.

69. Michel Serres with Bruno Latour, *Conversations on Science, Culture, and Time*, trans. Roxanne Lapidus (Ann Arbor: University of Michigan Press, 1995), 118, quoted in Keller, *Face of the Deep*, 176.

70. Keller, *Face of the Deep*, 181.

71. Ibid., 177, also drawing from Michel Serres, *Genesis*, trans. Geneviève James and James Nielson (Ann Arbor: University of Michigan Press, 1995), 6. Keller also finds support for this multiple reading of God in Lynn Bechtel, who translates *elohim* as

"differentiated unity . . . a group-orientation where individuality comes only embedded in collectivity and nature," in "Genesis 1:1-2:4a Revisisted: The Perpetuation of What Is," unpublished manuscript, 6, cited in Keller, *Face of the Deep*, 177; and Irigaray's meditation on angels, "Belief Itself," in *Sexes and Genealogies*, trans. Gillian C. Gill (New York: Columbia University Press, 1993), 42.

72. Keller, *Face of the Deep*, 181–82 (emphasis original).

73. The beginning of this trajectory can be found in Cooper-White, "Toward a Relational Theology: God-in-Relation," in *Shared Wisdom*, 181–93, including a summary of implications for pastoral praxis (186–93). In choosing to work with the Trinity as a living image, I disagree at this point with Keller, who characterizes the "logic of the Christian trinity" as "awkwardly frozen in an exceptionalism that only proves the rule of the One" in Keller, *Face of the Deep*, 177–78.

74. The two Gregorys and Basil are usually cited as the "Cappadocian Fathers." However, in his *Life of Saint Macrina*, trans. Kevin Corrigan (Toronto: Peregrina, 1996), by Gregory's own witness, their sister Macrina provided theological inspiration and correction to them both, as well as founding, together with their mother, the first Christian community of men and women. For a brief biography of Macrina, see any edition of the Episcopal Church's *Lesser Feasts and Fasts* (New York: Church Publishing) from 2000 forward (e.g., 2003).

75. LaCugna, *God for Us*, 270–71.

76. Ibid., 312n94. See also n174 in chapter 1 above (281).

77. Ibid.

78. Patricia Wilson-Kastner, *Faith, Feminism and Christ* (Philadelphia: Fortress Press, 1983), cited in LaCugna, *God for Us*, 272–73.

79. This line is from John Arthur, "This Is the Feast of Victory for Our God," *The Hymnal 1982*, #417, #418.

80. John Milbank, "Postmodern Critical Augustinianism: A Short *Summa* in Forty-two Responses to Unasked Questions," in *The Postmodern God*, ed. Graham Ward (Oxford: Blackwell, 1997), 274 (emphasis added).

81. Ibid., 267, also cited in Cooper-White, *Shared Wisdom*, 183 (emphasis added).

82. Milbank, "Postmodern Critical Augustinianism," 276.

83. John Milbank, "Pleonasm, Speech and Writing," in *The Word Made Strange: Theology, Language, Culture* (Oxford: Blackwell, 1997), 55–83; and idem, *Theology and Social Theory: Beyond Secular Reason* (Oxford: Blackwell, 1993), 267–309.

84. Milbank, "Postmodern Critical Augustinianism," 276.

85. Ibid., 268–69. For a further discussion of Irigaray's critique of equality, see also Susan Jones, "This God Who Is Not One: Irigaray and Barth on the Divine," in *Transfigurations: Theology and the French Feminists*, ed. C. Kim, S. St. Ville, and S. Simonaitis (Minneapolis: Fortress Press, 1993), 109–41; Grace Jantzen, "Luce Iragaray: Introduction," in *The Postmodern God*, ed. Graham Ward (Oxford: Blackwell, 1997), 191–97, cited also in Cooper-White, *Shared Wisdom*, 184.

86. See Jürgen Moltmann's influential idea of the Trinity as "divine society," in *The Trinity and the Kingdom*, trans. M. Kohl (San Francisco: Harper & Row, 1981).

87. Leonardo Boff states that "in the beginning is communion," in *Trinity and Society*, trans. Paul Burns (Maryknoll: Orbis, 1986), 9 et passim.

88. See Luce Irigaray's critique "Equal to Whom?" trans. Robert Mazzola, in *differences: A Journal of Feminist Cultural Studies* 1, no. 2 (1989): 39–62, reprinted in *The Postmodern God*, 198–214.

89. Milbank, "Postmodern Critical Augustinianism," 275.

90. Marin Buber, *I and Thou*. trans. Walter Kaufmann (New York: Scribner, 1970).

91. Keller, *Face of the Deep*, 178.

92. Elizabeth A. Johnson, *She Who Is: The Mystery of God in Feminist Theological Discourse* (New York: Crossroad, 1992), 210. For a detailed discussion of various historical interpretations of the Trinity and "freeing the symbol from literalness," also see 197–205.

93. Moltmann, *The Trinity and the Kingdom*.

94. Boff, *Trinity and Society*.

95. LaCugna, *God for Us*.

96. Johnson, *She Who Is*.

97. David S. Cunningham, *These Three Are One: The Practice of Trinitarian Theology* (Malden, Mass.: Blackwell, 1998).

98. Johnson, *She Who Is*, 192–93, also cited in Cooper-White, *Shared Wisdom*, 183.

99. Johnson, *She Who Is*, 210–11, also citing Hildegard of Bingen, *Illuminations of Hildegard of Bingen*, commentary by Matthew Fox (Santa Fe: Bear, 1985), 23.

100. Johnson, *She Who Is*, 210.

101. Sallie McFague, *Models of God: Theology for an Ecological, Nuclear Age* (Philadelphia: Fortress, 1987), 35 et passim.

102. John Macquarrie, *Principles of Christian Theology*, 2nd ed. (New York: Scribner's, 1977), 190–210.

103. Ibid., 210.

104. LaCugna, *God for Us*, 15.

105. The exception to this is in the earliest history of the idea of the Trinity. The pre-Nicene fathers had a more linear, or processional, understanding of the Trinity, with the Son and the Spirit as subordinate to the Father (although not articulated as different in *substance*, as in the Arian heresy). It was the Arian controversy that pushed the question at Nicaea of Christ being of "one substance with the Father," which further prompted the Cappadocian clarification of the Trinity as simultaneously "one substance, three persons." This history is detailed in LaCugna, *God for Us*, 21–79.

106. Johnson, 219, also citing Augustine, *De trinitate*, in *Nicene and Post-Nicene Fathers*, vol. 3, ed. Philip Schaff (Grand Rapids, Mich.: Eerdmans, 1956), 8.1.2.

107. Johnson, *She Who Is*, 216.

108. Ibid., 227.

109. Deleuze, *Difference and Repetition*, 228–30, also cited in Keller, *Face of the Deep*, 168.

110. Anselm, *Monologion* 78, in *Saint Anselm: Basic Writings*, trans. S. N. Deane (LaSalle, Ill.: Open Court, 1974), 142, cited in Johnson, *She Who Is*, 203.

111. I am grateful to Keller for her use, in passing, of the concept of *kenosis* in her construction of a "tehomic theology," particularly in reference to oceanic images the infinity of God as described in the mystical tradition of negative theology (*Face of the Deep*, 217). Keller also repeatedly refers to theology as "opening out" beyond classical doctrinal categories and images for God.

112. Cf., ibid., 274–75.

113. Cooper-White, "Higher Powers and Infernal Regions."

114. Borrowing from Cunningham's Trinitarian formulation in *These Three Are One*.

115. Gerard Manley Hopkins, *The Poems of Gerard Manley Hopkins*, 4th ed. Ed. W. H. Gardner and N. H. Mackenzie (London: Oxford University Press, 1967), 69.

116. Kaufman, *In the Beginning . . . Creativity*, 42, 46, 48–50, 53–70 et passim.

117. Ibid., 63ff. Here Kaufman takes up the question of evil and the destructive aspects of nature "red in tooth and claw" from process theology in relation to the concept of God as loving.

118. Ibid., 59.

119. Ibid., 56–57. Note that Kaufman refers to Darwin explicitly in his book on creativity.

120. Ironically, the title of this central tympanum (the other two depicting creation of day and of night), which depicts the creation of human beings, is titled "Ex Nihilo." Yet, in the turbulence of the image, there is clearly a circling "ground" of chaos, a stone *tohu-vabohu* of considerable substance, and not a nothing!

121. Dillard, *Pilgrim at Tinker Creek*, 145.

122. Ibid., 145.

123. Ibid., 145–46.

124. Bernard Loomer, *The Size of God: The Theology of Bernard Loomer in Context*, ed. William Dean and Larry E. Axel (Macon, Ga.: Mercer University Press, 1987).

125. This understanding of God is more compatible with C. G. Jung's insistence on "Wholeness" as the *telos*, or goal, of human development than the teleological focus of some Christian theologies, such as John Wesley's, on the spiritual journey as one toward "perfection." I have de-emphasized this distinction in this text because in my own thinking I am retreating from quite such a goal-oriented approach either in psychotherapy and human development or in theology, e.g., the more "progress"-suggestive versions of process theology.

126. E.g., first proposed by Carter Heyward in *The Redemption of God: A Theology of Mutual Recognition* (Lanhan, Md.: University Press of America, 1982), and elaborated in idem, *Touching Our Strength: The Erotic as Power and the Love of God* (San Francisco: HarperSanFrancisco, 1989).

127. Rita Nakashima Brock, *Journeys by Heart: A Christology of Erotic Power* (New York: Continuum, 1998).

128. Ibid., 67.

129. LaCugna, *God for Us*, 407–8.

130. Contra Jeffrey Zurheide, who takes a strong position in his pastoral theology, drawing heavily from Karl Barth and the Reform tradition, arguing that it is God's sovereignty that ultimately reassures the suffering, not God's weakness in solidarity (*When Faith Is Tested: Pastoral Responses to Suffering and Tragic Death*, Creative Pastoral Care and Counseling [Minneapolis: Fortress Press, 1997]).

131. Pamela Cooper-White, "Pastoral Implications," Easter, *Lectionary Homiletics* 15, no. 2 (February–March, 2005): 41ff.

132. Henri Nouwen, *Behold the Beauty of the Lord: Praying with Icons* (Notre Dame, Ind.: Ave Maria, 1987), 20.

133. Ibid.

134. Ibid., 19.

135. Cf. LaCugna, *God for Us*, 339: "Words and gestures of praise are 'performative'; their utterance makes actual the glory of God to which they refer and which they intend."

136. Jung Young Lee, *The Trinity in Asian Perspective* (Nashville: Abingdon, 1986), 95–123. Lee describes *ch'i* as in some sense subordinate to the Spirit, since energy and matter are both subordinate to God (98–100); he also distinguishes between the evil spirit that may participate in *ch'i* as pure energy, and the harmony and unity of the "Spirit as Godself," 100–102.

137. Luce Irigaray, "Divine Women," trans. Stephen Muecke, paper given at the Local Consumption conference in Sydney, Australia, 1986, 8.

138. Joem Lechte, "Luce Irigaray," in *Fifty Key Contemporary Thinkers*, http://www .envf.port.ac.uk/illustration/images/vlsh/psycholo/irigaray.htm.

139. Elizabeth Grosz, "Irigaray and the Divine," in *Transfigurations: Theology and the French Feminists*, ed. C. W. Maggie Kim, Susan St. Ville, and Susan Simonaitis (Minneapolis: Fortress Press, 1993), 210.

140. Augustine, *Confessions*, 10.27.38, trans. Henry Chadwick (Oxford: Oxford University Press, 1991), 201.

141. Thich Nhat Hanh, *Peace Is in Every Step: The Path of Mindfulness in Everyday Life* (New York: Bantam, 1992).

142. John Rippon, "How Firm a Foundation" (1787), *The Hymnal 1982*, #636, #637.

143. For a much more detailed discussion of transference and countertransference from a relational, intersubjective perspective, and its ethical implications for boundaries and care, see Cooper-White, *Shared Wisdom*, esp. "The Relational Paradigm: Postmodern Concepts of Countertransference and Intersubjectivity," 35–60.

144. Donnel B. Stern, *Unformulated Experience: From Dissociation to Imagination in Psychoanalysis* (Hillsdale, N.J.: Analytic Press, 1997).

145. Christopher Bollas, *The Shadow of the Object: Psychoanalysis of the Unthought Known* (New York: Columbia University Press, 1987).

146. T. S. Eliot, "Dry Salvages," in *The Four Quartets* (New York: Harcourt Brace Jovanovich, 1971 [1943]), 44.

Chapter 3: A Relational Understanding of Health and Unhealth

1. Philip Bromberg, "'Speak! That I May See You': Some Reflections on Dissociation, Reality, and Psychoanalytic Listening," *PD* 4, no. 4 (1994), 517–47, also cited in Pamela Cooper-White, *Shared Wisdom: Use of the Self in Pastoral Care and Counseling* (Minneapolis: Fortress Press, 2004), 49.

2. Paul Pruyser, *The Minister as Diagnostician* (Philadelphia: Westminster, 1976).

3. Nancy Ramsay, *Pastoral Diagnosis: A Resource for Ministries of Care and Counseling* (Minneapolis: Fortress Press, 1998).

4. Largely driven by managed care, a trend has arisen in the last decade or so that is variously called outcome-based practice or EVT (empirically validated treatment). (See, for example, Linda Seligman, *Selecting Effective Treatments: A Comprehensive, Systematic Guide to Treating Mental Disorders*, rev. ed. [San Francisco: Jossey-Bass, 1998].) It is a pragmatically oriented practice theory of sorts, a teleological theory in which the ends—as defined by the interests of insurers as much as by patients—not only justify but dictate the means. This is the approach adopted by the National Board for Certified Counselors, and by extension, most state licensure requirements. It appeals to the desire of legislators and the medical establishment to validate counseling practices from a positivist scientific model and to regulate practice from a risk-management perspective, that is, to minimize malpractice liability. In large part, however, it is a practice theory without a psychology, so in its worst manifestations, an EVT approach would suggest that the same therapist, based on quantitative outcome research, should be a cognitive-behaviorist with depressed patients, a behaviorist with anxious ones, a family systems therapist with couples in conflict, a psychopharmacologist with psychotic patients, and perhaps—only after cognitive methods have been tried first—a psychodynamic therapist working with traumatized patients. The inherent bias of this research is toward short-term interventions that restore a baseline of functioning but rarely focus on helping a client to reach any deeper understanding of the root causes of his or her problems.

5. Irvin Yalom, *Love's Executioner and Other Tales of Psychotherapy* (New York: Basic, 1989), 89, 232.

6. For an up-to-date guide, see Nancy McWilliams, *Psychoanalytic Case Formulation* (New York: Guilford, 1999).

7. Ibid., 11, see also 208–9.

8. Pamela Cooper-White, *Shared Wisdom: Use of the Self in Pastoral Care and Counseling* (Minneapolis: Fortress Press, 2004), 66–79, with case examples throughout.

9. Pamela Cooper-White, "Thick Theory: Psychology, Theoretical Models, and the Formation of Pastoral Counselors," Symposium on the Formation of Pastoral Counsel-

ors, ed. D. Bidwell and J. Marshall, *American Journal of Pastoral Counseling* 8, no. 3–4, in press.

10. Clifford Geertz, "Thick Description: Toward an Interpretative Theory of Culture," in *The Interpretation of Cultures* (New York: Basic, 1973), 3–32.

11. Christopher Bollas, "Freudian Intersubjectivity," *PD* 11, no. 1 (2001): 93–105.

12. Freud, "Three Essays on the Theory of Sexuality" (1905), in *SE* 7:125–245.

13. Nancy J. Chodorow, *The Reproduction of Mothering: Psychoanalysis and the Sociology of Gender* (Berkeley: University of California Press, 1978); idem, *Feminism and Psychoanalytic Theory* (New Haven: Yale University Press, 1989); Dorothy Dinnerstein, *The Mermaid and the Minotaur: Sexual Arangements and Human Malaise* (New York: Harper & Row, 1989); and Polly Young-Eisendrath and Florence Wiedemann, *Female Authority: Empowering Women through Psychotherapy* (New York: Guilford, 1987).

14. Jean Baker Miller, *Toward a New Psychology of Women*, 2nd ed. (Boston: Beacon 1987); and idem, "Connections, Disconnections and Violations," Work in Progress 33 (Wellesley, Mass.: Wellesley College/Stone Center, 1988).

15. Miller, *Toward a New Psychology of Women*; and Judith Jordan, Janet Surrey, Alexandra Kaplan, Jean Baker Miller, and Irene Stiver, *Women's Growth in Connection: Writings from the Stone Center* (New York: Guilford, 1991).

16. Carol Gilligan, *In a Different Voice: Psychological Theory and Women's Development* (Cambridge, Mass.: Harvard University Press, 1982).

17. For more on this point, see Joyce McDougall, "The Body-Mind Matrix," in *Theaters of the Body: A Psychoanalytic Approach to Psychosomatic Illness* (New York: Norton, 1989), 50–67.

18. Freud, *The Interpretation of Dreams* (1900), in *SE* 5: chap. 7.

19. George E. Vaillant, *Adaptation to Life* (Cambridge, Mass.: Harvard University Press, 1995 [1977]). Vaillant's work represented a milestone in adult development; at the same time, the study is limited to the degree that he generalized a universal developmental scheme from a study limited to white, privileged, Harvard-undergraduate, male subjects.

20. George E. Vaillant, *Ego Mechanisms of Defense: A Guide for Clinicians and Researchers* (Washington, D.C.: American Psychiatric Press, 1992). For a concise table, see also Glen O. Gabbard, *Long-Term Psychodynamic Psychotherapy* (Washington, D.C.: American Psychiatric Publishing, 2004), 26–28.

21. Ibid.

22. For a brilliant work problematizing the theme of primitivity in psychoanalysis, see Celia Brickman, *Aboriginal Populations in the Mind: Race and Primitivity in Psychoanalysis* (New York: Columbia University Press, 2003).

23. Freud, *Civilization and Its Discontents* (1930), in *SE* 21:59ff.

24. Such obsessive-compulsive symptoms are now recognized as having a physiological component and are treated with medication as well as psychotherapy. However, such symptoms may still convey unconscious meaning, alongside their biological predeterminants.

25. Similar formulations are detailed in Len Sperry, Jon Gudeman, Barry Blackwell, and Larry Faulkner, *Psychiatric Case Formulations* (Washington, D.C.: American Psychiatric Press, 1992). See also Nancy McWilliams, *Psychoanalytic Case Formulation* (New York: Guilford, 1999).

26. Glen O. Gabbard, "Psychoanalysis and Psychoanalytic Psychotherapy," in *Handbook of Personality Disorders: Theory, Research, and Treatment*, ed. W. J. Livesley (New York: Guilford, 2001), 359–76.

27. Stella Chess and Alexander Thomas, *Temperament in Clinical Practice*, rev. ed. (New York: Guilford, 1995).

28. Daniel Stern, *The Interpersonal World of the Infant: A View from Psychoanalysis and Developmental Psychology* (New York: Basic, 1985).

29. Ibid.; Frank Lachmann, "Some Contributions of Empirical Infant Research to Adult Psychoanalysis: What Have We Learned? How Can We Apply It?" *PD* 11, no. 2 (2001): 169.

30. Stephen Seligman, "Integrating Kleinian Theory and Intersubjective Infant Research Observing Projective Identification," *PD* 9, no. 2 (1999): 129–59.

31. W. R. D. Fairbairn, *An Object-Relations Theory of the Personality* (New York: Basic, 1952).

32. Melanie Klein, "Notes on Some Schizoid Mechanisms" (1946), in *Envy and Gratitude and Other Works* (New York: Delacorte, 1975), 1–24.

33. Thomas Ogden, *The Primitive Edge of Experience* (Northvale, N.J.: Aronson, 1989), 18–19.

34. Ibid., 20.

35. Melanie Klein, "A Contribution to the Psychogenesis of Manic-Depressive States, in *Contributions to Psycho-analysis 1921–1945* (London: Hogarth, 1935), 282–311; and idem, "Notes on Some Schizoid Mechanisms."

36. Ogden, *The Primitive Edge of Experience*, 28.

37. W. R. D. Fairbairn, *Psychoanalytic Studies of the Personality* (Boston: Routledge, 1952).

38. E.g., D. W. Winnicott, *The Maturational Processes and the Facilitating Environment* (London: Hogarth, 1965); and idem, *Playing and Reality* (New York: Basic, 1971).

39. Harry Guntrip, *Schizoid Phenomena, Object-Relations, and the Self* (New York: International Universities Press, 1961).

40. Stephen A. Mitchell, *Relational Concepts in Psychoanalysis: An Integration* (Cambridge, Mass.: Harvard University Press, 1988); J. M. Davies, "Multiple Perspectives on Multiplicity," *PD* 8, no. 2 (1992): 195–206; Robert Stolorow, George Atwood, Bernard Bradchaft, eds., *The Intersubjective Perspective* (Northvale, N.J.: Aronson, 1994); Donna Orange, George Atwood, and Robert Stolorow, *Working Intersubjectively: Contextualism in Psychoanalytic Practice* (Hillsdale, N.J.: Analytic Press, 1994); and Phillip Bromberg, *Standing in the Spaces: Essays of Clinical Process, Trauma, and Dissociation* (Hillsdale, N.J.: Analytic Press, 1998).

41. Hanna Segal, "Notes on Symbol Formation," in *The Work of Hanna Segal: A Kleinian Approach to Clinical Practice* (Northvale, N.J.: Aronson, 1981 [1957]).

42. Term from Peter Fonagy, Gyorgy Gergely, Elliot Jurist, and Mary Target, eds., *Affect Regulation, Mentalization, and the Development of Self* (New York: Other Press, 2002).

43. Ibid. See also Daniel Siegel, *The Developing Mind: How Relationships and the Brain Interact to Shape Who We Are* (New York: Guilford, 2001), and Beatrice Beebe, *Infant Research and Adult Treatment: Co-Constructing Interactions* (Hillsdale, N.J.: Analytic Press, 2002).

44. Bessel Van der Kolk, "The Body Keeps the Score: Memory and the Evolving Psychogiology of Post-Traumatic Stress," *Harvard Review of Psychiatry* 1 (1994): 253–65; and Jody Messler Davies and Mary Gail Frawley, *Treating the Adult Survivor of Childhood Sexual Abuse* (New York: Basic, 1994).

45. Term originally from Klein, "Notes on Some Schizoid Mechanisms."

46. Jerold Kreisman and Hal Straus, *I Hate You, Don't Leave Me: Understanding Borderline Personality* (New York: Avon, 1991).

47. Judith L. Herman, *Trauma and Recovery* (New York: Basic, 1992).

48. D. W. Winnicott, "The Use of an Object and Relating through Identifications," in *Playing and Reality* (New York: Basic, 1971), 86–94.

49. See also Michael Eigen, *The Psychotic Core* (Northvale, N.J.: Aronson, 1986).

50. Frances Tustin, "The Autistic Capsule in Neurotic Adult Patients," in *The Protective Shell in Children and Adults* (London: Karnac, 1990), 145–68.

51. Heinz Kohut, *Analysis of the Self: A Systematic Approach to the Psychoanalytic Treatment of Narcissistic Personality Disorders* (New York: International Universities Press, 1971).

52. Heinz Kohut and Ernest Wolf, "The Disorders of the Self and Their Treatment: An Outline," in *IJPA* 59 (1978): 413–25.

53. Heinz Kohut, *The Restoration of the Self* (New York: International Universities Press, 1977).

54. Followers of Kohut such as Ernest Wolf and others identified additional types of selfobjects, e.g., Ernest Wolf, *Treating the Self: Elements of Clinical Self Psychology* (New York: Guilford, 1988). Kohut himself introduced a third selfobject, the alter-ego or twinship selfobject in *The Restoration of the Self* (New York: International Universities Press, 1977).

55. Howard D. Baker and Margaret N. Baker, "Heinz Kohut's Self-Psychology: An Overview," *AJP* 144 (1987): 3, using the term "good enough" from D. W. Winnicott, "Ego Distortion in Terms of True and False Self" (1960), in *The Maturational Processes and the Facilitating Environment* (London: Hogarth, 1965), 145.

56. Ibid., 1–9.

57. Wolf, *Treating the Self*.

58. For a postmodern discussion of narcissism and its origins in lack (drawing on both

Freud and Lacan), see Gilles Deleuze, *Difference and Repetition*, trans. P. Patton (New York: Columbia University Press, 1994), esp. 110ff.

59. One notable exception to this is Mark Gehrie, "Empathy in Broader Perspective: A Technical Approach to the Consequences of the Negative Selfobject in Early Character Formation," in *Basic Ideas Reconsidered: Progress in Self Psychology*, vol. 12, ed. Arnold Goldberg (Hillsdale, N.J.: Analytic, 1996), 159–79. Gehrie considers how negative selfobjects are incorporated, resulting in malformation of psychic structure rather than simply deficit. Thanks to Lallene Rector for this clarification.

60. Lenore Terr, *Too Scared to Cry: Psychic Trauma in Childhood* (New York: Basic, 1990).

61. Ibid.; and Herman, *Trauma and Recovery*.

62. E.g., Frances Wickes, *The Inner World of Childhood: A Study in Analytical Psychology* (Boston; Sigo, 1988 [1927]).

63. Herman, *Trauma and Recovery*.

64. Leonard Shengold, *Soul Murder: The Effects of Childhood Abuse and Deprivation* (New Haven: Yale University Press, 1989), 541.

65. Michael Basch, *Understanding Psychotherapy: The Science behind the Art* (New York: Basic, 1988).

66. Donald L. Nathanson, *Shame and Pride: Affect, Sex, and the Birth of the Self* (New York: Norton, 1992).

67. Ibid.

68. Silvan S. Tompkins, *Affect, Imagery, Consciousness*, 4 vols. (New York: Springer, 1962, 1963, 1991, 1992). For updated information about ongoing research in affect theory, see the websites of the Tompkins Institute at http://www.tomkins.org/home/ and the Silvan Tompkins Research Group at http://www.silvantomkins.org/links.htm.

69. Basch, *Understanding Psychotherapy*, 72.

70. Nathanson, *Shame and Pride*.

71. Eve Kosofsky Sedgwick and Adam Frank, eds., *Shame and Its Sisters: A Silvan Tompkins Reader* (Durham: Duke University Press, 1995). For a pastoral theological study of shame, see Jill McNish, *Transforming Shame: A Pastoral Response* (Binghamton, N.Y.: Haworth Pastoral Press, 2004).

72. John Bradshaw, *Healing the Shame That Binds You* (Deerfield Beach, Fla.: Health Communications, 1988).

73. Helen Block Lewis, *Shame and Guilt in Neurosis* (New York: International Universities Press, 1971).

74. Alice Miller, *The Drama of the Gifted Child: The Search for the True Self*, trans. Ruth Ward, (New York: Basic, 1981); and idem, *For Your Own Good: Hidden Cruelty in Child-Rearing and the Roots of Violence*, 3rd ed. (New York: Farrar, Straus, and Giroux, 1990).

75. Nathanson, *Shame and Pride*.

76. Donald Nathanson in an interview by Gilbert Levin, also citing Silvan Tomkins, online at http://www.tomkins.org/pressroom/conversation.aspx.

77. Francis J. Broucek, *Shame and the Self* (New York: Guilford, 1991).

78. Andrew P. Morrison, *Shame, the Underside of Narcissism* (Hillsdale, N.J.: Analytic, 1989).

79. Lewis, *Shame, Guilt and Neurosis*.

80. Leon Wurmser, *The Mask of Shame* (Baltimore: Johns Hopkins University Press, 1981); see also Neville Symington, *Narcissism: A New Theory* (London: Karnac, 1993).

81. Carl D. Schneider, *Shame, Exposure, and Privacy* (Boston: Beacon, 1977).

82. Ibid.

83. Robert Karen, "Shame," *The Atlantic* 269 (February 1992): 40–61. See also idem, "Ugly Needs, Ugly Me: Anxious Attachment and Shame," in *Becoming Attached: First Relationships and How They Shape Our Capacity to Love* (Oxford: Oxford University Press, 1994), 238–47.

84. Thandeka, *Learning to Be White: Money, Race, and God in America* (New York: Continuum, 1999). See also an earlier psychoanalytic/political treatment of white racism by Franz Fanon, *Black Skin, White Masks*, trans. Charles Lam Markmann (New York: Grove, 1991 [1952]).

85. Nathaniel Hawthorne, *The Scarlet Letter and Other Writings*, ed. Leland Person, 4th ed., Norton Critical Editions (New York: Norton, 2005 [1850]).

86. Cited by Arthur Schlesinger Jr. in "Forgetting Reinhold Niebuhr: Why Has the Supreme American Theologian of the 20th Century Dropped Out of Our Religious Discourse?" *New York Times Book Review*, Sunday, 18 September 2005, 13.

87. Karl Menninger, *Whatever Became of Sin?* (New York: Hawthorn, 1973), 172.

88. Ibid., 228.

89. Schlesinger, "Forgetting Reinhold Niebuhr," 12.

90. Published as "I Do Not Do the Good I Want, But the Evil I Do Not Want Is What I Do: The Concept of the Vertical Split in Self Psychology in Relation to Christian Concepts of Good and Evil," *JPT* 13, no. 1 (2003): 63–84. Adapted here with permission.

91. David Tracy, *Blessed Rage for Order: The New Pluralism in Theology* (New York: Seabury, 1975), esp. 32–34.

92. Heinz Kohut, "The Two Analyses of Mr. Z," *IJPA* 60 (1979): 3–27. The vertical split was recently reconsidered in detail by Arnold Goldberg in *Being of Two Minds: The Vertical Split in Psychoanalysis and Psychotherapy* (Hillsdale, N.J.: Analytic, 1999).

93. Goldberg, *Being of Two Minds*, 10.

94. D. W. Winnicott, "The Antisocial Tendency" (1956), in *Through Paediatrics to Psycho-Analysis: Collected Papers* (New York: Brunner/Mazel, 1992), 306–15.

95. Discussed in detail by John Milbank, "Evil: Negative or Positive?" and "Forgiveness: Negative or Positive?" Paddock Lectures, General Theological Seminary, New York, N.Y., October 2000.

96. Kathleen Sands, *Escape from Paradise: Evil and Tragedy in Feminist Theology* (Minneapolis: Fortress Press, 1994), 2 et passim.

97. Augustine, *On the Free Choice of the Will (De libero arbitrio)*, trans. Thomas Williams (Indianapolis/Cambridge: Hackett, 1993); also *De correptione et gratia*, discussed in James Wetzel, "Predestination, Pelagianism, and Foreknowledge," in *The Cambridge Companion to Augustine*, ed. Eleonore Stump and Norman Kreztmann, (Cambridge: Cambridge University Press, 2001), 54–56.

98. Milbank, "Evil: Negative or Positive?" and "Forgiveness: Negative or Positive?"

99. Cited in Gilbert Meilander, "I Renounce the Devil and All His Ways," in *Sin, Death, and the Devil*, ed. C. Braaten and R. Jenson (Grand Rapids, Mich.: Eerdmans, 2000), 78.

100. Contra Gillian R. Evans, whose reading of Augustine, especially *De libero arbitrio*, asserts that "evil does not exist." ("Evil," in *Augustine through the Ages: An Encyclopedia*, ed. Allan Fitzgerald, O.S.A. [Grand Rapids, Mich.: Eerdmans, 1999]). However, Evans herself presents a more complex discussion of evil as a historical phenomenon and hence a "something" resulting from the willful turning away of fallen angels and human beings (in *Augustine on Evil*, Cambridge: Cambridge University Press, 1982, e.g., 100).

101. To be fair to the complexity of self psychology, it would be theoretically possible for someone to have an evil self-concept and disavow the good, but this is not the way it is usually understood or manifested in clinical application.

102. Augustine, *City of God*, XIV.XIII, in *Basic Writings of Saint Augustine*, vol. 2., ed. Whitney J. Oates (New York: Random House, 1948), cited in Marjorie Suchocki, *The End of Evil* (Albany: State University of New York Press, 1988), 6.

103. Kohut discussed the concept of "transmuting internalization" in all three of his major works. He first introduced it in *The Analysis of the Self: A Systematic Approach to the Psychoanalytic Treatment of Narcissistic Personality Disorders* (New York: International Universities Press, 1971), and elaborated in *The Restoration of the Self* (New York: International Universities Press, 1976) and (published posthumously) *How Does Analysis Cure?* ed. Arnold Goldberg and Paul Stepansky (Chicago: University of Chicago Press, 1984).

104. For the sake of clarity in this paper, I am omitting discussion of another positive or active conception of evil, that of Irenaeus, who viewed evil as an active force, but subsumed as a necessary part under God's plan, as a means of perfecting an immature creation, also espoused in modern times by John Hick in *Evil and the God of Love*, 2nd ed. (New York: Harper & Row, 1978). This might also be compared with Jung's notion of God even containing evil, especially in "Answer to Job," in *CW* 11.

105. There has been a recent resurgence of interest in the Albigensian Crusade, e.g., Michael Costen, *The Cathars and the Albigensian Crusade* (Manchester and New York: Manchester University Press, 1997).

106. See Elaine Pagels's exhaustive historical review of the word *Satan* as a name for the devil as "adversary" or "temptation" in *The Origin of Satan* (New York: Vintage, 1995).

107. For a lengthy discussion on Ignatius's discernment of spirits, see Jules Toner, S.J., *A Commentary on Saint Ignatius' Rules for the Discernment of Spirits* (St. Louis: Institute of Jesuit Sources, 1982).

108. Paul Ricoeur, *Fallible Man*, trans. C. Kelbley (New York: Fordham University Press, 1986).

109. Paul Ricoeur, *The Symbolism of Evil*, trans. E. Buchanan, (New York: Harper & Row, 1967), 146.

110. Ricoeur, *The Symbolism of Evil*, 155. Feminist theologian Kristine Rankka draws from this positive view of evil in her *Women and the Value of Suffering: An Aw(e)ful Rowing toward God* (Collegeville, Minn.: Liturgical, 1998), esp. 184–89.

111. E.g., Ricoeur, *The Symbolism of Evil*, 156. In her argument for evil as a "something," Rankka (184–85) notes the first two points Ricoeur makes about the positiveness of evil, cited above, but she omits Ricoeur's third point that evil is also subordinate to original goodness (*The Symbolism of Evil*, 156).

112. Ricoeur, *Fallible Man*, 145.

113. Milbank, "Evil: Negative or Positive?" and "Forgiveness: Negative or Positive?"

114. E.g., John Cobb and David Ray Griffin, *Process Theology: An Introductory Exposition* (Philadelphia: Westminster, 1976); David Ray Griffin, *God, Power, and Evil: A Process Theodicy* (Philadelphia: Westminster, 1976); and Edward Madden and Peter Hare, *Evil and the Concept of God* (Springfield, Ill.: Thomas, 1968).

115. See in particular Griffin's critique of Augustine in "Augustine and the Denial of Genuine Evil," in *God, Power, and Evil*, 55–71, also reprinted in Michael Peterson, ed., *The Problem of Evil: Selected Readings* (Notre Dame: University of Notre Dame Press, 1992), 197–214.

116. Harold Kushner, *When Bad Things Happen to Good People* (New York: Schocken, 1981).

117. Simone Weil, *Waiting for God*, trans. Emma Caufurd (New York: Putnam, 1951), cited in Alexander Nava, "The Mystery of Evil and the Hiddenness of God: Some Thoughts on Simone Weil," in *The Fascination of Evil*, ed. Hermann Haring and David Tracy, Concilium (Maryknoll: Orbis, 1998), 76. See also Terrence Tilley, *The Evils of Theodicy* (Washington, D.C.: Georgetown University Press, 1991); Kenneth Surin, *Theology and the Problem of Evil* (Oxford: Blackwell, 1986); and Gustavo Gutiérrez, *On Job: God-Talk and the Suffering of the Innocent*, trans. M. J. O'Connell (Maryknoll: Orbis, 1987); all cited in Todd Billings, "Theodicy as a 'Lived Question': Moving Beyond a Theoretical Approach to Theodicy," *Journal for Christian Theological Research* 5, no. 2 (2000): 1–9. Miroslav Volf has also rejected the category of "theodicy" on similar grounds, e.g., in "Memory, Suffering, and Redemption," lecture sponsored by the Philadelphia Theological Institute, 21 October 2001.

118. Nel Noddings, *Women and Evil* (Berkeley: University of California Press, 1989), 229. See also Rankka, *Women and the Value of Suffering*, 60ff.

119. Noddings, *Women and Evil*, 229–30.

120. Sands, *Escape from Paradise.*

121. E.g., Emilie Townes, ed., *A Troubling in My Soul: Womanist Perspectives on Evil and Suffering*, (Maryknoll: Orbis, 1993).

122. Peter Homans, "Response to Person, Culture, and Religion Panel on the 100th Anniversary of Freud's *Interpretation of Dreams*," American Academy of Religion, Boston, November 1999.

123. For a representative collection of articles by relational theorists, see Stephen Mitchell and Lewis Aron, eds., *Relational Psychoanalysis: The Emergence of a Tradition* (Hillsdale, N.J.: Analytic, 1999). Ongoing work in this school of thought is represented in the journal *Psychoanalytic Dialogues.*

124. Ana-Maria Rizzuto, *The Birth of the Living God: A Psychoanalytic Study* (Chicago: University of Chicago Press, 1979).

125. Jane Grovijahn, "A Theology of Survival" (PhD dissertation, Graduate Theological Union, 1997).

126. Betty Joseph, "Toward the Experiencing of Psychic Pain" (1981), in *Psychic Equilibrium and Psychic Change* (London: Routledge, 1989), 88–97.

127. Elizabeth Johnson, *She Who Is: The Mystery of God in Feminist Theological Discourse* (New York: Crossroad, 1992), 64. See also an earlier exposition of this theme by Valerie Saiving [Goldstein], "The Human Situation: A Feminine View," *Journal of Religion* 40 (1960): 100–112, reprinted in *Womanspirit Rising: A Feminist Reader in Religion* (San Francisco: Harper & Row, 1979), 25–42. Saiving proposes that patriarchal attention to sins of self-absorption are less relevant for women and suggests as alternatives the sins of "triviality, distractibility, diffuseness; lack of an organized center or focus; dependence on others for one's own self-definition; tolerance at the expense of standards of excellence; inability to respect the boundaries of privacy; sentimentality; and mistrust of reason." Saiving's proposals have more recently been debated as inadvertently reinforcing essentialist stereotypes of women and insufficiently critical of women's own participation in cultural evils, particularly racial and class oppression. See also Rankka, *Women and the Value of Suffering.*

128. Noddings, *Women and Evil*, 120–21.

129. Townes, *A Troubling in My Soul.*

130. Delores Williams, "A Womanist Perspective on Sin," in *A Troubling in My Soul: Womanist Perspectives on Evil and Suffering*, ed. Emilie Townes (Maryknoll: Orbis, 1993), 146.

131. David Tracy and Hermann Haring, introduction, in *The Fascination of Evil*, 1.

132. Billings, "Theodicy as a 'Lived Question'," 9:

Evil is not explained; it is protested against by acting as if a reign of peace were prior to this world of violence. As Gustavo Gutiérrez says in *On Job*, "Only if we take seriously the suffering of the innocent and live the mystery of the cross amid that suffering, but in the light of Easter, can we prevent our theology from being 'windy arguments' (Job 16:[103]）." The question of theodicy, and the life of the Christian, is lived between the suffering of the cross and the increasingly penetrating light of Easter. As such, the question of theodicy remains open and anomalous rather than answered and (hence) forgotten.

133. Edward Farley offers a convincing parallel discussion of the human hunger to eliminate vulnerability, insecurity, and contingency by relying on "mundane goods" (such as religions, sciences, nations, social movements, etc.), and in turn collapsing the "eternal horizon" (borrowing Ricoeur's terminology) into these goods, which is idolatry, in *Good and Evil: Interpreting a Human Condition* (Minneapolis: Fortress Press, 1990), 130–35.

134. Wendy Farley, *Tragic Vision and Divine Compassion: A Contemporary Theodicy* (Louisville: Westminster John Knox, 1996), 27–31; see also Rankka, *Women and the Value of Suffering*, esp. 174–81.

135. Rankka, *Women and the Value of Suffering*, 196.

136. Jürgen Moltmann, *The Trinity and the Kingdom* (Minneapolis: Fortress Press, 1993), 49.

137. D. W. Winnicott, "Ego Distortion in Terms of True and False Self" (1960), in *The Maturational Processes*, 145.

Chapter 4: The Therapeutic Process

1. Translation by Albert Outler (Philadelphia: Westminster, 1955). I depart here from the Henry Chadwick translation (Oxford: Oxford University Press, 1991) because Outler's historic translation is particularly evocative in relation to psychotherapy.

2. Fromm-Reichmann's actual term is *psychiatrist*, which she explains as follows: "There is no valid intensive psychotherapy other than that which is psychoanalytic or psychoanalytically oriented. For this reason the reader will find that the term 'psychiatrist' is used throughout this book in reference to the doctor who is engaged in psychoanalytic or dynamically oriented intensive psychotherapy" (x, footnote). Since the time Fromm-Reichmann wrote *Principles of Intensive Psychotherapy* (see n3), psychoanalytic institutes began to admit other doctoral-level practitioners besides MDs into training, and parallel institutes (e.g., Adlerian, Eriksonian, Jungian, and others, the Wright Institutes in California, institutes for Clinical Social Work, institutes for psychoanalytically oriented pastoral counseling such as the Blanton-Peale Institute in New York City and the Center for Religion and Psychotherapy in Chicago, etc.) also were founded to grant doctoral degrees and/or certificates in psychoanalytic psychotherapy and research, so the term *psychiatrist* to refer to analysts and analytically trained psychotherapists is now obsolete.

3. Frieda Fromm-Reichmann, *Principles of Intensive Psychotherapy* (Chicago: University of Chicago Press, 1960), x. Fromm-Reichmann was an exponent of the Sullivanian

or "interpersonal" school of psychoanalysis in the 1960s, in which the "relational" school has strong roots via the William Alanson White Institute. The teachers she named in her dedication included Sigmund Freud, Kurt Goldstein, Georg Groddeck, and Harry Stack Sullivan, identifying her psychoanalytic "family tree" as classical, interpreted through American and interpersonal psychoanalytic thought.

4. Exceptions to this occurring later in the treatment are referred to as Negative Therapeutic Reaction (NTR), first described by Freud in "The Ego and the Id" (1923), in *SE* 19:3–66, usually triggered by empathic ruptures or impasses at a time when previously buried unconscious material is touched in a way that feels too psychically dangerous to the patient to pursue. Occasionally NTR is also triggered by a deepening intimacy that in itself feels too threatening. For a review of the literature on NTR, see Janet Schumacher Finell, "A Challenge to Psychoanalysis: A Review of the Negative Therapeutic Reaction," *PR* 74, no. 4 (1987): 487–515; see also Joseph Sandler et al., "The Negative Therapeutic Reaction," in *The Patient and the Analyst: The Basis of the Psychoanalytic Process*, 2nd ed. (Madison, Conn.: International Universities Press, 1992).

5. Freud, "Analysis Terminable and Interminable" (1937), in *SE* 23:209–54.

6. Analogous to D. W. Winnicott's expression the "good enough mother," in "Ego Distortion in Terms of True and False Self" (1960), in *The Maturational Processes and the Facilitating Environment* (London: Hogarth, 1965), 145.

7. Attributed to Freud by Erik Erikson, *Childhood and Society* (New York: Norton, 1993 [1950]), 265.

8. This definition follows James Fowler's definition of *faith* as "a person's way of seeing him or herself in relation to others against a background of shared meaning and purpose," in *Stages of Faith: The Psychology of Human Development and the Quest for Meaning* (San Francisco: Harper & Row, 1981), 4.

9. Freud, "Lines of Advance in Psychoanalytic Therapy" (1919), in *SE* 17:166.

10. James Bugenthal, *Psychotherapy and Process: The Fundamentals of an Existential-Humanistic Approach* (New York: Random House, 1978), 60 (emphasis added).

11. Jung, *The Psychology of the Transference* (1946), in *CW* 16:163–326.

12. Term from Wilfred Bion, *Learning from Experience* (London: Tavistock, 1962).

13. For a thoughtful meditation on the relationship of chaos and change, especially in organizations, see Margaret Wheatley, *Leadership and the New Science: Discovering Order in a Chaotic World* (San Francisco: Berrett-Koehler, 2001).

14. Fromm-Reichmann, *Principles of Intensive Psychotherapy*, 7 (emphasis added).

15. Freud recommended against note-taking in "Recommendations for Physicians Practicing Psycho-Analysis," (1912), in *SE* 12:109–10.

16. This book assumes that the reader is acquainted through supervision and other readings with the basics of establishing a therapeutic frame. Two good up-to-date resources are Glen O. Gabbard, "The Nuts and Bolts of Psychotherapy: Getting Started," in *Long-Term Psychodynamic Psychotherapy* (Washington, D.C.: American Psychiatric Press, 2004), 41–58, and Nancy McWilliams, "Boundaries I: The Frame,"

in *Psychoanalytic Psychotherapy: A Practitioner's Guide* (New York: Guilford, 2004), 99–131. A very straightforward approach for beginners is also provided in Maxa Ott, *First Steps in the Clinical Practice of Psychotherapy: A Practice-Oriented Psychodynamic Approach* (Northvale, N.J.: Aronson, 2001.)

17. Summarized from Fromm-Reichmann, *Principles of Intensive Psychotherapy*, 7–31.

18. Heinz Kohut, *The Analysis of the Self: A Systematic Approach to the Psychoanalytic Treatment of Narcissistic Personality Disorders* (New York: International Universities Press, 1971).

19. E.g., American Association of Pastoral Counselors, Code of Ethics IV.D., http://www.aapc.org/ethics.cfm; American Association of Christian Counselors Code of Ethics ES1.400, http://www.aacc.net/About_us/media/aacc_code_of_ethics.doc; and American Counseling Association Code of Ethics 2005, Section B, http://www.counseling.org/Resources/CodeOfEthics/TP/Home/CT2.aspx?.

20. The use of case material for publication remains an unsettled issue. Anonymity and disguise are required by codes of ethics, and limiting the amount of material to what is strictly relevant is also advisable. Seeking the patient's consent is a matter of context and best decided in consultation, weighing the potential for harm to the patient and the treatment, and if the therapy is terminated, the ramifications of reopening issues and the limited ability to process. Constance O. Goldberg, personal communication, October 2005; Arnold Goldberg, Judy Kantrowitz, and Allanah Furlong, "Psychoanalytic Dialogues: In Strictest Confidence," panel at the American Psychoanalytic Association Winter Meeting, New York, 22 January 2005; Arnold Goldberg, "Writing Case Histories," *IJPA* 78 (1997): 435–38; Glen O. Gabbard, "Disguise or Consent: Problems and Recommendations Concerning the Publication and Presentation of Clinical Material," *IJPA* 81 (2000): 1,071–86 and http://www.ijpa.org/gabbardnov00.htm; Lewis Aron, "Ethical Considerations in the Writing of Case Histories," *PD* 10 (2000): 231–45; Stuart Pizer, "A Gift in Return: The Clinical Use of Writing about a Patient," *PD* 10 (2000): 247–59; J. Halpern, "Beyond Wishful Thinking: Facing the Harm That Psychotherapists Can Do by Writing about Their Patients," *Journal of Clinical Ethics* 14 (2003): 118–36; Judy L. Kantrowitz, "Writing about Patients: I. Ways of Protecting Confidentiality and Analysts' Conflicts over Choice of Method" and "II. Patients' Reading about Themselves and Their Analysts' Perceptions of Its Effect," *JAPA* 52, no. 1 (2004): 69–123; idem, "III. Comparisons and Attitudes of Analysts Residing in and outside of the United States," *IJPA* 85 (2004): 3–22; and idem, "IV. Patients' Reactions to Reading about Themselves," *JAPA* 53, no. 1 (2005), 83–129, and http://www.apsa.org/Portals/1/docs/JAPA/531/Kantrowitz-4-IV-pp.83-129.pdf.

21. A more lengthy practical discussion of the process of "socialization to therapy" is found in McWilliams, "Preparing the Client," in *Psychoanalytic Psychotherapy*, 73–98.

22. McWilliams, *Psychoanalytic Psychotherapy*, 77, also citing Jeremy Safran, "Breaches in the Therapeutic Alliance: An Arena for Negotiating Authentic Relatedness," *Psychotherapy: Theory, Research, and Practice* 30 (1993): 11–24. See also Safran and

J. Christopher Muran, *Negotiating the Therapeutic Alliance: A Relational Treatment Guide* (New York: Guilford, 2000).

23. Winnicott, "Ego Distortion in Terms of True and False Self" (1960), in *Maturational Processes and the Facilitating Environment*, 145.

24. Ibid.

25. Winnicott, "The Capacity to Be Alone," in *The Maturational Processes and the Facilitating Environment*, 29–37.

26. D. W. Winnicott, "The Use of an Object and Relating through Identifications" (1969), in *Playing and Reality* (New York: Basic Books, 1971), 86–94.

27. For a more extended discussion of literal and emotional safety in therapy for both patient and therapist, see McWilliams, *Psychoanalytic Psychotherapy*, 76–86.

28. Gabbard and colleagues make a distinction between obviously unethical, injurious boundary "violations" and boundary "crossings" in which the meanings and consequences may be more ambiguous. T. G. Gutheil and Glen O. Gabbard, "The Concept of Boundaries in Clinical Practice: Theoretical and Risk Management Dimensions," *AJP* 150 (1993): 188–96; and idem, "Misuses and Misunderstandings of Boundary Theory in Clinical and Regulatory Settings," *AJP* 155 (1998): 409–14; see also Glen O. Gabbard, *Psychodynamic Psychotherapy in Clinical Practice*, 3rd ed. (Washington: American Psychiatric Press, 2000).

29. The influence of unconscious narcissism in seemingly benign therapist enactments is discussed in light of empirical research in Pamela Cooper-White, "The Use of the Self in Psychotherapy: A Comparative Study of Pastoral Counselors and Clinical Social Workers," *AJPC* 4, no. 4 (2001): 5–35, which is summarized in Pamela Cooper-White, *Shared Wisdom: Use of the Self in Pastoral Care and Counseling* (Minneapolis: Fortress Press, 2004), 155–80.

30. For a clinical theory focusing on unconscious tests in the transference, see Joseph Weiss, Harold Sampson, and the Mount Zion Psychotherapy Research Group, *The Psychoanalytic Process: Theory, Clinical Observation, and Empirical Research* (New York: Guilford, 1986).

31. Ibid.

32. Pamela Cooper-White, "Soul-Stealing: Power Relations in Pastoral Sexual Abuse," *Christian Century* 108, no. 6 (1991): 196–99; and Peter Rutter, *Sex in the Forbidden Zone* (Los Angeles: Tarcher, 1989).

33. McWilliams, *Psychoanalytic Psychotherapy*, 126.

34. Barbara Pizer, "The Therapist's Routine Consultations: A Necessary Window in the Treatment Frame," *PD* 10, no. 2 (2000): 197–208. For a summary of warning signs in the countertransference outlined by Pizer as signaling a need for consultation, in the context of therapists' narcissistic vulnerabilities, see also Cooper-White, *Shared Wisdom*, 176–78.

35. Constance O. Goldberg, personal communication.

36. Winnicott, "Ego Distortion in Terms of True and False Self," 145.

37. Term coined by Hans Loewald, "On the Therapeutic Action of Psycho-Analysis," in *Essential Papers on Object Relations*, ed. Peter Buckley (New York: New York University Press, 1986 [1960]), 385–418.

38. Jay R. Greenberg, "The Problem of Analytic Neutrality," *CP* 22 (1986): 98; see also idem, "Theoretical Models and the Analyst's Neutrality," in *Relational Psychoanalysis: The Emergence of a Tradition*, ed. Lewis Aron and Stephen Mitchell (Hillsdale, N.J.: Analytic, 1999 [1986]), 131–52.

39. Sheldon Roth, "Understanding: The Soft, Persistent Voice of Reason," in *Psychotherapy: The Art of Wooing Nature* (Northvale, N.J.: Aronson, 2000 [1987]), 127–42.

40. Freud, "New Introductory Lectures" (1933), in *SE* 22:180.

41. Hanna Segal, "Notes on Symbol Formation" (1957), in *The Work of Hanna Segal: A Kleinian Approach to Clinical Practice* (Northvale, N.J.: Aronson, 1981).

42. This process was described concisely in Jody Messler Davies and Mary Gail Frawley, *Treating the Adult Survivor of Childhood Sexual Abuse: A Psychoanalytic Perspective* (New York: Basic, 1994); the movement from nonverbal to symbolic to verbal is not confined to the treatment of post-traumatic stress per se.

43. Kim Chernin, *A Different Kind of Listening: My Psychoanalysis and Its Shadow* (New York: HarperCollins, 1995), xxvi.

44. Allen Schore, *Affect Regulation and the Origin of the Self: The Neurobiology of Emotional Development* (Hillsdale, N.J.: Erlbaum, 1999); and Daniel J. Siegel, *The Developing Mind: Toward a Neurobiology of Interpersonal Experience* (New York: Guilford, 1999).

45. Bessel van der Kolk, "The Body Keeps the Score: Memory and the Evolving Psychobiology of Post-Traumatic Stress," http://www.trauma-pages.com/a/vanderk4.php.

46. Ibid., 10.

47. Bessel van der Kolk and Rita Fisler, "Dissociation and the Fragmentary Nature of Traumatic Memories: Overview and Exploratory Study," http://www.trauma-pages.com/a/vanderk2.php.

48. For further discussion see Michael Moskowitz, Catherine Monk, Carol Kaye, and Steven Ellman, eds., *The Neurobiological and Developmental Basis for Psychotherapeutic Intervention* (Northvale, N.J.: Aronson, 1997); and Louis Cozolino, *The Neuroscience of Psychotherapy: Building and Rebuilding the Human Brain* (New York: Norton, 2002). The progression in therapy from nonverbal to symbolic to verbal expression is also described specifically in relation to treatment of trauma in Davies and Frawley, *Treating the Adult Survivor of Childhood Sexual Abuse*. From a pastoral perspective see also David Hogue, *Remembering the Future, Imagining the Past: Story, Ritual, and the Human Brain* (Cleveland: Pilgrim, 2003).

49. Joseph Weiss, "The Patient's Plans, Purposes, and Goals," in Weiss, Sampson, and the Mount Zion Psychotherapy Research Group, *The Psychoanalytic Process*, 84–100.

50. Gabbard, *Long-Term Psychodynamic Psychotherapy*, 62–70.

51. For more on the psychodynamic use of supportive interventions, see Lawrence Rockland, *Supportive Therapy: A Psychodynamic Approach* (New York: Basic, 1992), and

idem, *Supportive Therapy for Borderline Patients: A Psychodynamic Approach* (New York: Guilford, 1992).

52. Bjørn Killingmo, "Affirmation in Psychoanalysis," *IJPA* 76 (1995), 508–13.

53. Margaret Little, *Psychotic Anxieties and Containment: A Personal Record of My Analysis with Winnicott* (Northvale, N.J.: Aronson, 1990); see also idem, *Transference Neurosis and Transference Psychosis* (Northvale, N.J.: Aronson, 1977).

54. Betty Joseph, *Psychic Equilibrium and Psychic Change: Selected Papers of Betty Joseph*, ed. Michael Feldman and Elizabeth Bott Spillius (London: Routledge, 1989). See especially "Toward the Experiencing of Psychic Pain" (1976), 88–100.

55. Harold Searles, *Collected Papers on Schizophrenia and Related Subjects* (London: Karnac, 1993 [1966]); and idem, *My Work with Borderline Patients* (Northvale, N.J.: Aronson, 1986).

56. Heinz Kohut, *Analysis of the Self: A Systematic Approach to the Psychoanalytic Treatment of Narcissistic Personality Disorders* (New York: International Universities Press, 1971). See also Hyman Spotnitz, *Psychotherapy of Preoedipal Conditions* (Northvale, N.J.: Aronson, 1987), and idem, *Modern Psychoanalysis of the Schizophrenic Patient*, 2nd ed. (Human Sciences, 1985).

57. E.g., Paul Williams, ed., *A Language for Psychosis: Psychoanalysis of Psychotic States* (New York: Brunner-Routledge, 2001); Arnold Goldberg, ed., "The Narcissistic Patient Revisited," *Progress in Self Psychology* 17 (2001); and Alan Bass, ed., "Symposium on the British Independents," special issue, *PD* 8, no. 4 (1998).

58. Lawrence Hedges, *Listening Perspectives in Psychotherapy* (Northvale, N.J.: Aronson, 1992 [1983]). On the use of self psychological themes over classical themes with different patients, see also Michael Basch, "Choosing a Therapeutic Approach," in *Practicing Psychotherapy: A Casebook* (New York: Basic, 1992).

59. E.g., John Bowlby, *A Secure Base: Clinical Applications of Attachment Theory* (London: Routledge, 2000 [1988]); Peter Fonagy, *Attachment Theory and Psychoanalysis* (New York: Other Press, 2000); Jude Cassidy and Phillip Shaver, eds., *Handbook of Attachment: Theory, Research and Clinical Applications* (New York: Guilford, 2002); and Mauricio Cortina and Mario Marrone, eds., *Attachment Theory and the Psychoanalytic Process* (London: Whurr, 2003). For application in couples and family therapy, see also Susan Johnson and Valerie Whiffen, eds., *Attachment Processes in Couple and Family Therapy* (New York: Guilford, 2003).

60. Winnicott, "Ego Distortion in Terms of True and False Self" (1960), in *The Maturational Processes and the Facilitating Environment*, 140–52.

61. Heinz Kohut, *How Does Analysis Cure?* (Chicago: University of Chicago Press, 1984), esp. 64–110.

62. This fluctuation of supportive and interpretative approaches has been explored in depth in recent years, e.g., Lawrence Josephs, *Balancing Empathy and Interpretation: Relational Character Analysis* (Northvale, N.J.: Aronson, 1995); Jeffrey Seinfeld, ed., *Interpreting and Holding: The Paternal and Maternal Functions of the Psychotherapist* (Northvale, N.J.: Aronson, 1993); and Martha Stark, *Modes of Therapeutic Action: Enhancement*

of Knowledge, Provision of Experience, and Engagement in Relationship (Northvale, N.J.: Aronson, 1999).

63. For further discussion of changing views toward therapeutic process and technique in contemporary analysis, see Spyros Orfanos, ed., "Symposium on Clinical Judgment in Relational Psychoanalysis," *PD* 8, no. 2 (1998): 183–246.

64. Sandor Ferenczi, "The Elasticity of Psycho-Analytic Technique" (1928), in *Final Contributions to the Problems and Methods of Psycho-Analysis*, ed. Michael Balint, trans. Michael Balint and Eric Mosbacher (London: Karnac, 2000 [1955]), 87–101.

65. Seinfeld, *Interpreting and Holding*; and Nancy McWilliams, "Mothering and Fathering Processes in the Psychoanalytic Art," *PR* 78 (1991): 525–45.

66. Ibid.

67. Berry Brazelton, "Joint Regulation of Neonate-Parent Behavior," in *Social Interchange in Infancy*, ed. Edward Tronic (Baltimore: University Park, 1982), 137–54; see also Berry Brazelton and Heidelise Als, "Four Early Stages in the Development of Mother-Infant Interaction," *Psychoanalytic Study of the Child* 34 (1979): 349–69.

68. McWilliams, "Mothering and Fathering Processes in the Psychoanalytic Art."

69. Freud's term for the failure to maintain an interpretive stance in therapy, "Wild Psycho-Analysis" (1910), in *SE* 11:139–53.

70. Letter to Sandor Ferenczi, quoted in Ernest Jones, *The Life and Work of Sigmund Freud: Years of Maturity, 1901–1919* (New York: Basic, 1955), 241, also cited in Beate Lohser and Peter Newton, *Unorthodox Freud: The View from the Couch* (New York: Guilford, 1996), 15.

71. Christopher Bollas, "Freudian Intersubjectivity," *PD* 11, no. 1 (2001): 93–105.

72. Jay R. Greenberg, "Self-disclosure: Is It Psychoanalytic?" *CP* 31 (1995): 197.

73. Glen O. Gabbard, "On Gratitude and Gratification," *JAPA* 48 (2000): 697–716.

74. Susan Fairfield, "Analyzing Multiplicity: A Postmodern Perspective on Some Current Psychoanalytic Theories of Subjectivity," *PD* 11, no. 2 (2001): 232–33.

75. Donnel Stern, "Unformulated Experience," *CP* 19 (1983): 71–99.

76. Donnel Stern, "The Analyst's Unformulated Experience of the Patient," *CP* 25 (1989): 1–33.

77. Freud, "Recommendations to Physicians Practicing Psycho-Analysis" (1912), in *SE* 12:111–20; and idem, "Two Encyclopedia Articles: A. Psycho-analysis" (1923), in *SE* 18:235–54.

78. Theodor Reik, *Listening with the Third Ear: The Inner Experience of a Psychoanalyst* (New York: Farrar, Straus, 1948).

79. E.g., Freud, *The Interpretation of Dreams* (1900), in *SE* 4–5; idem, "The Unconscious" (1915), in *SE* 14:159–204; and idem, "The Dynamics of Transference" (1912), in *SE* 12:99ff.

80. See http://www.hipaacomply.com/.

81. E.g., Gabbard, *Long-Term Psychodynamic Psychotherapy*, 41–58; and McWilliams, *Psychoanalytic Psychotherapy*, 46–131. For legal issues related to practice, see also Lawrence Hedges, *Facing the Challenge of Liability in Psychotherapy: Practicing Defensively*

(Northvale, N.J.: Aronson, 1996). Updated information on compliance with HIPAA regulations is found online at http://www.hipaacomply.com/.

82. Alice Miller, *The Drama of the Gifted Child: The Search for the True Self*, trans. Ruth Ward (New York: Basic, 1981).

83. Charles Figley, *Compassion Fatigue: Coping with Secondary Traumatic Stress Disorder in Those Who Treat the Traumatized* (New York: Brunner-Mazel, 1995); and Charles Figley and Patricia Smith, *Introduction to Compassion Fatigue in the Helping Professions* (New York: Brunner-Routledge, 2005).

84. McWilliams, *Psychoanalytic Psychotherapy*, 120.

85. This term was first attributed to Edward Bibring in 1937. It is elaborated by Elizabeth Zetzel in "Current Concepts of Transference," *IJPA* 37 (1956): 369–76.

86. Winnicott "The Use of an Object."

87. Joseph Weiss, "The Patient's Unconscious Work," in *The Psychoanalytic Process*, 107–13.

88. For example, see Charles Taylor's appropriate use of a Rational Emotive Therapy (RET) model for pastoral care in *The Skilled Pastor* (Minneapolis: Fortress Press, 1991), and Margaret Kornfeld's use of Solution-Focused Brief Therapy in *Cultivating Wholeness* (New York: Continuum, 1998).

89. HBO Original Programming, Brad Grey Television and Chase Films, *The Sopranos*, Season 2, Episode 16, "Toodle-F***ing-Oo." For an entertaining psychoanalytic review of this series, see Glen O. Gabbard, *The Psychology of "The Sopranos": Love, Death, Desire, and Betrayal in America's Favorite Gangster Family* (New York: Basic, 2002). Also, Naomi Goldenberg presented on psychoanalytic readings of *The Sopranos* at the Person, Culture, Religion Group of the American Academy of Religion, Denver, Colo., November 2001, and the Culture and the Unconscious Conference, University of East London and the Tavistock Clinic, London, July 2004.

90. *Tarasoff v. Regents of the University of California*, 17 Cal.3d 425 (1976). See http://en.wikipedia.org/wiki/Tarasoff_v._Regents_of_the_University_of_California for a good summary. Recent case law has extended Tarasoff to threats reported by a patient's family members in at least one state (*Ewing v. Goldstein*, 120 Cal. App. 4th 807 [2004] and *Ewing v. Northridge Hospital Medical Center*, 120 Cal. App. 4th 1289 [2004]). For discussion see Charles Patrick Ewing, "Judicial Notebook: Tarasoff Reconsidered," *Monitor on Psychology* 36, no. 7 (2005): 112, http://www.apa.org/monitor/julaug05/jn.html.

91. See http://www.hipaacomply.com/.

92. For an exploration of this theme by a pastoral psychotherapist who is also a trained spiritual director, see Thomas Hart, *Hidden Spring: The Spiritual Dimension of Therapy*, 2nd ed. (Minneapolis: Fortress Press, 2002).

93. DSM-IV-TR, V62.89 "Religious or Spiritual Problem," 741.

94. E.g., William Miller, ed., *Integrating Spirituality into Treatment: Resources for Practitioners* (New York: American Psychological Association, 1999); Thomas Plante and Allen Sherman, eds., *Faith and Health: Psychological Perspectives* (New York: Guilford, 2001); P. Scott Richards and Allen Bergin, eds., *A Spiritual Strategy for Counseling and*

Psychotherapy (Washington, D.C.: American Psychological Association, 1997); Michael C. Smith, *Psychotherapy and the Sacred: Religious Experience and Religious Resources in Psychotherapy* (Chicago: Center for the Scientific Study of Religion, 1995); and Froma Walsh, ed., *Spiritual Resources in Family Therapy* (New York: Guilford, 1999).

95. Norma Wood, "Pastoral Counseling and Spiritual Direction: Pastoral Theology's Stepchildren?" in *Spirituality: Toward a 21st Century Lutheran Understanding*, ed. Kirsi Stjerna and Brooks Schramm (Minneapolis: Lutheran University Press, 2004), 109–20. For a thoughtful reflection on the ways the roles of secular psychotherapist, pastoral counselor, pastor, and spiritual director may overlap, see also Thomas Hart, "Pastoral Counseling or Spiritual Direction: What's the Difference?" *Presence: An International Journal of Spiritual Direction* 11, no. 2 (2005): 7–13.

96. Freud, "Recommendations to Physicians Practicing Psycho-analysis," *SE* 12:118.

97. Lohser and Newton, *Unorthodox Freud*.

98. Analysis of John Dorsey in 1935, cited in Lohser and Newton, *Unorthodox Freud*, 112.

99. Sandor Ferenczi, *The Clinical Diary of Sandor Ferenczi*, ed. Judith Dupont, trans. Michael Balint and Nicola Zarday Jackson (Cambridge, Mass.: Harvard University Press, 1988).

100. Reik, *Listening with the Third Ear*, 23, also cited in McWilliams, *Psychoanalytic Psychotherapy*, 182.

101. Greenberg, "Self-Disclosure: Is It Psychoanalytic?" 197.

102. For a good general discussion of contemporary perspectives on self-disclosure, see also Glen O. Gabbard, "Employing Judicious Use of Self-Disclosure," in *Long-Term Psychodynamic Psychotherapy*, 140–42. For a more fluid Ferenczian approach, see Greenberg, "Self-Disclosure," 193–20; and Stephen A. Mitchell, "The Emergence of Features of the Analyst's Life," *PD* 8, no. 2 (1998): 187–98.

103. Greenberg, "Self-Disclosure," 197.

104. Gabbard, "Employing Judicious Use of Self-Disclosure," 142; see also idem, *Love and Hate in the Analytic Setting* (Northvale, N.J.: Aronson, 1996), 128–37.

105. See especially the case of the therapist "Sara" and her patient "Miranda" in Cooper-White, *Shared Wisdom*, 132–52, and related findings from my empirical research, 166–76. For more details on the research, see Cooper-White, "The Therapist's Use of the Self: Countertransference in Pastoral Counseling and Clinical Social Work" (PhD dissertation, Institute for Clinical Social Work, 2000), which is summarized in idem, "The Use of the Self in Psychotherapy: A Comparative Study of Pastoral Counselors and Clinical Social Workers," *AJPC* 4, no. 4 (2001): 5–35, and in idem, *Shared Wisdom*, 155–80.

106. For a useful clinical example and discussion, see Jody Messler Davies, "Getting Cold Feet, Defining 'Safe-Enough' Borders: Dissociation, Multiplicity, and Integration in the Analyst's Experience," *PQ* 68 (1999): 184–208.

107. Arnold Modell, "The Therapeutic Relationship as a Paradoxical Experience," *PD* 1 (1991): 26.

108. Winnicott, *Playing and Reality*. See also Thomas Ogden, "On Potential Space," *IJPA* 70 (1985): 129–41.

109. Gabbard, *Long-Term Psychodynamic Psychotherapy*, 51.

110. Glen O. Gabbard and Eva P. Lester, *Boundaries and Boundary Violations in Psychoanalysis* (New York: Basic, 1995), 78, 88–89 et passim; and Kenneth Pope, Janet Sonne, and Jean Holroyd, *Sexual Feelings in Psychotherapy* (Washington, D.C.: American Psychological Association, 1995), 180–82. The issue of the "slippery slope" in pastoral contexts is taken up in Cooper-White, *Shared Wisdom*, 103–22 et passim. For a sophisticated discussion of the complexities of this issue in actual practice, see also Jody Messler Davies, "Descending the Slippery Slopes: Slippery, Slipperier, Slipperiest," *PD* 10, no. 2 (2000): 219–30

111. Gabbard, *Long-Term Psychodynamic Psychotherapy*, 52.

112. Ibid., 65.

113. D. W. Winnicott, "Transitional Objects and Transitional Phenomena," in *Collected Papers: Through Paediatrics to Psycho-Analysis* (London: Tavistock, 1958 [1951]), 229–42; see also idem, *Playing and Reality*.

114. Cooper-White, "The Use of the Self in Psychotherapy," 155–80.

115. Ibid. These therapists were Board-certified Diplomates in Clinical Social Work.

116. Ibid.

117. Valerie DeMarinis, *Critical Caring: A Feminist Model for Pastoral Psychology* (Nashville: Westminster John Knox, 1993); David Hogue, "Shelters and Pathways: Ritual and Pastoral Counseling," *JSTM* 19 (1998–99): 57–67, also citing Otto van der Hart, *Rituals in Psychotherapy: Transition and Continuity* (New York: Ivrington, 1983); Hogue, "Living as if . . . Ritual, the Brain, and Human Experience"; and Herbert Anderson and Edward Foley, *Mighty Stories, Dangerous Rituals: Weaving Together the Human and the Divine* (San Francisco: Jossey-Bass, 2001). Regarding ritual in pastoral care see also Elaine Ramshaw, *Ritual and Pastoral Care*, ed. Don S. Browning (Philadelphia: Fortress Press, 1987); Kenneth Mitchell, "Ritual in Pastoral Care," *JPC* 43 (1989): 68–77; and Pamela Couture, "Ritual and Pastoral Care," in *Dictionary of Pastoral Care and Counseling*, ed. Rodney Hunter (Nashville: Abingdon, 1990), 1,089–90.

118. See also Cooper-White, "The Ritual Reason Why: Explorations of the Unconscious through Enactment and Ritual in Pastoral Psychotherapy," *JSTM* 19 (1998–99): 68–75.

119. Erik Erikson, *Toys and Reasons: Stages in the Ritualization of Experience* (New York: Norton, 1977), 80.

120. Constance O. Goldberg, "The Privileged Position of Religion in the Clinical Dialogue," *Clinical Social Work Journal* 24, no. 2 (1996): 125–36.

121. Ibid., 130–34, also citing William James's suggestion for exploring the "functionalist" or "pragmatic" view of religion and its adaptive uses, in *The Varieties of Religious Experience* (London: Longman Dreen, 1901–1902).

122. Ana-Maria Rizzuto, *The Birth of the Living God: A Psychoanalytic Study* (Chicago: University of Chicago Press, 1981); DeMarinis, *Critical Caring*, esp. "The Case of Heather," 67–81; and Antoine Vergote and Alvaro Tamayo, *Parental Figures and the Representation of God: A Psychological and Cross-Cultural Study*, Louvain Psychology Series Studia Psychiologicia (New York: Mouton de Gruyter, 1981).

123. Lallene Rector, "The Function of Early Selfobject Experiences in Gendered Representations of God," *Progress in Self Psychology* 12 (1996): 269–83. See also Carrie Doehring, *Internal Desecration: Traumatization and Representations of God* (Lanham, Md.: University Press of America, 1993).

124. Randall Mason, "The Psychology of the Self: Religion and Psychotherapy," and Joaquim Scharfenberg, "The Psychology of the Self and Religion," in *Advances in Self Psychology*, ed. Arnold Goldberg (New York: International Universities Press, 1980), 407–37; Diana Claire Hahn, "God as a Mirroring and Idealizing Selfobject Function: Its Influence on Self-cohesion and Mood: An Empirical Study" (PhD dissertation, California School of Professional Psychology, 1994); Steven Knoblauch, "The Selfobject Function of Religious Experience: The Treatment of a Dying Patient," *Progress in Self Psychology* 11 (1995): 207–17; idem, "The Patient Who Was Touched by and Knew Nothing about God," in *Soul on the Couch: Spirituality, Religion, and Morality in Contemporary Psychoanalysis*, ed. Charles Spezzano and Gerald Gargiuolo (Hillside, N.J.: Analytic Press, 2003); Pamela Holliman, "Religious Experience as Selfobject Experience," *Progress in Self Psychology* 18 (2002): 193–205; and Lallene Rector, "Mystical Experience as an Expression of the Idealizing Selfobject Need," *Progress in Self Psychology*, 17 (2001): 179–95.

125. Robert Randall, *Pastor and Parish: The Psychological Core of Ecclesiastical Conflicts* (New York: Human Services, 1988).

126. Randall Lehmann Sorenson, "Ongoing Change in Psychoanalytic Theory: Implications for Analysis of Religious Experience," Charles Spezzano, "Illusion, Faith, and Knowledge: Commentary on Sorenson's 'Ongoing Change in Psychoanalytic Theory,'" and Sorenson, "Reply to Spezzano," *PD* 4, no. 4 (1994): 631–72; and Marie Hoffman, "From Enemy Combatant to Strange Bedfellow: The Role of Religious Narratives in the Work of W. R. D. Fairbairn and D. W. Winnicott," *PD* 14, no. 6 (2004): 769–804.

Chapter 5: The Middle Phase and Termination

1. Freud, "The Unconscious" (1915), in *SE* 14:194.

2. For a good overview see Dan Buie, "Empathy: Its Nature and Limitations," *JAPA* 29 (1981): 281–307.

3. Freud described the neutrality of the analyst in terms of a "receiving organ" and a "mirror" in "Recommendations to Physicians Practicing Psycho-analysis" (1912), in *SE* 12:115, as well as a "blank screen" upon which patient's fantasies could be projected, in "The Ego and the Id" (1923), in *SE* 19:50. Note that Freud's actual practice, based on

firsthand accounts, e.g., Beate Lohser and Peter Newton, *Unorthodox Freud: The View from the Couch* (New York: Guilford, 1996), was more engaged than his published admonitions about the need for a surgeon's "emotional coldness" (Freud, "Recommendations to Physicians Practicing Psycho-analysis," 115). This admonition was written in a context of fear about sexual boundary violations, and C. G. Jung's relationship with the patient Sabina Spielrein in particular. For a detailed history, see A. Carotenuto, *A Secret Symmetry: Sabina Spielrein between Jung and Freud*, trans. A. Pomerans, J. Shepleyand, and K. Winston (New York: Pantheon, 1982); and Jean Kerr, *A Most Dangerous Method: The Story of Jung, Freud, and Sabina Spielrein* (New York: Vintage, 1993), also discussed in relation to the history of countertransference in Pamela Cooper-White, *Shared Wisdom: Use of the Self in Pastoral Care and Counseling* (Minneapolis: Fortress Press, 2004), 9–13.

4. Carl Rogers, "The Interpersonal Relationship: The Core of Guidance," *Harvard Educational Review* 32, no. 4 (1962).

5. Irvin Yalom, *Existential Psychotherapy* (New York: Basic, 1980); see also William Meissner, *What Is Effective in Psychotherapy? The Move from Interpretation to Relation* (New Haven: Yale University Press, 1996).

6. Freud, "Recommendations to Physicians Practicing Psycho-analysis," 115.

7. E.g., Lohser and Newton, *Unorthodox Freud*.

8. Carl R. Rogers, *A Way of Being* (Boston: Houghton Mifflin, 1980), 115–16.

9. Anna Freud, *The Ego and the Mechanisms of Defense*, rev. ed. (New York: International Universities Press, 1966 [1937]), 28.

10. Glen O. Gabbard, *Long-Term Psychodynamic Psychotherapy* (Washington, D.C.: American Psychiatric Press, 2004), 61.

11. Howard E. Book, "Empathy: Misconceptions and Misuses in Psychotherapy," *AJP* 145, no. 4 (1988): 423.

12. Howard Clinebell, *Basic Types of Pastoral Counseling* (Nashville: Abingdon, 1984 [1966]).

13. Edwin Kahn, "Heinz Kohut and Carl Rogers: A Timely Comparison," *American Psychologist* 40, no. 8 (1985).

14. Carl Rogers, *Client-Centered Therapy* (Boston: Houghton Mifflin, 1951); and idem, "A Theory of Therapy, Personality, and Interpersonal Relationships, as Developed in the Client-Centered Framework," in *Psychology: A Study of Science*, vol. 3, *Formulations of the Person and the Social Context*, ed. S. Koch (New York: McGraw-Hill, 1959), 184–256.

15. Heinz Kohut, "Introspection, Empathy, and Psychoanalysis: An Examination of the Relationship between Mode of Observation and Theory," *JAPA* 7 (1959): 459.

16. Heinz Kohut, "Introspection, Empathy, and the Semi-Circle of Mental Health," *IJPA* 63 (1982): 396–97.

17. E.g., Robert Stolorow, Bernard Brandchft, and George Atwood, *Psychoanalytic Treatment: An Intersubjective Approach* (Hillsdale, N.J.: Analytic Press, 1987).

18. Christopher Bollas, *The Shadow of the Object: Psychoanalysis of the Unthought Known* (New York: Columbia University Press, 1987), 201–2 (emphasis added).

19. Ibid., 202.

20. Wilfred Bion identified this phenomenon of being rendered unable to think (which he called "negative K") in "A Theory of Thinking, Second Thoughts," in *Learning from Experience* (London: Karnac, 1989 [1962]), 110–19, and "Attacks on Linking, in *Second Thoughts: Selected Papers on Psycho-Analysis* (London: Karnac, 1987 [1967]).

21. Bollas, *The Shadow of the Object*, 202–3.

22. Joseph Weiss, "The Patient's Plans, Purposes, and Goals," in Joseph Weiss, Harold Sampson, and the Mount Zion Psychotherapy Research Group, *The Psychoanalytic Process: Theory, Clinical Observation, and Empirical Research* (New York: Guilford, 1986), 84–100.

23. I have already written about this extensively elsewhere, e.g., in "Soul-Stealing: Power Relations in Pastoral Sexual Abuse," *Christian Century* 108, no. 6 (1991): 196–99, and *Shared Wisdom*, 151–52.

24. Franz Alexander, "Some Quantitative Aspects of Psychoanalytic Technique," *JAPA* 2 (1954): 685–701.

25. For a helpful discussion of the problems with this concept, see Patrick Casement, *Learning from the Patient* (New York: Guilford, 1985), 144–46, 269–71, 274–92.

26. Michael F. Basch, *Doing Psychotherapy* (New York: Basic, 1980).

27. Alice Miller, *The Drama of the Gifted Child: The Search for the True Self*, trans. Ruth Ward (New York: Basic, 1981), esp. 43–44 on mourning.

28. Ibid.

29. Gabbard, *Long-Term Psychodynamic Psychotherapy*, 165.

30. Basch, *Doing Psychotherapy*, 178.

31. E.g., Book, "Empathy," 420–24.

32. Freud, *The Dynamics of Transference* (1912), in *SE* 12:99ff.

33. Weiss, Sampson, and the Mount Zion Psychotherapy Research Group, *The Psychoanalytic Process*. For a good popular introduction, see also Lewis Engel and Tom Ferguson, *Hidden Guilt* (New York: Pocket, 1990).

34. Even some of the more conservative ego psychologists, such as Fred Pine, have increasingly advocated openness to diversity of approaches, as in Pine's most recent book, *Diversity and Direction in Psychoanalytic Technique* (New Haven: Yale University Press, 1998). See also Nancy McWilliams on "psychoanalytic pluralism," *Psychoanalytic Psychotherapy: A Practitioner's Guide* (New York: Guilford, 2004), 19–23.

35. Freud, "On Beginning the Treatment" (1913), in *SE* 12:135.

36. Christopher Bollas reflects further on the "Freudian pair" (his term) in "Freudian Intersubjectivity: Commentary on Paper by Julie Gerhardt and Annie Sweetnam," *PD* 11, no. 1 (2001): 93–105.

37. Freud, "Recommendations to Physicians Practicing Psycho-Analysis," 12:111–20.

38. Benoni Reyes Silva-Netto, "Cultural Symbols and Images in the Counseling Process," *PP* 42, no. 4 (1994): 272–84.

39. E.g., John M. Whitely, producer, "Carl Rogers Counsels an Individual on Anger and Hurt" (Washington, D.C.: American Personnel and Guidance Association Video, 1977); and Carl Rogers, with commentary by Maria Villas Boaz Bowen, "Jill: The Case of Jill," in *The Psychotherapy of Carl Rogers*, ed. Barry Faber, Debora Brink, and Patricia Raskin (New York: Guilford, 1996). Further primary source videos and resources are available through the Carl Rogers Center for Studies of the Person, 150 Silverado Street, Suite 112, La Jolla, CA 92037, http://www.centerfortheperson.org/.

40. Barry Faber, Debora Brink, and Patricia Raskin, eds., *The Psychotherapy of Carl Rogers* (New York: Guilford, 1996).

41. Basch, *Doing Psychotherapy*, 179.

42. Leon Wurmser, *The Mask of Shame* (Baltimore: Johns Hopkins University Press, 1981); Neville Symington, *Narcissism: A New Theory* (London: Karnac, 1993).

43. Pine, *Diversity and Direction in Psychoanalytic Technique*.

44. Term coined by Robert Fliess, "The Metapsychology of the Analyst," *PQ* 11 (1942): 211–27. See also James Grotstein, "Projective Identification Reappraised," *CP* 30, no. 4 (1994) and 31, no. 3 (1995); and idem, "Integrating One-person and Two-person Psychologies: Autochthony and Alterity in Counterpoint," *PQ* 66 (1997): 403–30.

45. D. W. Winnicott, *Playing and Reality* (New York: Basic, 1971).

46. Casement, *Learning from the Patient*, 38.

47. Philip Ringstrom, "Cultivating the Improvisational in Psychoanalytic Treatment," *PD* 1, no. 5 (2005): 727–54, http://psychematters.com/papers/ringstrom.htm.

48. Letter to Sandor Ferenczi, quoted in Ernest Jones, *The Life and Work of Sigmund Freud: Years of Maturity, 1901–1919* (New York: Basic, 1955), 241 (emphasis in the original), also cited in Lohser and Newton, *Unorthodox Freud*, 15.

49. Lohser and Newton, *Unorthodox Freud*, 16.

50. Freud, *On Beginning the Treatment* (1913), in *SE* 12:121–44.

51. D. W. Winnicott, "Ego Distortion in Terms of True and False Self" (1960), in *The Maturational Processes and the Facilitating Environment* (London: Hogarth, 1965), 145.

52. Basch, *Doing Psychotherapy*, 145.

53. Ibid.

54. Freud, "Psychopathology of Every Day Life" (1901), in *SE* 6. For a helpful interpersonal perspective, see also Frieda Fromm-Reichmann, *Principles of Intensive Psychotherapy* (Chicago: University of Chicago Press, 1960), 154–57.

55. Freud, *The Interpretation of Dreams* (1900), in *SE* 4–5.

56. Ibid. For a thoughtful history from a relational perspective, see Rosemarie Sand, "The Interpretation of Dreams: Freud and the Western Dream Tradition," *PD* 9, no. 6 (1999): 725–47.

57. J. Alan Hobson, *The Dreaming Brain* (New York: Basic, 1988).

58. Morton F. Reiser, "The Dream of Contemporary Psychiatry," *AJP* 158 (2001): 351–59, http://ajp.psychiatryonline.org/cgi/content/full/158/3/351; and Ramon Greenberg and Chester Pearlman, "The Interpretation of Dreams: A Classic Revisited," *PD* 9, no. 6 (1999): 749–65, with commentaries by Milton Kramer and Ernest Hartmann, 779–88. For a good general overview of the psychology of dreaming, see Kelly Bulkeley, *An Introduction to the Psychology of Dreaming* (Westport, Conn.: Praeger, 1997).

59. E.g., Kelly Bulkeley, *Visions of the Night: Dreams, Religion, and Psychology* (Albany: State University of New York Press, 1999); idem, *The Wilderness of Dreams: Exploring the Religious Meanings of Dreams in Modern Western Culture* (Albany: State University of New York Press, 1994); idem, ed., *Dreams: A Reader on Religious, Cultural and Psychological Dimensions of Dreaming* (New York: Macmillan, 2001); and idem, *Among All These Dreamers: Essays on Dreaming and Modern Society* (Albany: State University of New York Press, 1996). See also Kelly Bulkeley, *The Wondering Brain: Thinking about Religion with and beyond Cognitive Neuroscience* (New York: Routledge, 2004).

60. Fromm-Reichmann, *Principles of Intensive Psychotherapy*, 171.

61. James Grotstein, *Who Is the Dreamer Who Dreams the Dream? A Study of Psychic Presences* (Hillsdale, N.J.: Analytic Press, 2000).

62. Jung, "The Analysis of Dreams," "On the Significance of Number Dreams," "General Aspects of Dream Psychology," "On the Nature of Dreams," "Individual Dream Symbolism in Relation to Alchemy," and "The Practical Use of Dream-Analysis," *CW* 4, 8, 12, 16. See also James Hall, *Jungian Dream Interpretation: A Handbook of Theory and Practice* (Toronto: Inner City, 1983).

63. Jung, "The Practical Use of Dream-Analysis" (1934), in *CW* 16:139–62.

64. Charles Whitman, who was the "Texas Tower Sniper" (1 August 1966), http://en.wikipedia.org/wiki/Charles_Whitman.

65. Originally termed "world play" by Margaret Lowenfeld, *The Non-verbal Thinking of Children and Its Place in Psychology* (London: Institute of Child Psychology, 1964). The classic text on sandplay is by Dora M. Kalff, *Sandplay: A Psychotherapeutic Approach to the Psyche*, ed. Barbara Turner (Cloverdale, Calif.: Temenos, 2003 [1980]). For more information and resources see the website of Sandplay Therapists of America, http://www.sandplay.org/index.htm.

66. C. G. Jung, *Memories, Dreams and Reflections* (New York: Vintage, 1962), 174–75.

67. Thomas Ogden, "The Analytic Third: An Overview," in *Relational Psychoanalysis: The Emergence of a Tradition*, ed. Stephen Mitchell and Lewis Aron (Hillsdale, N.J.: Analytic Press, 1999), 487, http://www.fortda.org/Spring_99/analytic3.html. See also idem, "The Analytic Third: Working with Intersubjective Clinical Facts," *IJPA* 75 (1994): 3–20; and idem, *Reverie and Interpretation: Sensing Something Human* (Northvale, N.J.: Aronson, 1997).

68. Anne Lamott, *Plan B: Further Thoughts on Faith* (New York: Riverhead, 2005), 93–94.

69. Jane Grovijahn, "A Theology of Survival" (PhD dissertation, Graduate Theological Union, 1997).

70. W. R. D. Fairbairn, *Psychoanalytic Studies of the Personality* (Boston: Routledge, 1952).

71. Harry Guntrip, *Schizoid Phenomena, Object-Relations, and the Self* (New York: International Universities Press, 1961). Guntrip describes the process of retrieving memories of his own depressed mother holding his dead brother on her lap, and the ways this internal object lived through his own illnesses and depressions.

72. Jody Messler Davies, "Multiple Perspectives on Multiplicity," *PD* 8, no. 2 (1995): 196. Davies gives clinical examples of this process in this article and also in "Getting Cold Feet, Defining 'Safe-Enough' Borders: Dissociation, Multiplicity, and Integration in the Analyst's Experience," *PQ* 68 (1999): 184–208.

73. Ibid.

74. Ibid.

75. Philip Bromberg, "Standing in the Spaces: The Multiplicity of Self and the Psychoanalytic Relationship," *CP* 32 (1996): 535, reprinted in idem, *Standing in the Spaces: Clinical Process, Trauma, and Dissociation* (Hillsdale, N.J.: Analytic Press, 2001), 290.

76. For more discussion of this dynamic, see, e.g., Gabbard, "Gender Constellation and Transference," in *Long-Term Psychodynamic Psychotherapy*, 71–75. The relationship of this issue to neural networks of representation is further detailed in Glen O. Gabbard and D. Westen, "Developments in Cognitive Neuroscience II: Implications for Theories of Transference," *JAPA* 50 (2002): 99–134.

77. Primarily in Freud, *Three Essays on the Theory of Sexuality*, in *SE* 7:125–245.

78. E.g., Adrienne Harris, ed. "Symposium on Gender," special issue, *PD* 1, no. 3 (1991), including Virginia Goldner, "Toward a Critical Relational Theory of Gender," with commentary by John Gagnon; Jessica Benjamin, "Father and Daughter: Identification with Difference—A Contribution to Gender Heterodoxy," with commentary by Irene Fast; Emmanuel Kaftal, "On Intimacy between Men," with commentary by Irene Fast; and Muriel Dimen, "Deconstructing Difference: Gender, Splitting, and Transitional Space," with commentary by Juliet Mitchell and reply by Dimen. See also Judith Butler, *Gender Trouble: Feminism and the Subversion of Identity* (New York: Routledge, 1999); and Lynne Layton, *Who's That Girl? Who's That Boy? Clinical Practice Meets Postmodern Gender Theory*, 2nd ed. (Hillsdale, N.J.: Analytic Press, 2004). For a sophisticated nonessentialist critique of Butler from a Lacanian psychoanalytic perspective, see the following articles from *PD* 10, no. 5 (2000), 735–94: Cynthia Dyess and Tim Dean, "Gender: The Impossibility of Meaning"; Donnel Stern, "The Limits of Social Construction: Commentary on Paper by Cynthia Dyess and Tim Dean"; James Hansell, "Beyond Essentialism and Constructivism: Commentary on Paper by Cynthia Dyess and Tim Dean"; Ken Corbett, "Toward the Coexistence of Effort and Lack: Commentary on Paper by Cynthia Dyess and Tim Dean"; and Dyess and Dean, "Relational Trouble: Reply to Commentaries."

79. For a thoughtful essay on this issue, see Sheldon Roth, "Gender and Personality of the Therapist: Are All Therapists Equal?" in *Psychotherapy: The Art of Wooing Nature* (Northvale, N.J.: Aronson, 2000 [1987]), 207–22; see also the following psychoanalytic research articles: Serge Lecours, Marc-André Bouchard, and Lina Normandin, "Countertransference: Therapist Activity, Gender, Experience Differences," *PsP* 12 (1995): 259–80; B. F. Marcus, "Vicissitudes of Gender Identity in Female Therapist/Male Patient Dyads," *Psychoanalytic Inquiry* 13 (1993): 258–69; and Ellen S. Person, "Women in Therapy: Therapist Gender as a Variable," *IRPA* 10 (1983): 93–204.

80. E.g., Andrew Sung Park and Susan Nelson, *The Other Side of Sin: Woundedness from the Perspective of the Sinned-Against* (Albany: State University of New York Press, 2001); Andrew Sung Park, "A Theology of Enhancement: Multiculturality in Self and Community," *JPT* 13, no. 2 (2003): 14–33; Emmanuel Lartey, *In Living Color: An Intercultural Approach to Pastoral Care and Counseling*, 2nd ed. (London and Philadelphia: Kingsley, 2003); idem, "Global Views for Pastoral Care and Counselling: Post-modern, Post-colonial, Post-Christian, Post-human, Post-pastoral," address given at the 7th Asia-Pacific Congress on Pastoral Care and Counselling, Perth, 15 July 2001, http://www.icpcc.net/materials/globalvi_1.htm; Nancy Ramsay, "Navigating Race as a White Pastoral Theologian," *JPT* 12, no. 2 (2002): 11–27; Pamela Couture and Rodney Hunter, eds., *Pastoral Care and Social Conflict* (Nashville: Abingdon, 1995); Larry Kent Graham, *Care of Persons, Care of Worlds: A Psychosystems Approach to Pastoral Care and Counseling* (Nashville: Abingdon, 1992); and John Patton, *Pastoral Care in Context: An Introduction to Pastoral Care* (Louisville: Westminster John Knox, 1993).

81. Kimberlyn Leary, "Racial Enactments in Dynamic Treatment," *PD* 10, no. 4 (2000): 641, also citing Donnel Stern, *Unformulated Experience* (Hillsdale, N.J.: Analytic Press, 1997).

82. E.g., Mark Bracher, "Psychoanalysis and Racism," *Journal for the Psychoanalysis of Culture and Society* 2, no. 2 (1997): 1–11.

83. Philip Cushman, "White Guilt, Political Activity, and the Analyst," *PD* 10, no. 4 (2000): 607, critiquing Gordon Allport's social psychological approach in *The Nature of Prejudice* (Reading, Mass.: Addison-Wesley, 1979). See also Philip Cushman, *Constructing the Self, Constructing America* (Reading, Mass.; Addison-Wesley, 1995).

84. Clifford Geertz, "Description: Toward an Interpretive Theory of Culture," in *The Interpretation of Culture* (New York: Basic, 1973).

85. For a discussion of this "developmental lag" in psychoanalysis in addressing race socially as well as intrapsychically see Leary, "Racial Enactments in Dynamic Treatment," 648. See also Patricia Elliott, "Working through Racism: Confronting the Strangely Familiar," *Journal for the Psychoanalysis of Culture and Society* 1, no. 1 (1996): 63–72; Muriel Dimen, "Introduction: Symposium on Race," *PD* 10, no. 4 (2000): 569–78; Neil Altman, "Reply to Commentaries," *PD* 10, no. 4 (2000): 637; and Adrienne Harris, "Haunted Talk, Healing Action: Commentary on Paper by Kimberlyn Leary," *PD* 10, no. 4 (2000): 659.

86. Harris, "Haunted Talk, Healing Action," 660.

87. Celia Brickman, *Aboriginal Populations in the Mind: Race and Primitivity in Psychoanalysis* (New York: Columbia University Press, 2003).

88. Ibid. See also Neil Altman, "Black and White Thinking: A Psychoanalyst Reconsiders Race," *PD* 10, no. 4 (2000): 591.

89. Neil Altman, *The Analyst in the Inner City: Race, Class, and Culture through a Psychoanalytic Lens* (Hillsdale, N.J.: Analytic Press, 1995).

90. Thandeka, *Learning to Be White: Money, Race, and God in America* (New York: Continuum, 2000). See also Leary, "Racial Enactments in Dynamic Treatment."

91. Diane Jonte-Pace, "Psychoanalysis, Colonialism, and Modernity: Reflections on Brickman's Aboriginal Populations in the Mind," presented to the Person, Culture and Religion Group, American Academy of Religion, San Antonio, Tex., November 2004.

92. Franz Fanon, *Black Skin, White Masks* (London: Pluto, 1952); Anne Anlin Cheng, *The Melancholy of Race* (New York: Oxford University Press, 2001); and Juliet Mitchell, *Psychoanalysis and Feminism* (New York: Pantheon, 1974), cited in Jonte-Pace, "Psychoanalysis, Colonialism, and Modernity." See also Christopher Lane, *The Psychoanalysis of Race* (New York: Columbia University Press, 1998); Ann Pellegrini, *Performance Anxieties: Staging Psychoanalysis, Staging Race* (New York: Routledge, 1997); Muriel Dimen, ed., "Symposium on Race," *PD* 10, no. 4 (2000): 569–666; and David Eng and Shinhee Han, "A Dialogue on Racial Melancholia," *PD* 10, no. 4 (2000): 667–700. See also the following articles from *PD* 14, no. 5 (2004): 581–710: Susan Bodnar, "Remembering Where You Came From: Dissociative Process in Multicultural Individuals"; Gary Walls, "Toward a Critical Global Psychoanalysis"; Steven Botticelli, "The Politics of Relational Psychoanalysis"; Cleonie White, "Culture, Influence, and the 'I-ness' of Me: Commentary on Bodnar and Walls"; with replies by Bodnar, Walls, and Botticelli. See also Gillian Straker, "Race for Cover: Castrated Whiteness, Perverse Consequences"; and Melanie Suchet, "A Relational Encounter with Race," with commentary by Neil Altman and replies by Straker and Suchet, *PD* 14, no. 4 (2004): 405–56.

93. Sander L. Gilman, *Freud, Race, and Gender* (Princeton: Princeton University Press, 1993); and Cushman, "White Guilt, Political Activity, and the Analyst," 614.

94. Ibid.

95. Lynne Layton, "Cultural Hierarchies, Splitting and the Heterosexist Unconscious," in *Bringing the Plague: Toward a Postmodern Psychoanalysis*, ed. Susan Fairfield, Lynne Layton, and Carolyn Stack (New York: Other Press, 2002), cited in Leary, "Reply to Commentary," *PD* 10, no. 4 (2000): 664.

96. Jay R. Greenberg, *Oedipus and Beyond* (Cambridge, Mass.: Harvard University Press, 1991); Altman, *The Analyst in the Inner City*; Cushman, *Constructing the Self*; and Adrienne Harris, "Haunted Talk, Healing Action," 660.

97. Altman, "Black and White Thinking," 602.

98. Leary, "Racial Enactments in Dynamic Treatment," 652, also citing Toni Morrison, *Playing in the Dark: Whiteness and the Literary Imagination* (Cambridge, Mass.: Harvard University Press, 1992).

99. Little has been written specifically about the influence of class in psychoanalytic therapy. One exception is Bodnar, "Remembering Where You Come From," 589–93 et passim. See also Cushman, *Constructing the Self*; Rosemarie Perez Foster, Michael Moskowitz, and Rafael A. Javier, eds., *Reaching across Boundaries of Culture and Class: Widening the Scope of Psychotherapy* (Northvale, N.J.: Aronson, 1996).

100. Altman, "Black and White Thinking," 592–98. Altman describes how—as a Jewish therapist working with an African American patient—the complexity of his own racism and his internal conflicts over Jewish stereotypes infused his countertransference reactions, thus paralyzing his ability to listen and speak freely to his patient, especially when confronted by nonverbal testing and enactments.

101. "Hungry Ghost," http://en.wikipedia.org/wiki/Hungry_ghost.

102. Chinavoc, http://www.chinavoc.com/festivals/ghost.htm

103. "Hungry Ghost."

104. Harry Guntrip, "My Experience of Analysis with Fairbairn and Winnicott (How Complete a Result Does Psychoanalytic Therapy Achieve?)," *IRPA* 2 (1975): 145–56; and André Green, "The Dead Mother" (1980), in *On Private Madness* (New York: International Universities Press, 1986), 142–73.

105. Louise Demers, "Intergenerational Grief: Who's Mourning Whom?" in *Revue Canadienne de Psychoanalyse* 1, no. 1 (1993): 31, citing Nicholas Abraham and Maria Torok, *L'écorce et le noyau* (Paris: Aubier Montaigne, 1978) [*The Shell and the Kernel*, trans. Nicholas Rand (Chicago: University of Chicago Press, 1994)].

106. Ibid., 32.

107. Kate Heyhoe, "Feast of the Hungry Ghosts, Hong Kong, China," http://www.globalgourmet.com/food/kgk/1099/kgk103099.html.

108. Sándor Ferenczi, *The Clinical Diary of Sándor Ferenczi* (1931), ed. J. Dupont, trans. Michael Balint and Nicola Zarday Jackson (Cambridge, Mass.: Harvard University Press, 1988).

109. There is a long history to this development, beginning in the 1950s. For more detailed discussion of the history of the evolution of the concept and its use in therapeutic practice, and the evolution of the use of countertransference in pastoral care and counseling, see Cooper-White, *Shared Wisdom*.

110. Important contributions to the contemporary revival of this discussion include, from a relational perspective, Theodore J. Jacobs, *The Use of the Self: Countertransference and Communication in the Analytic Situation* (Madison, Conn.: International Universities Press, 1991); idem, "The Inner Experiences of the Analyst: Their Contribution to the Analytic Process," *IJPA* 74 (1993): 7–14; Lewis Aron, "One-Person and Two-Person Psychologies and the Method of Psychoanalysis," *PsP* 7 (1990): 475–85; and Bruce L. Smith, "The Origins of Interpretation in the Countertransference," *PsP* 7 (1990): 89–104. Similar contributions from a Kleinian perspective include André Green, "Discussion of 'The Inner Experience of the Analyst,'" *IJPA* 74 (1993): 1131–35; Thomas H. Ogden, *Subjects of Analysis* (Northvale, N.J.: Aronson, 1994); and idem, *Reverie and Interpretation*. For a more recent review of these developments, see also Jeanne Wolff

Bernstein, "Countertransference: Our New Royal Road to the Unconscious?" *PD* 9, no. 3 (1999): 275–99.

111. Freud, *The Unconscious* (1915), in *SE* 14:159–204.

112. Thomas H. Ogden, *The Primitive Edge of Experience* (Northvale, N.J.: Aronson, 1989); and Jill S. Scharff, *Projective and Introjective Identification and the Use of the Therapist's Self* (Northvale, N.J.: Aronson, 1992).

113. Scharff, *Projective and Introjective Identification and the Use of the Therapist's Self*, 45.

114. C. E. Watkins, "Countertransference: Its Impact on the Counseling Situation," *Journal of Counseling and Development* 63 (1985): 356–59.

115. This pattern of staying-leaving-returning was identified by Rebecca Emerson Dobash and Russell P. Dobash, *Women, Violence, and Social Change: A Case against the Patriarchy* (New York: Free Press, 1979), 231. See also Pamela Cooper-White, *The Cry of Tamar: Violence against Women and the Church's Response* (Minneapolis: Fortress Press, 1985), 116.

116. Freud, *Remembering, Repeating, and Working-Through* (1914), in *SE* 12:147ff.

117. Ibid.

118. A. Freud, *The Ego and the Mechanisms of Defense.*

119. Freud, *New Introductory Lectures on Psychoanalysis* (1916–17), in *SE* 15–16.

120. Freud, *The Aetiology of Hysteria* (1896), in *SE* 3:189ff. For discussion and critique of Freud's eventual recanting of the "seduction theory," see Florence Rush, "The Freudian Coverup," *Chrysalis* 1 (1977): 31–45; Jeffrey Moussaieff Masson, *The Assault on Truth: Freud's Suppression of the Seduction Theory* (New York: Farrar, Straus, and Giroux, 1984); Janet Malcolm, *In the Freud Archives* (New York: Knopf, 1984); and Judith L. Herman, *Trauma and Recovery* (New York: Basic, 1992).

121. For a recent relational symposium on enactment, see Lewis Aron et al., "Symposium on Enactment," special issue, *PD* 13, no. 5 (2003): 623–742.

122. Theodore Jacobs, "On Countertransference Enactments," *JAPA* 34 (1986): 289–307, and idem, "On Unconscious Communications and Covert Enactments: Some Reflection on Their Role in the Analytic Situation," *Psychoanalytic Inquiry* 21 (2001): 4–23.

123. E.g., Lewis Aron, *A Meeting of Minds: Mutuality in Psychoanalysis* (Hillsdale, N.J.: Analytic Press, 1996); Theodore Jacobs, "Posture, Gesture and Movement in the Analyst: Cues to Interpretation and Countertransference," *JAPA* 21 (1973): 77–92; "On Countertransference Enactments;" and idem, *The Use of the Self* (Hillsdale, N.J.: Analytic Press, 1989).

124. Freud, "Remembering, Repeating, and Working-Through" (1914), in *SE* 12:145–56.

125. Jacobs, "On Countertransference Enactments."

126. Anthony Bass, "'E' Enactments in Psychoanalysis," *PD* 13, no. 5 (2003): 660.

127. Ibid., 661.

128. Ibid.; see also Jacobs, "On Countertransference Enactments."

129. Cooper-White, *Shared Wisdom*, 56–58.

130. Ferenczi, *The Clinical Diary of Sándor Ferenczi*.

131. Judith Fingert Chused, "The Role of Enactments," *PD* 13, no. 5 (2003): 682–83.

132. Ibid., 683 (emphasis added).

133. Pamela Cooper-White, "The Use of the Self in Psychotherapy: A Comparative Study of Pastoral Counselors and Clinical Social Workers," *AJPC* 4, no. 4 (2001): 5–35, summarized in idem, *Shared Wisdom*, 155–80.

134. Miller, *The Drama of the Gifted Child*.

135. Cooper-White, *Shared Wisdom*, 174–80.

136. Kohut, "Introspection, Empathy, and the Semi-Circle of Mental Health."

137. E.g., Carter Heyward, *When Boundaries Betray Us: Beyond Illusions of What Is Ethical in Therapy and Life* (San Francisco: HarperSanFrancisco, 1995); Katherine Ragsdale, ed., *Boundary Wars: Intimacy and Distance in Healing Relationships* (Cleveland: Pilgrim, 1996); Roy SteinhoffSmith, *The Mutuality of Care* (St. Louis: Chalice, 1999); and Judith Orr, "Review of *The Mutuality of Care*, by Roy SteinhoffSmith," *JPT* 10 (2000): 126–29.

138. For a fuller discussion of professional ethics from a constructivist perspective, see Irvin Hoffman, "Practical Implications," in *Ritual and Spontaneity in the Psychoanalytic Process: A Dialectical-Constructivist View* (Hillsdale, N.J.: Analytic Press, 2002), 287–304. See also Karen Maroda, "Countertransference Techniques: Constructing the Interpersonal Analysis," in *The Power of Countertransference: Innovations in Analytic Technique* (Northvale, N.J.: Aronson, 1991), 110–56.

139. Hoffman, "Practical Implications," 303.

140. Ibid.

141. Winnicott, "Counter-Transference" (1960), in *The Maturational Processes and the Facilitating Environment*, 164.

142. Winnicott, "Ego Distortion in Terms of True and False Self," 145.

143. Kohut, *How Does Psychoanalysis Cure?* (Chicago: University of Chicago, 1984), 23, 66, 69–72 et passim; see also Winnicott on the ego-building aspects of frustration in *The Maturational Processes and the Facilitating Environment*, 141, 181. From a recent clinical perspective, see also Betty Berger, "Deprivation and Abstinence in Psychoanalytic Psychotherapy," *Israel Journal of Psychiatry* 36, no. 3 (1999), http://psychematters.com/papers/berger.htm.

144. Heinz Kohut, *The Analysis of the Self* (New York: International Universities Press, 1971); and idem, *How Does the Analyst Cure?*

145. Kahn, "Heinz Kohut and Carl Rogers."

146. Book, "Empathy," 424.

147. Ogden, "The Analytic Third: An Overview," 487. See also idem, "The Analytic Third: Working with Intersubjective Clinical Facts," 3–20, and idem, *Reverie and Interpretation*. Lewis Aron has added that the professional therapeutic community and psychoanalysis itself also functions as the "Third" to therapists' dyadic relationships with

patients, in "Clinical Choices and the Relational Matrix," *PD* 9, no. 1 (1999): 1–29, with further commentary by Arnold Cooper, Steven Knoblauch, Giuseppe Moccia, Gianni Nebbiosi, and Stuart Pizer, 31–72.

148. Cooper-White, *Shared Wisdom*, esp. 47–60.

149. Ogden, "The Analytic Third: An Overview," 487.

150. Stephen A. Mitchell, *Hope and Dread in Psychoanalysis* (New York: Basic, 1995), 228.

151. Ibid., 229.

152. Jody Messler Davies, "Transformations of Desire and Despair: Reflections on the Termination Process from a Relational Perspective," *PD* 15, no. 6 (2005): 783.

153. Ibid.

154. Gabbard, *Long-Term Psychodynamic Psychotherapy*, 168.

155. Marilyn Steele, personal communication.

156. Cooper-White, "Conclusion: Call to Reconciliation," in *The Cry of Tamar*, 253–62.

157. McWilliams, *Psychoanalytic Psychotherapy*, 137.

158. Irenaeus, *St. Irenaeus of Lyons, Against the Heresies (Adversus haereses)*, trans. Dominic Unger (New York: Paulist, 1992), 4.20.7.

Chapter 6: The Therapeutic Sensibility

1. Dante Alighieri, *Inferno*, trans. Henry Wadsworth Longfellow in *Inferno: The Longfellow Translation*, ed. Matthew Pearl (New York: Modern Library, 2003), 3, parallel text, http://www.divinecomedy.org/divine_comedy.html.

2. Theodor Reik, *Listening with the Third Ear: The Inner Experience of a Psychoanalyst* (New York: Farrar, Straus, 1948), cited in Nancy McWilliams, *Psychoanalytic Psychotherapy: A Practitioner's Guide* (New York: Guilford, 2004), 21.

3. Wilfred Bion, *Attention and Interpretation* (London: Tavistock, 1970), 32, 41–54.

4. Ibid., 125, citing a letter by John Keats to George and Thomas Keats, 21 December 1817.

5. Ibid.

6. Ibid., 32, 41.

7. First described in Wilfred Bion, *Transformations* (London: Heinemann, 1965).

8. Ibid., frontispiece.

9. Ibid., 32.

10. Bion, *Attention and Interpretation*, 26.

11. Rainer Maria Rilke, *Letters to a Young Poet*, trans. Stephen Mitchell (New York: Vintage, 1986 [1903]), 34.

12. Annie Dillard, *Pilgrim at Tinker Creek* (New York: Harper's Magazine Press, 1974), 145.

13. Frieda Fromm-Reichmann, *Principles of Intensive Psychotherapy* (Chicago: University of Chicago Press, 1960), 7.

14. Sheldon Roth, *Psychotherapy: The Art of Wooing Nature* (Northvale, N.J.: Aronson, 2000 [1987]), 441.

15. Martin Buber, *I and Thou*, trans. Walter Kaufmann (New York: Free Press, 1971).

16. E.g., Martin Bergmann, "Platonic Love, Transference Love, and Love in Real Life," *JAPA* 30 (1982): 87–111; Reuben Fine, *Healing of the Mind: The Technique of Psychoanalytic Psychotherapy*, 2nd ed. (New York: Free Press, 1982); Irvin Hoffman, *Ritual and Spontaneity in the Psychoanalytic Process: A Dialectical-Constructivist View* (Hillsdale, N.J.: Analytic Press, 2002); Julia Kristeva, *In the Beginning Was Love: Psychoanalysis and Faith*, trans. Arthur Goldhammer (New York: Columbia University Press, 1987); idem, *Art, Love, Melancholy, Philosophy, Semiotics, and Psychoanalysis*, trans. Kelly Ives (Kent, U.K.: Crescent Moon, 1998); Joseph Natterson, "Love in Psychotherapy," *PsP* 20 (2003): 509–21; and Daniel Shaw, "On the Therapeutic Action of Analytic Love," *CP* 39 (2003): 251–78.

17. Freud in a letter to Jung, 1906, in *The Freud/Jung Letters*, ed. William McGuire, trans. Ralph Manheim, and R. F. C. Hull (Princeton: Princeton University Press, 1974), 8–9. For further discussion, see Glen O. Gabbard, *Love and Hate in the Analytic Setting* (Northvale, N.J.: Aronson, 1996), 7–13.

18. Freud, "Some Character Types Met with in Psycho-analytic Work" (1916), in *SE* 14:312.

19. Irvin Yalom, *Existential Psychotherapy* (New York: Basic, 1980); see also William Meissner, *What Is Effective in Psychotherapy? The Move from Interpretation to Relation* (New Haven: Yale University Press, 1996).

20. Robert Stoller, *Sexual Excitement: Dynamics of Erotic Life* (New York: Pantheon, 1979); and idem, *Observing the Erotic Imagination* (New Haven: Yale University Press, 1985).

21. Winnicott, "Hate in the Countertransference" (1947), in *Through Pediatrics to Psycho-Analysis* (New York: Basic, 1975), 199.

22. Ibid., 201.

23. Ibid.

24. Mary Jacobus, "Clytemnestra's Daughters," *Didaskalia* 5, no. 3 (2002): http://www.didaskalia.net/issues/vol5no3/jacobus.html. Mary Jacobus is Professor of English at Cambridge. Her recent books include: *Psychoanalysis and the Scene of Reading* (Oxford: Oxford University Press, 1999), *First Things: The Maternal Imaginary in Literature, Art, and Psychoanalysis* (London: Routledge, 1996), and *Romanticism, Writing, and Sexual Difference* (Oxford: Oxford University Press, 1995).

25. D. W. Winnicott, "Ego Distortion in Terms of True and False Self" (1960), in *The Maturational Processes and the Facilitating Environment* (London: Hogarth, 1965), 145.

26. On the ambiguities of the therapist's role, see also Hoffman, *Ritual and Spontaneity in the Psychoanalytic Process*.

27. McWilliams, *Psychoanalytic Psychotherapy*, 161.

28. Ibid.

29. This more functional idea of therapeutic love is found in Hans Loewald, "Psychoanalytic Theory and Psychoanalytic Process" (1970), in *Papers on Psychoanalysis* (New Haven: Yale University Press, 1980), 277–301, and Roy Shafer, "The Interpretation of Transference and the Conditions for Loving," *JAPA* 25 (1977): 335–62, and idem, *Retelling a Life: Narration and Dialogue in Psychoanalysis* (New York: Basic, 1992), cited in Gabbard, *Love and Hate in the Analytic Setting*, 38.

30. Loewald, "Psychoanalytic Theory and Psychoanalytic Process," 297.

31. Jessica Benjamin, "Commentary on Paper by Jody Messler Davies," *PD* 14, no. 6 (2004): 751. See also idem, "Beyond Doer and Done-to: An Intersubjective View of Thirdness," *PQ* 63 (2004): 5–46.

32. Benjamin, "Commentary on Paper by Jody Messler Davies," 752–53.

33. Dante, *Inferno* (XXXIV:133–39), 170, parallel text http://www.divinecomedy.org/divine_comedy.html.

Glossary of Psychoanalytic Terms

The following are the author's definitions of terms used throughout this book and in common psychoanalytic parlance. There are many variations in the ways these terms are used, based on differing theoretical orientations. This list is intended to be neither exhaustive nor universally definitive, but a guide for readers and an invitation to further reading. When a term was first coined by a particular theorist, that individual's last name is included in parentheses. More detailed information and citations for most of these individuals are included in the book and its index and is widely available in published form.

Abstinence. A value, particularly in classical psychoanalysis, for refraining from excessive activity as the therapist, either verbal or nonverbal. It is now understood that the therapist makes a unique contribution as a person to the therapeutic relationship, and that nonverbal enactment is to some degree inevitable. Abstinence continues to be valued, however, as a caution against impulsivity or using the patient or the therapy itself for self-gratification on the part of the therapist. (Note: in psychoanalytic usage this term has nothing to do with avoiding alcohol or sex in general.)

Acting out. The process of converting split-off feelings, memories, impulses, or other mental contents into behavior, bypassing rational reflection and therefore generally considered undesirable because of its tendency to produce negative effects in relationships. In technical therapeutic terms, *acting out* refers to such behavior when it occurs outside the therapy, and *acting in* refers to unconsciously motivated impulsive behaviors occurring in the therapeutic relationship. *See also* Enactment.

Addiction. In psychoanalytic usage, addiction refers to the physiological process of habituation and dependency to a substance (such as alcohol, nicotine, narcotics, etc.) Psychological addictions are more usually understood psychodynamically as compulsions. *See also* Compulsion.

Affect. (Basch) The primary physiological state underlying emotion. The primary affects observed in infants (Tomkins) include interest/excitement, enjoyment/joy, surprise/startle, distress/anguish, fear/terror, anger/rage, shame/humiliation, dissmell (reaction to bad smell), and disgust. Other researchers have added boredom, contentment, and shame as primary affects. *See also* Emotion; Feeling.

Anal. (S. Freud) The stage of development following the oral stage, in which the child becomes preoccupied with the struggle to control his own productions (including but not limited to actual feces) in the face of parental and societal prohibitions. Unresolved conflicts at this stage result in problems with control, aggression ("anal-sadistic" behavior), and perfectionism masking a desire to smear or destroy.

Analytical psychology. The technical term used to refer to Jungian analysis and theory.

Archetype. (Jung) Similar to the Platonic idea, an archetype is a symbol, image, or constellation of images deriving from the collective experience of humanity and taking particular form through culture and the individual personality that represents a guiding idea or motivating force for both individual and collective beliefs and behaviors. These may be personified (e.g., the Hero, the Witch, the "Puer" [boy]) or more abstract (Wholeness, the Self). Abstract archetypes are often represented by symbols (such as the mandala for Wholeness, Jesus, or the Buddha for the Self), but the archetype itself is greater than the particular symbol.

Associations. Technical psychoanalytic term for thoughts, images, feelings, and fantasies that float to the patient's and therapist's minds in the course of therapy in connection (or association) with whatever is being discussed—however apparently unrelated they may seem. The flow of associations and the linkages among seemingly unrelated ideas give clues to the patient's unconscious processes and meanings. *See also* Free association.

Attachment. (Bowlby, Ainsworth) The bond between an infant and primary caretaker(s), which, when formed as a habitual mode of attachment, has lifelong implications for relating with others. The classic modes of attachment are secure (flexible), anxious (clingy), and avoidant (withdrawing). Current research has suggested further modes of attachment such as ambivalent, disorganized, and traumatic.

Attunement. (D. Stern) A term from infant observation research that describes the level of sensitivity and empathy initially given by the parent or primary caretaker toward the child; also used to describe the quality of sensitivity to the other in all relationships.

Autistic. As used in psychoanalytic theory, the term *autistic* does not refer to the developmental disorders on the autism spectrum in the DSM, but to a primal self-protective state of self-preoccupation and disregard for the reality of others. The "autistic-contiguous position" (from Ogden, extending Klein's developmental positions) is a state first occurring even earlier than the paranoid-schizoid position, in which the infant's experience of self is all-encompassing, and the first awareness of others as other occurs through tactile experience, that is, via the skin.

Blank screen. More a myth than a reality in psychoanalytic practice, the term *blank screen* refers to the supposed nonresponsiveness of the therapist toward the patient, in order to avoid contaminating the projections in the patient's transference. Sometimes related to Freud's recommendation that the analyst maintain a stance of surgical coldness. Contemporary psychoanalytic therapists recognize that although an effort is made to be nonreactive and nonjudgmental, a blank screen is not only impossible, but unempathic.

Borderline. Originally used to designate a category of diagnosis falling between neurotic and psychotic, *borderline* is now used as a diagnostic label (DSM) to describe a personality disorder characterized by a chronic psychological pattern of splitting (see Splitting), terror of abandonment, and a history of dramatic up-and-down relationships. Contemporary trauma theorists (Herman) now consider borderline to fall under the broad category of post-traumatic phenomena. As a term, *borderline* has become contested because it has often been used pejoratively, and disproportionately in association with women.

Catharsis/Cathartic. (S. Freud) The discharge of repressed emotion through recollection of an unconscious memory. Current psychoanalytic theory tends to downplay dramatic cathartic moments in favor of more sustained, incremental gains in insight and reflection.

Cathexis. (S. Freud) Strong attachment to another person, place, or thing formed by the internalization of that person as an inner object. Freud postulated that the melancholia of mourning was related to the sudden loss in external reality of a strongly cathected object.

Character/Characterological disorder. See Personality disorder.

Cognitive-behavioral. A nonpsychoanalytic form of therapy aimed toward the disciplined mental restructuring of self-defeating thoughts and desensitization of the patient toward situations that cause irrational anxiety and related unwanted behaviors. Although cognitive-behavioral therapy is focused on present-day life and functioning, many psychoanalytic therapists incorporate cognitive and behavioral strategies over the course of a longer-term insight-oriented therapy to aid in relief of symptoms.

Complex/Unconscious complex. (S. Freud, Jung) In classical psychoanalysis, a syndrome or enduring set of multiple neurotic symptoms; in Jungian analysis, to be "in complex" means to be in the grip of an archetype or other powerful unconscious dynamic force, manifested by atypical behaviors, lapses in judgment, or other parapraxes.

Compulsion. A behavior, often chronic, arising from an irresistible psychological pressure. *See also* Obsession/Obsessive-compulsive.

Conflict. (S. Freud) In psychoanalytic terms, *conflict* does not refer primarily to conscious interpersonal conflict in actual relationships but, rather, the inner struggle between id, ego, and superego, or, in object relations terms, conflicted feelings, thoughts, and impulses arising from internal objects with competing aims.

Conscious. (S. Freud) The region of mind theorized as accessible to ordinary awareness, in contrast to the preconscious and the unconscious. *See also* Preconscious; Unconscious.

Control-mastery. (Weiss and Sampson) A recent form of psychoanalytically informed therapy based on empirical research into unconscious transference "tests" by patients, and therapists' optimal responses.

Corrective emotional experience. (Alexander) An idea, mostly discredited in psycho-analysis, that the function of therapy is to reparent the patient or otherwise provide a new relationship that is curative in and of itself, apart from promoting insight.

Countertransference. (S. Freud) Clasically defined as unconscious, unresolved conflicts in the therapist that cause distortions in perceiving the patient accurately and errors in interpretation and behavior toward the patient (*classic countertransference*); more recently defined as the sum total of all the therapist's feelings, thoughts, fantasies, and behaviors in relation to the patient, including both the therapist's own unresolved issues and projections and other material that arises from shared pool of unconscious relationship between patient and therapist and from the patient's own internal world (*totalist countertransference*). Taken together, the patient's transference and the thera-pist's countertransference form a continuum of mutual perceptions, projections, and subjective experiences within the therapeutic relationship. *See also* Transference.

Crisis. An acute experience of stress in which one's normal coping mechanisms are inad-equate or become ineffective. The goal of crisis intervention is to help restore the person's normal baseline functioning.

Defenses/Defense mechanisms. (S. Freud, A. Freud) Unconscious strategies by which intolerable thoughts are repressed, anxiety is managed, and ego function is protected. In the mid-twentieth century, these were elaborated and organized into four levels (Vaillant): Level 4, "higher defenses" (including altruism, sublimation, conscious suppression, humor); Level 3, "neurotic defenses" (including intellectualization, repression, reaction formation, and displacement); Level 2, "immature defenses" (including fantasy, projection, passive aggression, hypochondriasis, and acting out); and Level 1, "primitive defenses" that almost always involve splitting (including delusional projection, denial, distortion, idealization, and devaluation). Classical and ego-psychology oriented therapists continue to use this as a standard way of under-standing and categorizing a patient's habitual style of thinking and relating, particu-larly under stress. Most contemporary therapists appreciate the role of defenses in preserving an individual's emotional equilibrium, and they caution against attempts by therapists to dismantle or abruptly expose them.

Denial. (1) (S. Freud) One of the defense mechanisms, denial is the unconscious process of not knowing what one actually knows to be true. For example, one knows that one's spouse is an alcoholic but continues to think, believe, and behave as if this were not the case. (2) (Kübler-Ross) One of the normal stages of dying; a normal (if transitory) aspect of grief.

Depressive position. (Klein) A state in which one is developmentally able to hold good and bad realities together in one's mind, involving both external reality and internal fantasy. It is depressive because it acknowledges the tragic reality of the juxtaposi-tion of one's own and others' aggression with love and attachment. For example, I can be angry and want to hurt the one I love; the mother who loves and feeds me is also the mother who doesn't always respond to my cries. *See also* Paranoid-schizoid position.

Desire. The term favored in contemporary psychoanalysis, following Lacan's translation (*désir*), for Freud's term (*Wunsch*, "wish"): a strongly motivating, unconscious hunger or longing, particularly at the unconscious level of the id. It is particularly used in reference to sexual or erotic desire but also refers more generally to all that is yearned for internally. *See also* Drive.

Development/Developmental stages. Expressed in a variety of theories, beginning with Freud's psychosexual stages (oral, anal, genital/phallic) and including Erikson's "eight stages of man," this term refers to various eras of maturation that are commonly observed in the growth of the human person. Structural theories, like Piaget's, focus on successive cognitive advances occurring in an exact sequential order; psychoanalytic theories emphasize multiple lines of development (A. Freud). The most recent theories emphasize moral thought (Kohlberg, Gilligan), capacity for relatedness (Kegan), and faith/meaning making (Fowler, Loder).

Dialectic-behavioral therapy. An integrative therapy designed especially for patients diagnosed with borderline personality disorder in which educative, cognitive, and behavioral strategies are combined with some insight-oriented supportive therapy.

Disavowal. A term used particularly in self psychology to refer to the process by which conscious knowledge about one's desires or behaviors that are unacceptable to a person's self-concept is split off from conscious awareness. It is not unconscious, as in repression, but denied. See Vertical split.

Dream analysis/interpretation. A technique used in virtually all forms of psychoanalytic practice, although with some variations in method, in which dreams are recalled and examined for clues about the patient's unconscious.

Drive. (S. Freud—*Triebe*, also sometimes called "instinct") Freud identified two innate, biologically based motivations toward survival that underlie all human behaviors: procreation (sex) and self-defense (aggression). Object relations theorists recast Freud's drive theory to emphasize object-seeking (relational attachment to others) over sex and aggression. Late in his life, Freud posited that aggression becomes the death instinct (instinct toward cessation of all striving and the tensions caused by libido). *See also* Desire.

DSM (*Diagnostic and Statistical Manual*). The established American reference book for officially recognized diagnostic categories. While some of the writers of the DSM are psychoanalytic in orientation, the manual is intended to be purely descriptive, without reference to etiology, and a DSM diagnosis does not constitute a full psychodynamic evaluation. The current edition of the DSM is DSM-IV-TR (4th ed., text revision).

Ego. The most conscious of the three "institutions of the mind" Freud eventually identified in his structural model of the mind, the ego (literally from the Latin, "I," a translation from Freud's simpler colloquial German *Ich*) is the conscious executive function that is capable of self-conscious thought, knowledge, evaluation, and decision. The goal of classical analysis is to give increasing mastery to the ego, which is the seat of reason. In Jungian theory, the ego is an archetype representing the executive center or nucleus of consciousness, but it is a relatively small (and unduly self-important) region of the whole Self. *See also* Id; Superego; Self.

Ego ideal. (S. Freud) An object that unconsciously represents what/whom the ego emulates or would like to be. *See also* Idealization.

Ego psychology. The offshoot of classical psychoanalysis that held sway in American psychoanalysis through much of the mid-twentieth century and continues to undergird much of what has become orthodox or mainstream psychoanalytic theory and practice. Based on the work of A. Freud and followers, ego psychology stresses defense mechanisms and the adaptive or maladaptive functioning of personality. *See also* Defenses/Defense mechanisms.

Emotion. (Basch) The highest level of cognitive processing of affect, including both associated memory and the meaning assigned to it. *See also* Affect; Feeling.

Empathy. In Rogerian therapy, understanding accompanied by nonpossessive warmth and nonjudgment; For Kohut, a technical term used to refer to understanding the other person/the patient as if one were standing inside his or her perspective (in contrast to sympathy, which is care or concern from the outside). Empathy in itself is not necessarily equivalent to being warm or nice, as empathy can be used coldly by sociopaths to control others. However, empathy, as understanding coupled with care, is in itself therapeutic, since people long to be understood. Empathy is not innate intuition but a developmental achievement and a skill that can be learned.

Enactment. Used as a technical term, particularly in relational psychoanalytic therapy, to refer to the nonverbal cues and communications that occur in the therapeutic relationship that always carry unconscious meanings. Enactments are considered an inevitable and often overlooked aspect of the therapeutic process. *See also* Acting out.

Evenly hovering attention. (S. Freud—*gleichschwebende Aufmerksamkeit*, sometimes also translated as "evenly suspended" or "free-floating" attention) Freud's recommendation for the therapist's maintaining a flexible state of equal attentiveness toward the patient's verbalizations, nonverbal communications/enactments, and thoughts, feelings, fantasies, and associations arising in the therapist him- or herself.

Facilitating environment. (Winnicott) The environment created by the the primary caretaker in which an infant is securely held and given space, through play, to grow.

False self. (Winnicott) An enduring identity formed early in childhood in compliance with external expectations but at the expense of being oneself. See True self.

Fantasy/Phantasy. (S. Freud, Klein) The inner, unconscious imaginal life of the patient in which wishes and perceptions of objects are taken as literal facts, as in a dream; in therapy, fantasy also represents what is being imagined, akin to a daydream, and as such may be explored for unconscious meaning. Note that fantasy is not limited to sexual wishes or daydreams.

Feeling. (Basch) The conscious awareness of an affect. *See also* Affect; Emotion.

Flight into health. A form of resistance in which the patient avoids further therapeutic work by declaring that s/he is feeling fine and does not need any more sessions.

Free association. (S. Freud) Freud's "fundamental rule" of therapy, that the patient should say whatever crosses his or her mind, however seemingly irrational or irrelevant. The particular flow of associations, and any blockages that occur (signaling "resistance"), are as important as the content of the associations themselves.

Gestalt. (Perls) Literally, from German, "whole." An offshoot of classical psychotherapy in which inner objects are acted out in therapy. Gestalt therapy is also noted for its integrative attention to manifestations of the patient's psychological structure in the physical body.

Good-enough. (Winnicott) The quality of parenting that facilitates growth. Reliability, rather than perfection, is what is valued in this phrase. The *good-enough* parent reliably provides nurture and holding and in his or her occasional, normal lapses allows for "optimal frustration" by which the child can gradually achieve differentiation and self-sufficiency.

Guilt. The feeling of having done something bad or wrong. In the therapeutic sense, this feeling is healthy to the degree it corresponds with reality and neurotic to the degree that it is unrealistic, generated by a harsh or overly punitive superego or parental introject. *See also* Shame.

Holding environment. See Facilitating environment.

Hysteria/Hysterical. A now outmoded term used technically in classical psychoanalysis to describe the conversion of repressed sexual and/or aggressive wishes into physical symptoms. Contemporary research validates Freud's original observations (later recanted) that many symptoms of hysteria are post-traumatic reactions (in the case of his hysterical female patients, to sexual abuse; similar reactions were also observed and recorded in the early twentieth century as "war neurosis.") *See also* Psychosomatic.

Id. (S. Freud) The most unconscious of Freud's three "institutions of the mind" in the structural model, the id (literally "it," or *Es* in Freud's original German) carries the instinctual drives of sex and aggression. Because sexual and aggressive wishes are considered unacceptable and are suppressed or controlled by the process of socialization, most or all of the id is driven into the unconscious via repression.

Idealization/Idealizing function. (Kohut) One of the two primary functions of the early selfobjects, idealization is the process by which the child first comes to internalize the parent as reliable and good, and eventually begins to emulate. Idealization is the foundation for healthy aspirations, ambition, and nonpathological narcissism/self-esteem. The therapist must allow the patient to use him or her as an idealizing object as one aspect of the transference-countertransference relationship. *See also* Mirroring.

Identification. (S. Freud) An unconscious process by which one internalizes another or adopts patterns of thought and behavior in order to join in similarity or sameness with another. Identification may also be conscious, as in "I identify with her values," but it is more forceful psychodynamically when identifications are unconscious, as in "identification with the oppressor" (A. Freud).

Interpersonal. The term given to the form of psychoanaysis practiced by Sullivan and his followers, focusing on the mutual experience of the relationship between therapist and patient; the "interpersonal school" (e.g., the William Alanson White Institute in New York).

Interpretation. Considered the central activity of the therapist in many branches of psychoanalysis, interpretation is the process of bringing unconscious material to consciousness by making connections between present and past events, and external and internal realities in the patient's life. The goal of interpretation is insight, leading to reduction in suffering and in unconsciously driven patterns of self-defeating behavior. In contemporary psychoanalytic therapy, interpretation is understood more in terms of *exploration of meaning*, which is a shared activity of both therapist and patient, guided by both the therapist's expertise and the patient's knowledge and experience of him- or herself.

Intersubjectivity. The area of shared feeling, experience (conscious and unconscious), and meaning-making that develops between two people in relationship; a theory arising from self psychology in contemporary psychoanalysis that emphasizes the mutual psychic influence and construction of meaning in the therapeutic relationship.

Law of the Father. (Lacan) The rules and prohibitions of society—represented by the father in the oedipal triangle and conveyed through the medium of language—by which each individual is irrevocably alienated by the process of socialization from a direct, unmediated experience of self.

Mentalization. (Fonagy) Similar to Piaget's concepts of object permanence and reciprocal operations, mentalization is the developmental capacity to hold stable representations of both oneself and another person in one's own mind (also called object constancy), as well as the capacity to know that the other is doing the same, and to imagine what the other might be thinking.

Mirror. (1) In Rogerian therapy and in counseling theory, the listening skill of empathically and concisely saying back to the patient what the therapist has heard, sometimes selectively emphasizing a word or phrase that seems to carry particular affective intensity; (2) in self psychology, one of two earliest selfobject functions in childhood (*see also* Idealizing), the primary caretaker's empathic recognition of the child's growth and being, a self-sustaining function that is also provided later in life by other selfobjects (including the therapist toward the patient); (3) in Lacanian theory, the primal recognition of oneself in the mirror as not-me, leading to the first experience of alienation between the experience of self and all forms of representation, symbolization, and expression of the self, including language.

Narcissism/Narcissistic. A term with various shades of meaning in different psychoanalytic theories, *narcissism* refers overall to one's own attachment to oneself. All infants are born with "primary narcissism" (S. Freud), the literally self-centered worldview that cannot yet differentiate self from environment. Pathological narcissism results from lack of parental mirroring and increasingly modulated admiration in early childhood (Kohut) and involves inflated self-regard and a sense of entitlement that defensively covers over a lack of self-esteem and pervasive sense of shame, depression, and inadequacy. Healthy or mature narcissism involves adaptive forms of self-protection and self-advancement in the world (modulated aggression).

Neurosis/Neurotic. (S. Freud) An umbrella term for all forms of psychological distress ("inner conflict") caused by pressure from the id to break through the repression barrier, creating anxiety. Neurotic symptoms are compromise formations that simultaneously express or gratify the intolerable wish in disguised form while also pushing it back into the unconscious. Classic neurosis is characterized by excessive guilt and anxiety.

Neutrality. A technical term, particularly used in classical psychoanalysis and ego psychology, referring to the recommended stance of the therapist as nonjudgmental and nonreactive toward the patient. From A. Freud, neutrality means maintaining mental equidistance among the patient's ego, id, superego, and external reality.

Object. (Klein) A technical term referring to the internalized representations of others in the environment, beginning with primary caretakers. Objects are not equivalent to actual other people—they are a blend of actual experiences of others and internal fantasies.

Object constancy. The developmental capacity to hold a stable representation of an external object in mind, even when that person, place, or thing is not present. *See also* Mentalization.

Object relations. An umbrella term for the psychoanalytic theorists following Klein, including Fairbairn, Winnicott, and Guntrip, who emphasize the conscious and unconscious relations with others beginning in infancy (over and against Freud's drive theory), the formation of internal representations of others as constitutive of self and personality, and the pathogenic function of splitting in mental life.

Object use. (Winnicott) The mental activity by which an individual becomes able to relate to an actual other person rather than relating largely through projection to his or her unconscious fantasies of the other; to be able to take in "other-than-me" feedback from the other.

Obsession/Obsessive-compulsive. An obsession is a repetitively or chronically occurring thought that one cannot "get out of one's head," often linked to compulsions or ritualized behaviors that function to discharge or ward off anxiety caused by the obsession, as in obsessive-compulsive disorder. An obsessive personality style is related to perfectionism and preoccupation with details. *See also* Compulsion.

Oedipal. (S. Freud) The developmental crisis, named after the Greek tragic protagonist Oedipus, in which the (male) child around age five or six, wishes to kill his father in order to possess his mother for himself. This crisis is considered to be resolved optimally when the boy (or man) is able to renounce his grandiose desire and accommodate himself to reality; neurosis is theorized to arise from unduly harsh prohibitions and violent repression of the oedipal wish in an unmetabolized form, or pathological gratification of the wish in which the boy is allowed to take the place of the father in the mother's affections. The generalizability of the theory to girls is a contested area of theory. In a more gender-neutral contemporary understanding, the oedipal crisis refers to the developmental demand that one move beyond simple (and at times symbiotic) dyadic relationships to navigate more complex and relationally demanding triadic ones.

Optimal frustration. (Winnicott) A healthy amount of frustration generated in the child by the primary caretaker's inevitable inability to be perfectly responsive, which stimulates growth in the child in the effort to meet his or her own needs. Optimal frustration is frustration that is neither so overwhelming that it far exceeds the child's coping capacities, nor so insufficient that it fails to promote growth. *See also* Good enough.

Oral. (S. Freud) The earliest phase of infant development, in which sexual and aggressive needs and impulses are experienced through the mouth (e.g., sucking, biting, tasting). Conflicts stemming from this period involve unsatisfied hunger (literal and symbolic), forms of oral aggression such as uncontrolled greed or excessive speech, and issues with oral gratification (both sexual and other forms of oral gratification). *See also* Anal; Phallic.

Paranoid-schizoid position. (Klein) The more "primitive" (earliest in infancy) of Klein's two developmental "positions," in which good and bad (both in fantasy and in external reality) are mentally split apart in order to preserve the good as pure in fantasy. *See also* Depressive position.

Parapraxes. Behaviors by which the unconscious "slips out" or is communicated, such as slips of the tongue or the pen, accidents that convey unconscious communications, etc.

Personality. An enduring set of beliefs, thoughts, behaviors, and tolerated feelings that characterize a person's habitual attitudes and practices in the world and vary little from setting to setting. Used more or less interchangeably in psychoanalytic theory with *character* or *character structure*.

Personality disorder. An impairment in personality or character that is pervasive rather than situational and tends to globally affect the person's self-image and functioning in all relationships, both personal and professional. In DSM diagnosis, it is recorded on a separate axis from other mental disorders, and it often may coexist with or underlie other problems such as depression or anxiety. Unlike neurosis, which is experienced by a patient as a problem within him- or herself, a person with a personality disorder is likely to regard his or her problems as belonging outside the self, that is, caused by someone else.

Phallic. (S. Freud) The third developmental stage (sometimes also called "genital") in Freud's theory, following the anal stage, in which the child strives for power and mastery. This is played out in the oedipal crisis. The gender laden imagery of this theoretical construct was intended by Freud, resulting in his further theory of "penis envy" in girls. In contemporary psychoanalytic theory, the focus is more generally on the phallus as a symbol for power or the desire for power, accompanied by envy for whatever one cannot possess (whether penis, breast, mother, father, or other desires), and the poignancy of grief over what is lost (in reality or in fantasy).

Potential space. (Winnicott) The "space" (sometimes called "transitional space") that is created initially between the child and the mother/primary caretaker, as it appears in both the child's fantasy and in the actual relation between child and mother. This space is facilitative to the extent that it expands and allows for the child to play and to develop his or her creative potential while at the same time it is protected by the safety of the holding function provided by the parent. The space is transitional in the sense that it functions as a bridge between the child's own subjectivity, in which the mother is an entirely internal object of fantasy, and the experience of the actual mother. It is in part the "rub" between fantasy and reality that promotes growth and new mental capacities in the child.

Preconscious. (S. Freud) The region of mind theorized as falling between conscious and unconscious in which mental contents are accessible if given attention but otherwise lie beneath ordinary conscious awareness. *See also* Conscious; Unconscious.

Projection. The unconscious process by which one's internal fantasy or inner object is externalized onto an actual other person, and then the other person is related to as if s/he were the internal object.

Projective identification. The unconscious process by which one's projection is, in turn, internalized and acted out by the other person—a projection "into" rather than merely "onto" the other person.

Psychoanalytic. The umbrella term for all psychological, interpretive approaches deriving from Freud's theories of the unconscious.

Psychodynamic. The term for psychological approaches that attend to the unconscious movements and relationships among internal objects and between people in interpersonal relationships.

Psychosexual. (1) In Freud's usage, referring to the unconscious infantile sexual wishes and impulses that constitute a person's sexual identity, attitudes, and behavior; (2) in contemporary usage, any reference to the psychological dimension of sexuality, including thoughts, feelings, fantasies, memories, identity, desires, and motivations for sexual behavior.

Psychosis/Psychotic. Form of pathology marked by a pervasive and involuntary departure from consensual reality, usually not recognized as such by the individual affected. Clinically, the primary symptoms of psychosis include delusions; hallucinations; grossly disorganized or stereotyped thoughts, speech, or behavior; and inappropriate affect. Psychosis is generally regarded as a disorder of thought, as distinct from an emotional disorder (such as depression or anxiety). It may be chronic or episodic, and it may coexist with affective disorders such as depression or anxiety.

Psychosomatic. Literally, "soul/psyche-body": physical effects or symptoms caused, at least in part, by unconscious feelings, memories, thoughts, wishes, etc., that cannot be allowed into consciousness; psychologically generated effects or symptoms that are manifested in the body.

Real relationship. (Greenson) The aspect of the therapeutic relationship based on conscious, reality-based perceptions. As Greenson used the term, it is also a contested concept describing a conscious or ego-to-ego relationship between therapist and patient that lies *outside* the transference-countertransference relationship and functions to order and protect the work of the therapy—in some sense, the business relationship of the therapy. Many question the possibility of any aspect of the therapeutic relationship that is untouched by the transference-countertransference dynamic, or is entirely conscious. The "real relationship" has also been used to rationalize boundary crossings as falling outside the transference relationship (Gabbard).

Relational/Relational-psychoanalytic. (1) Term used to refer to a contemporary movement in psychoanalysis that grew out of object relations; emphasizes the co-construction of meaning and reality, the mutuality of psychic influence in the therapeutic relationship within a framework of asymmetrical responsibility; and focuses on the use of the therapist's self (countertransference) as a useful tool for understanding and empathy. (2) *Relational* is also the term used to refer to the feminist form of interpersonal therapy developed at the Stone Center at Wellesley College, following J. Miller.

Representation. In psychoanalysis, a technical term for the mental images of one's inner objects, sometimes referred to as "object representations" or "mental representations." *See also* Mentalization.

Repression. The process by which intolerable or socially unacceptable wishes (in Freudian theory, sexual and aggressive) are pushed back into the unconscious.

Resistance. (S. Freud) In Freud's earliest use (carried into some practices of classical analysis), the manifestation of repression in the form of blockage of the flow of associations, and more generally, a paradoxical unconscious refusal to cooperate with the very help the patient is seeking. From Freud's later work onward, *resistance* is understood empathically as a self-protective or defensive function that is best approached by an attempt to understand rather than to confront or dismantle.

Sandplay/Sand tray. A projective technique used in Jungian analysis in which patients can arrange small objects in a box filled with sand, creating a form of dreamscape or external representation of internal images that can then be analyzed. Over time, photographs of successive sand trays may reveal trends or developments in the patient's inner life.

Self. (1) In self psychology, the underlying psychological structure of a person's ongoing sense of identity, purpose, and personal cohesion (or lack thereof); (2) in Jungian psychology, the Self is the whole person, encompassing the ego, the personal unconscious, the collective unconscious, and at its outer edges touching what humans experience as the transcendent or divine.

Self psychology. The branch of psychoanalysis, similar to object relations, following the theory and practice of Kohut from the late 1950s to the present. Self psychology emphasizes the role of empathy in therapy, the role of others ("selfobjects"), and the importance of mirroring and idealizing in development. It has been particularly helpful in addressing narcissistic pathology.

Selfobject. Term from self psychology to refer to significant external others (objects) as they are unconsciously internalized both in early development and across the lifespan, functioning intrapsychically to build and/or support a cohesive self structure through the primary functions of mirroring and idealizing, and other functions identified in ongoing self psychological research.

Shame. A feeling of being bad, often triggered by feeling unwittingly exposed. *See also* Guilt.

Somaticization. The process by which split-off feelings, memories, or other mental contents become manifested in physical symptoms, sometimes also referred to as "psychosomatic." See Psychosomatic.

Splitting. (Klein) The process of keeping mental contents, particularly "good" and "bad," separate in order to preserve the fantasied purity of the good. Splitting may occur in relation both to one's self-representations and in the form of projections onto or into others, resulting in all-or-nothing thought patterns of oscillating idealization and denigration.

Structural model. (S. Freud) Freud's later model of mind, in which regions of conscious and unconscious are overlaid by the three parts or "institutions" of ego, id, and superego. *See also* Topographical model.

Superego. (S. Freud) One of the three "institutions of the mind" in Freud's structural model, the superego (above the "I") represents the internalization of parental and societal prohibitions and taboos, and functions with varying degrees of harshness as the primary motivator of a person's conscience, or moral sense of right and wrong.

Symbolization. The process by which formerly unconscious material is brought into awareness in the form of images and nonverbal representations (symbols). It is often the first intermediate step between the unconscious and verbalization.

Therapeutic alliance. (Zetzel) The aspect of the therapeutic relationship in which the patient and the therapist consciously or unconsciously agree to join together in the work of therapy, with a shared goal of healing and/or growth for the patient. The therapeutic alliance depends upon a positive rapport between patient and therapist and protects the therapy from dissolving when the work becomes stressful or conflictual. Sometimes also referred to as the "working alliance" (Greenson) and related to the "real relationship."

Topographical model. (S. Freud) Freud's first graphic depiction of the mind, in which conscious, preconscious, and unconscious were shown as successive layers, or regions, in the mind. *See also* Structural model.

Transference. (S. Freud) Freud's term for the patient's projections, or transferring of experiences of parents and other authority figures from childhood, onto the person of the therapist (or other helping professional or authority figure). *See also* Countertransference.

Transference neurosis. (S. Freud) The formation of an enduring pattern of transference reactions in the therapeutic relationship. Freud considered the formation and resolution of the transference neurosis to be key to the therapeutic process.

Transference psychosis. A pattern of transference reactions in the therapeutic relationship in which the "as-if" quality drops away, and the therapist is related to as the original primary caretaker him- or herself. (In the shift from transference neurosis to psychosis, "You are just like my mother" becomes "You *are* my mother.")

Transitional object. (Winnicott) An object to which a child becomes attached (such as a teddy bear or blanket) that can serve as a soothing connection to the primary caretaker in his or her absence.

Transmuting internalization. (Kohut) The therapeutic process by which ruptures in the empathic connection between therapist and patient are processed and interpreted, leading to internal healing and structure-building in the patient.

Trauma. An acute or repeated experience of terror or horror in which one believes one's life is threatened and/or normal coping mechanisms are overwhelmed.

True self. (Winnicott) The sense of self that corresponds with one's innate and actual gifts, inclinations, and desires; also related to the capacity for play and spontaneity.

Unconscious. First theorized by Freud, the unconscious is an umbrella term for the region(s) in the mind in which thoughts, feelings, fantasies, memories, and other mental contents are pushed back out of awareness. Truly unconscious mental contents are absolutely inaccessible to ordinary thought processes and come to light only through the careful observation of associations, dreams, somatic reactions, and various forms of atypical enactments or parapraxes (such as slips of the tongue, accidents, etc.). *See also* Conscious; Preconscious.

Vertical split. (Kohut) A process emphasized by Kohut in which mental contents are removed from awareness through the process of disavowal rather than repression. Such contents are still accessible to consciousness but normally blocked from awareness (often because they do not fit the individual's ordinary sense of self or are sources of shame), unlike repressed material, which is unconscious and inaccessible to ordinary mental recall.

Working through. (Freud) The process central to the middle phase of therapy in which unconscious material is brought to conscious awareness through interpretation/ exploration and affective reexperiencing.

Index of Names

Index of Subjects

Index of Biblical References